AMERICAN LITERATURE IN TRANSITION, 1770–1828

This volume presents a complex portrait of the United States of America grappling with the trials of national adolescence. Topics include (but are not limited to): the dynamics of language and power, the treachery of memory, the lived experience of racial and economic inequality, the aesthetics of Indigeneity, the radical possibilities of disability, the fluidity of gender and sexuality, the depth and culture-making power of literary genre, the history of poetics, the cult of performance, and the hidden costs of foodways. Taken together, the essays offer a vision of a vibrant, contradictory, and conflicted early U.S. Republic resistant to consensus accountings and poised to inform new and better origin stories for the polity to come.

WILLIAM HUNTTING HOWELL is Associate Professor of English at Boston University. He is the author of *Against Self-Reliance: The Arts of Dependence in the Early United States* (University of Pennsylvania Press, 2015) and the coeditor (with Megan E. Walsh) of Frank J. Webb's *The Garies and Their Friends* (Broadview Press, 2016). His essays have appeared in *American Literature, The William & Mary Quarterly, Early American Studies, Common-place*, and *Avidly*, among others.

GRETA LAFLEUR is Associate Professor of American Studies at Yale University. LaFleur is the author of *The Natural History of Sexuality in Early America* (Johns Hopkins University Press, 2018). Her writing appears in *Early American Literature, Early American Studies, American Quarterly, American Literature*, and on the *Los Angeles Review of Books* and *Public Books* websites.

NINETEENTH-CENTURY AMERICAN LITERATURE IN TRANSITION

Editor
Cody Marrs, University of Georgia

Nineteenth-Century American Literature in Transition provides an omnibus account of American literature and its ever-evolving field of study. Emphasizing the ways in which American literature has been in transition ever since its founding, this revisionary series examines four phases of American literary history, focusing on the movements, forms, and media that developed from the late eighteenth to the early twentieth century. The mutable nature of American literature is explored throughout these volumes, which consider a diverse and dynamic set of authors, texts, and methods. Encompassing the full range of today's literary scholarship, this series is an essential guide to the study of nineteenth-century American literature and culture.

Books in the series

American Literature in Transition, 1770–1828 edited by WILLIAM HUNTTING HOWELL & GRETA LAFLEUR
American Literature in Transition, 1820–1860 edited by JUSTINE MURISON
American Literature in Transition, 1851–1877 edited by CODY MARRS
American Literature in Transition, 1876–1910 edited by LINDSAY RECKSON

AMERICAN LITERATURE IN TRANSITION, 1770–1828

EDITED BY

WILLIAM HUNTTING HOWELL
Boston University

GRETA LAFLEUR
Yale University

CAMBRIDGE
UNIVERSITY PRESS

CAMBRIDGE
UNIVERSITY PRESS

University Printing House, Cambridge CB2 8BS, United Kingdom

One Liberty Plaza, 20th Floor, New York, NY 10006, USA

477 Williamstown Road, Port Melbourne, VIC 3207, Australia

314–321, 3rd Floor, Plot 3, Splendor Forum, Jasola District Centre, New Delhi – 110025, India

103 Penang Road, #05–06/07, Visioncrest Commercial, Singapore 238467

Cambridge University Press is part of the University of Cambridge.

It furthers the University's mission by disseminating knowledge in the pursuit of education, learning, and research at the highest international levels of excellence.

www.cambridge.org
Information on this title: www.cambridge.org/9781108475860
DOI: 10.1017/9781108675239

First published 2022

A catalogue record for this publication is available from the British Library.

Library of Congress Cataloging-in-Publication Data
NAMES: Howell, William Huntting, editor. | LaFleur, Greta, 1981- editor.
TITLE: American literature in transition, 1770–1828 / edited by William Huntting Howell, Greta LaFleur.
DESCRIPTION: Cambridge ; New York, NY : Cambridge University Press, 2022. | SERIES: Nineteenth-century American literature in transition ; volume 1 | Includes bibliographical references and index.
IDENTIFIERS: LCCN 2021060661 (print) | LCCN 2021060662 (ebook) | ISBN 9781108475860 (hardback) | ISBN 9781108469180 (paperback) | ISBN 9781108675239 (epub)
SUBJECTS: LCSH: American literature–Colonial period, ca. 1600–1775–History and criticism. | American literature–1783–1850–History and criticism. | Literature and society–United States–History–18th century. | Literature and society–United States–History–19th century. | BISAC: LITERARY CRITICISM / American / General
CLASSIFICATION: LCC PS193 .A45 2022 (print) | LCC PS193 (ebook) | DDC 810.9/002–dc23/eng/20220208
LC record available at https://lccn.loc.gov/2021060661
LC ebook record available at https://lccn.loc.gov/2021060662

ISBN 978-1-108-47586-0 Hardback

Contents

Contributors

SARI ALTSCHULER is Associate Professor of English and Director of the Health, Humanities, and Society Initiative at Northeastern University. She is the author of *The Medical Imagination: Literature and Health in the Early United States* (University of Pennsylvania Press, 2018) and coeditor of *Keywords for Health Humanities* (under contract with New York University Press). Her essays have appeared in *Early American Literature*, *Nineteenth-Century Literature*, *American Literature*, *American Literary History*, *PMLA*, and the *Lancet*.

ANNA MAE DUANE, Associate Professor of English at the University of Connecticut, is the author or editor of five books that explore the intersection of race, age, and national identity. Her most recent book, *Educated for Freedom: The Incredible Story of Two Fugitive Schoolboys Who Grew Up to Change a Nation* (New York University Press, 2020), follows the lives of James McCune Smith and Henry Highland Garnet from their attendance at the New York African Free School through their adult accomplishments in literature, medicine, and oratory.

EMILY GARCÍA is Associate Professor of English and Latina/o/x and Latin American Studies at Northeastern Illinois University. Her research has appeared in *Early American Literature* and the collection *The Latino Nineteenth Century*, edited by Jesse Alemán and Rodrigo Lazo.

MATTHEW GARRETT is author of *Episodic Poetics: Politics and Literary Form after the Constitution* (Oxford University Press, 2014) and editor of *The Cambridge Companion to Narrative Theory* (Cambridge University Press, 2018), and his essays have appeared in *American Literary History*, *American Quarterly*, *Critical Inquiry*, *ELH*, the *Journal of Cultural Economy*, and other journals and edited collections. He teaches English and American Studies at Wesleyan University, where he directs the Certificate in Social, Cultural, and Critical Theory.

SANDRA M. GUSTAFSON is a longtime member of the English faculty at the University of Notre Dame. She is the author of works on American literature and culture including *Imagining Deliberative Democracy in the Early American Republic* (University of Chicago Press, 2011), *Eloquence Is Power: Oratory and Performance in Early America* (University of North Carolina Press, 2000), and essays on William Apess, James Fenimore Cooper, Jonathan Edwards, and Margaret Fuller. She is the editor of *The Norton Anthology of American Literature*, Vol. A (9th edition) and advisory editor of the MLA-affiliated journal *Early American Literature*, as well as the coeditor of *Cultural Narratives: Textuality and Performance in American Culture before 1900* (University of Notre Dame Press, 2010), and guest editor of a special issue of the *Journal of the Early Republic* on political writing and literature. A faculty affiliate of Notre Dame's Center for Civil and Human Rights and a faculty fellow at the Kroc Institute for International Peace Studies, she is completing a book about the nineteenth-century American novel and the early peace movement.

SEAN P. HARVEY is Associate Professor of History at Seton Hall University. His publications include *Native Tongues: Colonialism and Race from Encounter to the Reservation* (Harvard University Press, 2015) and "Native Views of Native Languages: Communication and Kinship in Eastern North America, ca. 1800–1830," *The William & Mary Quarterly* (October 2018). An earlier article, "'Must not their languages be savage and barbarous like them': Philology, Indian Removal, and Race Science," *Journal of the Early Republic*, won the Ralph D. Gray prize for best article from the Society for Historians of the Early American Republic in 2011. He served as Co-Editor of Reviews for the *Journal of the Early Republic* from 2014 to 2017. He is currently working on a book-length project on Albert Gallatin and the US early republic in the Atlantic world.

ELIZABETH HOPWOOD is a Lecturer in English at Loyola University Chicago, where she also directs the Center for Textual Studies and Digital Humanities. Her research focuses on long nineteenth-century foodways in the space of the United States and the Atlantic, digital archives, and digital humanities design.

WILLIAM HUNTTING HOWELL is Associate Professor of English at Boston University. He is the author of *Against Self-Reliance: The Arts of Dependence in the Early United States* (University of Pennsylvania

Press, 2015) and the coeditor (with Megan E. Walsh) of Frank J. Webb's *The* Garies *and Their Friends* (Broadview Press, 2016). His essays have appeared in *American Literature, The William & Mary Quarterly, Early American Studies, Common-Place,* and *Avidly,* among others.

JOHN MAC KILGORE is Associate Professor of English at Florida State University. JM's first book, *Mania for Freedom: American Literatures of Enthusiasm from the Revolution to the Civil War* (University of North Carolina Press, 2016), is a study of "political enthusiasm" and its literatures – texts devoted to mobilizing action against tyranny and supporting inspired cultures of democratic dissent. JM is currently working on two book projects: one on the literature of Old Florida and the contemporary politics of public memory, another on the anti-capitalist literary history of the United States, 1776–1876.

THOMAS KOENIGS is Associate Professor of English at Scripps College in Claremont, California. He is the author of *Founded in Fiction: The Uses of Fiction in the Early United States* (Princeton University Press, 2021).

GRETA LAFLEUR is Associate Professor of American Studies at Yale University. LaFleur is author of *The Natural History of Sexuality in Early America* (Johns Hopkins University Press, 2018). LaFleur is also the editor (with Kyla Schuller) of a special issue of *American Quarterly,* "Origins of Biopolitics in the Americas"; the editor, with Benjamin Kahan, of a special issue of *GLQ* on "The Science of Sex 'Itself'"; and the editor, with Anna Klosowska and Masha Raskolnikov, of *Trans Historical: Gender Plurality before the Modern* (Cornell University Press, 2021).

KIRSTEN LEE is a doctoral candidate in English at the University of Pennsylvania. Her research and teaching interests include early African American literature, class struggle, abolition, and gender and sexuality. She is currently completing a dissertation on the meaning and location of borders and borderlands in long nineteenth-century African American literature.

DREW LOPENZINA is an Associate Professor of English at Old Dominion University and teaches in the intersections of Early American and Native American literatures. He is the author of three books: *The Routledge Introduction to Native American Literature* (Routledge, 2020), *Through an Indian's Looking Glass: A Cultural Biography of William Apess, Pequot* (University of Massachusetts Press, 2017), and *Red Ink: Native Americans Picking up the Pen in the Colonial Period* (SUNY Press, 2012).

MICHAEL A. MCDONNELL is Professor of History at the University of Sydney and the author of *Masters of Empire: Great Lakes Indians and the Making of America* (Hill & Wang, Macmillan, 2015) and *The Politics of War: Race, Class, and Conflict in Revolutionary Virginia* (Omohundro Institute of Early American History and Culture and University of North Carolina Press, 2007). He also is an editor or coeditor of three other works on the Age of Revolution, including *Facing Empire: Indigenous Experiences in a Revolutionary Age*, with Kate Fullagar (Johns Hopkins University Press, 2018), and *Remembering the Revolution: Memory, History, and Nation-Making from the Revolution to the Civil War*, with Frances Clarke, Clare Corbould, and W. Fitzhugh Brundage (University of Massachusetts Press, 2013). McDonnell is currently at work on several projects, including an examination of the place of the American Revolution in Black American life (with Clare Corbould), a study of Revolutionary War memoirs written by lower-class veterans of the conflict, and a three-volume *Cambridge History of the American Revolution*.

DON JAMES MCLAUGHLIN is an assistant professor of nineteenth-century and early American literature at the University of Tulsa. His research focuses on literary movements in the Americas, genealogies of queer health, the medical humanities, disability studies, the LGBTQ past, and the history of emotions. His writing has been published in *American Literature*, *J19: The Journal of Nineteenth-Century Americanists*, and *Literature and Medicine*.

LORI MERISH is Professor of English at Georgetown University. She is the author of *Sentimental Materialism: Gender, Commodity Culture, and Nineteenth-Century American Literature* (Duke University Press, 2000) and *Archives of Labor: Working Class Women and Literary Culture in the Antebellum United States* (Duke University Press, 2017). She is currently writing a book about cultural depictions of poverty and the poor in nineteenth-century American literature, performance, and photography.

HEATHER S. NATHANS is the Chair of the Department of Theatre, Dance, and Performance Studies, and the Alice and Nathan Gantcher Professor in Judaic Studies at Tufts University. Publications include *Early American Theatre from the Revolution to Thomas Jefferson* (Cambridge University Press, 2003), *Slavery and Sentiment on the American Stage, 1787–1861* (Cambridge University Press, 2009), and *Hideous Characters and Beautiful Pagans: Performing Jewish Identity on the Antebellum*

American Stage (University of Michigan Press, 2017), which received the 2018 Barnard Hewitt Award (ASTR) and the John W. Frick Book Award (ATDS). In 2018, Nathans also received the Betty Jean Jones Award for teaching and mentorship from ATDS. Nathans is the editor of the *Studies in Theatre History and Culture* series from the University of Iowa Press.

WENDY RAPHAEL ROBERTS is Associate Professor of English at the University at Albany, SUNY, and author of *Awakening Verse: The Poetics of Early American Evangelicalism* (Oxford University Press, 2020). Her research on revival poetry has been supported by grants from the American Antiquarian Society, the Massachusetts Historical Society, the Huntington Library, the McNeil Center for Early American Studies, the Woodrow Wilson Foundation, and the New England Regional Fellowship Consortium.

MICHELLE SIZEMORE is Associate Professor of English at the University of Kentucky. She is the author of *American Enchantment: Rituals of the People in the Post-Revolutionary World* (Oxford University Press, 2018). Her articles have appeared in *Studies in American Fiction, Legacy,* and other venues. She is currently working on two book projects. *Democratic Dispositions* examines the temperaments, moods, and tendencies of nineteenth-century American political life. *Figures* explores the literature and culture of mathematics in the eighteenth- and nineteenth-century Atlantic world.

MARAMA WHYTE received her PhD from the University of Sydney in 2020. She is now a research associate at the University of Melbourne and a research assistant on the Australian Research Council Discovery Project *War Stories: The Meaning of the American Revolution* at the University of Sydney. She is currently working on her first book, which examines feminist activism by women journalists in the United States during the 1970s.

Series Preface

In the past few decades, as American literary studies has changed and evolved, the long nineteenth century has proven to be a crucial pivot point. *American Literature: The Long Nineteenth Century* captures the dynamism of both this critical moment and the historical period it engages. Emphasizing the ways in which American literature has remained in transition ever since its founding, these four volumes comprise a significant act of literary-historical revisionism. As suggested by the overlapping dates (i.e., 1770–1828, 1820–1860, 1851–1877, 1876–1910), these volumes challenge traditional ways of periodizing literature. This series argues for the contingency and provisionality of literary history in general and of nineteenth-century American literary history in particular. The transitional and mutable nature of American literature is explored throughout these volumes, which address a wide range of topics, methods, and areas of interest, and examine the myriad forms, movements, and media that developed across this era. By drawing together leading and emerging scholars and encompassing the full range of today's American literary scholarship, this series provides an omnibus account of nineteenth-century American literature as well as its ever-evolving field of study.

Acknowledgments

[GL & WHH:] First and foremost, we want to thank the many people whose consolidated efforts made this volume – and the broader series of which it is a part – possible. We thank especially General Editor Cody Marrs, whose work to herd this volume and its three companions into production was exemplary. His deft touch became even more important with the arrival of the COVID-19 pandemic, which made all of our jobs and lives so much more difficult. We also want to thank Lindsay Reckson and Justine Murison, the editors of two of the other *American Literature in Transition: The Long Nineteenth Century* volumes, who were, predictably, thoughtful and cheery fellow travelers through this process. At Cambridge University Press, we thank Ray Ryan and Edgar Mendez, who did the indispensable work of getting our contributors their contracts and ushering the series into production.

With respect to this volume, in particular, we would like thank all of our contributors – those who were ultimately able to get us their submissions, and those who were not. As editors, it was an enormous pleasure to work with this sharp and excited group of people, and what we gained from it far exceeds the capacity of the pages that follow.

We also want to thank the Department of Women's, Gender and Sexuality Studies at Yale University, whose Fund for Lesbian and Gay Studies Fellowship supported editing costs that made it possible for this volume to become the best version of itself. Relatedly, we thank Angela Terrill for her excellent (and very efficient!) work on this project; it is a better and cleaner manuscript for her efforts.

***

[GL:] Many thanks are due to my colleagues in the Department of American Studies at Yale University, as well as to my colleagues in eighteenth- and nineteenth-century studies elsewhere who have shaped my understanding of this era and these fields. I also want to acknowledge Kyla Schuller, Anna Klosowska, Masha Raskolnikov, Benjy Kahan, and Serena Bassi – all current and former colleagues on editing projects – whose collaboration has helped me identify my priorities in editorial work, itself a strange and specific genre of intellectual labor. Finally, the bulk of my work on this project landed squarely in the year when I went up for tenure and fortunately received it, and I thus want to thank all of my friends and family members who stuck around despite my stress and complaints.

***

[WHH:] For good advice and peerlessly sympathetic ears throughout the process, I would like to thank Cathy Kelly, Kasey Evans, Coleman Hutchison, Jay A. Grossman, Tara Bynum, Chris Hunter, and Joe Shapiro. I would also like to acknowledge the unwavering support of my friends and colleagues in the English Department and the American and New England Studies Program at Boston University. And I would like to thank my parents for doing all the parenting things that seem straightforward until you yourself actually have to *do* them. Not unrelatedly: Matthias James McDonough Howell and Edgar Thomas McDonough Howell both came into this world between the start of this project and its finish; I thank them for their forbearance, their indomitability, and their contagious wonder. Lastly, endlessly: Marie Satya McDonough for everything.

CHAPTER I

Introduction
Transitions

William Huntting Howell and Greta LaFleur

For scholars and citizens alike, the period between 1770 and 1828 is generally acknowledged to be one of the most – if not *the* most – important eras in the political history of the United States. It was also for quite a long time something of a dead spot in literary scholarship. For better or for worse, the writing of the late eighteenth- and early nineteenth-century United States has for generations been treated as relentlessly *minor*: formulaic novels, grim sermons, creaky plays, secondhand civic theory, and third-rate poetry that all suffer from comparison with contemporary writing in the British Isles, Continental Europe, and East Asia. The cultural moment may be crucial and the philosophical stakes high, but the texts that constitute it are best approached in the aggregate (or as popular myth and symbol) rather than in their details. Indeed, one could skip from Thomas Paine's *Common Sense* (1776) to James Fenimore Cooper's *Last of the Mohicans* (1826) and still tell a compelling story about the early republic: insofar as they foreground questions of democracy and liberal subjectivity, theorize the righteousness of settler colonialism and Manifest Destiny, and pass blithely over a whole host of structural inequalities in the name of imagining a new nation, Paine and Cooper yield up handy frameworks for explaining the literatures of this period all by themselves.

There are consequences to this sort of step-skipping. For our purposes in *American Literature in Transition, 1770–1828, Volume 1*, the most important of these consequences is the illusion of historical smoothness, stability, or consensus. (This is what gives The Founding its capital-F and its definite article, for example, or designates a particularly complicated cultural period by the name of a particularly dreadful president, as in the "Age of Jackson.") Of late, a sense of early republican rectitude has been particularly robust in the thinking of those on the ideological right, for whom the American Revolution and its aftermath present a vision of perfect probity and clarity. As the *Washington Post* pointed out in a story offering to decode the symbols on display during the storming of the US

Capitol on January 6, 2021, a number of "Trump allies and surrogates . . . referred to Jan. 6 as Republicans' '1776 moment.'"[1] The Proud Boy–affiliated "1776.shop" website (now shuttered) sold ten different T-shirts with Revolutionary-era flag designs – not just the Gadsden flag (whose "Dont Tread on Me" has featured in the Tea Party's iconography since its inception), but also the Pine Tree flag (with its Lockean "Appeal to Heaven") and the flag of George Washington's headquarters (thirteen stars on a blue field). Among more high-flown expressions of conservative fantasy, we might think of the Federalist Society's expedient fiction of judicial originalism, which posits a frozen and fetishized Constitution – to be interpreted solely according to the putatively manifest "intent" of its original Framers – as a rationale for countering any and all non-regressive legislation. That such ideas are transparently fatuous – white-supremacist, historically vacant, and casting chauvinistic ignorance as a virtue – in no way diminishes their power.

The appeal of Revolutionary-era dates and symbols for the American right is straightforward: How better to frame a ruthlessly partisan and utterly contemporary ideology than with a veneer of almost universally acclaimed "tradition"? How better to recall a cultural moment in which power and property accrued more or less exclusively to white men? That said Of course, linking the early republic with righteous simplicity has never been an activity limited to conservatives. For instance, we might think of Mary Antin, a Jewish immigrant whose family moved to Boston from Belarus in the late nineteenth century. Enrolled in a public school, Antin found herself drawn irretrievably to the figure of George Washington: she wrote poems about him, gave speeches about him, and fabricated a new "American" subjectivity in what she cast as his likeness. For Antin, whose life's work consisted in public advocacy for Progressive causes – particularly those related to the treatment of immigrants and the alleviation of poverty – Washington served as a kind of paragon of radical equality, proof that birth and worth were in no way correlated. "I had relatives and friends who were notable people by the old standards . . . but this George Washington, who died long before I was born, was like a king in greatness, and he and I were Fellow Citizens."[2] Washington may have done special things, but his most important act was his participation in the republic; his greatness affirms the possibility of *her* greatness – and of everyone's. It's not at all surprising that Washington's ambivalent relation-ship to slavery (including his own enslavement of several hundred people at Mt. Vernon) doesn't come up in Antin's account; neither does his role in the displacing of Indigenous peoples. Washington is a radiant and uncomplicated hero for Antin, whose static iconicity – impressed ad infinitum on every quarter (since 1932) and every dollar bill (off and on since 1869) – remains part of the fabric of US life.

Broadly, then: people occupying a vast range of positions on the political spectrum have long associated the turn of the nineteenth century with a kind of prelapsarian rectitude or *certainty* – it was a time before all of the trouble started, whatever that trouble might be. The all-too-recent *1776 Commission Report* – produced by the Trump administration partly in response to Nikole Hannah-Jones's *1619 Project* for the *New York Times* – frames a particularly acidulous version of consensus historiography: "The facts of our founding are not partisan. They are a matter of history. Controversies about the meaning of the founding can begin to be resolved by looking at the facts of our nation's founding. Properly understood, these facts address the concerns and aspirations of Americans of all social classes, income levels, races and religions, regions and walks of life."[3] Breathtaking tautology aside, this notion that all "controversies" about the first years of the United States require resolution into a singular "proper" and universally applicable understanding – and that such resolutions would be the natural and inevitable outcome of "looking at the facts" – is, of course, both absurd and dangerous. Historical "fact" is not a kind of fossil, to be pulled up glittering and self-evident from the ooze, always already primed for integration into a stable explanatory system that confirms the justness and inevitability of the present. The pastness of the past doesn't mean that it all makes perfect sense; it should be no more totalizable than the now.

In the spirit of resisting consensus history and making space for new and better ways of imagining the American project, this volume rejects grand narratives in favor of the contingent, the provisional, the temporary. There is always more to do and say about this (or any) set of cultural moments; *American Literature in Transition, 1770–1828, Volume 1*, is not designed to be the last word on the early Republic, but rather a set of provocations, landmarks, or models for future inquiry. Hence, the titular emphasis on "transition": in what follows, we describe a field that is constantly changing and, with it, a shifting landscape of questions, archives, foci, and more. We take as a starting assumption a belief in the possibilities of unknowing, a sense of the importance of exploring – without explaining away – the vast range of opacities that have shaped what and how we think about the United States. And insofar as new areas of uncertainty are often the progenitors of new methods, new histories, and new archives, the aspiration of this volume is not *more* certainty but rather a closer and more molecular perspective on the period's knottier historical problems.

Many silent transitions inform what we have tried to do here. In a traditional historiographic sense, this period is perhaps the most obviously transitional of the four volumes in the series. The years 1770–1828 encompass the shift from the eighteenth to the nineteenth century, the shift from a colonial to an early national or republican period, the shift from locally concentrated authority to something like federal governance, and the shift from manuscript and manually operated printing technologies to something nearing industrial print production. But there are a great many more moving parts: we have attempted, in this collection, to move at least sporadically away from these received political and historical frameworks in order to think about how else we might see and understand the literature of this period. Sometimes, that means centering new texts or other objects of study; at other points, it means developing underexamined networks of production, reception, and engagement. In all cases, we hope this volume (and the series that it commences) will pose larger questions about what American literature – a phrase that, at best, describes a loose, unwieldly conglomerate of print, manuscript, and other material sources – was, is, and could be.

Accordingly, the essays in this volume take as axiomatic the intransigent messiness of the period. The early republic was a moment without a monoculture. There were scores of languages spoken, Indigenous and Indo-European and African; there were also syncretic mixes, like Gullah and Louisiana Creole. Even among anglophone white folks, there were significant regional barriers to communication. (This is why Noah Webster gets so wound up about an American English dictionary in the late eighteenth century – he perceives the need to *make* a unitary American language, not the need to record it.) There was considerable economic disparity, and a great deal of conversation about whether mercantile or agricultural interests ought to claim precedence in the affairs of the republic. There was religious difference, too; Judaism, Catholicism, Quakerism, Protestant Congregationalism, African Methodist Episcopalianism, Charismatic Pentecostalism, Yoruba, Islam, and an irreducible variety of indigenous faiths shared space (if not equal power) under the federal tent. Most importantly, some people were enslaved and others were free; some people claimed the right to displace others for the purposes of capitalist enclosure. The ceaseless structural conflict framed by the interested fictions of white supremacy and Manifest Destiny meant that there could never be such a thing as a singular Early Republic.

The collection features essays on classic topoi of the Founding as well as on issues that have garnered increasingly sustained scholarly attention but that still cannot claim the centrality to the field as a whole that we think they merit: Hispanophone and other non-Anglophone literatures, disability aesthetics and analytics, queer care, and the origins of white supremacist cultures in the United States.[4] Still: there are just as many fields and subfields, geographies and questions that are *not* represented in what follows. Curating a collection of essays that purports to represent five complex decades not only lends itself to but actually *requires* omissions, absences, and gaps. We have sought to represent a wide spectrum of archives, sources, methods, and genres in a critical stance that announces a belief in the pedagogical value of exposure and assemblage over cohesion. But we have also tried our best to set up useful conversations among the pieces. To that end, we have loosely organized the essays that follow into three broad fields, in an effort to corral what we believe are some of the unique contributions of this volume into frameworks – some very traditional to literary criticism, others less so – that showcase some of the current transitions in the study of the literatures of the early United States. What we hope will emerge from this volume are questions: difficult, unresolved, but newly thinkable with the help of the essays it contains – a generative and deeply interesting cacophony instead of a triumphal march.

Form and Genre

Part I of the book is devoted to essays that might be said to turn on questions of expressive form. A great deal of important writing from the time of the Founding falls outside of now-conventional parameters of literary art: we thus seek to acknowledge and celebrate the considerable formal diversity of the period. Indeed, it's hard to overstate the richness and variety of literary and para-literary texts in the early Republic; people consumed daily and weekly newspapers and monthly magazines; they bought English and Continental imprints as well as American ones; they sent each other letters and assembled common-place books; they wrote and read almanacs and catechisms and political histories and natural histories and cookbooks and dictionaries and murder ballads and political pamphlets and hymnals and missals and philosophical essays and novels and poems and satires and on and on. The essays in this section are meant to suggest angles of approach to this multitude; although the techniques they deploy and the conclusions they draw might be quite distinct, they share a commitment to the possibilities of generic reading.

We begin with documents involved in the creation of the state. In "The Law of Form and the Form of the Law," Matthew Garrett takes up the rhetorical niceties critical to instantiating a democracy in which the actual power of the people is radically curtailed. Moving through the series of documents that amount to the bureaucratic Founding of the United States (the Declaration of Independence, the Articles of Confederation, the US Constitution, *The Federalist*), he shows how a propertied elite arrogated sovereignty to itself under the sign of representative government burdened with a "responsibility" to the People – those abstracted guarantors of moral and political authority – instead of a crass accountability to actual squabbling and (as the elite imagined them) unwashed constituents.

Even if the notion of the People was a useful fiction for constraining actual demotic power, speaking to the public mattered a great deal. The idea that governmental action relied on securing the appearance of popular consent meant that the ancient arts of charisma and rhetorical persuasion claim a new and remarkable importance in the project of holding the United States together. Sandra Gustafson's examination of the genre of the "The Statesman's Address" considers the early republican interest in the potency of the spoken word, exploring the remarkable continuities between neoclassical aesthetics, religious revivalism, and Indigenous diplomacy. This dynamic becomes especially vivid in the first decades of the nineteenth century, Gustafson argues, with the recording and wide dissemination of congressional debates; the cultural elevation of men like Daniel Webster and John C. Calhoun on the basis of their rhetorical ability is an essential part of the fantasy of the United States as a deliberative polity.

In another turn on the relationship between language and hegemony, Sean Harvey uses Indigenous vocabularies to isolate and specify some of the stakes of linguistic study under the conditions of settler colonialism. Among the parties devoted to the work of recording Native American languages and translating them into English were traders, missionaries, government administrators, and natural philosophers. As such a list might suggest, no matter what form the collection of words took, the results were far from neutral – with consequences both intimate and global. A knowledge of Native speech might be used to press a commercial advantage, convert a "heathen" soul to Christianity, seize a territory, or build a Eurocentric theory of human cultural evolution. Critically, though, these word lists can also frame facets of Indigenous resistance and perseverance in the face of assimilationist or exterminationist fantasies. (For a companionate claim about Indigenous oratorical traditions, see Lopenzina's essay below.)

The next three chapters shift to a consideration of belletristic forms. Thomas Koenigs's "The Genteel Novel in the Early United States" explores late eighteenth- and early nineteenth-century attempts to reframe fictional entertainments as essential ideological tools. Although the genre of the novel had often been treated as dangerous in the eighteenth century – as the sort of thing that put bad ideas in the heads of readers, that encouraged sympathy for or identification with the vicious and depraved – Koenigs shows how early US novelists leveraged suspicions about the form and about gentility itself to imagine or consolidate something like an aristocracy of virtue disarticulated from an aristocracy of wealth. That is, the novel becomes a crucial site both for testing definitions of "refinement" and "virtue" and – at least in theory – for metacognitive thinking about how fiction might inculcate those ideas into an irregularly educated and unevenly distributed population.

The next essays continue in a similarly demotic vein. Heather Nathans's "The State of Our Union: Comedy in the Post-Revolutionary US Theater" finds in comic stage performance an overlooked archive for reading social tensions in the postwar moment – especially those tensions related to the absurdities of racial and class inequality. American theater audiences in the last decades of the eighteenth century were extremely keen on comedies of manners, whether by British or American playwrights, especially those that mobilized cultural otherness as part of the humor. At a time when the playhouse was perhaps the most important setting for popular entertainment, the runaway success on the American stage of stock figures like the fop, the bumpkin, and the ethnic "type" makes concrete – and often ironizes – the broader power relations that structure the culture. Along these same popular lines, in "'To assume her Language as my own': The Revival Hymn and the Evangelical Poetess in the Early Republic," Wendy Roberts explores the contours of pietistic poetry produced by women in the late colonial and post-Revolutionary eras. Deeply conventional and so ubiquitous as to be more or less invisible to scholars, gendered hymnody has not often been considered worthy of extended critical attention. For Roberts, however, these poems document the necessarily aesthetic nature of Protestantism; the ecstasies of belief rendered in verse by various Poetesses are key to understanding the lived religion of the First and Second Great Awakenings. Roberts also locates in the poems of Phillis

Wheatley Peters a vital critique of the figure of the totalizing (and implicitly white) Evangelical Poetess. Wheatley Peters's refusal to produce the
hymns that the dominant culture expected of poetically inclined women –
in favor, for example, of neoclassical epyllia – coupled with her unconventional adaptations of some of hymnody's signature tropes, puts her at the
center of an anti-white-supremacist tradition.

Part I concludes with a literary look at foodways. Elizabeth Hopwood's
"Ambiguities and Little Secrets: Taste-Making and the Rise of the
American Cookbook" takes up the ideological complexity of early
republican cookbooks, finding in recipes and their framing a vision of
domestic tranquility dependent on the mystification of enslaved labor and
international trade. Commodities such as ginger and sugar came to market
denuded of the whole bloody history of their cultivation and preparation;
cookbooks stand as manuals for recasting extractive processes in terms of a
wholesome narrative of sustainability, feminine capability, and household
independence. If there is no practical separation in the household manual
between the government of the kitchen and the government of the polity,
then the stakes of baking are quite high; the house is not merely a
metaphorical "little commonwealth" but a critical site for the fantasies that
sustain the big commonwealth itself.

Networks

Shifting from an emphasis on genre to an emphasis on the conditions of
production, we have organized Part II around the idea of the network –
the dynamic interconnection between people, geographies, texts, and
cultural infrastructures. This is not, itself, a new idea. Scholars from
Lisa Brooks to Michael Warner, Caroline Wigginton to Joseph Rezek
have all, and quite differently, taken as a point of departure the critical
importance of networks to various sorts of cultural production: history,
print, letters, and diplomacy. Scholarship in book history, in particular,
has emphasized the immense influence of networks on the production
and circulation of print and manuscript materials. Recent work in Black
and Indigenous studies has charted the critical importance of networks
for a wide range of technologies of communication – from periodicals
to oratory, sermons to songs, novels to "true histories," craftwork
to print. These networked technologies, in turn, become central to
fugitivity, negotiation, political consciousness-raising, and collective
resistance.[5]

The contributors to this part of the volume – Emily García, Drew Lopenzina, Anna Mae Duane, John Mac Kilgore, and Kirsten Lee – all build on the importance of eighteenth- and nineteenth-century networks to fascinating and innovative ends. Each of these pieces has a distinct archive and a different aim, but they share an appreciation of relationality – be it local, regional, or circumatlantic. Framing the means and modes of the *circulation* of ideas as vital corollaries to the ideas themselves, these essays foreground the intricate mediations at the center of early Republican sociability.

The section begins with Kilgore's "Modern Bigotry: The War for the Ohio, the Whiskey Rebellion, and the Settler Colonial Imagination in the Early Republic," which shows how networks of print entertainment, political influence, and armed resistance became absolutely indispensable to the emergence of a consolidated white identity and the attendant growth of shared white supremacist and settler colonial sentiment. These networks, Kilgore argues, structured the arrangements of power both within and between regions, and stretched from the so-called frontiers to the metropoles. Reading well-studied writers such as Hugh Henry Brackenridge in light of these networks allows connections between distant locations and seemingly unrelated political conflicts (here, the United States wars against the United Indian Nations and the Whiskey Rebellion) to come into focus, and brings into relief facets of some of these texts that might be otherwise difficult to trace.

It is also possible to read these colonialist networks against the grain. As Drew Lopenzina details in his essay, "'This Politick Salvage': Defining an Early Native American Literary Aesthetics," the extensive textual records of British settler colonial violence – in the form of travel writings, colonial reports, and natural histories – also document Indigenous diplomacy. Lopenzina follows a particular tropology through white accounts of diplomatic relations, noting that settlers often represented Indigenous peoples as exceedingly politically savvy while consistently remarking on the unlikeliness that they could be politically savvy at all. He names this representational technique "*unwitnessing*, a rhetorical mode in which the very thing being commented upon for some pragmatic purpose of exposition must then be repeatedly and forcefully retracted to serve prevailing colonial ideologies of conquest." As an example, Lopenzina points us to the unwitting account of the widespread Native understanding of the "common pot," or agreement to shared, negotiated use of land, that appears in George Washington's description of a speech he attended by the Seneca orator Tanaghrisson in 1754. While Washington seems unable to understand the oratory as an elaboration of Native-settler politics, we can see precisely the kinds of diplomacy of which Indigenous communities were imagined to be incapable.

The rewards of this attention to circulation, across and among regions and historical periods, are not merely the richness and specificity that comes with historical detail. Indeed, as Emily García argues in her essay, "Logics of Exchange and the Beginnings of US Hispanophone Literature," the particularity of *place* significantly affects the tools of literary composition – metaphor, imagery and other tropes, and political and economic logic – that in turn shape the content of the work. "Logics of Exchange" focuses on bilingual Hispanophone writers and printers in Philadelphia, a city with a flourishing print industry and with mercantile ties to both the Spanish Caribbean and Central America. Taking up this political economy, García argues, we are better able to draw out what she terms the "logics of exchange" of early nineteenth-century Hispanophone print.

Focusing on networks, as opposed to single authors, also allows us to repurpose old questions to new ends. Indeed, sustained focus on the connections between writers, printers, and thinkers – especially when scholars take a durational approach to these communities, examining them over the span of decades – allows previously un- or underexamined features of their conversations to come into view. In her essay, "The Emigrationist Turn in Black Anti-Colonizationist Sentiment," Kirsten Lee's attention to Black periodicals – newspapers produced by Black writers and editors for an intended Black audience – exposes some of the more granular politics informing debates about the resettlement of free and enslaved Black Americans in Liberia, Sierra Leone, or elsewhere. Her careful consideration of these intracommunity dialogues, rather than relying exclusively on writings by proponents or members of the (white-founded and white-led) American Colonization Society, allows a more nuanced perspective on the public reception of back-to-Africa efforts – all too often the choice of well-meaning white abolitionists and white enslavers alike. What this research reveals is that Black skepticism about resettlement elsewhere provided the foundations for Black separatist movements aimed at founding Black-governed and Black-populated communities *inside* the United States and Canada. By drawing readerly attention to the subtleties of these conversations – between white and Black proponents of colonization, Black proponents and opponents of colonization, and distinctions between colonizationist versus emigrationist political visions – the intellectual work of negotiating competing theories of political emancipation, abolition, and civic enfranchisement comes into stark relief.

Just as importantly, lesser-studied conversations between and within political organizations and charitable societies dedicated to different forms of service work afford us a sense of how politics of all kinds were shaped by the simultaneous development of philanthropic and municipal infrastructures in American cities. These infrastructures, as scholars such as Donna Andrew have argued, represented a boon in private support for needy individuals – but that support was almost inevitably contingent on forms of transactional control aimed at managing ostensibly troublesome populations.[6] Certain philanthropic organizations, such as the Magdalen Societies, moreover, expanded, opening sites in cities up and down the East Coast. These infrastructural networks can be slippery and difficult to chart. But Anna Mae Duane embarks on just such an effort in her essay, "The Black Child, the Colonial Orphan and Early Republican Visions of Freedom." Duane uses things like school recitations to track the metaphorics of childhood out of its pride-of-place as the cherished idiom for describing the new US Republic and *into* philanthropic efforts to address the realities of Black children who would be manumitted in their majority. In particular, Duane considers exchanges between members of the American Colonization Society and students at the New York African Free School; for the ACS, the institutional education of Black youth was a critical site of intervention in their maturation into adulthood, but also an important opportunity for procolonizationist propaganda. In contradistinction to Lee's essay, Duane finds Black *children* coming toe-to-toe with a political platform that would make their emancipation contingent on their deportation. Attention to the strategic use of charitable infrastructures for the dissemination of colonizationist literatures, then, exposes the ambivalent character of early nineteenth-century print, and its use as a tool for achieving insidious ends.

Methods for Living

The final constellation into which the contributions of this volume seemed to cluster was an abiding concern with representations and theorizations of the practice and negotiation of ordinary life. In spite of fantasies about national unity in the afterglow of the ratification of the Constitution and a renewed Era of Good Feelings in the wake of the War of 1812, this was a moment of frontier violence, widespread economic instability (including the Embargo of 1807, the Panic of 1819, and the controversies over the establishment of the First and Second Banks of the United States), and a deeply uneven distribution of resources. Despite the generally middling-to-wealthy status of most protagonists of canonical early nineteenth-century literatures, a great many residents of the pre-industrial United States were people without guaranteed access to their everyday needs: skilled and unskilled laborers (whether free, bonded, or enslaved), subsistence farmers, the poor and indigent. How do we make sense of the practical strategies that individuals brought to the problem of navigating hard and uncertain times?

Essays by Michelle Sizemore, and Michael McDonnell and Marama Whyte take up the question of what Sizemore calls "The Affective Postwar," wherein residents of what had previously been the British North American colonies struggled to make sense of both their own experiences and the shifts in statecraft that attended the Revolution. Each essay is keenly interested in the emotional dimensions of this moment, although the texts at the center of the pieces differ significantly. While McDonnell and Whyte take up the explosion of memoirs and biographical writing that followed the end of the war, Sizemore argues that we need to expand the historiographic span of the Revolution itself, in order to account for how this event "generat[ed] national feelings long after its conclusion." In both pieces, attention to the emotional dimensions of narration – considering tone and tropologies of representation, as well as explicit and lengthy descriptions of the subjective experiences of writers and protagonists – allows for the generation of something like an Annales school treatment of the *longue durée* effects of the Revolutionary War for everyday people, an account sensitive to cultural shifts in what some have described as the *mentalité* of the moment.

Along the same affective lines, Lori Merish's "Literature of Poverty and Labor" takes a narrow-gauge, almost microhistorical approach to the literary representation of the rampant problem of poverty and lack of available work (especially for women) in early nineteenth-century Philadelphia. Where Sizemore and McDonnell and Whyte's archive suggests both the challenges and the promises of the long post-Revolutionary moment, Merish's essay elaborates the brutal reality of early republican inequality. Focusing on the narratives of poor free people seeking – often in vain – work that could sustain themselves and their families, Merish's essay points to the insights that can be derived from a close attention to the figures that tend to remain in the background of novels, essays, newspaper articles, and the papers of wealthy Americans. As she suggests, these narratives reveal the almost total ubiquity of class and labor struggle.

A reorientation toward such archives helps us more accurately populate our vision of early national life; it can also model reading strategies that encourage critiques of the aestheticization of poverty – the way that poor people and their struggles are abstracted into techniques used to set scenes and evince readerly pathos, rather than represented as realities meriting narrative exploration in their own right.

Finally, Sari Altschuler's "Neuroqueering the Republic: The Case of Charles Brockden Brown's *Ormond*" and Don James McLaughlin's "A Queer Crip Method for Early American Studies" both put early nineteenth-century American literature to work to consider how various narrative strategies tried – and often failed – to represent what Altschuler calls "different bodyminds[,] during a time when there were not yet adequate narrative means for doing so." While Altschuler finds in Charles Brockden Brown's *Ormond* a narratological experiment that seeks to redraw the boundaries of culturally thinkable neurodiversity, McLaughlin suggests that techniques for representing non-normative bodyminds may already exist – but that they have tended to be misread as simply moments of queerness. For both Altschuler and McLaughlin, disability studies offers a critical framework for approaching literary questions; they each draw important tools from the long-nineteenth-century texts at the center of their essays for recognizing what narrative – and critique itself – is not yet equipped to represent or even to know. For McLaughlin, a focus on the adult cradle – literally, a rocking device, more or less identical to a baby cradle but simply sized for adults – allows a glimpse into the everyday reality of a world in which people were frequently in great and chronic pain. His treatment of the material culture that appears unmarked in novels, papers, and other texts helps us register forms of connection and care that appear widely in texts from this era but are frequently either unseen or merely subsumed under the umbrella of queer history. These eclectic essays, as a whole, allow the quotidian and even the banal to assume pride of place as important frameworks for literary historical analysis. While each is quite different, taken together they nonetheless announce a singular, aggregate transition for literary study, in which the ordinary rather than the exceptional provides the foundations for future scholarly conversations.

A Note on the Text

As writers and scholars, each of us has been counseled by many an editor to avoid references to current events, especially in the introduction to a book.

Such references, the story goes, make the work feel dated, which is to say that they make impossible the feeling of timelessness that is supposedly one of the hallmarks of great scholarship.

Even so: Let us start by stating that the majority of the essays collected here were written, submitted, edited, revised, and revised again during the global COVID-19 pandemic. While the editorial team for this series as a whole was in no way relieved from the unique pressures of what can probably no longer be called a "moment" – working from home, extremely limited access to archives, balancing teaching and writing with the full-time care of small children or other family members, to say nothing of the stress, outrage, anxiety, and straight-up drudgery that has attended it – through our work as editors, we were also witnesses to the disparate and far-reaching effects that the pandemic wrought on our contributors as well. While many of the absences in this volume are simply the product of both our editorial choices and the makeup of the field as a whole, we also lost a range of solicited contributions from scholars whom we think of as doing some of the most exciting work in the field today to the immense pressures of care work, illness, and death. That the current pandemic represents not only a global emergency but also an unquestionably racialized public health crisis – one that has disproportionately impacted Black, Latinx, Native, and/or poor people – has been especially visible to us, as editors, throughout this process. While many of the essays in this collection in fact address, showcase, and explore the conditions that provided the historical foundations for those very disparities, literary research also seems like cheap and bitter consolation.[7] This was buttressed by two other forms of political upheaval that made Americanist scholarship an at best complicated endeavor: in the United States, another spate of murders of Black people by police officers and several months of global, critically important protests; and a presidential election (in 2020) in which, for those of us writing in the United States (but no less than for those writing elsewhere) the potential of an increasingly authoritarian future seemed to hang in the balance. We assembled this volume in a moment in which it was difficult to think, write, and commit time to scholarship when so many other things felt so much more important. In a moment of widespread misinformation, legitimate fear, and general precarity, we have all had to improvise with whatever analytic tools seemed promising.

Such a demand for an improvisational and eclectic response, however, may nonetheless have provided an important, if clumsy, set of instructions for the production of this volume. As we lived the transitions of the past several years, we have learned a great deal about how to think with and through the constancy of cultural instability. This moment has demanded flexibility and intellectual openness, and we hope that we have brought that ambivalent inheritance into the collection that follows.

Notes

1 *Washington Post* (January 15, 2021). www.washingtonpost.com/nation/inter active/2021/far-right-symbols-capitol-riot/.

2 Mary Antin, *The Promised Land* (Boston: Houghton Mifflin, 1925), 224.

3 President's Advisory 1776 Commission, *The 1776 Report* (Washington, DC, 2021), 1. https://web.archive.org/web/20210119000821/https://www .whitehouse.gov/wp-content/uploads/2021/01/The-Presidents-Advisory-1776-Commission-Final-Report.pdf.

4 For just a taste of the foundational scholarship in these fields, see Kirsten Silva Gruesz, *Ambassadors of Culture: The Transamerican Origins of Latino Writing* (Princeton, NJ: Princeton University Press, 2002), and her forthcoming *Cotton Mather's Spanish Lessons: Language, Race, and American Memory* (Cambridge, MA: Harvard University Press, 2021); Rodrigo Lazo's *Letters from Filadelfia: Early Latino Literature and the Trans-American Elite* (Charlottesville: University of Virginia Press, 2020) and Lazo, ed., *The Latino Nineteenth Century* (New York: New York University Press, 2016); and Lawrence Rosenwald, *Multilingual America: Language and the Making of American Literature* (Cambridge: Cambridge University Press, 2008).

5 See Michael Warner, *Letters of the Republic: Publication and the Public Sphere in Eighteenth-Century America* (Cambridge, MA: Harvard University Press, 1990), and Caroline Wigginton, *In the Neighborhood: Women's Publication in Early America* (Amherst: University of Massachusetts Press, 2016). See also Joseph Rezek, *London and the Making of Provincial Literature Aesthetics and the Transatlantic Book Trade, 1800–1850* (Philadelphia: University of Pennsylvania Press, 2015); Kacy Tillman, *Stripped and Script: Loyalist Women Writers of the American Revolution* (Amherst: University of Massachusetts Press, 2019); Lisa Brooks, *Our Beloved Kin: A New History of King Philip's War* (New Haven, CT: Yale University Press, 2018); Derrick Spires, *The Practice of Citizenship*: Black Politics and Print Culture in the Early United States (Philadelphia: University of Pennsylvania Press, 2019); and Alejandra Dubcovsky, *Informed Power: Communication in the Early American South* (Cambridge, MA: Harvard University Press, 2016).

6 Donna Andrew, *Philanthropy and Police* (Princeton, NJ: Princeton University Press, 1989).

7 A number of Americanists, alongside historians of science (and epidemiology in particular), have curated lists of resources – books, essays, think-pieces, etc. – that might serve as historical guides for thinking about a range of facets of the COVID-19 pandemic. Perhaps most notably, in March 2020, Alondra Nelson, as well as Sari Altschuler (contributor to this volume) and Elizabeth Maddock Dillon, posted Twitter threads with guides to how to think about the cultural politics of epidemics – including their racial, national, gendered, and economic dimensions.

Form and Genre

CHAPTER 2

The Law of Form and the Form of the Law

Matthew Garrett

Expressly political literature in the period of the Revolution and early republic attempts to balance, synthesize, or overcome the contradiction between the language of universal freedom and the nascent and evolving national institutions of domination, exploitation, and general unfreedom. The division between ruling and dominated classes was itself of course far from novel in the eighteenth century; but the early United States was historically distinctive because its formative political philosophy and legal documents – along with the larger part of its literary production – insisted at once on the necessity of the common people to the vitality of the polity and the propriety of their exclusion from power. The function of the people, in this new situation, was to legitimate a state apparatus organized to greater or lesser degrees against their interests and well-being. Although historians quibble over the precise tempering of the early national instrument, all by now recognize the basic restriction of its tonal range: "The framers of the Constitution embarked on the first experiment in designing a set of political institutions that would both embody and at the same time curtail popular power, in a context where it was no longer possible to maintain an exclusive citizen body. Where the option of an active but exclusive citizenry was unavailable, it would be necessary to create an inclusive but passive citizen body with limited scope for its political powers."[1] The shift from active and exclusive to inclusive but passive is, crucially, a mutation from the social logic of domination to that of exploitation, a shift in which US state formation functions as a hinge between historical epochs.

Inclusive but passive: the combination may be stated as a starkly political solution to the problem, but it was profoundly dependent on the expressive forms through which these political institutions were articulated – described, endorsed, interpreted, and defended. In the early republic, a traditional historiographical division between political substance and literary expression is invalidated by the conditions themselves.

For in undertaking to produce an inclusive but passive common citizenry, early national political literature was required to shape itself to its task: to speak with a historically original forked tongue.

Consider, first, the relationship between the two lasting documents of the early national period: the Declaration of Independence and the Constitution. Notoriously, the Declaration has no legal standing, but rhetorically the two texts have operated together since the ratification period in 1787–1788, above all because of their gestural incipits, which are themselves best understood in relation to the mediating text of the Articles of Confederation.

The Declaration of Independence (1776):

> When in the Course of human events, it becomes necessary for one people to dissolve the political bands which have connected them with another, and to assume among the powers of the earth, the separate and equal station to which the Laws of Nature and of Nature's God entitle them, a decent respect to the opinions of mankind requires that they should declare the causes which impel them to the separation. – We hold these truths to be self-evident, that all men are created equal, that they are endowed by their Creator with certain unalienable Rights, that among these are Life, Liberty and the pursuit of Happiness.

The Articles of Confederation (1781):

> To all to whom these Presents shall come, we the under signed Delegates of the States affixed to our Names send greeting.

The Constitution (1787):

> We the People of the United States, in Order to form a more perfect Union, establish Justice, insure domestic Tranquility, provide for the common defence, promote the general Welfare, and secure the Blessings of Liberty to ourselves and our Posterity, do ordain and establish this Constitution for the United States of America.

The movement from 1776 to 1787 is the development of agential sentences. The infamous passive construction that begins the Declaration in fact enunciates only its own speech. The break with Britain is taken as given, "we" or the "one people" who enact the break announce only that they will "declare the causes" that have forced it. The "necessary" is thus doubly historical. On the one hand, the text marks the history of political events (the dissolving of political bands); on the other, as Paul Downes has sharply shown, the writing annotates the historicity of its grammatical procedures: "The Declaration ... declares that a time comes in the course of human events when the equivocal agency of the third-person passive construction becomes necessary."[2] The Declaration's style of involution is the coiling of a grammatical problem, the question of political subjecthood, that is unfurled in its juridical sequels. That is, at the moment of the discursive (i.e., linguistic but not yet institutional) emergence of the new nation, political agency is recognizable as a problem of political sentence-making; a subsequent series of grammatical adjustments in the early national documents seeks to fix, revise, refine, and redefine the basis from which a national authority may be legitimated through reference to its citizen-subjects.

Diplomatic diction replaces grammatical flourish in the Articles of Confederation, which speak in the modest tenor of the state functionary at the consul's table. The delegates of the states "agree to certain articles of Confederation and perpetual Union" between the states themselves, and indeed the bulk of the preamble to the Articles is simply the list of states, which is given twice (once as paratextual identification of the agents, once within the marked textual boundary of the Articles themselves). Significantly, when stylistic play and ambiguity disappear, concern with style erupts as a basic theme of the text, which begins properly with the question of naming in Article I: "The Stile of this confederacy shall be 'The United States of America.'" If, as Downes puts it, being "a subject of the American Revolution" is to be "bound to negotiate a relationship to this disembodying (or body-doubling) substitution, this linguistic sleight-of-hand, this revolutionary grammar," then to be a subject of the nation-building that immediately follows is to be located, diminutively, among a multiplicity of other grammatical agents.[3] The plural "united states" acts contingently on the basis of agreement.

Viewed in the context of the grammatical dynamics of the three documents, the usurping phrase "We the People of the United States" assumes a sharper grade of contrasts than stock thematic political analysis observes. For the Declaration's grammatical stridency – that is, the boldness of grammar itself, wielded as a fully realized instrument of expression in its own right – returns here dialectically, in inverted form. No sentence could be clearer about its enunciating subject: this first-person utterance identifies itself for the reader's convenience. But whereas the hidden actor in the Declaration delivered nothing but its circumstances, the abundantly articulated subject of the Constitution does nothing but secrete its own. The interplay between the two styles of writing, and the deepening ambiguity of their connection with each other, has been an important part of their circulation as legitimating documents in US history. The collective first person who holds certain truths to be self-evident is grafted onto the first-person People of the Constitution, which is therefore assumed to hold fast to those same principles, and the necessity of historical rupture binds itself to the necessity of national consolidation. The meek delegates in between perish from sight: they never stood a chance.

All of this is politics writ small, in the microstructures of language, dependent on the ramifications of three related but distinct deployments of the first-person plural, inflected in three different ways by the dynamics of the three texts. At three moments in the movement from revolutionary rupture to national consolidation (from constituent power to the constitution), the language of the emergent state slaloms between exclusive and inclusive expressions of citizenry, active and passive constructions of the subject.[4] Taken in sequence, the sentences indicate something additional: namely, that in a significant way, this language *is* politics in the period. Such political writing responds to the pressures of social conflict, which determine its distortions (its contortive grammars, its rhetorical concessions to and appropriations of the activity of the included but passive subjects), but it attempts to seal off politics from the common people who remain its essential reference.

Nevertheless, the putative truth of the Constitution's preamble could be "made manifest," as Benjamin Franklin put it, through the contest for ratification: state delegates would vote to accept or reject the Constitution that had been drafted in secrecy in Philadelphia.[5] Yet the question of ratification, too, amounted to a dispute within the possessing class. Thus the literature of the ratification debate extends and intensifies the problems of representation expressed in the early documents. Pointedly, participants in the debate understood their arguments to be a national and international spectacle, observed by their nonpossessing counterparts within the new nation and by their allies and antagonists abroad. In the opening number of *The Federalist*, Alexander Hamilton registered the world-historical stakes of the argument as a means of establishing the texture – the standards and tonality – of the deliberation: "The subject speaks its own importance: comprehending in its consequences nothing less than the existence of the UNION the safety and welfare of the parts of which it is composed, the fate of an empire in many respects the most interesting in the world."[6] Here *The Federalist* shares, in its initiating move, the epistemology of self-evidence announced in the Declaration of Independence, but with a decisive difference: in the context of the ratification debate, self-evidence obtains not as the ground of political *substance* (natural rights) but rather as a measure of the political *significance* of the conjuncture. From substantive, the grammar has morphed into modifier: we have traveled from noun to adjective. The first truth here held to be self-evident is that the US Constitution is important as the test of political history against political philosophy, of "whether societies of men are really capable or not of establishing good government from reflection and choice, or whether they are forever destined to depend for their political constitutions on accident and force."[7] This small but consequential adjustment in accent coheres with the dialectical reversal the Constitution performs on the Declaration's grammar: having seized the first-person plural, the Constitution – and now *The Federalist* – must add volume to its draught of the polity by reframing the conditions of argument. Its first, and recurring, concern is with the *medium* of debate: the definition of the agent (the People) that speaks through the self-evident subject of ratification.

At issue here is the inseparability of the federalist political position from the federalist mode of position-taking. That is, *The Federalist* is necessarily driven to reflect again and again on its conditions of writing and the ethos behind them, to contrast its "enlightened zeal" with the "torrent of angry and malignant passions" that it predicts will be "let loose" during the debate.[8] Abhorring both "democracy" and all "levelling" – egalitarian – politics, partisans of the new Constitution weave their loathing for the mass of the people into their enactment of the People.[9] Reworking Lockean and Protestant sectarian conceptualizations of enthusiasm, the paradox of enlightened zeal not only enables *The Federalist* rhetorically to align its passions with its asserted disinterestedness, but it also consolidates its speaking subject into a singular, coherent, and elevated personality.[10] Publius, the pseudonym under which Hamilton, James Madison, and John Jay published *The Federalist*, is the avatar of the Constitution's "People."

As avatar, the Publius pose fuses the category of the People with the Constitution's inclusive but passive citizenry. Publius speaks with enlightened zeal: a controlled passion that guarantees rather than impairs federalist refinement. As the final installment in the series puts it:

> I have addressed myself purely to your judgments, and have studiously avoided those asperities which are too apt to disgrace political disputants of all parties and which have been not a little provoked by the language and conduct of the opponents of the Constitution. The charge of a conspiracy against the liberties of the people which has been indiscriminately brought against the advocates of the plan has something in it too wanton and too

malignant not to excite the indignation of every man who feels in his own bosom a refutation of the calumny. The perpetual changes which have been rung upon the wealthy, the well-born, and the great have been such as to inspire the disgust of all sensible men. And the unwarrantable concealments and misrepresentations which have been in various ways practiced to keep the truth from the public eye have been of a nature to demand the reprobation of all honest men. It is not impossible that these circumstances may have occasionally betrayed me into intemperances of expression which I did not intend; it is certain that I have frequently felt a struggle between sensibility and moderation; and if the former has in some instances prevailed, it must be my excuse that it has been neither often nor much.[11]

"Enlightened zeal" means more than prim conservatism or distaste for open class struggle. Throughout, The Federalist figures both the common and the plural as decisive enemies of the republic. In the debate, too much passion (unenlightened zeal) spurs too many people (of the common kind) to dissent. Importantly, dissent in this case is fidelity to the existing Confederation and resistance to the federalist aspiration to hegemony. Indeed, it is more accurate to say that, in The Federalist's rhetorical rendering of the debate, the insidious fluency of that passion itself generates the bad people by infecting them with what is "too wanton and too malignant." The pleonasm – what would be adequately wanton and malignant? – symptomatizes the problem. The Federalist deploys its own expressiveness to excise the malignancy and smother the human "conflagration" it has enflamed.[12] The characteristic double movement of federalist argumentation, achieving full literary flower in The Federalist itself, is to disperse the multiplicity of the people first, then consolidate them into a unified national government – "government" understood in the specifically eighteenth-century sense of restriction, guidance, or binding.[13] That consolidation is only meaningful, only effective, when it unifies components whose complexity would otherwise overwhelm or subvert centralization itself. Notably, this centralizing text embraces signs of its own disorganization, and of the piecemeal quality of pro-Constitution argument, reworking the variegated, the partial, and the dispersive into an episodic form of unification.

Dispersal and consolidation, the two aspects of that mode of unification and the two faces of federalist nation-building, require scrutiny because the overwhelming political effect of ratification has been to freeze what was a process into an apparently static form. The federalist position came to be identified quickly in the 1787–1788 moment with the movement of consolidation, but this act of self-nominalization was itself part of the federalist strategy, since it reversed the accepted meaning of the very word "federalist," which originally designated a supporter of the new US Confederation (and so a partisan of a relatively loose and compromise-based sharing of power among the states). "Indeed, a principle objection to the Constitution was that it set up a national, not a federal, government."[14] Contrasting the rhetorical and material operations of *The Federalist* with those of Thomas Paine's revolutionary pamphlet *Common Sense*, which itself aspired to organize a national polity (and in so doing created a myth of textual saturation), Trish Loughran has accented the former's function of gathering up the fictional fragments of a notional nation:

> The myth of *Common Sense* is based on a trope of diffusion, but *The Federalist* organizes itself around tropes of collection. . . . Paine sought to saturate a vast but always self-identical space through acts of reading that would have enabled a densely participatory (if still textually mediated) political culture. But *The Federalist* posits a new mechanics of government that allows the part to stand in completely for the whole. . . . [T]he irony of American nationalism is that the Revolution had to be undone in just this way in order to be remembered by the many later generations that would legitimate it as the authentic origin of "their" nation (rather than a failed experiment, like the Confederation).[15]

Painean dissemination would be the counterpoint, in terms of constituent power, to *The Federalist*'s constitutional seizure of political power.

Yet consolidation itself tends to be a consolidating category, aspiring as it does to obliterate the activity of solidifying (Latin *consolidare*: to make solid together) the otherwise liquid and various materials it claims, retroactively, to have identified as a binding whole. Certainly, *The Federalist* strove synecdochally to replace the disparate and contentious classes and regions of the Confederation with the "part" of the federalist ruling class. At the same time, the rhetorical – as well as the institutional – operations of consolidation required an enumeration and even an amplification of the disparateness of the parts themselves. A first moment of dispersion was the prerequisite for a successful national consolidation. The proper name for that eminently literary synthesis is *episodic* because it organizes the component parts into an imaginary whole on the basis of their simultaneous autonomy and collective functionality. A political plot is woven out of many episodes.[16]

Uniting these two moments into a single dynamic figure, *The Federalist* seeks both to assume what it calls a "comprehensive" view of the ratification debate – a view that rhymes with its political argument for "extending the sphere" of the republic – and to "refine" both the political and the rhetorical forms of representation to ensure an effective distance from the people themselves.[17] The elevated, refined prospect provides the vantage from which the new national politics may be properly understood (evaluated, explained, defended, endorsed) and from which it may be enacted in practice. Significantly, this federalist discourse is largely aligned with that of a key strain of elite Anti-Federalist argument. Whereas Hamilton and Madison insist on distance from the people purportedly to avoid "the danger of corruption and demagoguery," propertied Anti-Federalists like Richard Henry Lee sought the same outcome through the Confederation itself. By combining federal extension with local control that concentrated power among the ruling elites, "the states provided models of small republics in which liberty and virtue could both flourish"; a national constitution would, in this view, lead to the most dangerous outcome of all, "only hasten[ing] democratization."[18] Again, we recognize that the ratification debate was, by and large, a dispute within the possessing class.

As we have seen, the intra-elite character of the debate did not foreclose the determination of its language by the class struggle. On the contrary, the victory of the men of property was realized at the cost of a certain distortion, a certain rhetorical swerving toward and envelopment of the problematic of the people. The people did not have the power, but they remained power's elemental reference. At the same time, overt clashes of class positions were not entirely absent, and a large but largely forgotten movement of plebeian anticonstitutionalists and radical democrats expressed itself with clarity. In terms of the linguistic atmosphere of the ratification debate, we may home in on an example of the incompatibility of competing concepts in this contest between classes, incompatibility that tells us much about the relation between social conflict and literary-political expression in the period.

Consider the curious career of the eighteenth-century usage of "responsibility," a term that has been misunderstood because apprehended only within the discourse of the dominant class. Working from the "comprehensive" and "refined" perspective of *The Federalist*, an influential line of interpretation has seen the underlying concept of responsibility as the bearer of a new etiolation of individual agency and accountability in the early US republic. For *The Federalist*, the notion operates in two directions at once: in Madison's treatment of senatorial terms (in *Federalist* 63), it designates the ability of the elected official to respond to the demands of the constituency: "Increased accountability must follow increased autonomous power." But in Hamilton's defense of the office of president, which was widely understood among Anti-Federalists to reinstate many of the worst aspects of monarchy, the term operated in the opposite direction: "The dangers of concentrating power are outweighed by the necessity of concentrating 'responsibility,' by the crucial obligation to locate accountability definitively in an individual who takes 'responsibility' for the complex process." The upshot of this argument is that the agency of the individual subject in general has become undecidable in 1787–1788, and the term bends to accommodate the new historical mood: "Responsibility refers primarily to the condition of being answerable, and only secondarily, and thus not necessarily, to the condition of being personally involved or morally culpable."[19] According to this reading of *responsibility*, a historically new separation appears between the capacity to act and the exposure to blame, and the federalist state-building project should be understood as part of a larger, late eighteenth-century destabilization of the liberal subject. Yet while such an interpretation is effective as a reading of *The Federalist*, by acceding to that text's evasion of reality it fails to grasp the semantically denser collective context for the word as an ongoing site of struggle within language. That is, rather than accept *The Federalist*'s version of "responsibility" as the definitive source for the understanding the concept in this period, we do well to explore its animation within the contested field of social meaning. Doing so generates a more precise historical concept and a richer sense of the political stakes of responsibility within the constitutional moment.

Samuel Bryan's widely reprinted *Centinel* series of essays against the Constitution delivers the necessary corrective to the overvaluation of agential ambiguity. For Centinel, the Confederation was the guarantee – or the best existing guarantee – of a national democracy, precisely because it held out the promise of both the protection of liberties and effective representation within the legislature. In this most "assertive and class-conscious" series of Anti-Federalist essays, Centinel elaborated on this perspective through both a negative critique of the proposed Constitution and a positive articulation of the alternative.[20] Throughout, and in keeping with his eponymous character's name, Bryan trains his polemicist's eye on both concrete class actors and their structural antagonism; under such scrutiny, the prevarications of federalist "responsibility" wilt like so many false blooms. For Centinel's lesson is that the claim of diminished agency is always deceitful when deployed by men of power – by, that is, the men who are agents by definition because they command the activity (the labor, the freedom, the political prospects) of others. In place of specious ambiguity is ringing clarity. Specifically, in arguing for a unicameral legislature organized on the principles of the Pennsylvania state constitution, Centinel restores the meaning of "responsibility" within the conflict over agency in a divided society:

> If you complicate the plan by various orders, the people will be perplexed and divided in their sentiments about the source of abuses or misconduct, some will impute it to the senate, others to the house of representatives, and so on, that the interposition of the people may be rendered imperfect or perhaps wholly abortive. But if, imitating the constitution of Pennsylvania, you vest all the legislative power in one body of men (separating the executive and the judicial) elected for a short period, and necessarily excluded by rotation from permanency, and guarded from precipitancy and surprise by delays imposed on its proceedings, you will create the most perfect responsibility, for then, whenever the people feel a grievance they cannot mistake the authors, and will apply the remedy with certainty and effect, discarding them at the next election. This tie of responsibility will obviate all the dangers apprehended from a single legislature, and will the best secure the rights of the people.[21]

The word "responsibility" here is not the vehicle for a new, free-floating historical meaning. On the contrary, it is itself a site of conflict. Men of power evade responsibility with speculations high and deep, speculations that also (as we saw in the shifting grammars of the founding documents) draw their attention to styles of expression at the cost of accuracy on the ground of social reference. Centinel's counterclaim secures both sides of the question, assessing the rhetorical nuances of the debate as a means of more surely understanding its material conditions.

Rereading *The Federalist*'s Publius pose according to Centinel's protocols, one better recognizes the methodical evasion of agency that is integral to its style of ruling-class mystification. When *Federalist* 85 performatively glosses Publius's tone by stating that "circumstances may have occasionally betrayed me into intemperances of expression which I did not intend," the language at once embraces its material power (I may have expressed myself intemperately, I can express myself intemperately) and disavows responsibility for that power. The effect is to *concentrate power* in the person of Publius. Contrary to the stated claim that some self-same agency is undermined by the overdetermination of "circumstances," the force of the sentence impels its meaning toward the concavity of a self-identical agent fully in command of its intentions and its social capacities. Far from a dominated subject of power, at the mercy of events, the Publius pose enacts political power *as such*. It does so through a linguistic act of splitting – the speaker versus the circumstances, the "struggle between sensibility and moderation" – that precisely reiterates Centinel's analysis of the bicameral legislature, with a situational and too-sensible "house of representatives" against a moderate and centered speaking ego (a "senate"): "If you complicate the plan by various orders, the people will be perplexed and divided in their sentiments about the source of abuses or misconduct, some will impute it to the senate, others to the house of representatives, and so on, that the interposition of the people may be rendered imperfect or perhaps wholly abortive." *The Federalist*'s achievement in its sentence is also the achievement of the Constitution in its formidable opening sentence: not just an interruption of the people's capacity to intervene but an ingestion of the people themselves, an absorption of the polity into the body of the "authors." Centinel's "most perfect responsibility" evaporates into the ether of the "more perfect Union."

Ingestion is a radical mode of inclusion, all but guaranteeing the passivity of the included citizenry. The US Constitution and its propagandists during the ratification debate were also adept at crafting an *exclusive* citizenry, yet it is important to note that the federalist digestive system was already at work in these exclusions in 1787–1788: in the incorporation of Indigenous and enslaved people (in Article 1, Sections 2 and 9, of the Constitution, the former of which also provided for the inclusive exclusion of incarcerated people "bound to Service for a Term of Years"), the more diffuse regulation of gender positionalities (as in *Federalist* 6's identification of the Shaysites with "female" "bigotry," "petulancy," and "cabal"), and the more profound "isolation" of both the economy and the wider field of social relations from the framework of the national law.[22] In the dialectics of inclusion and exclusion, activity and passivity, we ultimately find a sweeping historical novelty in the constitutional consolidation: the invention of a state apparatus that is uniquely suited not primarily to overt domination over citizen-subjects but rather to their exploitation by private actors formally extrinsic to the state. We have seen the rhetorical or literary version of this style of exploitation in the federalist position in the ratification debate; its institutional consequences are beyond the scope of a study of language and rhetoric. But the early republic initiates a considerably new phase in the nexus of rhetorical expression and social power, and the preceding examination of the texts situates us to grasp the signature of US state formation: its function

> to disorganize the dominated classes politically, and at the same time to organize the dominant classes politically ... Its principal contradiction is not so much that it "calls" itself the state of all the people, although it is in fact a class state, but that, strictly speaking, it presents itself in its very

institutions as a "class" state (i.e. the state of the dominant classes which it helps to organize politically), of a society which is institutionally fixed as one not-divided-into-classes; in that it presents itself as a state of the bourgeois class, implying that all the "people" are a part of this class.[23]

In this modern, specifically capitalist form of national law, the literary vehicle is inseparable from the material form, and whether or not Centinel's "tie of responsibility" can be woven from such materials is a question for the future, not for a study of the literary-historical past.

Notes

1 Ellen Meiksins Wood, "The Demos versus 'We, the People': From Ancient to Modern Conceptions of Citizenship," in *Democracy against Capitalism: Renewing Historical Materialism* (London: Verso, 2016), 214. See also the piquant assessment of Karl Polanyi, *The Great Transformation: The Political and Economic Origins of Our Time*, new ed. (Boston: Beacon Press, 2001), 233–234, and the significant theorization of Antonio Negri, *Insurgencies: Constituent Power and the Modern State*, trans. Maurizia Boscagli (Minneapolis: University of Minnesota Press, 1999), 141–189. The specialized historiography on the subject is vast: the references to Meiksins Wood, Polanyi, and Negri provide a sense of its world-historical resonance, beyond the US national perspective.

2 Paul Downes, *Democracy, Revolution, and Monarchism in Early American Literature* (New York: Cambridge University Press, 2002), 16. The charge of the Declaration's linguistic field is evident in its rhetorical capture of the would-be Loyalist parody *Counter-Declaration*, published in New York in 1781, which in acceding to the Declaration's grammar finds itself in "the very place, so to speak, from which U.S. political independence was launched" (Philip Gould, *Writing the Rebellion: Loyalists and the Literature of Politics in British America* [New York: Oxford University Press, 2013], 79).

3 Downes, *Democracy, Revolution, and Monarchism*, 16.

4 The constitution is what attempts to foreclose constituent power, to end revolution, though "constituent power resists being constitutionalized" (Negri, *Insurgencies*, 1). The heuristic value of Negri's distinction outweighs the provocative but sometimes questionable yield of his local historical claims.

5 Benjamin Franklin, "Speech at the Conclusion of the Constitutional Convention, Philadelphia, September 17, 1787," in *The Debate on the Constitution: Federalist and Anti-Federalist Speeches, Articles, and Letters during the Struggle over Ratification*, ed. Bernard Bailyn (New York: Library of America, 1993), 1: 4. The richest study of the recourse to speech in the period remains Christopher Looby, *Voicing America: Language, Literary Form, and the Origins of the United States* (Chicago: University of Chicago Press, 1996). See also Michael Warner, *The Letters of the Republic: Publication and*

the Public Sphere in Eighteenth-Century America (Cambridge, MA: Harvard University Press, 1990).

6 James Madison, Alexander Hamilton, and John Jay, *The Federalist Papers*, ed. Isaac Kramnick (Harmondsworth: Penguin, 1987), 87. Enduring literary-critical studies of this text include Albert Furtwangler, *The Authority of Publius: A Reading of the Federalist Papers* (Ithaca, NY: Cornell University Press, 1984); Robert A. Ferguson, "The American Enlightenment, 1750–1820," in *The Cambridge History of American Literature*, vol. 1: *1590–1820*, ed. Sacvan Bercovitch (New York: Cambridge University Press, 1994); and Joseph Fichtelberg, "The Aesthetics of *The Federalist*," *Early American Literature* 49 (2014): 89–119. Eric Slauter has provided a wide cultural context for the 1787–1788 moment in *The State as a Work of Art: The Cultural Origins of the Constitution* (Chicago: University of Chicago Press, 2009).

7 Madison, Hamilton, and Jay, *The Federalist*, 87.

8 Ibid., 88.

9 In a letter to the manor lord Robert Livingston, Hamilton wrote regarding New York politics that "the situation of the state at this time is so critical that it is become a serious object of attention to those who are concerned for the *security of property* or the prosperity of government, to endeavour to put men in the Legislature whose principles are not of the *levelling kind*. The spirit of the present Legislature is truly alarming, and appears evidently directed to the confusion of all property and principle" (Alexander Hamilton to Robert Livingston, April 25, 1785, *The Papers of Alexander Hamilton, vol. 3: 1782–1786*, ed. Harold C. Syrett [New York: Columbia University Press, 1962], 609; emphasis in original). The indispensable study of the class politics of the US Constitution and its ongoing inflection of national law is Jennifer Nedelsky, *Private Property and the Limits of American Constitutionalism: The Madisonian Framework and Its Legacy* (Chicago: University of Chicago Press, 1990). Charles Post's synthesizing verdict is lucid: the "Constitutional Settlement of 1787 … established the political dominance of mercantile capitalists and created state-institutions (a corps of tax-collectors and a federal army) capable of implementing pro-merchant state-policies" (Charles Post, *The American Road to Capitalism: Studies in Class-Structure, Economic Development and Political Conflict, 1620–1877* [Chicago: Haymarket, 2012], 77).

10 John Locke, *An Essay Concerning Human Understanding* (Oxford: Clarendon Press, 1975), book IV, chapter 19. On enthusiasm within eighteenth-century Protestantisms, see Nancy Ruttenburg, *Democratic Personality: Popular Voice and the Trial of American Authorship* (Stanford, CA: Stanford University Press, 1998), and Jordy Rosenberg, *Critical Enthusiasm: Capital Accumulation and the Transformation of Religious Passion* (New York: Oxford University Press, 2011).

11 Madison, Hamilton, and Jay, *The Federalist*, 483.

12 Ibid., 128.

13 *Oxford English Dictionary*, s.v. "government."

14 Jackson Turner Main, *The Anti-Federalists: Critics of the Constitution, 1781–1788*, new ed. (Chapel Hill: University of North Carolina Press, 2004), xxv. "They are called Antifederalists, but it should be made clear at once that they were not antifederal at all. In reality they were determined to preserve the Confederation, and the name, far from being their own choice, was imposed on them by their opponents, the so-called Federalists. The attachment to them of a word which denotes the reverse of their true beliefs, and which moreover implies that they were mere obstructionists, without any positive plan to offer, was part of the penalty of defeat" (xxiii).

15 Trish Loughran, *The Republic in Print: Print Culture in the Age of U.S. Nation Building, 1770–1870* (New York: Columbia University Press, 2007), 224, 225–226.

16 Matthew Garrett, *Episodic Poetics: Politics and Literary Form after the Constitution* (New York: Oxford University Press, 2014), 21 and passim.

17 Madison, Hamilton, and Jay, *The Federalist*, 90, 126, 127.

18 Saul Cornell, *The Other Founders: Anti-Federalism and the Dissenting Tradition in America, 1788–1828* (Chapel Hill: University of North Carolina Press, 1999), 73. Sandra Gustafson has considered how the elite political dilemmas of national unification versus federation and elite consolidation versus individual rights were enacted in the embodied performance of the speeches at the Philadelphia convention itself; the spectacle of the expressive body, in this case, concentrated the political questions within the speaker himself, in a complex amalgam of gender and power that drew on aristocratic representative publicity even as it instantiated republican "manhood." The combination, regardless of the political orientation of the speaker, was quintessentially federalist. See Sandra M. Gustafson, *Eloquence Is Power: Oratory and Performance in Early America* (Chapel Hill: University of North Carolina Press, 2000), 210–213; Dana D. Nelson, *National Manhood: Capitalist Citizenship and the Imagined Fraternity of White Men* (Durham, NC: Duke University Press, 1998); and Julie Ellison, *Cato's Tears and the Making of Anglo-American Emotion* (Chicago: University of Chicago Press, 1999). See also Jay Grossman, *Reconstituting the American Renaissance: Emerson, Whitman, and the Politics of Representation* (Durham, NC: Duke University Press, 2003), 53–55. For a counterpoint claim about "democratic" styles of embodied speech, see Ruttenburg, *Democratic Personality*. Most stimulating as a commentary on gender, sexuality, and the (imaginary) body in the historiographical uptake of the "founding fathers," especially Alexander Hamilton, is Michael J. Drexler and Ed White, *The Traumatic Colonel: The Founding Fathers, Slavery, and the Phantasmatic Aaron Burr* (New York: New York University Press, 2014), 35–39.

19 Jay Fliegelman, *Declaring Independence: Jefferson, Natural Language, and the Culture of Performance* (Stanford, CA: Stanford University Press, 1993), 148, 149. Notably, the *Oxford English Dictionary*, which includes Hamilton's use as a notable early print example, does not support the claim for ambivalence,

pointing rather to unambiguous "obligation" (*Oxford English Dictionary*, s.v. "responsibility").

20 Cornell, *The Other Founders*, 100.

21 *Centinel* I, *Independent Gazetteer*, Philadelphia, October 5, 1787, in *The Debate on the Constitution*, 1: 56.

22 Madison, Hamilton, and Jay, *The Federalist*, 105; Polanyi, *The Great Transformation*, 234.

23 Nicos Poulantzas, *Political Power and Social Classes*, trans. Timothy O'Hagan with David McLellan, Anna de Casparis, and Brian Grogan (London: Verso, 1978), 189.

CHAPTER 3

The Statesman's Address

Sandra M. Gustafson

Critics have long noted that American literature bears a strong relationship to oral forms and styles. The complex relationship between oral and written language shapes the style and themes of Benjamin Franklin and Charles Brockden Brown. It informs both the essays that Ralph Waldo Emerson developed out of his sermons and lectures and the relationship between Margaret Fuller's political writings and her formal conversations. Oral styles animate the vernacular idioms of Mark Twain and William Faulkner as well as the oratorical poetry of Walt Whitman and Allen Ginsberg. Political speech figures prominently in American fiction, from Harriet Beecher Stowe, Herman Melville, and Nathaniel Hawthorne to Ralph Ellison, Leslie Marmon Silko, and Chang-Rae Lee. In the period covered by this volume, oratory figures importantly in such notable novels as *Modern Chivalry* (1792–1815), *Wieland* (1798), and *Last of the Mohicans* (1826). Indeed, political speech was far more central to the literary culture of the day than the novel. Writing in *Professing Literature: An Institutional History* (1987), a classic history of the changing shape of English departments and their role in American higher education, Gerald Graff observed that "oratorical culture" was central to the "teaching of English" before 1875.

The formative role that political oratory played in the literary culture of the early republic was the subject of John Quincy Adams's inaugural lecture as the first Boylston Chair of Rhetoric and Oratory at Harvard University, published in 1810. Echoing views shared by his father, former President John Adams, the new Boylston Chair proclaimed that "eloquence was power" in ancient Greece and Rome. He went on to describe how "under governments purely republican, where every citizen has a deep interest in the affairs of the nation ... the voice of eloquence will not be heard in vain." Focused on the classical tradition, Adams failed to recognize the longer history of oratory in Britain's colonies and the early republic. The native peoples who inhabited the North American continent had distinctive and highly elaborated traditions of spoken eloquence, and they adapted these traditions to the new world of European colonialism. Africans in North America came from societies where oratory held a place of importance. The interaction of European, Indigenous, and African oratorical traditions produced rich examples of an increasingly prominent form of verbal art. To cite one example, Henrick Aupaumut's career as a diplomat for the Washington administration in the 1790s hinged on the creative adaptation of treaty council rhetoric. Aupaumut was a Revolutionary War veteran and Christian Indian, as well as a dedicated leader of his Mahican community and preserver of its traditions. Though he was not a "statesman" as the term is usually understood, Aupaumut envisioned a statesman-like role for himself as US ambassador to the Northwest Indian nations. Drawing on ancient Mahican rituals of diplomacy, he employed the oral forms of the treaty council to negotiate on behalf of the "15 sachems of the United States."[1] His account of his mission focuses on scenes of diplomatic speech, and he presents himself as a cultural ambassador as well as a political negotiator.[2]

The rising cultural prominence of oratory in general, and of the statesman's address as a genre, can be traced to the early years of the American Revolution. Looking back on the events that led up to the anticolonial movement, John Adams singled out James Otis's Writs of Assistance speech of 1761 as the first salvo in the war of words that escalated into military combat. Writs of assistance were controversial legal instruments of British authority that enabled customs agents to search for illegal goods, without requiring specific information on the items being sought. Describing the historical events with dramatic flair, Adams presented the Writs of Assistance trial in the council chamber of Boston's Old Town House as the occasion for outbursts of primal eloquence that created a patriot identity and formed a new political community. The substance of Otis's argument, challenging English authority and hinting at a natural rights philosophy, shaped emerging arguments for independence. Adams highlighted the style of Otis's speech, using Pentecostal imagery to describe its effects on his listeners: "Otis was a flame of Fire! With the promptitude of Classical Allusions, a depth of Research, a rapid Summary of Historical Events and dates, a profusion of legal Authorities, a prophetic glare of his eyes into futurity, and a rapid Torrent of impetuous Eloquence, he hurried away all before him; American independence was then and there born." Describing how "every man of a crowded audience appeared to me to go away, as I did, ready to take up arms against writs of assistance," Adams drastically collapsed the sequence of events leading to war with Britain.[3]

In this mythic narrative of American national origins, Adams transformed a courtroom speech into a catalytic event. Overstating the importance of this single occasion for heightened effect, he captured the impact of Otis's argument as it shaped colonial political debate. The decision to highlight the occasion of the speech, rather than to focus on the argument alone, points to the new prominence of political eloquence in colonial public life. Revolutionary political oratory contributed to the formation of a national public sphere with both material and symbolic dimensions. Scholars have highlighted the effect of a burgeoning print culture on the patriot movement; at the same time, vernacular political oratory – including the statesman's address – emerged as a formal genre with a national audience. These developments in verbal form were accompanied and heightened by a pattern of imagery influentially expressed in a phrase drawn from the Bible: "the letter killeth but the spirit giveth life" (2 Cor. 3:6). In the speeches of patriot orators such as James Otis and Patrick Henry, the living American word triumphed over the dead letter of British law.

Lawyers played a crucial role in the rise of the partisanship that characterized radical politics, transforming narrow legislative and legal arguments into broad and stirring assertions of colonial rights. Newly sophisticated and professionalized attorneys such as Otis spoke *to* laypeople, and increasingly they claimed to speak *for* them. "I ... now appear not only in obedience to your order," he told the Massachusetts court in 1761, "but also in behalf of the inhabitants of this town ... and out of regard to the liberties of the subject" (*EIP* 141). Otis and other patriot leaders distinguished their art from its antecedents in the pulpit, the courtroom, and the legislature when they broke the elite frame of the Assembly, religious congregation, or court chamber in order to address a wider public. This notion of speaking for the people had precedents rooted in Greek and Roman antiquity, but it acquired new prominence and developed practical and symbolic significance in the context of the independence movement.

The classical world was one source of inspiration for the emerging culture of eloquence. Among the ancients, Pericles and Demosthenes were celebrated Athenian orators and statesmen, while the Roman Republic offered many exemplary figures, Cicero preeminent among them. As both a celebrated speaker and an influential theorist of oratory's central role in self-governing societies, Cicero profoundly shaped the ideal of the eloquent statesman. A Cicero revival sparked by Conyers Middleton's

1741 biography informed political and intellectual developments on both sides of the Atlantic. James Otis and John Adams both celebrated Cicero, and John Quincy Adams championed Cicero's legacy in his *Lectures on Rhetoric and Oratory* (1810), delivered during his service as the first Boylston Chair of Rhetoric and Oratory at Harvard University. This renewed interest in Cicero was closely tied to the rise of the modern republic.[4]

Complementing these Greek and Roman precursors were two additional influences: the example of Native American political culture and the passionate religious oratory of the Great Awakening. Native American oratory entered European culture from early in the contact period, as authors included scenes of Indigenous eloquence in their narratives of encounter. Public speech was often a central feature of these narratives, as Native communities acknowledged the arrival of the newcomers and negotiated with them over security, resources, power, and land. Later, diplomatic speech loomed large in treaty reports and other printed accounts of colonial negotiations.[5] Rising interest in classical republican thought sharpened the focus on Indigenous oratory. In *History of the Five Indian Nations*, the first extended English-language history of a Native American people, Cadwallader Colden fused the classical and Indigenous traditions to present a hybrid form of republicanism. Colden was a Scottish-born New York official prominent in Indian affairs and a member of the transatlantic republic of letters. He corresponded extensively with scientists and intellectuals including Benjamin Franklin, who shared his interest in Native America. Colden identified the Haudenosaunee (or "Iroquois") with ancient republicans, noting in his dedication that "The Greeks and Romans ... [were] once as much Barbarians as our *Indians* now are," and commenting that "The People of the *Five Nations* are much given to *Speech-making*, ever the natural Consequence of a perfect Republican Government: Where no single Person has a Power to compel, the Arts of Persuasion alone must prevail." The first edition of Colden's *History* (1727) appeared in New York, shortly after Thomas Gordon and John Trenchard published an extended series of essays called *Cato's Letters* (1720–23), which elevated republican thought. Trenchard and Gordon named their series for the icon of the Roman Republic who had been celebrated in Joseph Addison's celebrated play of 1712. Colden's Roman-like "Iroquois" lent republican history an American flavor. A significantly expanded version of Colden's work appeared in three London editions of 1747, 1750, and 1755 and was widely extracted in the periodical press.[6]

In the later editions of the *History*, Colden included excerpts from the Lancaster Treaty of 1744, whose proceedings were first published by Pennsylvania's official printer, Benjamin Franklin. These treaty proceedings had already achieved unusually wide circulation throughout the colonies and in England. Colden and Franklin both emphasized the difference between English and Native American standards for public speech, particularly in a diplomatic setting. The stately drama of an "Iroquois" oration could convey a rich range of meanings, from studied assertion to sly humor to angry denunciation. But the formal restraints on treaty oratory precluded the quick retort or the witty rejoinder valued among the English. Colden observed that "every sudden Repartee, in a publick Treaty, leaves them with an Impression of a light inconsiderate mind," while Franklin noted the "great Order and Decency" of "Iroquois" proceedings, whose norms emphasizing attentive silence set them apart from the often-tumultuous conduct of the British Parliament. In his 1783 essay "Remarks Concerning the Savages of North-America," Franklin elevated Indigenous conventions as more favorable to reasoned deliberation than parliamentary protocols.[7]

Evangelical preaching was a second major influence on Revolutionary eloquence. Compared with Indigenous oratory, evangelical influence was more direct and less tied to the history or theory of republicanism. Perhaps its greatest impact was on the way that speeches came to be delivered. Solomon Stoddard's *The Defects of Preachers Reproved* (1723) marked a watershed moment in the emergence of the extemporaneous preaching style that would eventually contribute to the tone and style of Revolutionary oratory. For fifty-five years Stoddard occupied the pulpit at Northampton, wielding considerable spiritual and social power in the surrounding frontier region of western Massachusetts up until his death in 1729. Stoddard was an early champion of a vigorous, animated style of delivery who rejected the practice of reading a sermon from a manuscript or notes. In *Defects* he signaled a willingness to challenge metropolitan cultural power, attacking preachers who substituted learning and morality for the authority of divine grace. "Men of Learning may be led aside by reading erronious Books," he warned. "Learned Education will not deliver Men from carnal Reason." Stoddard's message became a touchstone of the New Light movement: the best preaching sprang from the minister's personal familiarity with the workings of the spirit, not from book learning.[8]

The tension about sermon delivery erupted into open partisanship in New England and throughout the colonies with the arrival of the British evangelist George Whitefield in 1739. Whitefield made affective extemporaneous preaching of the sort advocated by Stoddard into a sign of evangelical commitment. He presented the sacred orator as passionate, embodied, and directly engaged with his viewers. In a passage that resonates with Adams's description of Otis as a "flame of fire," a Connecticut farmer named Nathan Cole described Whitefield's "bold undaunted Countenance" as giving the English preacher the appearance of being "Cloathed with authority from the Great God." "My old Foundation was broken up," Cole explained, "and I saw that my righteousness would not save me." In a similar vein, Josiah Smith of South Carolina observed that Whitefield appeared "deeply affected and impressed in his own heart. How did that burn and boil within him, when he spake of the things he had made, touching the King?" The themes of a higher authority authorizing a radical change, and of social and psychological turmoil, would later figure in the patriot movement as extemporaneous speech became a feature of revolutionary rhetoric.[9]

The legal profession was disproportionately represented among patriot leaders, and lawyers transformed themselves into revolutionary orators by adapting the impassioned spiritual rhetoric of the Great Awakening. Though James Otis was not an evangelical Protestant, his oratory showed its imprint. As already noted, Adams emphasized Otis's extemporaneous fluency in his account of the Writs of Assistance hearing, and this emphasis emerged in contrasting Otis with his main opponent Jeremiah Gridley, who defended the writs of assistance with "great Learning" and a "majestic Manner." Gridley's stateliness distinguished him from Otis, who was "quick and elastic," with an "Apprehension ... as quick as his Temper"; his play of features reflected the rapidity of his thought. While Gridley won the case, successfully arguing that the writs of assistance were covered by legal precedent and so permissible, Otis established a more important point that became central to revolutionary thought when he emphasized that "ALL PRECEDENTS ARE UNDER THE CONTROUL OF THE PRINCIPLES OF THE LAW." That is, Otis introduced the concept of fundamental principles of law that preexist and sanction codified law. As a champion of fundamental (or natural) law, Otis shaped the developing argument against parliamentary authority in the colonies, including the controversy over taxation without representation. Otis further contributed to the transformation of early national political theory and practice when he successfully advocated for opening the proceedings of the Massachusetts General Court to the public, paving the way for the open galleries in Congress and state legislatures that provided space for an audience. Even more than the example of his Writs of Assistance speech, this institutional transformation contributed to the rising importance of the statesman's address as a genre.[10]

In Virginia as in Massachusetts, patriot eloquence inspired popular passion and political action, disrupted established hierarchies and institutions, and drew on natural law and feeling for its insights. Patrick Henry figures in Thomas Jefferson's Revolutionary mythology in a roughly analogous way to Otis's place in the patriot lore of John Adams. Writing in 1805 to Henry's biographer William Wirt, Jefferson celebrated Henry as "the man who gave the first impulse to the ball of revolution," calling him "the greatest orator that ever lived." Elsewhere Jefferson rhapsodized that Henry spoke "as Homer wrote." He attributed Henry's immense popularity to his "consumate knowlege of the human heart," a connection that resembles Stoddard's call for preachers to speak from experience. Henry fostered the image of himself as a man of vocal power: a poorly educated, self-made man of the people, a leader with sources of knowledge deeper and truer than mere books. His speech was rhapsodic, drawing listeners away from mundane realities, and transformative, making them into patriots and heroes. Virtually every description of Henry begins with his physical and cultural limitations and seeks to analyze the transformation that occurred as he spoke, extending it to the political movement that he came to embody. More than any other Revolutionary orator, Henry enacted the transfer of the evangelical model of transfigured, vocal, public selfhood into the political domain. His most famous oration – the "Liberty or Death" speech delivered to the Virginia Convention in 1775 – was a semi-secularized variant of the evangelical sermon. Edmund Randolph compared Henry on this occasion to Paul preaching at Athens. Seeking to convict, convert, and assure the hesitant legislators and the public that military preparation was essential for the preservation of Virginia's political liberties, he "transferred into civil discussions many of the bold licenses which prevailed in the religions." These included not only the basic conversion structure but also the wealth of scriptural references and the animated, extempore delivery. An eyewitness described Henry's elaborate theatrics: slave-like gestures of submission and bondage, the shattering of chains, and the plunging of an invisible dagger into his breast.[11]

American patriot orators like Otis and Henry created novel modes of nationalist identity based on their public performances. In later years, historians told the story of the Revolution in biographies of its great orators, and elocution became a popular activity involving the recitation of famous speeches. The generations of schoolchildren who recited

Henry's "Liberty or Death" speech reproduced a sense of national identity that lent itself to critique as well as celebration. A notable example of critique directed at the nation appears in Henry Highland Garnet's "An Address to the Slaves of the United States" (1843) – also known as the "Call to Rebellion" speech – which takes Henry's words as an inspiration for enslaved people. Advocating "physical resistance" as a means to end slavery, Garnet described the effects in memorable terms: "The sentiments of their revolutionary orators fell in burning eloquence upon their hearts, and with one voice they cried, Liberty or Death. Oh what a sentence was that! It ran from soul to soul like electric fire, and nerved the arm of thousands to fight in the holy cause of Freedom." In a rhetorical gesture that became popular in abolitionist speeches and writings, Garnet repeats Henry's famous phrase to call for revolution against the slave system.[12]

***

As a genre, the statesman's address is most closely associated with scenes of political deliberation. The Revolutionary vogue for extemporaneous oratory meant that records of such scenes were often sparse. Recalling his service in the Continental Congress from 1774 to 1778, John Adams noted that "the Orators ... appeared to me very universally extemporaneous, and I have never heard of any committed to writing before or after delivery." For Adams, the absence of crucial records rendered the task of writing an authentic history of the American Revolution impossible. "Who shall ever write the history of the American revolution?" he asked Thomas Jefferson in 1815. "Who can write it? Who will ever be able to write it?" Jefferson agreed, noting that without records of the proceedings, "the life and soul of history must for ever be unknown." He described Adams as the Declaration's "ablest advocate and defender" in Congress and singled out for praise an unrecorded rejoinder to John Dickinson, which gained a reputation as Adams's greatest oration. Jefferson described the speech in terms that elevate its power to move the audience over its artfulness. "He was not graceful nor elegant, nor remarkably fluent," Jefferson wrote, "but he came out occasionally with a power of thought and expression, that moved us from our seats." Adams himself regretted the ephemerality of his rhetorical achievement, noting that it was one of only a very few of his speeches that he wished had been "literally preserved."[13]

In contrast to the Continental Congress, which met behind closed doors, the state constitutional conventions were open to the public. Here the records are extensive. The audiences at these conventions served as the imaginary body of "the people," which materialized in thirteen discrete scenes of oratorical performance. Attendees both performed (through their presence) and witnessed (in the contributions of their representatives) their own creation as a political "people." Records of the proceedings reveal that images of oral powers, capable of nurturing or destroying the social body, structured many arguments about the Constitution, both pro and con. An Antifederalist commonplace warned that the national government would "swallow up" the states. In one striking moment, Pennsylvania Federalist leader James Wilson described the proposed national government as "a new body, capable of being encreased by the addition of other members; – an expanding quality peculiarly fitted to the circumstances of America." Oral imagery often figured in contexts that connected republican government to an unwritten ethic of virtuous citizenship. Drawn from classical republican thought, this emphasis on virtuous speech and action as necessary supplements to the written Constitution addressed the fundamental amorality of its institutional and procedural emphasis. The federal convention that produced the constitution identified the supplementary relationship between that document and elected representatives in its discussion of the need to fill national offices with "Continental Characters," that is, men of sufficient stature and knowledge to overcome regional biases and transfigure discrete local communities into a unified nation.[14]

George Washington was the preeminent "Continental Character" who embodied the qualities of republican virtue, including moderation, self-control, deliberation, and civility. Despite his graceful demeanor and masterful physical presence – he was 6'2", an acclaimed horseman, and elegant dancer – he did not aspire to fame as an orator. His voice was "agreeable rather than strong," and he lacked the classical education that James Otis and Patrick Henry used to fashion themselves into eloquent statesmen. Washington's inability or unwillingness to become a fluent orator illuminates a central fact of his public career: his self-effacing persona enabled him to navigate and sometimes resolve the contradictions of republican authority. Washington's tact and personal reserve carried political benefits in the transition from imperial colonies to independent republic. Avoiding offense and creating an enigmatic authority, he developed a reputation for standing above partisan conflict.[15]

Despite his limitations as a speaker, Washington contributed to an emerging republican style of address. His skills as a public speaker resided not in his mastery of language but in his ability both to publicly manifest emotion and to display his struggles to control intense feelings. Observers at his First Inaugural Address interpreted his obvious discomfort in contradictory ways. William Maclay, a political leader from Pennsylvania, complained that "this great man was agitated and embarrassed" as he delivered the address. "He trembled, and several times could scarce make out to read, though it must be supposed he had often read it before." Maclay found the president's efforts at oratorical gesture to be especially inappropriate, preferring that "this first of men had read off his address in the plainest manner." The features of Washington's delivery that bothered Maclay struck the Massachusetts Federalist Fisher Ames quite differently, as captured in this description: "His aspect grave, almost to sadness; his modesty, actually shaking; his voice deep, a little tremulous, and so low as to call for close attention." Ames interpreted the president's manner not as proof of ineptitude, but as awareness of the moment's significance. He saw in the performance "an allegory in which virtue was personified, and addressing those whom she would make her votaries. Her power over the heart was never greater, and the illustration of her doctrine by her own example was never more perfect."

The fact that Washington's first performance as president evoked such conflicting responses may have contributed to his decision to circulate his Farewell Address as a text rather than resign orally. In a political culture where gentlemen did not openly seek public office, he feared that he would appear to be soliciting reelection if he announced his intention to retire in a speech before Congress. Though he had resigned his army command and delivered his State of the Union messages in person, he left Philadelphia hours before his Farewell Address appeared in print. Appealing directly to "Friends and Fellow Citizens" over the heads of Congress, the text warned against party spirit, regionalism, and demagoguery, and tied these domestic concerns to the influence of foreign powers. During Washington's second term, contested relations with France and Britain had shaped disputes over the legacy of the American Revolution and fueled the emergence of the first party system that set the Federalists against the Jefferson-led Democratic Republicans. It was in this context that congressional oratory first emerged as high drama in the 1790s.

In the United States, citizens could expect to hear for themselves the deliberations that produced and interpreted the laws that governed them. Following the example of Massachusetts, Congress opened many of its proceedings soon after it was founded. Major congressional debates and arguments before the Supreme Court drew large audiences of women and men, and in later years foreign visitors (including Fanny Wright and Alexis de Tocqueville) made a pilgrimage to Capitol Hill to hear the deliberations there. The growth in the numbers and power of deliberative bodies, and the fact that many were publicly accessible for the first time, transformed the chamber floor into a unique type of stage where real-life political dramas were enacted. The agon on the House and Senate floors became an absorbing spectacle of national significance. Viewing the performances from the galleries and reading reports of them in their newspapers, Americans came to imagine congressional debates as the dramatic enactment and negotiation of political differences that they, through the electoral process, had embodied in their representatives and placed on the national stage.

The rise of congressional eloquence was tied in important ways to the political career of Fisher Ames, who developed a style of deliberative oratory that transformed central qualities of Washington's presidential address – notably, his strategies for asserting authority in a self-effacing manner – into a form of representative speech intended to clarify and enlarge the popular voice. For Ames, this approach involved a theory of political hegemony based on emotional control. He summed up his theory of republican leadership in his funeral oration for the first president, highlighting the way that Washington displayed his effort to control powerful feelings. Ames noted further how that personal struggle made Washington an exemplary republican leader, for if he could control his own emotions, he could govern those of others. Post-Revolutionary America needed a leader "who possessed a commanding power over the popular passions, but over whom those passions had no power," and "that man was Washington," Ames concluded. He went on to describe his own "unutterable" feelings upon hearing of Washington's death, a form of silence that highlighted Ames's own capacity for self-control.[16]

Ames enacted his theory of public feeling in his most famous oration, the 1796 speech to the House of Representatives in support of the treaty negotiated by John Jay to resolve lingering hostilities with Great Britain. The most celebrated instance of congressional eloquence in the new republic's first decade, Ames's Jay Treaty speech created an immediate sensation, was reprinted in several editions, and continued to influence aspiring statesmen for years to come. His performance influenced both Daniel Webster, who memorized the address and modeled his style on it, and Abraham Lincoln, who knew and admired the speech. Widely known to support Jay's Treaty, Ames was gravely ill and remained silent until the concluding days of the debate. He transformed the circumstance of his illness into a performance of the loosening of restraint and the breaking forth of speech at great personal cost. He began his speech by stating, "I would have resisted if I could" and stressing that he felt "unprepared for debate" but could no longer remain silent. He ended by appealing to the House to fund the treaty and warned that without such funding, "even I, slender and almost broken as my hold upon life is, may outlive the government and Constitution of my country." Equating the orator's body with the body of the state, Ames offered his life to sustain the federal government founded on the Constitution.[17]

***

After 1800, a system for reporting congressional debates matured as the press became more diverse and accessible and as the methods of capturing and disseminating speech through the medium of print became increasingly sophisticated. Semiofficial accounts of House and Senate debates appeared in the *National Intelligencer* (from 1800), the *Register of Debates* (from 1824), and the *Congressional Globe* (from 1833), while a variety of newspapers sent their own reporters to cover the proceedings, often in imperfect or highly partisan ways. The speakers themselves sometimes contributed to distortions in the printed records by editing their addresses. While some journalists focused on representing congressional debates, others commented on the proceedings in printed letters. The letter form was also employed in semiprivate settings, with Congressmen and spectators offering descriptions of the debates in manuscripts intended for circulation.

Deliberative speech in Congress and the courts achieved an unusual prominence on the national scene in these years. This elevation of deliberative oratory was in part a consequence of the fact that executive speech was muted as the earliest occupants of the White House wrestled with the question of what role that a president should play in the republic. Thomas Jefferson's decision to deliver his State of the Union addresses in writing was a watershed moment marking a shift toward a quieter, if not less powerful, executive. The House debates drew more attention in the early years because they were livelier and faster paced, but beginning in the 1820s the Senate emerged as the home of celebrity orators including Daniel Webster, Henry Clay, John Calhoun, Thomas Hart Benton, and Edward Everett.

Statesmanlike oratory was a popular subject for *The North American Review* (*NAR*), a Boston-based periodical that frequently featured writing on political eloquence. Founded in 1815, the *Review* was modeled on great British periodicals such as *The Edinburgh Review* and *The Quarterly Review*. Contributors to the *NAR* included men who were, or who later became, prominent educators, diplomats, religious leaders, and politicians. One such author was Edward Tyrrel Channing, who followed in the footsteps of John Quincy Adams when he became the Boylston Professor of Rhetoric and Oratory at Harvard, where he counted Ralph Waldo Emerson, Henry David Thoreau, and Wendell Phillips among his pupils. In an 1817 essay for the *NAR* on "The Abuses of Political Discussion," Channing warned against "false excitement and corrupt eloquence." He noted that the ancient republics had been driven to "madness" by "stormy and troubled eloquence," and he stressed that modern republicans could be encouraged to avoid such a course and instead "respect deliberation, order, and settled habits."

Alexis de Tocqueville saw a different danger arising from the central place that the statesman's address had come to hold in the political culture of the United States. In the second volume of *Democracy in America* (1840), Tocqueville commented on the weaknesses of congressional eloquence, contrasting it with Revolutionary oratory. While revolutionary orators in America and France spoke about universal truths, routine public debates in Congress were more limited in focus, and consequently less stimulating, in part because elected representatives varied widely in intellect and ability. Americans resigned themselves to the uneven quality of congressional oratory, Tocqueville concluded, because they viewed it as an inevitable side effect of the Constitution and the party system. "They bear witness to their long experience of parliamentary practice not by refraining from dull speeches," he observed, "but by summoning their courage to listen to them." What distinguished an aesthetically pleasing "statesman's address" from one of these dull congressional speeches? The ability to articulate large principles and to project a sweeping vision were two important criteria, while the setting and context contributed to the overall effect. "There is nothing more wonderful or more impressive than a great orator discussing great affairs in a democratic assembly," Tocqueville wrote. The experience of speaking "to the whole nation, for the whole nation ... heightens both his thought and his power of expression."[18]

During the first half of the nineteenth century, competing national visions were put forward by the "Great Triumvirate" of John Calhoun, Henry Clay, and Daniel Webster, who first served together in the House of Representatives during the 1810s and were together in the Senate from 1832. All three were noted orators, whose styles were analyzed and contrasted in contemporary studies on the "Golden Age of American Oratory" (the title of an 1857 book by Edward Griffin Parker). Webster surpassed Calhoun (who was better known for logic than rhetoric) and even outshone the celebrated Clay in his reputation for eloquence. For Webster, eloquence proved to be a cornerstone of his political influence and an enduring part of his cultural legacy.

Webster's long-lived reputation as the preeminent aesthetician of modern republican eloquence was forged in the period between 1815 and 1835. He achieved this rhetorical prominence with a series of well-received speeches that included his commemorative orations at Plymouth (1820) and Bunker Hill (1825), which highlighted the sources of republican ideology and emphasized the political imagination needed to fulfill its ideals; his eulogy for Presidents Adams and Jefferson (1826), celebrating the shared ideals of the friends and political rivals; and his deliberative orations on the Greek Revolution (1824) and the Congress of Panama (1826), which presented a broad field for the spread of republican values. In these addresses, and with rising urgency in the Second Reply to Hayne (1830), he sought to build a consensus that would resist the centripetal forces of nullification – a states' rights cause spearheaded by Calhoun – that were then threatening the American republic. The Second Reply to Hayne is the source of one of Webster's best-known phrases: "Liberty *and* Union, now and for ever, one and inseparable." In this speech he took on the role of Defender of the Constitution, presenting himself as the modern Cicero who sought to protect the republic from destruction by southern nullifiers who put the state above the nation.

Many of these nationalist themes were already present when Webster gave the commemorative address at the bicentennial celebration of the landing at Plymouth on December 22, 1820. Webster was then thirty-eight, a Boston-based lawyer with noted successes arguing before the US Supreme Court, a former congressman from New Hampshire, and a member of the Massachusetts Constitutional Convention meeting to revise the state constitution. In his Plymouth address, Webster described a set of foundational values, related those values to regional and national publics, and framed a tradition based on memory and sentiment. For an audience that included former president John Adams, one of his central influences, Webster considered republicanism from the vantage point of colonization and identified the institutions that had fostered republican mores in New England. Comparing Plymouth to Marathon, the scene of the Greek triumph against Persia that ushered in a period of growth under Pericles, Webster described both sites as origin points for social and political developments of world-historical importance. The central distinction that he drew between the Greek colonies and the colonists of New England was moral and intellectual. The settlements of British North America represented the convergence of "the settlement of a new continent" with "an age of progressive knowledge and improvement," allowing them to uniquely advance human culture beyond anything accomplished by the Greeks. Webster identified the wide possession of personal property, deliberative and representative government, an educated citizenry, and Christianity as the features of New England life that shaped his ideal of the modern republic. He particularly celebrated the local administrations of New England and, as Tocqueville would later do in *Democracy in America*, he singled out for particular praise the town hall meetings, stating that "they are so many councils or parliaments, in which common interests are discussed, and useful knowledge acquired and communicated."

Webster's (and later Tocqueville's) advocacy for New England republicanism was based on his analysis of the features required for a modern republic to succeed: commerce, Christianity, and deliberation. As an advocate for deliberative and participatory institutions, Webster emphasized the need to use restraint and avoid inflammatory rhetoric, including the language of political enslavement. In his Plymouth address, he highlighted the fact that slavery was not merely a dead political metaphor when he painted a word picture of forging real chains and fetters: "I hear the sound of the hammer, I see the smoke of the furnaces where manacles and fetters are still forged for human limbs. I see the visages of those who by stealth and at midnight labor in this work of hell, foul and dark, as may become the artificers of such instruments of misery and torture." Webster called on justices, ministers, and merchants to suppress "this inhuman and accursed traffic" in human beings. He made a special appeal to the "fair merchant" for whom the ocean represents "a field of grateful toil," asking him to imagine that same ocean as it appears to "the victim of this oppression." This exercise in perspectivalism contributed to an emerging concern with the experiences of the oppressed.[19]

Having celebrated New England as a locus of national origins at Plymouth, Webster shifted his emphasis to focus on the forging of national values in his "Discourse in Commemoration of the Lives and Services of John Adams and Thomas Jefferson" (1826). Famously, Adams and Jefferson had died within a few hours of one another on July 4, 1826 – the fiftieth anniversary of the Declaration of

Independence. In his commemorative address, Webster stressed how these two men, one from New England and the other from Virginia, had jointly shared the revolutionary moment and contributed to the post-revolutionary state. He ignored the well-known frictions between the two former presidents, emphasizing instead the collaborative work that united North and South in support of the Revolutionary cause and the principles of the Declaration. The centerpiece of Webster's speech was an account of the Continental Congress, where Adams and Jefferson first worked together. He celebrated the Congress's proceedings as the perfect blend of philosophy and action, where the "deliberations" included "every thing which political philosophy, the love of liberty, and the spirit of free inquiry" had produced, wedded to "new and striking views," and the whole applied with "irresistible force, in support of the cause which had drawn them together." The main narrative section of the address includes an account of how Jefferson came to draft the Declaration and a re-creation of Adams's speech supporting it. In the absence of records of the proceedings, Webster was free to speculate about the qualities that made Adams effective and to theorize about the nature of "true eloquence." He concluded that eloquence "must exist in the man, in the subject, in the occasion"; it arises at the moment when "words have lost their power, rhetoric is vain, and all elaborate oratory contemptible." True eloquence goes beyond logic and urges speaker and audience toward "action, noble, sublime, godlike action." Adams's signal achievement on this occasion was not in any particular thing that he said, but rather in his success at persuading Congress to act by declaring independence from Great Britain.[20]

Webster's speech on Adams and Jefferson marks the closing of the era when the statesman's address emerged as a central aesthetic element in the political and literary culture of the modern republic. In succeeding decades there was a marked shift toward a more colloquial style, as white manhood suffrage took root and the United States experienced rising conflicts over slavery, colonial expansion, women's rights, and economic inequality.[21]

The statesman's address of the early United States remains an ideal type that is periodically reinvigorated, most recently by President Barack Obama, whose dramatic rise was propelled by the eloquence with which he expressed democratic republican ideals of the common good. Obama indirectly referenced Webster's Bunker Hill Monument oration by way of a quotation from John F. Kennedy in his 2009 speech accepting the Nobel Prize for peace. During his service as a senator from Massachusetts,

Kennedy had worked to revive Webster's reputation in *Profiles in Courage* (1956), and his rhetoric often echoed the language of his predecessor. This passage from the peroration of the Bunker Hill Monument oration resonates in Kennedy's statesmanlike rhetoric in his 1963 speech at American University, and from there it echoes in Obama's Nobel address:

> In a day of peace, let us advance the arts of peace and the works of peace. Let us develop the resources of our land, call forth its powers, build up its institutions, promote all its great interests, and see whether we also, in our day and generation, may not perform something worthy to be remembered. Let us cultivate a true spirit of union and harmony.

The rhetorical and intellectual tradition linking Daniel Webster to Barack Obama includes not only John F. Kennedy, but also Frederick Douglass, Abraham Lincoln, and Martin Luther King, Jr. As this partial list suggests, the genre of the statesman's address has had an influence on the literature of the United States whose considerable breadth and depth have yet to be fully measured.[22]

Notes

1 This essay draws liberally from my previously published work, especially *Eloquence Is Power: Oratory and Performance in Early America* (Chapel Hill: University of North Carolina Press for OIEAHC, 2000) (cited parenthetically as *EIP*) and *Imagining Deliberative Democracy in the Early American Republic* (Chicago: University of Chicago Press, 2011) (cited parenthetically as *IDD*). This paragraph draws from the introduction to *EIP*, especially xiii–xiv and xix.

2 Hendrick Aupaumut, *A Narrative of an Embassy to the Western Indians* ..., in Historical Society of Pennsylvania, *Memoirs*, II (Philadelphia, 1827), 61–131.

3 My discussion of James Otis and Patrick Henry comes from the discussion of "oratorical public culture" in chapter 4 of *EIP*.

4 I discuss Cicero and the Cicero revival in both *EIP* (including an examination of embodiment in Cicero's writings on 276–78) and *IDD* (esp. 15–17 and 71–79).

5 For additional detail, see *EIP* 1–12 and chapter 4.

6 *EAL* 114–17. The passage from Colden is from *History of the Five Indian Nations*, 3rd ed. (London, 1755), I: 15.

7 An extended analysis of the Lancaster Treaty appears in *EIP*, 119–39, with mention of "Remarks concerning the Savages" on 127; in *IDD* I discuss Franklin's treatment of religious speech in "Remarks" on 86–87.

8 *EIP* 45–46; the quoted passage is from Stoddard's *The Defects of Preachers Reproved* ..., 2nd ed. (Boston, 1747), 5.

9 *EIP* 46.

10 *EIP* 153–54; on the opening of galleries, see *EIP* 150.

11 *EIP* 158–70.

12 Henry Highland Garnet, "An Address to the Slaves of the United States," 4. https://digitalcommons.unl.edu/cgi/viewcontent.cgi?article=1007&context= etas (accessed April 10, 2020).

13 *EIP* 201–4.

14 *EIP* 207–9.

15 My discussion of Washington in this paragraph and the two following paragraphs is drawn from *EIP* 213–32.

16 Ames is treated in *EIP* 235–46.

17 *EIP* 241–43.

18 Here as well as in the preceding three paragraphs, the text is condensed from *IDD*, 21–29.

19 My discussion of Webster's Plymouth oration is drawn from *IDD*, 43–46.

20 *IDD* 107–8.

21 These developments are outside the chronological scope of this essay. They are well treated in Kenneth Cmiel's *The Fight for Popular Speech in Nineteenth-Century America* (New York: William Morrow & Co., 1990).

22 *IDD* 219–20.

CHAPTER 4

Vocabularies and Other Indigenous-Language Texts

Sean P. Harvey

Linguists and ethnohistorians have long used vocabularies and other Native-language texts (including dictionaries, grammars, and spelling books) to investigate dialectical variation across space, linguistic change over time, psychological associations and worldviews, and social norms related to language use. Only in the past few decades have other kinds of scholars begun to turn their attention to these often difficult sources. Intellectual historians and literary critics – including Anthony Pagden, Walter D. Mignolo, and Edward Gray – explained how they manifest Euro-American language philosophies and ideologies. These include theories about language's origin, development, and differentiation; the kinship or not of particular tongues; pejorative dichotomies distinguishing oral and written, rude and cultivated languages; and whether the use of specific forms of speech or writing should be promoted or suppressed.[1] Laura J. Murray urged scholars to move beyond the realm of ideas and ideologies, arguing that careful reading of this "elusive genre" reveals the motives that inspired the creation of these texts and "the dynamics of cross-cultural talk and translation ... the tenor and lineaments of the dealings, disputes, and chit-chat that characterized relations between Aboriginal and white people." Scholars have extended this approach to other contexts as well.[2] More broadly, a host of recent work suggests the value in approaching these kinds of texts as facets of the adaptation of Indigenous literacies and practices of intercultural communication and mediation.[3]

Given this strong multipart foundation, few scholars would question the value of these sources for a range of historical and literary questions and, indeed, scholarly interest in these kinds of sources has surged in the last decade. In this new scholarship one can also discern different emphases and perhaps deeper disagreements about how to read these sources. While numerous studies have shown how Euro-Americans defined Indigenous languages and minds as "savage," Sarah Rivett has suggested ways that the

recognized difference of Native languages from European tongues desta-
bilized Euro-American epistemologies and ideologies.[4] While Cameron
Strang urges scholars to see vocabulary collecting, at least under certain
conditions, as a challenge to imperialism, my own work has examined the
role linguistic knowledge played in different facets and phases of US
colonialism – including exchange, evangelization, diplomacy, administration, and language eradication – as well as the significance of linguistic
theories for developing notions of race.[5] Several scholars, moreover, have
elucidated the ways vocabularies and other Native-language texts usually
hinged on the linguistic expertise of Indigenous consultants and were often
silently coauthored by Native people themselves, who used their work as
tutors, philologists, and sometimes authors to pursue ends for themselves
and for their people not always aligned with those of the whites they
"assisted."[6]

Various figures in the early United States eagerly collected linguistic
information to further specific economic, political, or religious ends, or to
participate in global efforts of linguistic collection and comparison. Often
those categories blurred. In the early republic this collecting impulse
became linked to a "salvage" project that aimed at recording the tongues
of a supposedly vanishing people, narrating an ancient national past, and
discovering linguistic ties among peoples useful to missionaries and administrators. Provincial insecurity and cultural nationalism frequently mingled
with the conviction that one's local situation – in other words, one's status
as a colonizer – validated one's authority on questions relating to
Indigenous subjects. The "true full and correct knowledge of America
and all that belongs to it," the immigrant philologist Peter S. Du
Ponceau told fellow linguistic collector Thomas Jefferson, "can only be
obtained in and from America."[7] What resulted were countless word lists
and vocabularies, many of which made their way in some form to scholars,
who devised theories of the way all "savages" spoke and thought in
different times and places, theories of racially distinct languages and
psychologies, theories of "Indian" origins based on supposed linguistic
affinities between Native people in North America and counterparts in
Asia (or, less frequently, Europe or Africa), and theories of which
Indigenous North Americans shared similarity or kinship in language
families.[8]

To illustrate the evidence and modes of interpretation that scholars can
find on this subject, what follows introduces different kinds of Indigenous-
language texts and then focuses on three particular linguistic projects in the
US early republic for which we have substantial documentation: American

contributions to a global collection project initiated by Catherine the Great of Russia in the 1780s; a project directed by Thomas Jefferson that began with a focus on Indian origins that same decade but shifted, after he ascended to the presidency in 1801, to focus on relations among Natives; and a set of intertwined projects in the 1820s that demonstrate the expanding and deepening of linguistic knowledge in the removal era. Convincingly interpreting the resulting texts usually requires moving beyond the genre itself to glean more information about production and use from private letters, official or business correspondence, or published works. Each project represented attempts to know Indigenous people through their language in which curiosity and the intent to benefit from colonialism mingled. The latter two projects also represented attempts to control Indigenous people through language. Each reveals Indigenous strategies of maintaining their language and, through it, peoplehood and sovereignty.

***

From the Atlantic to the Pacific, for those who lived, or expected to make a living, in or on the fringes of Indian country, the ability to communicate with one's suppliers, customers, and hosts facilitated trade and held out the hope of preventing misunderstandings, suspicion, and conflict. Whether the ultimate result was merely a scant and ad hoc word list or a copious vocabulary, acquiring linguistic knowledge began with the collection of words.[9] For traders, such lists were usually resolutely concrete, as in a vocabulary taken in 1819 from Demasduit (or Mary Marsh), a Beothuk woman captured to serve as an interpreter for British settlers in Newfoundland. Its hundreds of English and Beothuk words almost exclusively denote objects, things in nature, and bodily actions. Such a list highlights the prevailing extent, and limits, of exchange to the physical, what was easily indicated or performed.[10] Other vocabularies display the same focus while hinting at the tensions that could structure exchange and, as a result, the ever-present possibility of violence. A Nootka vocabulary taken in 1791 at Nootka Sound, present-day Vancouver Island, provides an example. Its compiler and consultant are unknown, but the tensions of a still-new trading relationship emerge repeatedly in the roughly 300 entries.[11]

Sukneh	to Abuse with Bad language
Honoah	to Be angry
I ti Ive	Is A Liying fellow
Shuokshittle	to Strike

The geographic distance separating these Indigenous vocabularies, and the sharply varying levels of power among those who participated in the production of the linguistic texts – from captives to Native people secure enough to threaten the newcomers – indicates the variation across time and space that one can find in extant vocabularies.

Vocabularies also emerged from more official settings and actors. The US Indian Agency and federal trading "factory" at Fort Wayne, Indiana Territory, compiled forty pages of Ottawa (or Odawa) words between 1809 and 1815. It begins with dozens of entries for fur-bearing animals, then dozens more of fowl and fish. The vocabulary continued through body parts, emotions and states of being, numerals, and colors. Some words, improbably, had no Ottawa equivalent in the corresponding space on the page, such as "war" and "dance." It could indicate an unwillingness on the part of the agent or the Indigenous consultant to broach the subject of war (and its associated ceremonies) as US efforts to expand and redirect the fur trade, and to increase Native debt, land cessions, missionary education, and white settlement, prompted some Ottawas and diverse other Native people to resist these efforts by joining the coalition led by the Shawnee brothers Tenskwatawa and Tecumseh. In 1811, US forces attacked the pan-Indigenous settlement at Prophetstown and war ensued. Toward the end of the vocabulary are questions and phrases related to travel (where, when, why, for what purposes) and trade ("have you any skins," "you sell too dear"), and hints of sex and violence ("I love you, do you love me"; "she is handsome, she is ugly, he is handsome, I was drunk last night, you was drunk, you beat me, you struck me, I am angry").[12] This document illustrates the effort devoted to acquiring linguistic knowledge and casts light on the range of activities, and emotions, that characterized this crucial node through which the United States conducted both its diplomacy and trade with Native nations in the Lake Erie and Lake Huron drainage, and the people who lived there or visited on the eve of the War of 1812 and during that conflict.

For missionaries, however, linguistic knowledge of the merely physical was insufficient. A Moravian among Cherokees in the early nineteenth century, John Gambold, described a missionary's perspective on this process. Traders and most others accustomed to acting as interpreters could go "no further than such things as occur in Commerce." To save an Indigenous soul, "to Translate him out of Death into Life," missionaries had to seek "Conversation." If a missionary proved himself open to accepting Native instruction, "Learning ... as Children do," some Cherokees were "willing to help them to the words ... & it is a Pleasure to them when a Brother first begins to stammer in their language."[13] Nevertheless, despite living among Cherokees for several decades, Gambold never learned their language.

Others were more successful, few more so than his older colleague David Zeisberger. In his decades as a missionary, Zeisberger learned Onondaga, one of the languages of the Haudenosaunee (or Iroquois League), and Lenape (or Delaware), prepared manuscript lexicons and grammars of those languages, and produced numerous scriptural translations and pedagogical books. These included the *Essay of a Delaware-Indian and English Spelling-Book: For the Use of the Schools of the Christian Indians on Muskingum River* (1776; rev. ed. 1806), which was an alphabetical listing of Delaware words, with their English equivalents, grouped according to the words' total number of syllables. It included thousands of words and phrases, in addition to some short scriptural and liturgical translations. Texts such as these enriched the spiritual and earthly lives of those affiliated with the mission. These texts also served a range of other purposes. They provided tangible evidence of missionaries' efforts that could be deployed as props in speeches. They could inspire distant colonists, citizens, and Europeans to support the mission. They would instruct missionary successors. In time they would also make their way to scholars.[14]

While particular economic, political, or religious motives drove these efforts at language collection, diverse individuals appropriated the resulting texts for divergent purposes. Zeisberger, for instance, sent his spelling book to Josiah Harmar, a US general, to fill a request from Catherine II of Russia, who was hoping to a compile a "Universal dictionary." The philosophical theories of Gottfried Wilhelm Leibniz and others, which posited that languages contained the best evidence for understanding the shared descent and differentiation of nations, and that humanity may have originated in a part of Asia within the Russian Empire, inspired the enlightened empress.[15]

That the world's peoples were divided by the languages they spoke was a commonplace at least as old as the biblical story of the Tower of Babel. The idea that the descent and kinship of peoples could be traced through their languages received philosophical legitimacy in the eighteenth century alongside the view that languages were, at least in part, conventional, consisting of labels that human beings applied to things. According to this theory, a given people would name the things they experienced early in their history. Subsequent encounters might lead them to adopt another people's labels for previously unknown things, but not for what they had long since named. By this logic, if one designed a vocabulary that collected words specifically for things that a people would have named at the earliest date – words for family members, celestial bodies, flora and fauna, and numerals – one could, in theory, collect only original words and not words that were the result of exchange. Catherine the Great's vocabulary sought to do just that, devising a list of dozens of such words, beginning with "God," that peoples would have possessed near the beginning of their histories. Through comparison of multiple philosophical vocabularies, one could discover similarities that could only have resulted from two or more peoples' shared ancestry. The absence of such similarities, on the other hand, suggested that two peoples were unrelated or related only distantly. Taking such logic further, through the presence or absence of words denoting particular practices or technologies one could trace the progress of arts and sciences from one people to another. Languages could be adopted or abandoned, and in early modern Europe language more likely indicated belonging to a particular state than some ancestral nation. Yet the philosophically minded looked to language as the most reliable evidence for the lineage of peoples.[16] From one angle, Indigenous participation in the creation of philosophical vocabularies could be seen to support colonialist efforts to delegitimate Indigenous claims to emergence from the land, or divine placement on the continent, through philosophical efforts to link them to the peoples of Asia. In practice, however, these vocabularies mostly convinced those who examined them that the Native languages of the Americas possessed no clear affinities with languages spoken elsewhere in the world. Participating in creating a vocabulary, moreover, provided an opportunity for an Indigenous consultant to establish or deepen a relationship with an influential white man.

Projects that were self-consciously philosophical or philological both appropriated texts that had been compiled for other purposes and produced new kinds of texts. These demonstrate colonialist ideologies and how linguistic expertise gained in one context could be transferred to another, but also Indigenous knowledge and Indigenous determination to remain on their lands. The most remarkable set of US texts for the Russian project came from Richard Butler, an Irish-born former Indian trader and officer in the army. He was already accustomed to adding his mite to philosophical projects, as when he sent a forty-page manuscript vocabulary of Shawnee to Pierre Eugène Du Simitière, a Philadelphia-based polymath collecting materials for a "History of the Indian Languages" as part of a broader antiquarian project.[17] The empress's request came to Butler, superintendent of Indian affairs in the Ohio Country, from George Washington.[18] Besides a vocabulary of Shawnee and Delaware, Butler enclosed two additional texts that disclose his familiarity with distinct registers of Shawnee speech and diplomatic protocol and his dismissal of their claims to the land. One of these enclosures was "a kind of Dialogue" to illustrate Shawnee speech norms in particular situations. In it, a Shawnee man who has long lived among whites arrives at a Shawnee village bearing a message. This "Messenger," whose name is Setting Sun, meets a "Conductor" who takes him to the village "Chief." They smoke a pipe while waiting for other chiefs to arrive, a necessary precondition before he could deliver his formal address appropriately. This dialogue, which one can follow in parallel columns of Shawnee and English, culminates with Setting Sun reprimanding his countrymen for the "folly" of how they lived and for making war against whites and threatening them with white assault on their towns; he urged them to make peace. Underlining how peace could lead to cultural assimilation, but also conforming to a convention of linguistic collection, immediately following this dialogue Butler inserted a translation of the Lord's Prayer.[19] The drama enacted what Butler, who served as a commissioner at each of the treaties at which the United States asserted conquest of the Ohio Valley and its peoples in the 1780s, could not achieve with Shawnees in council. The other enclosure combined Butler's knowledge of linguistic similarities among diverse Algonquians with selective use of Shawnee oral tradition, colonial- and revolutionary-era Indian affairs, and familiarity with western earthworks. It was a speculative essay on Indian origins and antiquity that narrated the conquest of and subsequent dispersal of Algonquians from the Ohio Valley, a historical precedent for US assertions.[20] Some of Butler's material appeared in the German philological compendium *Mithridates* in 1816.[21] Butler, however, had been scalped and his heart possibly eaten, when the Native northwestern confederacy crushed the US Army's attempt to conquer the Ohio Country at the Battle of the Wabash in 1791.[22]

By the late eighteenth century, the comparative vocabulary emerged as the preferred tool for arranging linguistic knowledge for the purpose of determining the kinship of peoples. This tabular form of linguistic representation arranged words from multiple languages in parallel columns to facilitate analysis, allowing one to see a single language by reading vertically down a given column and to see a single word across multiple languages by reading horizontally across columns. It was what Washington had asked Butler to supply, instructing that he need only "insert English words & the names of things in one column – & the Indian therefor in others on the same line, under the different heads of Delaware, Shawanese, Wiendots, &c."[23] He was unable to secure the participation of a Wyandot speaker, but Butler and the Princeton-educated Delaware chief John Killbuck, who had advocated his nation's neutrality during the War for Independence, produced a 281-term comparative vocabulary of English, "Shawano," and "Lenoppea, or Delaware," to which Butler added more than three dozen more words, mainly illustrating how Shawnees counted.[24] To appreciate the convenience of the comparative vocabulary for comparison, one need only contrast it with a work that was based on substantial collection, but which eschewed the comparative table. The naturalist Benjamin Smith Barton collected many hundreds of words from any Indigenous language he could obtain from missionaries, officials, or Native delegations passing through Philadelphia. He published his speculations on the relatedness of all Native languages and the ancient peopling of the Americas from all corners of the world in *New Views of the Origin of the Tribes and Nations of America* (1797; rev. ed. 1798), which also contained a kind of table of his linguistic evidence. But its arrangement used the words of Catherine the Great's vocabulary as section heads, beneath which he listed all the corresponding words from Native languages that he had been able to collect. "God" could be found in twelve Native languages and eight Asian languages and dialects on pages 1–2; "I (Ego)" could be found in seventeen Native languages and ten Asian languages and dialects on pages 78–80; and in between those terms a patient reader would find fifty-two other terms similarly arranged.[25] It allowed reasonably convenient comparison of a given word across languages, but it inhibited comparison of entire languages. As a result of their greater usefulness, comparative vocabularies became increasingly prominent in the late eighteenth and nineteenth centuries, as stand-alone manuscripts, such as the one Butler prepared for Catherine the Great, or printed in travel narratives, histories, and in nineteenth-century works of ethnology and philology.[26]

Thomas Jefferson devised and pursued the most important vocabulary project in the new nation. As early as *Notes on the State of Virginia* (1787), he had boldly (many thought scandalously) suggested that the linguistic diversity of North America indicated that the continent's Indigenous people had been in North America longer than other peoples had inhabited the other continents. Perhaps, he suggested, North America was the cradle of the human race. Jefferson urged gentlemen in or near Indian country to collect what linguistic evidence they could. To further the uniformity and reach of such efforts, Jefferson devised his own vocabulary.

He printed it as a broadside and sent it to naturalists, Indian agents, missionaries, and continental explorers, including Meriwether Lewis and William Clark. Collectors of "specimens" of Native languages could simply fill in equivalents in the blank spaces next to the printed words. The vocabulary consisted of four columns containing 280 words denoting "the most common objects in nature ... which must be present to every nation barbarous or civilized." While Jefferson early on determined to compare the results with those of the Russian project, his own vocabulary departed from the one that Catherine II had devised. Especially notable, Jefferson's vocabulary began with the four classical elements rather than "God," a term the philosopher-statesman excluded altogether.[27]

After Jefferson became president, comparison of the languages of North America and Asia remained a distant goal, but he subordinated it to the more immediate aim of determining relations among the Indigenous people of North America. As he pressed his western agents to obtain linguistic information, Jefferson was unconcerned with communication as such. When the US Indian agent John Sibley sent a report describing the complex language-scape of lower Louisiana that documented which peoples used Mobilian Jargon or a European tongue as a lingua franca, Jefferson instructed him, "it is their original languages I wish to obtain."[28] Understanding the lines of kinship evident in language (in theory) promised those directing US colonialism a stronger grasp of the linguistic and sociopolitical divisions that the administration routinely exploited in land cession treaties north of the Ohio River and, farther west after the Louisiana Purchase, the ostensibly hereditary animosities and alliances among peoples with whom the United States was only just beginning to establish trade. Decades after Jefferson's retirement, the Long Expedition to the Rocky Mountains carried Jefferson's blank vocabulary forms too.[29] The meager results of Jefferson's project belie the effort that went into it. Most of the resulting vocabularies were lost or destroyed. In separate incidents, either Barton or his estate lost the Lewis and Clark vocabularies; an enslaved man threw most of Jefferson's other vocabularies into the James River while searching for valuables; and deserters made off with the horses carrying the saddlebags that held most of the vocabularies Thomas Say had recorded on the Long Expedition.[30]

The extant vocabularies that Jefferson solicited are rich sources for varied questions. One can find blank spaces, non-entries often accompanied with explanatory notes. The Federalist politician William Vans Murray's vocabulary of Nanticoke, spoken on the Eastern Shore of Maryland, provides an example. "You will find they have no word for

the personals *he* and *she*," Murray informed Jefferson. "They were much at
a loss for all terms to express abstract ideas. It is a little surprising they had
a word for *Truth*." The question of abstraction and its relevance for
theories concerning the relative sophistication of rational thought among
the world's peoples was fundamental to Enlightenment moral
philosophy.[31] If he was unconvinced of the poverty of Native languages
when he began his collecting, Jefferson came to accept this view. Though
he had once attributed the linguistic diversity of North America to the
antiquity of Native settlement, an undated comment inserted in his
personal copy of *Notes on the State of Virginia* "hazard[ed] a conjecture"
that it was the result of nothing more than Native pride and savagery, as
disagreements would lead to schism, which would lead to new tongues.
Despite the countervailing evidence of English-speaking US citizens,
Jefferson believed that savage separatists would refuse to continue speaking
a language they had shared with those from whom they parted. "They have
use but for few words," Jefferson wrote, and only "a small effort of the
mind" would be necessary to invent new words to replace old ones.[32] On
the one hand, Murray provided an example of the Indigenous "anti-
lexica," the words that Native languages and the concepts that Native
minds supposedly lacked, which Europeans had been recording since the
sixteenth century. Rather than stressing the language ideology that
Jefferson, Murray, and many other whites held, however, we might follow
Sarah Rivett in recognizing how Nanticoke speakers challenged that ideology. Nanticoke determination to preserve their language – "They speak
their language exclusively among themselves," Murray told Jefferson – and
the decision of one or more Nanticoke consultants, including the "queen"
Mrs. Mulberry, to participate in recording a vocabulary forced Murray to
question the legitimacy of presuppositions and prejudices about the natu-
ralness of pronouns distinguishing male from female and the inability of
savages to grasp abstract "truth." Jefferson even questioned the philosophical rationale that undergirded his project of using language to determine
kinship, which relied on the premise that peoples would retain labels for
things long named.[33]

Many of these vocabularies provide allusions to or specific information
about Native consultants who participated in the creation of what were
often intercultural texts. The Indian agent Benjamin Hawkins, for example, explained the extent to which he relied on Native participation to
compile an extensive comparative vocabulary of Creek, Chickasaw,
Choctaw, and Cherokee. As he told Jefferson, "The Creek is obtained
from the purest source, one of my assistants an interpreter, a chief of the

nation, one of our greatest orators, aided by some chiefs selected for the purpose and by Mr. Barnard an assistant and interpreter. The Choctaw words were obtained by me some time past from a lad of that nation who spoke English. The Chickasaw from a Chickasaw who has resided several years among the Creeks, and had formerly acted as interpreter between the two nations."[34] Other sources suggest the texture of interactions, not always smooth, in which whites recorded these vocabularies. For instance, when Lewis and Clark attempted to record a vocabulary from Mandans, Siouan-speaking villagers on the Missouri River, they reportedly suspected the expedition of "a wicked design upon their country." In stark contrast, when Thomas Say struggled to record a Kiowa vocabulary on the Long Expedition, his consultant pronounced the Kiowa words and "smiled at our awkward attempts to imitate them, whilst we were engaged in committing them to paper."[35]

Some of the most striking descriptions of the social contexts of collection were those that referred to the ostensibly pending death of a language. When he visited Long Island, New York, in 1791, Jefferson paused to record Unkechaug words, the only Indigenous vocabulary he is known to have recorded himself. Ironically, he had to jot down the desired English words on the back of an envelope because he had brought no copies of his printed form. Despite noticing "a young woman . . . who knew something of the language," he insisted that "There remain but three persons of this tribe now who can speak it's language. These are old women." Several of Jefferson's correspondents also combined their vocabularies and linguistic observations with comments about dead or dying languages in the Tidewater and lower Louisiana. Cataloguing this ostensible language death was not simply an abstract memorializing of supposedly savage peoples imagined to be vanishing before civilization. It took added significance from the dual convictions that Native communities were distinguished by language and that the United States assumed title to the land of any "extinct" Native group. The disappearance of Native languages signified the acquisition of land.[36]

Projects that aimed to collect and describe Native languages proliferated, extended their reach, and deepened their aims in the 1820s–1830s, a period of intensified federal efforts at "civilizing" Native peoples, removal of eastern Indigenous peoples across the Mississippi River, and expanding networks of trade and settlement in the West. Unquestionably, the most important of these projects was that initiated by the Philadelphia philologist Peter S. Du Ponceau in 1816. Working initially with the retired Moravian missionary John Heckewelder, Du Ponceau explained Lenape grammatical forms, emphasizing their beauty and regularity, while at the same time insisting that the same grammatical features that united all of the Indigenous peoples of the Americas as a racial group divided them from other human beings. This work engaged crucial philological and ethnological debates in Europe, prompted a bevy of new editions of colonial-era missionary texts, and catalyzed a decades-long missionary-philological effort across North America that produced hundreds of vocabularies, dictionaries, translations, and other Native-language books. It was made possible only through the orthographic, lexical, and grammatical labors of Natives who chose to tutor white missionaries in their tongues and partner with them to produce Indigenous-language texts. The new philology inspired opponents as well. Concerned that it unduly elevated whites' opinions of Native people as Congress debated removal, the US superintendent of Indian Affairs for Michigan Territory, Lewis Cass, launched his own extensive linguistic-ethnographic collection project, aimed at the dual purposes of proving Native savagery and understanding degrees of relationship among Native groups. It too relied on Native participation. It was in this project, but only because he married into an Ojibwe family, that the Indian agent Henry R. Schoolcraft first began his career as an ethnologist.[37] Because the new philology sought a much deeper knowledge of language than what had been required for the mere recording of isolated words, Du Ponceau, Schoolcraft, missionary-philologists, and others pursuing this kind of linguistic collection relied on Indigenous consultants, and sometimes Natives who were themselves philologists, for knowledge of their language's grammatical mechanisms, aesthetic features, and similarity (or not) to other Indigenous tongues.

The surge of scholarly and missionary philology in the 1820s and subsequent decades produced a diverse array of Indigenous-language texts that reveal Indigenous frameworks as well as colonialist views. Scholarly treatises, religious translations, and the intermingling of philology in genres as diverse as lyceum lectures, epic poetry, captivity narratives, white appropriations and reworkings of Indigenous oral literature, and varying degrees of wholesale literary fabrication (as in the "Walam Olum" of Constantine S. Rafinesque) proliferated in these years, as did vocabularies and dictionaries.[38]

The dictionary, as a genre, is more imperious than a vocabulary. It aims toward a complete cataloguing of the words of a language. Close attention to these sources shows that they hold evidence for Native spiritual conceptions.[39] In his *Chippewa Primer*, the Presbyterian missionary Peter Dougherty listed "Reptiels, Lizards, etc." under "TERMS APPLIED TO

SPIRITUAL BEINGS," a categorization more reflective of Ojibwe beliefs about spiritual power than his own.[40] Similarly, these sources provide an entry point for recovering Indigenous political perspectives through attention to words that denote affiliation, allegiance, authority, and sovereignty. In a Creek vocabulary compiled by the Baptist missionary Lee Compere, purchased for the US Indian office by its director, Thomas L. McKenney, Compere recorded that he could find no equivalent for the English term "confederacy." Given the frequency with which whites labeled the Creek polity by that term, Compere's claim that it was "not understood" is striking and perhaps linked to the deliberate efforts of Creek nationalists in the previous decades to create a more centralized government as a means to resist white encroachment.[41] One can also find Native ethnonyms and, sometimes in accompanying materials, explanations of Native experiences of languages other than their own and the social or political significance they derived from ideas of shared descent or ongoing relations.[42]

It is difficult to overstate the richness of the material that one can find in these texts, maybe especially in grammars. The prefatory remarks – such as those in Du Ponceau's "Translator's Preface" to his edition of Zeisberger's Delaware grammar – range from close engagement with philosophical, philological, and ethnological debates to remarks on particular issues related to the administration of colonialism.[43] The grammatical content of these texts can also yield important insights for historians and literary scholars. Grammars of Native languages produced by non-Natives can vacillate between modest effort to convey the existing system of a language and claims to impose a system on unruly speech, as in *Indian Grammar Begun; or, An Essay to Bring the Indian Language into Rules*, a book published by the Puritan missionary John Eliot in 1666 and reissued with extensive annotations by Du Poneau and John Pickering in 1822. In such texts, however, we find – often guided by specific prefatory remarks or explanatory notes within the body of the text – commentary on the possible significance of what philologists found in a language. Some of these reflect a degree of relativism, as when Du Ponceau declared that a true "Universal Grammar" should include Lenape's distinct words for whether "we" included or excluded the listener. Others, however, reflect a more pernicious essentialism.[44] In his *Theoretical and Practical Grammar of the Otchipwe Language*, the Jesuit missionary Frederic Baraga linked the Ojibwe "dubitative" mood, which requires speakers to mark whether they had observed what they described or knew the information merely by hearsay, to the dubious claim that "the habit of lying is a strong trait in the Indian character."[45] To disprove such misrepresentations, to aid missionary or philological efforts, and to acquire authorial reputations, some missionary-schooled Indigenous philologists produced their own grammars and other philological works, including John Summerfield (Ojibwe) and Eleazer Williams, the Mohawk grandson of colonial Deerfield's "unredeemed captive."[46]

Most Native-language texts meant for scholarly purposes included an explicit discussion of orthography: how one chose letters or other characters to record the unfamiliar sounds of Native languages. Two Miami vocabularies completed using Jefferson's form illustrate the point. Both came courtesy of the chief Little Turtle and his son-in-law William Wells, a former captive turned US interpreter. While the philosophical traveler Constantin-François Volney, who had devised an alphabetic system to transliterate Asian languages, used the roman alphabet to record Miami sounds, William Thornton, inventor of his own system of writing, used distinct characters to convey sounds that English letters, he thought, failed to convey.[47]

Choices further proliferated after 1825, when whites learned of Sequoyah's invention of a syllabic system of writing Cherokee. Where white systems of recording Indigenous languages were almost invariably alphabetic, Sequoyah devised eighty-five characters to denote the syllables that composed the language's words. The number of characters exceeded those of the roman alphabet, but while alphabetic letters denote elementary sounds, each of Sequoyah's characters (save one) represented an entire syllable. It dramatically simplified reading and, therefore, the time and effort necessary to become literate, even for adults. Sequoyah opposed white territorial and cultural encroachment and was among the so-called voluntary emigrants across the Mississippi decades before the Trail of Tears. The syllabary, accordingly, provided the benefits of writing for conveying information across distance and generations while countering missionaries' use of literacy instruction to teach Christianity to Cherokee youths. These practical benefits and ideological advantages led a majority of Cherokees to learn and use the syllabary within a decade of its invention. But not all who used the syllabary shared all of Sequoyah's aims. The Cherokee missionary-philologist David Brown (or A-wih), who had previously used a missionary-devised alphabet as the acknowledged coauthor of *Tsuluki Sqcluclu: A Cherokee Spelling Book, for the Mission Establishment at Brainerd* (1819) and a more precise philologist-invented alphabet as the unacknowledged coauthor of the incompletely published *Grammar of the Cherokee Language* (1825), used the syllabary when he translated Cherokee laws and the New Testament between 1827 and his death in 1829. Although alphabetic systems continued to prevail for myriad practical and ideological reasons, in the wake of Sequoyah's success missionaries experimented with numerous syllabic and other nonalphabetic systems. On the one hand, such efforts sometimes partook in a degree of racialization, as white missionaries and scholars wondered if these better suited "Indian" tongues; but in some cases, as among Cherokees and later Crees, it was a frank acknowledgment of Native demands for their own mode of writing, distinct from that used by whites.[48] In this context, the orthography of an Indigenous-language text offers important clues about the author, intent, and audience.

Finally, this period also saw the introduction of new tools to aid linguistic collection and to help officials, missionaries, and scholars in making sense of the resulting information, including taxonomic tables and ethnographic maps. A crucial figure in this respect was Albert Gallatin, who had begun his ethnological work while serving as Jefferson's treasury secretary. Gallatin successfully pressed the War Department to initiate the most coordinated attempt to date at federal linguistic collection before mid-century. Indian agents, missionaries, traders, and others received several items, including some 600 words and short phrases that he produced in (occasionally grudging) collaboration with Du Ponceau; an explanation for how to use John Pickering's "uniform orthography," a recent invention already in use from New York to Hawai'i; a broadside containing Gallatin's classification, the *Table of Indian Tribes of the United States, East of the Stony Mountains, Arranged According to Language and Dialect* (1826), by far the most comprehensive and accurate linguistic classification of the Indigenous people of North America up to that time; and "a coloured map where the boundaries of languages are marked" to accompany it.[49] Unlike the *Table*, which enumerated the members of language families, the map flattened centuries of empirical observations to offer a sweeping visualization of undifferentiated language families covering the continent just as Congress was debating expelling eastern Indigenous peoples from their homelands.

Such taxonomies promised a window into the lineal relations of Native people that overcame much of the confusion of linguistic and cultural diversity, including the multilingualism and linguistic variation that had occurred alongside cultural exchange and intermarriage. As the Secretary of War James Barbour told his Indian superintendents and agents when he sent them Gallatin's materials, the project "would assist us in finding out the ancient boundaries of certain tribes." In the following decade, with removal a reality and officials seeking ways to simplify its administration and facilitate overland migration, Secretary of War Lewis Cass relied on such taxonomies as he sought to consolidate linguistically related peoples in federal agencies in the 1830s; soon afterwards, commissioners of Indian Affairs pushed distinct but linguistically related peoples onto shared reservations. The relations that philologists had uncovered in previous decades justified such programs and had made them possible.[50]

***

Acquiring knowledge of Native languages usually began with those who were pursuing specific aims in Indian country, mainly traders and missionaries who took deliberate steps to learn the languages of potential customers or converts. Beyond those immediate purposes, such materials often made their way to individuals pursuing philosophic aims, and, by the 1780s, scholars became a driving force behind the extension and deepening of knowledge of Native languages. They did so through the collection, compilation, and analysis of vocabularies and other Native-language texts. These are rich sources, teeming with significance in terms of intellectual history and sociopolitical significance with respect to US colonialism. Close reading promises insight into the dynamics of trade and missionary work. These texts illustrate theories about language on its own terms and theories that used language as a key to understanding Indigenous psychologies and genealogies, in frameworks that were alternately developmentalist, degenerationist, or essentialist; monogenist or polygenist. These sources show not only the ways various colonizers deployed linguistic knowledge (knowledge that could be shallow or deep) to justify dispossession in ideological terms, but also how some used it to achieve practical ends of colonization. Yet, crucially, these sources also provide unmatched possibilities for recovering Indigenous intellectual and sociopolitical frameworks. In large part that is because these texts ultimately depended on willing Native participation in the production of linguistic knowledge. These are *not* transparent sources. Interpreting their significance in the early republic often requires reading beyond the source itself, in philological publications and in extant manuscript correspondence involving those that produced, sought, or subsequently used them.

Notes

1 Anthony Pagden, *European Encounters with the New World* (New Haven, CT: Yale University Press, 1993), 117–140; Walter D. Mignolo, *The Darker Side of the Renaissance: Literacy, Territoriality, and Colonization* (Ann Arbor: University of Michigan Press, 1995); Edward G. Gray, *New World Babel:*

Languages and Nations in Early America (Princeton, NJ: Princeton University Press, 1999).

2 Laura J. Murray, "Vocabularies of Native American Languages: A Literary and Historical Approach to an Elusive Genre," *American Quarterly* 53 (2001): 590–623, at 591–92. For an exemplary reading of violence and intimacy in a St. Domingue enslaver's vocabulary of the west Central African language of Kikonga, see Sara E. Johnson, "'Your Mother Gave Birth to a Pig': Power, Abuse, and Planter Linguistics in Baudry des Lozière's *Vocabulaire Congo*," *Early American Studies* 16.1 (Winter 2018): 7–40.

3 For a review of the literature on intercultural communication, Indigenous literacies, and their significance for such projects, see Sean P. Harvey and Sarah Rivett, "Colonial-Indigenous Language Encounters in North America and the Intellectual History of the Atlantic World," *Early American Studies* 15.3 (Summer 2017): 442–473, esp. 447–460.

4 Pagden, *European Encounters with the New World*, 117–140; ; Mignolo, *Darker Side of the Renaissance*; Gray, *New World Babel*; Sean P. Harvey, *Native Tongues: Colonialism and Race from Encounter to the Reservation* (Cambridge, MA: Harvard University Press, 2015), 19–48, 82–84, 113–181; Sarah Rivett, *Unscripted America: Indigenous Languages and the Origins of a Literary Nation* (New York: Oxford University Press, 2017).

5 Cameron Strang, "Scientific Instructions and Native American Linguistics in the Imperial United States: The Department of War's 1826 Vocabulary," *Journal of the Early Republic* 37.3 (Fall 2017): 399–427; Harvey, *Native Tongues*. Speaking of linguistics in India, the anthropologist Bernard Cohn described the relationship between "the command of language and the language of command." See Bernard Cohn, *Colonialism and Its Forms of Knowledge: The British in India* (Princeton, NJ: Princeton University Press, 1996), 15–56. For comparative purposes, see also Joseph Errington, *Linguistics in a Colonial World: A Story of Language, Meaning, and Power* (Malden, MA: Blackwell, 2008).

6 Alejandra Dubcovsky and George Aaron Broadwell, "Writing Timucua: Recovering and Interrogating Indigenous Authorship," *Early American Studies* 15.3 (Summer 2017): 409–441.

7 Peter S. Du Ponceau to Thomas Jefferson, December 11, 1817, Letter Books of the Historical and Literary Committee, 3 vols., 1: 63, American Philosophical Society, Philadelphia. See also Gray, *New World Babel*, chap. 6.

8 Gray, *New World Babel*, chap. 5; Rivett, *Unscripted America*, chap. 7; Harvey, *Native Tongues*, chaps. 2, 6.

9 For traders' overt statements of the need for linguistic knowledge, see, for example, John W. Jordan, ed., "James Kenny's 'Journal to yᵉ Westward,' 1758–59," *Pennsylvania Magazine of History and Biography* 37.4 (1913): 395–449, at 420; John Dunn, *History of the Oregon Territory and British North-American Fur Trade; with an Account of the Habits and Customs of the Principal Native Tribes on the Northern Continent* (London, 1844), 250. On traders' language learning and use, see also Laura J. Murray, "Fur Traders in

Conversation," *Ethnohistory* 50.2 (2003): 285–314; Sean P. Harvey, "An Eighteenth-Century Linguistic Borderland," *Pennsylvania Magazine of History and Biography*, 136.4 (October 2012): 495–498.

10 "Vocabulary. New-foundland Native Red Indian Language. 1819," Houghton Library, Harvard University, Cambridge, MA. On Demasduit, see Ingeborg Marshall, *A History and Ethnography of the Beothuk* (Montreal: Queens-McGill University Press, 1996), 160–180.

11 "A Vocabulary of Nootka-Sound Language on the Northwest Part of America in the Latit[.] For the year 1791," American Antiquarian Society, Worcester, MA. This vocabulary was subsequently published. See Franz Boas, ed., "Vocabularies from the Northwest Coast of America," *Proceedings of the American Antiquarian Society at the Semi-Annual Meeting Held in Boston April 12, 1916*, n.s. 26 (1916): 185–202. On the theme of trade and mutual distrust, see Murray, "Vocabularies," 596–97; Harvey, *Native Tongues*, 22–23.

12 Fort Wayne Indian Agency, Ottawa Vocabulary, [c. 1809–1815], William L. Clements Library, Ann Arbor, MI. On the factory system that operated between 1795 and 1823, and on the Fort Wayne agency and factory more specifically, see David Andrew Nichols, *Engines of Diplomacy: Indian Trading Factories and the Negotiation of American Empire* (Chapel Hill: University of North Carolina Press, 2016), 47–49, 107–111. On Ottawas' attraction to prophetic resistance and eventual disillusionment with Tenskwatawa, see Richard White, *The Middle Ground: Indians, Empires, and Republics in the Great Lakes Region, 1650–1815* (New York: Cambridge University Press, 1991), 486, 506–513; Gregory Evans Dowd, *A Spirited Resistance: The North American Indian Struggle for Unity, 1745–1815* (Baltimore: Johns Hopkins University Press, 1992), 144.

13 John Gambold, "A Short Account concerning the Labours of the Brethren among the Heathen in General. Translated into English," [n.d.], Box 3500, folder 17, Moravian Archives, Bethlehem, PA.

14 David Zeisberger, *Essay of a Delaware-Indian and English Spelling-Book, for the Use of the Schools of the Christian Indians on Muskingum River* (Philadelphia, 1776). For a list of Zeisberger's published and manuscript works, see Edmund de Schweinitz, *The Life and Times of David Zeisberger: The Western Pioneer and Apostle of the Indians* (Philadelphia, 1870), 686–692. For the language philosophy of the Moravians' missionary effort, see Patrick Erben, *A Harmony of the Spirits: Multilingualism, Translation, and the Language of Community in Early Pennsylvania* (Chapel Hill: University of North Carolina Press, 2012), 1–62, 301–324. For the work of Moravians (especially Zeisberger and Heckewelder) with scholars, see Harvey, *Native Tongues*, 56, 67, 80–82, 92, 96–111.

15 Washington to Lafayette, January 10, 1788, in *Papers of George Washington, Confederation Series*, 6:31; Marquis de Lafayette to Benjamin Franklin, February 10, 1786; Josiah Harmar to Franklin, March 19, 1787; Franklin to Lafayette, April 17, 1787, in *Papers of Benjamin Franklin*, at http://

franklinpapers.org/framedNames.jsp, accessed January 30, 2019; David Zeisberger to Josiah Harmar, January 13, 1788, Misc. MSS. Collection, American Philosophical Society, Philadelphia. On Zeisberger's uneasiness at this kind of role, see Letter of David Zeisberger to the Brethren of the Helpers' Conference – On the Cayahaga River, February, 23, 1787, box 153, folder 10, no. 14, Moravian Archives, Bethlehem, PA. For examinations of US responses to Catherine the Great, see Gray, *New World Babel*, 112–115; Harvey, *Native Tongues*, 56–57, 66–67.

16 Thomas R. Trautmann, *Languages and Nations: The Dravidian Proof in Colonial Madras* (Berkeley: University of California Press, 2006), 10–12, 22–41, provides the best description of the logic of philosophical vocabularies. On languages and states, see Burke, *Languages and Communities*, 160–166.

17 "No. 11. Vocabulary of the Shawano Tongue. 1781," Du Simitière Scraps, No. 134, Library Company of Philadelphia. For Du Simitière's project, see "No. 12. Materials for a History of the Indian Languages," note pasted in "Chickasaw etc. Vocabulary," Du Simitière Scraps, No. 137; "Letter to de Lisle de Sales," Du Simitière Scraps, No. 141.

18 George Washington to Richard Butler, November 27, 1786, in *The Papers of George Washington, Confederation Series*, ed. W. W. Abbott (Charlottesville: University Press of Virginia, 1992–), 4:398–400.

19 "Richard Butler, November 30, 1787, Indian Vocabulary," George Washington Papers, Series 8, Miscellaneous Papers ca. 1775–99, Subseries 8D, Extracts, Abstracts, and Notes, 1738–1799: Extracts, Abstracts, and Notes, 1760–1799. The first page is at www.loc.gov/resource/mgw8d.124_0238_0796/?sp=413, accessed April 4, 2019.

20 Butler to Washington, November 30, 1787, Enclosure II, in *Papers of George Washington, Confederation Series*, 5:461.

21 Johann Christoph Adelung and Johann Severin Vater, *Mithridates oder allgemeine Sprachenkunde mit dem Vater Unser als Sprachprobe in beynahe fünfhundert Sprachen und Mundarten*, vol. 3 (Berlin, 1816), 349, 359–362.

22 Washington to Lafayette, January 10, 1788, in *Papers of George Washington, Confederation Series*, 6:30. On Butler's scalp and heart, respectively, see Kelsay Isabel Thompson, *Joseph Brant: Man of Two Worlds* (Syracuse, NY: Syracuse University Press, 1984), 457; Wiley Sword, *President Washington's Indian War: The Struggle for the Old Northwest, 1790–1795* (Norman: University of Oklahoma Press, 1985), 188.

23 George Washington to Richard Butler, November 27, 1786, in *The Papers of George Washington, Confederation Series*, 4:398–400.

24 Butler to Washington, November 30, 1787, Enclosure I, in *Papers of George Washington, Confederation Series*, 5:458. Unfortunately, for the first enclosure, the editors included transcriptions only of Butler's explanatory note and of the first page of the manuscript comparative vocabulary. The full manuscript of the comparative vocabulary is available at the Library of Congress and as digital images online, though one has to click through each image separately. See "Richard Butler, November 30, 1787, Indian Vocabulary."

25 Benjamin Smith Barton, *New Views on the Origin of the Tribes and Nations of America* (Philadelphia, 1797), 1–2, 78–80. Benjamin Smith Barton, *New Views on the Origin of the Tribes and Nations of America*, rev. ed. (Philadelphia, 1798), "Appendix," 20, contained a brief comparative table of Delaware and the languages of the Six Nations.

26 For examples of comparative tables, see Jonathan Edwards [Jr.], *Observations on the Language of the Muhhekaneew Indians* (New Haven, CT, 1788), 6–9; Edward Umfreville, *The Present State of Hudson's Bay, Containing a Full Description of That Settlement, and the Adjacent Country, and of the Fur Trade* (London, 1790), table titled "A Specimen of Sundry Indian Languages ..." following p. 202; J. Long, *Voyages and Travels of an Indian Interpreter and Trader, Describing the Manners and Customs of the North American Indians* (London, 1791), 184–211.

27 Thomas Jefferson, *Notes on the State of Virginia* (London, 1787), 164. See also Jefferson to Ezra Stiles, September 1, 1786, in *The Papers of Thomas Jefferson*, ed. Julian P. Boyd et al. (Princeton, NJ: Princeton University Press, 1950–), 10:316. For Jefferson's blank vocabulary, see American Philosophical Society Historical and Literary Committee, American Indian Vocabulary Collection (Mss. 497.V85), no. 18, American Philosophical Society, Philadelphia. The Society provides links to digital versions of this vocabulary and several completed vocabularies at https://search.amphilsoc.org/collections/view?docId= ead/Mss.497.V85-ead.xml, accessed June 14, 2018. For analyses of Jefferson's project, with respective emphases on Jefferson's interest in Indian origins and American antiquity, on the administrative uses with respect to knowledge of relations among Indians, and on the ways in which Native languages frustrated Jefferson's philosophical efforts, see Gray, *New World Babel*, chap. 5; Harvey, *Native Tongues*, chap. 2; Rivett, *Unscripted America*, chap. 7.

28 Thomas Jefferson to John Sibley, May 27, 1805, in *The Writings of Thomas Jefferson*, ed. Andrew A. Lipscomb, 20 vols. (Washington, DC, 1903–5), 11:79 (hereafter *WTJ*). For Sibley report, see John Sibley, "Historical Sketches of the Several Indian tribes in Louisiana, South of the Arkansas River, and between the Mississippi and River Grande" [1805], in *American State Papers, Class II. Indian Affairs*, 2 vols. (Washington, 1834), 2:721–725.

29 Jose Correa da Serra, April 26, 1816, in Donald Jackson, ed., *Letters of the Lewis and Clark Expedition with Related Documents, 1783–1854* (Urbana: University of Illinois Press, 1962), 611–613; "Concerning Inquiries to Be Made by Major Long of the Indians"; US War Department to Robert Walsh, April 7, 1819, American Philosophical Society Archives.

30 On these vocabularies' varied misfortunes, see Jefferson to Barton, September 21, 1809, in J. Jefferson Looney, ed., *The Papers of Thomas Jefferson: Retirement Series* (Princeton, NJ: Princeton University Press, 2004–), 1:555–56; Jefferson to Du Ponceau, November 7, 1817, in Jackson, ed., *Letters*, 631–633; Gallatin to William Clark, March 31, 1826, Gallatin Papers; Edwin James, *Account of an Expedition from Pittsburgh to the Rocky Mountains,*

Performed in the Years 1819, 1820 ... under the Command of Maj. S. H. Long
[1823], in *Early Western Travels, 1748–1846*, ed. Reuben Gold Thwaites
(Cleveland: Arthur H. Clark Company, 1904), 16:263–264.

31 William Vans Murray to Jefferson, September 18, 1792, in *Papers of Thomas
Jefferson*, ed. Boyd et al., 24:390. On the intellectual context, see David B.
Paxman, "Language and Difference: The Problem of Abstraction in
Eighteenth-Century Language Study," *Journal of the History of Ideas* 54
(1993): 19–36; Gray, *New World Babel*, chap. 4.

32 Thomas Jefferson, *Notes on the State of Virginia*, ed. William Peden (Chapel
Hill: University of North Carolina Press, 1954), 282 n. 12.

33 Murray to Jefferson, September 18, 1792, in *Papers of Thomas Jefferson*, ed.
Boyd et al., 24:390; Pagden, *European Encounters with the New World*, 127;
Rivett, *Unscripted America*, 232–234. The primary consultant may have been
Mrs. Mulberry, the only Nanticoke Murray named; but he claimed to have
recorded the vocabulary "in a Wigwam" and, while there were four such
wigwams in the community, he noted that Mulberry lived in a framed house.

34 Benjamin Hawkins to Jefferson, July 12, 1800, in *Papers of Thomas Jefferson*,
ed. Boyd et al., 32:50–52. See also American Indian Vocabulary Collection,
no. 5.

35 Charles Mackenzie, "The Missouri Indians: A Narrative of the Four Trading
Expeditions to the Missouri, 1804–1805–1806, for the North-West
Company," in *Les bourgeois de la Compagnie du Nord-Ouest: Récits de voyages,
Lettres et Rapports inédits relatifs au Nord-Ouest Canadien*, vol. 1, ed. L. R.
Masson (1889; New York: Antiquarian Press, 1960), 336–337; James,
Account of the Long Expedition, 16:210.

36 "Jefferson's Vocabulary of the Unquachog Indians," in *Papers of Thomas
Jefferson*, ed. Boyd et al., 6:467–470. See also Jefferson, *Notes*, 96; Murray
to Jefferson, September 18, 1792, in *Papers of Thomas Jefferson*, ed. Boyd
et al., 24:389–390; Sibley, "Historical Sketches," 725; Thomas L. McKenney
to Supts. of Indian Affairs, Indian Agents, and Supts. of Indian Schools,
August 22, 1825, in Records of the Office of Indian Affairs, Letters Sent,
2:131. On "extinction" and Indian title, see Jefferson to William H. Harrison,
February 27, 1803, in *Writings of Thomas Jefferson*, ed. Lipscomb, 10:371. Cf.
Gray, *New World Babel*, 112–138, which examines only the philosophical and
literary aspects of this "science of the vanished." On observations of Indians'
"lasts," see Jean M. O'Brien, *Firsting and Lasting: Writing Indians Out of
Existence in New England* (Minneapolis: University of Minnesota Press,
2010).

37 On the Du Ponceau and Cass projects, missionary efforts, and on Native
linguistic opinions in those contexts, see Harvey, *Native Tongues*, chaps. 3–5.

38 For the mass of vocabularies that Du Ponceau collected, see American
Philosophical Society Historical and Literary Committee, American Indian
Vocabulary Collection (Mss. 497.V85); Peter S. Du Ponceau, "Indian
Vocabularies, 1820–1844" (Mss. 497.In2); "Vocabularies of the Okonagan,
Attnaha, and Walla Walla Languages, [and] Vocabularies of the Languages of

Indians Inhabiting N.W. America, 1834–1836" (Mss. 497.3 T66), American Philosophical Society. On Rafinesque, see Harvey, *Native Tongues*, 166, 171.

39 See the discussion in Harvey and Rivett, "Colonial-Indigenous Language Encounters," 458–459.

40 Peter Dougherty, *A Chippewa Primer* (New York, 1844), 12. Another missionary from this period noted, "The efficacy of some Med[icine] is attributed to . . . snakes. The Great Horned Snake wh[ic]h lives in the water is the greatest Manito." See Theresa M. Schenck, ed., *The Ojibwe Journals of Edmund F. Ely, 1833–1849* (Lincoln: University of Nebraska Press, 2012), 429.

41 Lee Compere, "Vocabulary and Grammar of the Muskhoghe Language (1827)," 9, New-York Historical Society. For the Indian office's purchase, see Thomas L. McKenney to James Barbour, December 1, 1827, in Records of the Office of Indian Affairs, Letters Sent, 4:163. On Creek nationalism, see Steven C. Hahn, *The Invention of the Creek Nation, 1670–1763* (Lincoln: University of Nebraska Press, 2004); Kevin Kokomoor, *Of One Mind and of One Government: The Rise and Fall of the Creek Nation in the Early Republic* (Lincoln: University of Nebraska Press, 2018).

42 Sean P. Harvey, "Native Views of Native Languages: Kinship and Communication in Eastern North America, ca. 1800–1830," *William and Mary Quarterly*, 3rd ser., 75.4 (October 2018): 651–684.

43 David Zeisberger, *Grammar of the Language of the Lenni Lenape or Delaware Indians*, trans. Peter S. Du Ponceau (Philadelphia, 1827).

44 Peter S. Duponceau, "A Correspondence between the Rev. John Heckewelder, of Bethlehem, and Peter S. Duponceau, Esq," *Transactions of the Historical and Literary Committee of the American Philosophical Society* 1 (1819): 435. See also "Notes and Observations on Eliot's Indian Grammar. Addressed to John Pickering, Esq.," *Collections of the Massachusetts Historical Society*, 2nd ser. 9 (1822): xix.

45 Frederick Baraga, *A Theoretical and Practical Grammar of the Otchipwe Language, the Language Spoken by the Chippewa Indians; Which Is also Spoken by the Algonquin, Otawa and Potawatami Indians, with Little Difference. For the Use of Missionaries, and Other Persons Living among the Indians of the above Named Tribes* (Detroit, 1850), 95–96.

46 John Summerfield, alias Sahgahjewagahbahweh, *Sketch of Grammar of the Chippeway Language, to Which Is Added a Vocabulary of Some of the Most Common Words* (Cazenovia, 1834); Eleazer Williams, "Grammar of the Mohawk Dialect of the Iroquois Language, of the Five Ancient Confederated Nations. Containing Rules and Exercises, Intended to Exemplify the Indian Syntax, According to the Best Authorities, Preceded by Succinct Rules Relative to the Pronunciation," Missouri Historical Society, Columbia [American Philosophical Society microfilm]. On the philology of Summerfield and Williams, see Harvey, *Native Tongues*, 101–102, 111, 133–134, 160, 162. On Indigenous "proprietary authorship," see Philip Round, *Removeable Type: Histories of the Book in Indian Country, 1663–1880* (Chapel Hill: University of North Carolina Press, 2010), chap. 6.

47 American Indian Vocabulary Collection, nos. 3 and 9. See also [William Thornton], "Cadmus, or A Treatise on the Elements of Written Language, Illustrating, by a Philosophical Division of Speech, the Power of Each Character, Thereby Mutually Fixing the Orthography and Orthoepy. With an Essay on the Mode of Teaching the Deaf, or Surd and Consequently Dumb, to Speak," *Transactions of the American Philosophical Society* 3 (1793).

48 On whites' experience of Native sounds, how they addressed problems of orthographies, and the proliferation of syllabaries after 1825, see Harvey, *Native Tongues*, 113–144.

49 Albert Gallatin, *A Table of the Indian Tribes of the United States, East of the Stony Mountains, Arranged According to Languages and Dialects* (1826); Albert Gallatin to Peter S. Du Ponceau, May 9, Peter Stephen Du Ponceau Papers, 1663–1844, box 1, folder 8, Historical Society of Pennsylvania, Philadelphia. The resulting materials and the map were published a decade later in Albert Gallatin, "A Synopsis of the Indian Tribes within the United States East of the Rocky Mountains, and in the British and Russian Possessions in North America," *Archaeologia Americana: Transactions of the American Antiquarian Society* 2 (1836). For close considerations of the project and its context, see Strang, "Scientific Instructions and Native American Linguistics"; Harvey, *Native Tongues*, 148–156; Sean P. Harvey, "'The Indian Republic of Letters': Scholarly Networks and Indigenous Knowledge in Philology," in *Indigenous Languages and the Problem of the Archives*, ed. Adrianna Link, Abigail Shelton, and Patrick Spero (Lincoln: University of Nebraska Press, 2021).

50 James Barbour, "Department of War, May 15, 1826," [2], in Albert Gallatin Papers (New York University microfilm collection), reel 36. On linguistic consolidation in the removal era, see Harvey, *Native Tongues*, 190–194. On linguistic taxonomy, maps, and "erasure," see Judith T. Irvine and Susan Gal, "Language Ideology and Linguistic Differentiation," in *Regimes of Language: Ideologies, Polities, and Identities*, ed. Paul V. Kroskrity (Santa Fe, NM: School of American Research Press, 2000), 37–39, 50–55.

CHAPTER 5

The Genteel Novel in the Early United States

Thomas Koenigs

From the 1770s through the late 1820s, the US novel, as a genre, was preoccupied with its own gentility. Faced with the new nation's well-documented suspicion of fiction, many early US novelists, in both their paratexts and narratives, sought to establish the terms on which certain novels might be deemed appropriate reading for respectable persons, advocating, with varying degrees of explicitness, for the acceptance of their works as part of polite culture in the early republic.[1] These novelists, however, were deeply ambivalent about the genre's potential gentility. Even as they tried to position their novels as a respectable part of polite culture, they also sought to distance these works from the genre's association with fashionable frivolity and aristocratic leisure.[2] For this reason, these novels crystallize, as well as any genre, the republic's conflicted attitude toward gentility as such; early novelists worked to associate their works with an emerging mode of bourgeois gentility that both drew on and defined itself in contradistinction to European aristocracy.[3] The novel was one of the key sites at which early US writers negotiated what would define gentility in the new democratic nation.

As early US novelists argued for the social respectability of *select* novels, there emerged a class of what the editors of this volume have dubbed "Genteel Novels" – those novels that self-consciously distanced themselves from the racy, violent, and sometimes supernatural narratives characteristic of what the editors have called the "lurid novel." Although the "genteel novel" is a capacious, heterogeneous category that might encompass a variety of recognizable subgenres – from seduction tales to domestic fiction to historical romances – these novels often focused on domestic arrangements and almost always justified their narratives in terms of their edifying effects rather than the titillation and sensational entertainment associated with the lurid novel. The line dividing genteel novels from lurid ones, however, is frequently difficult to discern, and a clear conceptual distinction between them often breaks down when applied to a specific novel.

Many genteel novels teeter on the edge of the lurid, always threatening to tip over into racy sensationalism. Genteel novelists sought to harness the appeal of the very lurid tales that they explicitly disavowed, even as they also sought to contain this luridness within their projects of education and edification. Given the challenge of separating the lurid from the genteel in early US novels, I would propose an expansive definition of the "genteel novel" as any novel that, either explicitly or implicitly, argues for its respectability and advocates its inclusion in polite culture.

The "genteel novel" is an especially appropriate topic for a volume on American literature in transition, as the half-century following independence was a period of dramatic evolution for both the genteel novel and US attitudes toward the novel more generally. This era's genteel novels both participated in and reflected a transformation of the novel's social status: whereas in the 1780s and 1790s, the genre was generally regarded as an anathema to republican society, by the late 1820s certain types of novel had come to be widely accepted as respectable, even edifying, reading material.[4] Such changing attitudes reveal a subtle but significant shift in the kind of gentility associated with the genre, as novels gradually and unevenly lost their association with fashionable, aristocratic frivolity and instead came to be associated with middle-class domesticity in the antebellum period.[5] More than merely reflecting such changes, these genteel novels played a central role in this recasting of gentility as bourgeois respectability.[6] Because many – though certainly not all – genteel novels were socially or politically conservative in their themes and commitments, it can be easy to overlook the genre's sustained literary experimentation across this period, as novelists imagined and then reimagined the role that novels might play in the nation's emergent middle-class culture.

The Ambivalent Gentility of the Early US Novel

As David Shields and Richard Bushman have shown, the upper classes of eighteenth-century British America strove to cultivate their refinement, civility, and politeness as a means of making clear their gentry status and their authority in both cultural and political life. Drawing on a tradition of gentility that had been revitalized in the Renaissance and spread through European courts to its upper classes, colonial elites displayed their refinement in their manners, in how they dressed, in how they constructed and decorated their homes, in the societies in which they participated, and, perhaps most importantly, in how they educated their children. While the spread of gentility in the British colonies is evident in the proliferation of such diverse phenomena as parlors, silverware, and conduct manuals focused on manners, this refinement campaign was, until near the end of eighteenth century, primarily confined to the wealthy, and, as such, gentility served as the visible sign of what was widely regarded as a natural division of society and thus reinforced the established social hierarchy.[7]

The Revolution, however, complicated attitudes toward gentility. As the United States embraced republican governance, gentility's association with European aristocracy suddenly made it seem suspicious. Some republican writers pointed out the incongruity of aspiring to aristocratic forms of refinement in a republic; some argued that the fashions associated with genteel refinement were frivolous luxuries that had no role in a republican society; some even denounced such aspirations to gentility as signs of corruption and grave threats to the republic's virtue.[8] But, as both Shields and Bushman make clear, such republican critiques of gentility did not dampen the desire of many US citizens for greater refinement. Even the genteel entertainments most closely associated with European aristocracy, such as courtly balls, continued to have considerable attraction for the newly minted Americans.[9] If anything, the late eighteenth century saw an increasing number of Americans drawn to the refinement of an aristocratic past, as an emerging middle class of merchants, clerks, and even small-town farmers began to aspire to a degree of gentility.[10] The early republic, then, was characterized by its vexed, incongruous attitudes toward gentility: more and more Americans sought to cultivate gentility, even as the voluble republican press decried such refinement as a corrupt, aristocratic luxury inconsistent with the values of true republicanism.

Anxieties about aristocratic frivolity and luxury pervade early US condemnations of novel-reading. The republic's suspicion of fiction in general and the novel in particular might be one of the most familiar stories in US literary history, but it is worth revisiting briefly, because it is crucial for understanding the development of the genteel novel. In the early United States, novels and fiction were regarded as a double threat to readers' social respectability. First, critics contended that fiction's lack of basis in actual persons and events rendered it an unreliable source of knowledge and argued that fiction gave readers, especially young women, unrealistic, even delusive, expectations for the "world as it is." The false pictures of fiction, these critics argued, would lead directly to immoral behavior, especially licentiousness. Second, even many critics who did not see novel-reading as inherently harmful nevertheless regarded it as a distraction from religion, business, domestic duties, and political life. The early US novel thus emerged in dialectical relation to both the suspicion that novels were too genteel (in the sense of frivolous and fashionable) and the widespread belief that they were a profound threat to the gentility (in the sense of respectability) of its readers, because it would compromise their virtue.[11]

In the face of these anxieties, early US novelists developed elaborate arguments for why their particular novels should be considered respectable, edifying, or, at very least, not dangerous. The book that is generally regarded as the first American novel – William Hill Brown's *The Power of Sympathy, Founded in Truth* (1789) – exemplifies the extensive textual and paratextual apparatuses novelists constructed in an attempt to associate their novels with the right kind of gentility. A summary of its plot suggests that *The Power of Sympathy* is an exemplary lurid novel – it is a sensational tale of seduction, incestuous love, and suicide. Brown, however, embeds this nearly Gothic tale within a series of dialogues on female education between cultivated ladies and gentleman at a rural retreat that resemble contemporary conduct manuals. These dialogues return repeatedly to the question of what qualifies as acceptable, edifying reading material for young women and it gives particular attention to the question of novel-reading.

Brown's novel echoes many contemporary periodical essays in associating novel-reading with the decidedly frivolous kind of gentility. The conversations about novel-reading are sparked by the "genteel" Miss Bourn, who displays the foibles of refinement: she dresses elegantly yet awkwardly, spends a lot of time with company but does not have polished manners, and does not have the appropriate "modesty of her sex." In short, she exemplifies a fashionable yet superficial gentility that Brown opposes to the true refinement of other characters, such as the suggestively named Mr. Worthy and Mrs. Holmes. Brown links Miss Bourn's surface-level cultivation to her reading: "I read as much as anybody," she says of her novel-reading, "though it may afford amusement . . . I do not remember a single word." While the "genteel" Miss Bourn's awkward pretensions to a fashionable refinement and her time-wasting novel-reading are presented as relatively minor, correctable weaknesses, Brown makes clear how dangerous such habits become if they are left unchecked by referring to "The Story of Miss Whitman," a woman whose love for "novels and romances," in Brown's account, taught her to be "vain and coquettish," leading to her seduction and death in childbirth.[12] *The Power of Sympathy* insists that indiscriminate novel-reading is not only a genteel frivolity but also a profound threat to a young woman's chastity, respectability, and even her life.

The Power of Sympathy's warning against novel-reading, however, represents neither a categorical rejection of the genre nor a wholesale dismissal of gentility as a social ideal: the problem, rather, is that reading the wrong novels produces the wrong kind of gentility. Brown's avatar, Mr. Worthy, clarifies that he "does not condemn" every novel, but he insists that young women – or, rather, their guardians – must select the novels they read judiciously, because, as the assembled company all agrees, only those novels "which teach us a knowledge of the world are useful to form the minds of females."[13] Brown's novel, then, laments the frivolity and warns against the dangers of novel-reading, even as it also encourages the genre's critics to recognize that there are, in fact, laudable and instructive exceptions to the genre's general perniciousness. *The Power of Sympathy's* opening paratexts set it forth as just such an exception – it is an attempt to reform a suspicious genre from within by making it conformable to "truth" and, therefore, capable of giving young women an edifying "knowledge of the world." Reading such books, Brown suggests, will not produce the superficial gentility of Miss Bourn, but will give readers a moral knowledge that will help them cultivate the refined respectability of Mrs. Holmes.

The distinction between gentility as thoughtless fashionability and gentility as respectable moral refinement is a persistent theme in early US novels. While these novels' protagonists were drawn almost exclusively from the middle and upper classes – with a few exceptions such as Sarah Savage's *The Factory Girl* (1814) – these novels insistently staged the difference between the virtuous "better classes" to which their heroes and heroines belonged and the urbane, aristocratic (and faux-aristocratic) rakes, seducers, and villains that threatened the republic's sexual and political virtue.[14] As a means of establishing this distinction, many early US novels centered on either an orphan whose genteel origins are revealed only later in the novel—such as Judith Sargent Murray's serialized "The Story of Margaretta" (1792–94), William Hill Brown's *Ira and Isabella* (1807), Meredith Margaret Read's *Margaretta* (1807), and the anonymous *Rosa, American Genius and Education* (1810)—or a genteel child who has fallen in wealth or status as a result of misfortune or the mismanagement of an older generation, such as Susanna Rowson's *Sincerity* (1803–4), S. S. B. K. Wood's *Dorval, or The Speculator* (1805), Rebecca Rush's *Kelroy* (1812), and Catharine Maria Sedgwick's *A New-England Tale* (1822). These plots provided novelists with a means of establishing an opposition between fashionable, urban social life and the pastoral bourgeois gentility that these novels advocated without challenging the class stratification of US society. Such plots about genteel orphans, that is, offered a means of critiquing the fripperies of upper-class life by associating its protagonists, especially

its heroines, with the modest virtues of the lower class without inverting
class hierarchy. Reflecting the republic's conflicted attitude toward gentility, novelists went to great lengths to reconcile, at the level of plot, the
competing, even contradictory, attractions of aristocratic refinement and
republicanism and even stage their compatibility: in Read's *Margaretta*,
when the virtuous English aristocrats, Lord and Lady Warren – in fact,
Margaretta's true parents! – arrive in the United States, their hearts
are so "warmed with a noble enthusiasm for the rights and liberties of
the citizens of Columbia" that they "assumed the plain appellation
of Mr. and Mrs. Warren, laying their title on the altar of liberty as a
sacrifice to equality, peace, and independence."[15] Few moments better
capture early US novelists' simultaneous attraction to the cultivated
refinement of aristocratic culture and sense of its inappropriateness for
a republican society.

But in order to align their novels with the kind of bourgeois gentility
suitable for a republic, US novelists had to first undo the novel's association with the frivolity, fashion, and luxury of aristocratic social life.
Anxieties about the link between novel-reading and unhealthy, even
delusional, fixation on aristocratic life haunted early US novels. The most
dramatic example is Tabitha Tenney's *Female Quixotism* (1801). *Female
Quixotism* is the story of Dorcasina Sheldon, a young woman, who lives
with her father in the Pennsylvania countryside. While the Sheldon family
exemplifies the kind of rural, bourgeois gentility that many US novels
celebrate, Dorcasina, bereft of a mother's guiding influences, contracts a
taste for novel-reading that leads her to form quixotic expectations for her
life based on European romances. For Tenney, the dangers of novel-
reading involve not only the genre's epistemological unreliability, but also
its association with an aristocratic social order: Dorcasina's dreams of
meeting a lord disguised as a commoner or being rescued by a passing
nobleman expose her to myriad threats to both her person and her
respectability. *Female Quixotism*'s generic anxieties are closely tied to class
anxieties: Dorcasina's novel-reading produces a delusive desire for an
aristocratic courtship that, counterintuitively, leaves her vulnerable to the
schemes of social climbers and conmen who ape its conventions in an
attempt to secure her fortune.

While Tenney's antinovel novel presents novel-reading as a threat to
republican gentility – in *Female Quixotism*, this is a republican gentility of
a decidedly conservative, Federalist cast – other novelists sought to recode
novel-reading's social associations in order to align it with the same

virtuous, rural elite that Tenney believed were threatened by it. In Brown's second novel, the posthumously published *Ira and Isabella, a Novel, Founded in Fiction*, the very isolated reading that produces Dorcasina's social order-threatening delusions protects its protagonist Ira from the corruptions of fashionable city life. Brown's novel echoes the conventional association of novel-reading with a licentious, faux-aristocratic, urban social life when it describes the novel's villainous, Italianate rake Florio as having "turned over more pages of novels than of Roman history."[16] But it complicates this generic coding by also setting up an opposition between Ira's virtuous private reading and the worldly experience of Florio and Ira's other libertine friends. These libertines lament Ira's substitution of reading for worldly experience: "Learn, my friend, a little self-knowledge of the world, and unlearn a great deal of your book-knowledge. For books only instruct us in the interests of human nature, the duties of philanthropy, or, in other words, to regard others, and forget ourselves."[17] By having his rakish libertines voice arguments that recall condemnations of quixotic novel-reading, Brown recodes such reading as a means of preserving innocence and avoiding worldly corruption. This is a remarkable remaking of the antifictional critique that novel-reading separates readers from the "world as it is" in a private, illusory world of fancy. Many early US novels, including Brown's *Power of Sympathy*, had tried to establish their ability to provide readers with a reliable substitute experience of the "world" by asserting their firm foundation in "Truth" and "Fact." But in *Ira and Isabella*, Brown seizes upon another resonance of "the world" – the *beau monde*, or the urban world of stylish gentility.[18] This allows him to appropriate the concern that fiction separates readers from the "world" as a virtue and set forth his own novel – the only early US novel that claims in its subtitle to be "Founded in Fiction" – as an alternative to the corrupting influences of fashionable urban society. Setting Ira's private reading against the dissipation of city life, Brown realigns the novel – a genre often associated with exactly such frivolous dissipation – with the *otium* ideal of rural, literary retirement and posits the genre as a means of cultivating the natural sensibility, morality, and modesty that fashionable urban society corrupts.[19]

Rebecca Rush's *Kelroy, a Novel* is both one of the richest examples of the early US novel's ambivalent relationship to gentility as a category and one of the most elaborate attempts to recode the genre's relationship to genteel social life. *Kelroy* is a novel of manners, with pronounced Gothic undertones, that satirizes the vanities of social life in turn-of-the-century Philadelphia.

The novel's chief villain, the sinister Mrs. Hammond, seeks to rebuild her lost fortune and restore her lost social status by guiding her two daughters into profitable marriages. While Mrs. Hammond successfully arranges the marriage of worldly Lucy to the wealthy Englishman Walsingham, the younger Emily frustrates her mother's ambitions with her distaste for fashionable society and her love for the poor poet, Kelroy. The novel traces the deceptive schemes, including intercepted and forged letters, through which Mrs. Hammond breaks up their engagement, steering the heartbroken Emily into a more profitable union. Emily discovers her mother's plot when Mrs. Hammond's sudden death leaves her unable to destroy the evidence. Emily dies disillusioned and heartbroken shortly thereafter.

Kelroy is an insider's portrait of the vanities of upper-class social life in Philadelphia. The novel's satire is expansive, mocking the vulgar nouveaux riches' pretensions to refinement, the grasping ambition of social climbers, and the superficial gentility of Philadelphia's established elite. Raised in isolation from society in the country, Emily's humility and modesty are set in opposition to this fashionable, urban social world. Such a distinction would have been familiar in early US culture, but *Kelroy* stands out for how it positions Emily's novel-reading in *opposition* to this urbane society: "whilst Emily [was] busied in works of fancy or turning over ... the pages of a favorite author, Lucy was shut up in her chamber, practicing cotillions, and admiring herself in the glass."[20] *Kelroy*'s opposition of fiction-reading to the vanities of urban social life might echo *Ira and Isabella*, but this metageneric argument is complicated by how Emily's ultimate disillusionment reproduces, in a qualified form, the disciplining of the female quixote found in Tenney's novel. Emily's isolated reading and aversion to fashionable society might produce her exemplary virtue and modesty, but this bookish education has also given her a naïve view of her fellow humans. In a prophetic exchange, Lucy's husband – the admirably genteel Walsingham – warns Emily about the dangers of her inaccurate, if moral, worldview: "It would be happy for you ... if you could be translated to a world filled with creatures as innocent, and undesigning as yourself; for I fear there is many a hard lesson awaiting you in this rough, and crooked one of ours.... Experience will teach you the real characters of beings who chiefly compose your species."[21] Emily's private reading of "works of fancy" might have helped her cultivate an innocence and moral purity that sets her apart from Philadelphia's fashionable set, but this same exemplary innocence leaves her vulnerable to the deceptions and schemes of the city's grasping social climbers, including her own mother.

Kelroy is an exemplary genteel novel in that it is deeply ambivalent about both gentility and novels. Even as Rush's novel satirizes the frivolity of upper-class Philadelphia society, the alternatives she presents are neither the lower nor the rising merchant classes – who are ridiculed for their bungling attempts at gentility – but a more established, rural gentry, best exemplified by the virtuous Walsingham, a genuine English nobleman. And even as *Kelroy* celebrates the moral purity that Emily has cultivated, in part, through private reading, it also demystifies the naïve worldview that Emily has developed through this reading. The tragedy of *Kelroy* is that, in Rush's account, novel-reading produces a kind of refinement that renders readers unfit to navigate the fallen social world of genteel Philadelphia.

The Novel as Vehicle for Genteel Education

In opposing novel-reading to the fashionable vanities of urban society, *Kelroy* participates in this period's recoding of the genre's social associations, but it remains conflicted about one of the central questions that preoccupied novelists of this era: Could the novel ever be a vehicle for genteel education? And if so, what kind of gentility would it produce? For in spite of the conflicted attitudes toward gentility evident in their plots, many early US novelists presented their novels as a means of helping readers, especially young women, cultivate their own refinement. Throughout this period, however, this remained a controversial project, as there was no consensus about the two central questions on which such didactic projects hinged. The first was the question of whether novels could be reliable vehicles for instruction. The second was the question of whether gentility was something that could be learned.

The idea that novels could serve as didactic vehicles that might allow any reader to cultivate her gentility and, by extension, transform her class status came out of the Richardsonian tradition that flourished in the early republic.[22] Early US novels often reproduced what Nancy Armstrong influentially identified as the bourgeois project of Richardsonian fiction – the displacement of an earlier aristocratic form of desire focused on the body by the bourgeois conception of desire based on virtuous interiority. (To the Richardsonian drama of aristocratic seducer and virtuous, bourgeois victim, many early US novels added a drama of national difference, with English, Creole, or especially French seducers representing a particular threat to the young women of the republic.) As Armstrong has shown, Richardson's refiguration of desire in *Pamela* opened up new possibilities for social mobility, as Pamela's interiorized virtue transforms her from a target of seduction to a desirable wife for the aristocratic Mr. B. *Pamela*, however, did not simply tell a story of class mobility, but also offered its heroines as an instructive model for readers to imitate.[23] In other words, the Richardsonian novel both offered a condemnation of the vices of an older genteel, aristocratic order *and* offered itself as a didactic vehicle through which readers could potentially achieve a new degree of gentility themselves.

Richardsonian fiction's promise of transformative instruction made it influential, popular, and controversial in the American colonies and early republic. Critics argued that fiction's illusory nature – its lack of firm basis in fact and actuality – meant that it could never impart true knowledge and that readers who relied on fiction for instruction in gentility would obtain only a superficial refinement. John Trumbull's satiric poem *The Progress of Dulness* (1771–73) offered one of the most elaborate versions of this argument in its portrait of Harriet Simper. The poem takes as one of its chief objects of satire contemporary female education that, according to Trumbull, focuses on "modern style and fashion" to the exclusion of true knowledge, producing young women who prove the maxim that the "half-genteel are least polite."[24] Trumbull makes clear that the fashionable coquetry that these young women mistake for gentility has been produced, in part, through their romance reading: "For while she reads romance, the Fair one / Fails not to think herself the Heroine.... Thus *Harriet* reads, and reading really / Believes herself a young *Pamela*."[25] According to critics such as Trumbull, novel-reading produces not the refinement and class mobility promised by *Pamela* and its many US descendants, but a delusional, if fashionable, faux-gentility and dangerous coquetry.

Faced with such criticisms, however, US novelists did not abandon their didactic projects or their ambitions to cultivate genteel readers, but instead included extended defenses of their instructional projects, explaining exactly what differentiated *their* novel from the mass of dangerous novels. There is not space here to explore the competing theories of novelistic education advocated by different novelists, but I want to suggest that one of the defining characteristics of the genteel novel is not only its didacticism but its metadidacticism – its explicit participation in debates about *how* the novel might best serve as an instrument of education.[26] Judith Sargent Murray's ambivalently novelistic fiction, "The Story of Margaretta," is exemplary. Murray's narrative of the orphan Margaretta's upbringing by Mr. and Mrs. Vigilius offers a model for the education of a genteel young woman: it includes extended descriptions of appropriate training for manners, dancing, and, of course, reading. Mrs. Vigilius does not believe in rejecting novels altogether, but she closely monitors Margaretta's novel-reading, both selecting appropriate works and teaching her how to distinguish fiction from reality. In its original publication in *The Massachusetts Magazine*, Murray also incorporated fictional letters from readers, usually either young women in need of education or the guardians overseeing such educations, in which she even more explicitly lays out how her own narrative might be used to instruct young readers. This metadidactic apparatus is perhaps the most elaborate found in early US fiction, but almost every genteel novel took up the question of *how* novels might best instruct.

These genteel novels also make clear how anxieties about both novels and gentility were gendered in the early republic. Scholars have long noted the gendered nature of antinovel arguments, as critics contended that women's overactive imaginations and heightened sensibilities made them especially susceptible to the moral and epistemological pitfalls of novel-reading.[27] Scholars have also noted women's privileged role in discourses of gentility as exemplars of delicacy and refinement. This era's conduct writers increasingly assigned women dominion over the key site for the cultivation of gentility – the household – and taxed them with overseeing the family's refinement.[28] What I want to underscore here is how intimately intertwined these two discourses were: the sense that female novel-reading undermined, as one commentator put it in 1801, "the peace and happiness of society" was bound up with the emergent idea that women should serve as the guardians and models of the right kind of refinement.[29] In this context, the quixotic faux-gentility that Harriet Simper developed through novel-reading was not only a personal failing but a threat to the social fabric of the republic.

The didactic novel's promise to democratize gentility by offering a model for cultivation to anyone who could read also threatened to compromise gentility as a visible manifestation of an established, purportedly natural, social hierarchy.[30] What did it mean for gentility's status as a sign of society's just divisions if anyone could learn it from a book – if any Harriet could become genteel by imitating Pamela? While most early US novelists argued for the qualified instructional efficacy of some novels, they were far more ambivalent about whether true gentility was innate or could be learned. The paratexts of genteel novels might emphasize the shaping power of education – for both good and ill – but their endings often complicated this emphasis with revelations of secret genteel or noble identities. James Fenimore Cooper's 1820s novels, notably *Precaution* and *The Pioneers*, offer the most famous instances, but such concluding revelations are legion in earlier novels as well. Read's *Margaretta*, for example, seems to be a classic *Pamela*-style narrative, in which the poor, modest Margaretta repeatedly proves her exemplary chastity and virtue, converting a would-be seducer into a suitor. But this tale of class mobility through virtue and education, however, is complicated by the revelation that Margaretta is, in fact, the secret daughter of English nobility. While her noble parents ultimately disclaim their nobility in favor of American democratic principles, this revelation nonetheless troubles the narrative's emphasis on education by suggesting that Margaretta's exemplary virtue might be a result of her innate gentility, even nobility, rather than a product of her modest upbringing.

The novel that took up this opposition most explicitly is, as its subtitle suggests, 1810's anonymous *Rosa, or American Genius and Education*. But *Rosa*'s closing revelations of secret parentage have a very different force than in most genteel novels: the heroine is, in fact, the secret daughter of a Incan man, who has arranged for her to be raised by the wealthy Mrs. Charmion in order to "convince the world that the faculties of the native Americans might be as susceptible of improvement as those of the natives of Europe."[31] Although *Rosa* is unusual in its emphasis on nurture *over* nature, especially across racial lines, the pairing of *Margaretta* and *Rosa* crystallizes the genteel novel's preoccupation with and uncertainty about the relative influence of birth* and education.[32]

This ambivalence about the determinative effects of education versus birth reflects the genre's own controversial status in the early republic, as novelists who sought to justify their productions often emphasized their own narrative's instructive power even as they also sought to preclude anxieties about the genre's destabilizing effects on society by constructing conservative narratives that affirmed the existing social order. Because of such tensions, the genteel novel crystallizes, in an especially dramatic way, the vexed class politics of the early US novel more generally. Cathy Davidson's still field-defining account of the early US novel argued that the novel was a fundamentally democratic, even radical genre.[33] In recent years, however, scholars have challenged and qualified Davidson's account by both drawing attention to the limits of these novels' democratic inclusiveness and highlighting the conservatism of many early novels.[34] The early US novel was shaped by the nation's self-conscious rejection of British aristocracy, but it was also influenced by the conservative Federalism of novelists such as Tenney and Read: the genteel novel's fantasies of class mobility, its didactic promises, and its address to an expanded audience often rubbed uncomfortably against a conservative emphasis on the inherent refinement of the upper classes that reinforced the existing social order.[35]

The genteel novel's competing emphases on education and innate gentility are best exemplified by Catharine Maria Sedgwick's foundational *A New-England Tale*.[36] Sedgwick's "Moral Tale" centers on the virtuous orphan Jane Elton, who is forced to live with her cruel, hypocritical relatives when her parents die insolvent, because of their extravagant lifestyle. Living as an unofficial servant in her wealthy aunt's family, Jane has ample opportunities to develop and display the exemplary pious modesty that Sedgwick encourages her readers to imitate. Jane's piety attracts the attention of the wealthy and virtuous Mr. Lloyd, and the novel ends with their marriage. This *Pamela*-esque narrative, however, is complicated by how Jane's class-transforming marriage also represents a return to an earlier status quo: Jane not only returns to her former class, but even moves back into the very manor house in which she grew up! Genteel novels might emphasize education's ability to transform social fates and they often posited novels as vehicles for such transformative instruction. But by presenting this power chiefly in relation to those who had previously fallen in the social hierarchy, they suggested that such education in gentility was meant, first and foremost, for those who were already genteel.

The Genteel Novel in Transition

Between the early 1780s and the late 1820s, US attitudes toward fiction shifted considerably. Whereas ministers, pedagogues, and politicians of the 1780s and 1790s had decried novel-reading in sermons, conduct manuals, and periodical essays, by the late 1820s, many of these cultural authorities sanctioned and even lauded certain novels, if not the genre as a whole.[37] While warnings against novel-reading would endure in conduct manuals and some religious writings throughout the antebellum period, the anti-novel discourse had decreased in both its virulence and its pervasiveness by the 1820s.[38] During this decade, in fact, some writers even began to look back on the US suspicion of fiction as a (somewhat embarrassing) relic of an earlier era: "it appears but yesterday, that the grave, the serious, the religious, and the prudent, considered novel-reading as an employment utterly beneath the dignity of the human mind ... How surprising is the change we now witness."[39] I do not have space here to explore the myriad factors that contributed to such changing attitudes, including the rise of a leisured middle class with a thirst for entertainment; the emergence of new conceptions of domesticity that valorized private life; developments in printing, publishing, and bookselling; the explosion of a periodical press that often printed and championed fiction; and the development of a more robust aesthetic culture in the United States more generally. Instead, I simply want to suggest that the genteel novels of the early nineteenth century – a period oft-elided in our histories of US fiction[40] – also played a role in such shifting attitudes, as they theorized, in their different ways, the novel's potential value as a vehicle for edification and advocated for the inclusion of select novels as part of polite culture. If, by the 1830s, the novel genre was no longer haunted by its association with aristocratic gentility, it was, in part, because these genteel novels had remade the genre, so that it fit the mode of bourgeois respectability that, as Bushman has shown, displaced and absorbed earlier aristocratic conceptions of gentility over the first half of the nineteenth century.[41] Or even more than this, these novels themselves contributed to this wider shift in which gentility was gradually stripped of its aristocratic associations, much as *Margaretta*'s Lord and Lady Warren renounced their titles when they encountered the republican charm of a quaint Maryland village.

As the aristocratic ideal of gentility gradually morphed into a bourgeois ideal of respectable domesticity, the cultural importance of gentility in the US might seem less obviously paradoxical, but the contradictions of republican gentility endured. In their conflicted class commitments and deep ambivalence about the desirability of a more democratic society, genteel novels both brought such submerged tensions to the surface and attempted to manage them. Seeking to establish their own social respectability, these novels emphasized the transformative potential of their educational projects even as their plots often affirmed the existing social order. The genteel novel was a conservative genre insofar as it sought to legitimate itself within this existing social order: these were novels that argued against the widespread panic that the popularity of novel-reading threatened the stability of republican society. The genteel novel's strategic disavowal of its own novelty, however, should not obscure the remarkable literary experimentation that characterized the genre over the half-century following independence, as writers developed novel arguments about how this suspicious genre might function within, serve, and even help reproduce the existing, if ever evolving, social order.

Notes

1 On the antifictional discourse, see G. Harrison Orians, "Censure of Fiction in American Romances and Magazines, 1789–1810," *PMLA* 52.1 (1937): 195–214; Herbert Ross Brown, *The Sentimental Novel in America, 1789–1860* (New York: Pageant, 1959), 3–28; Terence Martin, *The*

Instructed Vision: Scottish Common Sense Philosophy and the Origins of American Fiction (New York: Kraus, 1961); Paul Gutjahr, "No Longer Left Behind," *Book History* 5 (2002): 209–236; and especially Cathy Davidson, *Revolution and the Word: The Rise of the Novel in America* (New York: Oxford University Press, 1986; revised 2004).

2 On how republican ideology shaped the antifictional discourse, see Michael Warner, *Letters of the Republic: Publication and the Public Sphere in Eighteenth-Century America* (Cambridge, MA: Harvard University Press, 1990).

3 For an expansive overview of gentility in the early United States and the conflicted attitudes toward its aristocratic associations in the republic, see Richard Bushman, *The Refinement of America* (New York: Knopf, 1992). See also David Shields, *Civil Tongues and Polite Letters in British America* (Chapel Hill: University of North Carolina Press, 1997).

4 On this shift in attitudes toward fiction, see Davidson, *Revolution and the Word*, 118–19, and Orians, "Censure of Fiction," 196–97. See also Nina Baym, *Novels, Readers, and Reviewers: Responses to Fiction in Antebellum America* (Ithaca, NY: Cornell University Press, 1984), 27–28, and James Machor, *Reading Fiction in Antebellum America* (Baltimore: Johns Hopkins University Press, 2011), 29.

5 On the association of the novel with domestic privacy during the antebellum period, see Baym, *Novels, Readers, and Reviewers*, and Richard Brodhead, *Culture of Letters* (Chicago: University of Chicago Press, 1993), 48–60. On the role of fiction in cultivating domestic gentility in the mid-nineteenth century, see Bushman, *Refinement of America*, 280–313.

6 On the more general shift from gentility to respectability as a cultural ideal in the United States from eighteenth to nineteenth century, see Bushman, *Refinement of America*.

7 Ibid., esp. xi–180.

8 See Warner, *Letters*; Shields, *Civil Tongues*, 308–28; and Bushman, *Refinement of America*, 181–203.

9 For an exemplary instance, see Shields's discussion of the Philadelphia ball celebrating the dauphin of France (*Civil Tongues*, 1–6).

10 Bushman, *Refinement of America*, xiii–xix.

11 On epistemological anxieties about fiction, see especially Martin, *Instructed Vision*. On the gendered nature of the antinovel discourse, see especially Davidson, *Revolution and the Word*. On republican suspicions of the novel, see especially Warner, *Letters*.

12 William Hill Brown, *The Power of Sympathy* (New York: Penguin, 1996), 22–24.

13 Ibid., 23.

14 On the interconnection of sexual and political virtue (and the attendant gendered anxieties about seduction) in republican political discourse, see Shirley Samuels, *Romances of the Republic* (Oxford: Oxford University Press, 1996), esp. 3–22.

15 Meredith Margaret Read, *Margaretta*, ed. Richard Pressman (San Antonio, TX: Early American Reprints, 2012), 320.

16 William Hill Brown, *Ira and Isabella* (Boston, 1807), 80.

17 Ibid., 25.

18 On the "world" and the *beau monde*, see Shields, *Civil Tongues*, 11–54.

19 On the importance of *otium* themes for Federalist writers of this era, see William Dowling, *Literary Federalism in the Age of Jefferson* (Columbia: University of South Carolina Press, 1999).

20 Rebecca Rush, *Kelroy*, ed. Dana D. Nelson (New York: Oxford University Press, 1992), 11.

21 Ibid., 86.

22 On the influence and reception of the Richardsonian novel (and its underlying Lockean pedagogy), see Jay Fliegelman, *Prodigals and Pilgrims* (Cambridge: Cambridge University Press, 1982), 13–29. For an account of the important ways in which early American seduction fiction diverges from the Richardsonian model, see Leonard Tennenhouse's "The Sentimental Libertine," in *The Importance of Feeling English: American Literature and the British Diaspora, 1750–1850* (Princeton, NJ: Princeton University Press, 2007), 43–72.

23 Nancy Armstrong, *Desire and Domestic Fiction: A Political History of the Novel* (Oxford: Oxford University Press, 1987).

24 John Trumbull, *The Satiric Poems of John Trumbull*, ed. Edwin Bowden (Austin: University of Texas Press, 1962), 83.

25 Ibid., 88.

26 For a discussion of one such metadidactic project, see Thomas Koenigs, "*Wieland's* Instructional Fictionality," *ELH* 79.3 (2012): 715–45.

27 See especially Davidson, *Revolution and the Word*, 101–50.

28 See Bushman, *Refinement of America*, esp. 440–46. He charts the various ways that the attribution of "superior gentility" to women "both exalted and restricted them" (440).

29 *Philadelphia Repository and Weekly Register* (June 1801): 238.

30 On how gentility functioned as a sign of the existing social order, see Bushman, *Refinement of America*, xii–xiii.

31 *Rosa, American Genius and Education* (1810), 67. Text prepared by Duncan Faherty and Ed White for *Just Teach One*, No. 11; *Common-Place: The Journal of early American Life* (Fall 2017). Online.

32 As White and Faherty put it in their introduction, "*Rosa* is a noticeable exception to the commonplace trope in early US fiction of privileging nature over nurture; within this text social and ethical values are learned behaviors and have no inherent connection to heredity" (1).

33 Emphasizing the more expansive readership of novels, the genre's promise of education, and its polyvocal nature, Davidson read the antinovel discourse as a conservative reaction to the democratic energies unleashed by the "rise of the novel" in the new nation (*Revolution and the Word*, 101–50).

34 Where Davidson had argued for the democratic, even radical, politics inherent in the genre, recent critics, most notably Ed White, have emphasized early US novelists' often explicitly conservative social and political commitments. See

especially White's "Divided We Stand: Emergent Conservatism in Royall Tyler's *The Algerine Captive*," *Studies in American Fiction* 37.1 (2010): 5–27.

35 There have been a number of important accounts of early US novels' engagement with questions of class, property, and economics. The most sustained discussion of the class politics of the early US novel, Joe Shapiro's *The Illiberal Imagination: Class and the Rise of the US Novel* (Charlottesville: University of Virginia Press, 2017), convincingly shows how many early US novels "work to naturalize class inequality among whites" and "endorse, and ratify structures of economic inequality" (4–5). On how early US novels reveal the intertwined sexual and economic desires and anxieties of the emergent bourgeoisie, see Karen Weyler, *Intricate Relations* (Iowa City: University of Iowa Press, 2004). See also Stephen Shapiro's world-systems approach to the early US novel in *The Culture and Commerce of the Early American Novel* (State College: Pennsylvania State University Press, 2009), which situates the emergence of the US novel within a longer history of global commerce. See also Jennifer Baker's account of the relationship between the credit economy and sympathetic identification in *Arthur Mervyn* (*Securing the Commonwealth* [Baltimore: Johns Hopkins University Press, 2005], 119–36). Finally, Armstrong and Tennenhouse have recently published *Novels in the Time of Democratic Writing* (Philadelphia: University of Pennsylvania Press, 2018), which compellingly argues that early American novels "challenged the assumption that 'property' could form a stable basis of society" that undergirded many contemporary British novels (9).

36 An archetypal example of both antebellum domestic fiction and liberal religious fiction, *A New-England Tale* began as an anti-Calvinist religious tract that was later expanded into Sedgwick's first extended fiction. On its foundational place in these two traditions, see Baym, *Woman's Fiction* (Urbana-Champaign: University of Illinois Press, 1978), and David Reynolds, *Faith in Fiction: The Emergence of Religious Literature in America* (Cambridge, MA: Harvard University Press, 1981), respectively.

37 On such changing attitudes toward novels, see Orians, "Censure of Fiction," 196–97; Baym, *Novels, Readers, and Reviewers*, 27–28; Davidson, *Revolution and the Word*, 118–19; and Machor, *Reading Fiction in Antebellum America*, 29. On the evolving attitudes of Protestant clergy, see Reynolds, *Faith in Fiction*.

38 Jennifer L. Brady, Dawn Coleman, and María Carla Sánchez, however, have recently qualified the conventional wisdom that this period brought the uniform "triumph of the novel" – to use Baym's memorable phrase – by drawing attention to the condemnations of fiction- and novel-reading that run through antebellum conduct literature. Brady, "Theorizing a Reading Public: Sentimentality and Advice about Novel Reading in Antebellum America," *American Literature* 83.4 (2011): 719–746; Coleman, *Preaching and the Rise of the American Novel* (Columbus: Ohio State University Press, 2013); Sánchez, *Reforming the World: Social Activism and the Problem of Fiction in Nineteenth-Century America* (Iowa City: Iowa University Press, 2008), esp. 28–87.

39 James McHenry, "On the Causes of the Present Popularity of Novel Writing," *American Monthly Magazine* (July 1824): 1–2.

40 The most self-conscious recent attempt to bridge this gap is Ed White and Michael Drexler's *The Traumatic Colonel: The Founding Fathers, Slavery, and the Phantasmatic Aaron Burr* (New York: NYU Press, 2014). See also White's "Trends and Pattern in the US Novel, 1800–1820," in *The Oxford History of the English Novel* (Oxford: Oxford University Press, 2014), which situates the novels of this era in relation to the aftermath of the election of 1800. On the shift from seduction to sentimental domestic fiction across this period, see Winfried Fluck, "Novels of Transition: From Sentimental to Domestic Novel," in *The Construction and Contestation of American Cultures and Identities in the Early National Period* (Heidelberg: University of Heidelberg Press, 1999), 97–119. Weyler's account of the "intricate relations" between sex and property in the early American novel focuses largely on this neglected era. See also the foundational accounts of Davidson and Henri Petter, *The Early American Novel* (Columbus: Ohio State University Press, 1971).

41 Bushman shows how the democratization of gentility across the late eighteenth and early nineteenth century – the way in which middle-class persons and families increasingly laid claim to this formerly aristocratic ideal – broke down long-standing class hierarchies between the elite gentry and the emergent bourgeoisie even as it often reinforced, in more and more humiliating ways, the divide between these refined classes and the lower classes (*Refinement of America*, esp. xv–xvii and 232–37).

CHAPTER 6

The State of Our Union
Comedy in the Post-Revolutionary US Theater

Heather S. Nathans

"May every happiness attend this union of virtue and honor," proclaims Captain John Smith in George Washington Parke Custis's 1830 comedy *Pocahontas, or The Settlers of Virginia*, as he presides over the marriage of Pocahontas and John Rolfe. While his wish seems a familiar one for a newly married couple, the ceremony takes a surprising turn when Smith drapes a chain of gold around Pocahontas's neck (as a thanks for saving his life), and asks her if she accepts it, along with the allegiance it implies. Somewhat disturbingly, Pocahontas replies (using the third person), "She will most cheerfully submit to wear the chain which binds her to the honour'd master of her fate, even tho' the chain were of iron instead of gold."[1] Indeed, in that same wedding scene, the bond uniting Pocahontas and Rolfe is described as a "shackle," again, perhaps not an uncommon humorous metaphor for marriage, but one that becomes deeply troubling in the colonial context in which it appears, as Pocahontas willingly submits to being bound to the British empire.

Beginning a chapter on *comedy* with a discussion about shackles, imperial visions, and the eventual genocide of millions of Indigenous peoples seems a peculiar choice. Yet many of the comedies of the post-Revolutionary era relied on strategies of defining who was allowed to be "inside" or "outside" the joke. That insider/outsider status appears in an early review of Custis's comedy. The *Alexandria Gazette* lauded the play, stating, "As Virginians, we feel a deep and intense interest in the historical events on which this play is based."[2] As the *Gazette*'s comments underscore, white spectators of 1830 saw the history and subject matter as *theirs*, rather than belonging to the indigenous characters in the play. They also clearly saw the native characters as comic fodder (a motif that would recur throughout early American drama). Throughout this chapter, I turn to scenarios like the one above that will strike the contemporary reader as far from funny. For example, I also follow the shifts in the British comedy *Inkle and Yarico*, a work about race and colonization, through multiple

American iterations from farce to tragedy between 1789 and 1830. I argue that tracing its rapid arc within less than fifty years reveals the instability of the comic form and the care that scholars need to take in theorizing a work's impact on prospective audiences.

Comedies rely on the union of opposites – whether those opposites might be literally characters of two different races, or oppositional ideas about the fate of the young nation. Comedy often rests on juxtapositions in which incongruity creates a sense of the absurd. However, with the distance of time, the humor becomes harder to read. It may be because the comedy now appears offensive to contemporary audiences in the ways it approaches material related to identity – whether it be race, gender, ethnicity, sexual orientation, or religion. It may also be because the context has shifted and the barb of the joke no longer strikes home. Any contemporary audience member who has scratched their heads listening to Shakespearean monologues about mustard, pancakes, or horse diseases will certainly understand how time makes some quotidian comedy incomprehensible. Similarly, anyone who has watched an episode of *Saturday Night Live* from a decade ago may well find themselves lost in trying to follow the political impersonations and riffs on the nightly news. The moment has passed and the urgency of the comedy becomes hard to recapture.

How can a theater scholar hope to conjure a vanished world of comedy from the early national period – an era in which some of the jokes are so historically specific that they would require five paragraphs of explanation (and a modern audience member *still* might not find them funny)? What tools can be used to excavate the comedies of this transitional period in US history? And what do those comedies of all different genres, including comic operas, pantomimes, minstrel shows, and romances, reveal about the audiences that consumed them? This chapter explores a combination of American-authored comedies and popular British works that continued to circulate in the American repertoire throughout the early national period. It also touches on some forms of comedy – particularly, circus and pantomime performance – that audiences imagined as more "democratic" and accessible. However, comedy offers more than escapist entertainment. It can allow audiences to acknowledge their anxieties by seeming to make fun of them (like the film comedies during the Great Depression that showed characters laughing through hardship, or *SNL* sketches that lampoon political figures). Comedy releases anger. It unites. It divides and declares allegiances. There can be a lot at stake in being silly.

"The Best Company in Town"

The colonial American stage overflowed with British comedies.[3] Favorites such as *Miss in Her Teens*, *The Recruiting Officer*, *The Way of the World*, *The Beaux' Stratagem*, and *The West Indian* delighted audiences by evoking elegant scenes from British society and, perhaps more importantly, by pitting cosmopolitan characters against more countrified ones. These plays remained in the theatrical repertoire, and despite the boycotts on British goods in the tense years leading up to the Revolution, they also remained for sale by colonial booksellers, suggesting that audiences savored their humor both in public in the playhouse and in the privacy of their own homes. New York bookseller Hugo Gaine (who also sold theater tickets) boasted a list of more than eighty British plays for sale at his bookshop – all plays that audiences could have seen at the city's Nassau Street, Chapel Street, or John Street theaters at various points in the city's colonial history.[4] Following the trajectory of one of these popular comedies may suggest how audiences used the silliness onstage to position themselves in pre- and postwar culture.

Theatergoers in colonial Philadelphia, New York, Charleston, or Williamsburg could identify with the sophisticated tricksters of George Farquhar's *The Beaux' Stratagem* (1707), which decades after its debut still delighted audiences with its tale of Aimwell and Archer, two adventurers cutting a wide swath through country towns in quest of wealthy and gullible heiresses. One of the first advertisements for a colonial production of *The Beaux' Stratagem* appeared in *The Virginia Gazette* on September 10, 1736. The "Young Gentlemen of the College [of William and Mary]" planned to perform the comedy at the Williamsburg Theatre. These "young gentlemen" clearly identified with the witty adventurers, always ready with a bon mot. Their humor depends on an invocation of city life, London locales, and the language of fops and flirts in high society, as this opening scene between them suggests:

Arch. Tis still my maxim, that there is no scandal like rags, nor any crime so shameful as poverty.
Aim. The world confesses it every day in its practice though men won't own it for their opinion. Who did that worthy lord my brother, single out of the side-box to sup with him t'other night?
Arch. Jack Handicraft, a handsome, well-dressed, mannerly, sharping rogue, who keeps the best company in town.
Aim. Right! And, pray, who married my lady Manslaughter t'other day, the great fortune?

Arch. Why, Nick Marrabone, a professed pickpocket, and a good bowler; but he makes a handsome figure, and rides in his coach, that he formerly used to ride behind.

Aim. But did you observe poor Jack Generous in the Park last week

Arch. Yes, with his autumnal periwig, shading his melancholy face, his coat older than anything but its fashion, with one hand idle in his pocket, and with the other picking his useless teeth; and, though the Mall was crowded with company, yet was poor Jack as single and solitary as a lion in a desert.

Aim. And as much avoided for no crime upon earth but the want of money.[5]

The two bemoan their exclusion from the trappings of city life: side-boxes at the theater, the Mall (the site for fashionable parades of the well-to-do), gaming houses, elegant clothing, and rides in magnificent coaches. The colonial audience watching the "young gentlemen" of William and Mary could only have fantasized about the luxuries described in the play as they sat in the Williamsburg Theatre. Built between 1714 and 1716, the original Williamsburg playhouse would have appeared homespun and simple beside the lavishly appointed playhouses of London and Bath. Might they have imagined themselves as Aimwell and Archer, exiled from the metropolis to the rustic setting of Lichfield, like the two heroes in the play?

By 1762 the professional theater circuit had blossomed in the colonies and audiences could have enjoyed *The Beaux' Stratagem* and other comedies in more refined settings. As *The New-York Mercury* proudly informed its readers, the new theater in Chapel Street (located on the Lower East Side of Manhattan, now Beekman Street) offered "new partitions to divide the side-boxes from one another and thereby render them more commodious for select parties."[6] Thus, wealthy colonial audience members hearing Aimwell's joke about his lordly brother singling out a party in a theater side-box could have pictured themselves seated alongside London's bon ton. Even the edicts from the Continental Congress that banned theatergoing (1774 and 1778) failed to banish Aimwell and Archer from the stage. The occupying British forces hosted their own amateur theatricals, featuring performers drawn from the army and also from the loyalists who lingered in town. The wartime newspaper, the *Royal Gazette*, proudly advertised numerous productions of *The Beaux' Stratagem* throughout the conflict. As audience perspective on the comedy shifted, might the British soldiers onstage and in the loyalist crowd watching have pictured themselves as the cultured Aimwell and Archer, mocking the country bumpkins (or Yankee Doodles) around them?

The close of the war brought a return of professional theater to the US stage along with the opening of new, purpose-built playhouses in cities from Savannah to Boston. It also brought *The Beaux' Stratagem* back into the American repertoire. An advertisement in the *New-York Packet* invited audiences to see "A comedy not performed here these 14 years." The fourteen-year gap refers to the absence of the Old American Company, the professional troupe driven out by the congressional anti-theater ban.[7] However, postwar theatergoers would have found much that seemed familiar about this new "American" production. Tickets remained for sale at Mr. Gaine's bookshop and box seats remained available for the wealthy. However, this advertisement concluded with a declaration that marked a significant change from the play's earlier history: "Vivat Respublica."[8]

"Nothing Can Authorize a Laugh"

Just two years before *The Beaux' Stratagem* made its triumphant return clad in the trappings of republican virtue, another comedy about manners and morals caused a violent outburst in the city of Boston.[9] An anonymously published satire entitled *Sans Souci. Alias Free and Easy; or, An Evening's Peep into a Polite Circle* (1785) mocked Bostonians who aspired to elite fashions and behavior. Embracing Lord Chesterfield's rules of conduct as her lodestar, the character of Little Pert declares to her companion Young Forward,

> When I was at New-York, among the British, I was ashamed to acknowledge myself a Bostonian – we had such a particular character – we were always pictured as a set of canting Presbyterians who began Sundays before sun set on Saturday, and held out praying until Monday morning at sunrise – that all our diversions were singing psalms, and going to Thursday-Lectures. – But thank Heaven we can now hold up our heads amidst the most polite circle at Raneleigh, or join with full *éclat* the brilliant assembly at Vauxhall.[10]

Little Pert rejoices that her city has adopted card playing and other British social diversions, while a character named simply "Republican Heroine" deplores the "excesses of dissipation" and, claims she, "could hardly refrain from tears" at the prospect of wealthy Bostonians making such a spectacle of themselves, "at so early a period after the war."[11]

While the anonymous author's comic pamphlet may have been intended as a jesting rebuke to Boston's postwar elite Tea Assembly, or to be read among circles that would have appreciated the inside joke, it prompted a violent reaction. According to the *Falmouth Gazette and Weekly Advertiser*, the announcement of its publication by the offices of the *Massachusetts Centinel* sent a group of men armed with clubs to the

Centinel's printing shop to stop the playlet's circulation.[12] According to *Fowle's New-Hampshire Gazette*, at least two members of the opposing parties came to blows and "were considerably bruised." The paper claimed that "a judicial inquiry ... was to take place yesterday afternoon." The paper offered an ironic coda to the report, suggesting that the controversy had only sparked *more* interest in the play: "The pamphlet, we understand, was published according to advertisement, and met with a rapid sale."[13]

Perhaps it is not surprising that a city that had suffered under a military blockade for the 1773 dumping of British tea into the Boston harbor would balk at the creation of a members-only tea club so soon after the war. As David Shields notes, "The name Sans Souci ('without worry') invoked simultaneously the aesthetic ideals of the art of sociability (ease and liberty of expression) and the extravagances of the French court (Sans Souci was the name of Marie Antoinette's palace). The amusements enjoyed there – dancing, tea drinking, card playing – were vices ... marked with the epithet 'polite.'"[14] For Shields, "The peril posed by the Sans Souci seemed new precisely because the integrity of public culture of the United States was new."[15]

Sans Souci offers the quintessential example of a comedy most intelligible to its immediate circle and contingent on intimate knowledge of the real-life figures disguised as "Little Pert," the "Republican Heroine," and others. From the distance of time it reads as mildly entertaining along the lines of moralizing comedies such as British playwrights Colley Cibber and John Vanbrugh's *The Provok'd Husband*, a 1728 comedy about a flirtatious wife named Lady Townly besotted by gambling and the pleasures of the town. However, as Christopher Lukasik argues, *Sans Souci* reveals a deep anxiety about "the more radical impulses of democracy." Intriguingly, the characters in *Sans Souci* view manners as the key to social mobility in a cosmopolitan culture, and see American society as aligned against that type of transformation.[16] Lukasik suggests that in *Sans Souci*, "America becomes a nation ... because it disavows the fluidity of its own social space."[17] Thus, the comedy points to critical challenges in the regulation of postwar culture.

In 1787, the same year that *The Beaux' Stratagem* returned to the New York stage, a new comedy by a young American playwright made its debut. Royall Tyler's *The Contrast* remains one of the best-known comedies of the early national period. Though set in the post-Revolutionary era among American characters, the play clearly owes a significant debt to its British predecessors in its representations of flirts and fops, foolish servants and dictatorial parents. As Jeffrey Richards notes, Tyler performed in illicit college theatricals during his time at Harvard before the Revolution, and thus would have been well-acquainted with British comedies. The *Massachusetts Gazette* proudly published an audience member's account from New York, which declared that the play possessed "the true requisites of Comedy in a very great degree" and that its debut had been attended by "many of the first characters in the United States."[18] Whatever lineage might be traced to its British ancestors, *The Contrast*'s predominantly white American audiences seemed eager to claim it as a product of "native genius."

The Contrast centers on the love story between Colonel Manly, a veteran of the war, and Maria Van Rough (betrothed to the wastrel Billy Dimple). Dimple has been spoiled by his recent travels to London and his obsession with the rules of gentlemanly behavior outlined by Lord Chesterfield (just like the characters in *Sans Souci*). Dimple fancies himself a rake, and despite his looming engagement to Maria, dallies with Charlotte (Manly's coquettish sister) and her friend Letitia. Ultimately Dimple's perfidy is exposed; Maria's father becomes reconciled to her marriage to Manly; and, as the play closes, Manly declares, "I have learned that probity, virtue, honor, though they should not have received the polish of Europe, will secure an honest American the good graces of his fair countrywomen."[19]

Not surprisingly, Tyler's comedy focuses on "the contrast" between British and American virtues. However, the play also underscores the difference between British and American *humor*. At the top of Act III, Dimple's servant, Jessamy (who apes his employer's manners) hears the housemaid Jenny laughing offstage. He exclaims with affected disgust, "Ha! that's Jenny's titter. I protest I despair of ever teaching that girl to laugh; she has something so execrably natural in her laugh that I declare it absolutely discomposes my nerves." Jessamy calls Jenny into the room and begs her, "Jenny, don't spoil your fine face with laughing." He reminds her that, according to Chesterfield, "You may smile ... but nothing can authorize a laugh."[20] Tyler also mocks the way that members of the elite "giggle and simper" by "tortur[ing] some harmless expression into a double meaning."[21] He creates British-influenced characters unable to appreciate "natural" humor and enamored with elaborate practical jokes, puns, and tricks. While definitions of what constitutes "natural"[22] behavior are always contingent on historical context, the post-Revolutionary period witnessed a reaction against the overly mannered style of British elites as "republican simplicity" became the hallmark of the era. For Tyler, the *un*natural humor of a character like Jessamy or Dimple relies on cruelty and condescension. By contrast (pun intended), American humor involves the ability to gently mock oneself, as Manly and Jonathan do throughout the play. Tyler's best-known contribution from *The Contrast* remains the character of Jonathan, the Yankee. Clumsy and awkward, yet gifted with common sense, Jonathan would become a foundational figure in American comedies, inspiring similar characters that often served as both comic relief and *raisonneur*. The character's "Yankee" ingenuity became a hallmark of the figure, as well as a useful comic strategy. The Yankee – represented as both white and Christian – could serve as a comic yardstick against which other stage types might be measured.

"A Humorous Dialogue between a Sailor, Master of the Horse, and a Clown"

Much of the comedy of the early national period and early nineteenth-century relied on witty verbal banter to establish "inside" and "outside" figures. But there were other methods that relied on physical comedy rather than text. As Lynn Matluck Brooks has argued, early national theater revealed a fascination with staging "otherness" – whether of race, ethnicity, or religion – and often for comic effect. Brooks explores the career of John Durang, one of the country's earliest clowns and dancers, to imagine the ways in which American performers used humor and embodied performance to define white national identity against a panoply of other stage types inherited from Europe.[23] Durang, who toured throughout the eastern states and into Canada, appearing with circuses and with various theatrical companies, relied on movement, costume, and music far more than text to convey the humor of his characters. His work suggests development of a physical and visual comic lexicon on American stages, as well as a scripted one.[24] In addition to performing comic dances such as "La Fricasee" (likely based on a French folk tune), Durang relied on his skills as a physical comedian in pantomimes such as the popular ballet *La Fôret Noire* (1795).[25] The fairytale-like plot of *La Fôret Noire* centers on Lucille, secretly married to a soldier named Lauredan and mother to their son, Adolphus (whom she keeps hidden). Her father, Geronte, insists that she marry the Abbé (a vain buffoon). She refuses. Geronte orders his servants to take Adolphus into the woods and kill him. A band of robbers intervene and rescue the child. The robbers are pursued by soldiers, who chase them back and forth across the stage. Durang played one of the soldiers in the original Boston production. Although many dance scholars describe *La Fôret Noire* as one of the first "serious" ballets on the US stage, some of the descriptions of the fights between the soldiers and robbers in the play read like a Keystone Cops chase in a Mack Sennett movie as they lead each other into ambushes, capture the Abbé and strip him down to his underwear, and so on. In his diary from the 1790s, Dr. Alexander Anderson recalls seeing a double bill of *La Forêt Noire* and John Durang's celebrated comic "Dwarf Dance" afterward.[26]

During a career that spanned three decades Durang embraced what Brooks describes as a "theatrical project" of crafting characters that audiences would immediately recognize by their racial or ethnic markers embodied in movement or dance. In addition to playing a soldier and comic dwarves, Yankees, and American sailors, Durang also played French, Dutch, German, Scottish, Spanish, Native American, and Black characters. Sometimes Durang's performances incorporated a range of identities in a single evening, potentially sowing confusion about which one (if any) could be defined as "authentically" American. For example, in 1804 Baltimore's *Telegraphe and Daily Advertiser* announced a July 4 performance entitled *The American Wigwam, or The Temple of Liberty*. It featured Durang in the "redface" character of Tammany, the Indian chief, performing "War" and "Scalp" dances, followed by an amusing sailor's hornpipe (a lively dance that gained popularity in the last decade of the eighteenth century).[27] Those pieces remained in Durang's repertoire for many years (through his retirement in 1819). Two years later, Durang played in Baltimore again, still featuring the "War" and "Scalp" dances, but this time expanded to include "the Osage War and Rejoicing Dances, the Chipeway's [*sic*] Eagle Tail dance, [and] the Mohawk Scalp dance." He contrasted these entertainments with a recital of the classic 1769 comic monologue, "Bucks Have at Ye All," Thomas King's satire on the behavior of refined British audiences, and a "Ballad Dance" described as "founded on a humorous German story" by a resident of Lancaster, Pennsylvania, and set in a small town in Pennsylvania.[28] This particular evening's performances reflect the wide range of comic material available on postwar US stages. Though it obviously had its roots in various European comic stereotypes, Durang's presentation of immigrant and indigenous cultures offers a piquant contrast to King's cosmopolitan commentary on louche British audiences of a century before. In his study *Theatrical Nation: Jews and Other Outlandish Englishmen*, Michael Ragussis illuminates the ways in which comic outsiders (Jews, Scots, Irish, Turks, and others) peopled the British stage in the mid-eighteenth century at the height of an economic crisis when nonwhite characters became ciphers for British political, social, and economic anxieties. Ragussis's study documents the adaptability of these comic types, as they were repurposed again and again for white, predominantly Gentile Anglo audiences.[29] I see a similar pattern emerging in early American theater. For example, the popularity of Durang's redface "War" and "Scalp" dances, alongside his vernacularized Scottish and German comedies, suggests the emergence of an audience seeking humor that seemed more "American" in its representation and synthesis of numerous cultural influences. Yet Durang's humor still relied on familiar patterns of "othering" racial or ethnic "outsiders" (even if they were indigenous characters).

"Between the Play and the Farce"

In January 1796, the *Massachusetts Mercury* advertised an upcoming performance of the comic opera *Inkle and Yarico*, including a "Celebrated Negro Dance" and, "between the play and the farce,"[30] a new piece by Chestnut Street Theatre composer Alexander Reinagle, entitled "The Grateful Lion, or Harlequin Shipwreck'd." As Jeffrey Ravel has noted, harlequin performers often used black masks (or blacked up their faces),[31] following a long-standing European tradition. (Durang's portraits of himself in harlequin costumes often depict him with a blackened face or mask.) Thus this evening's lineup suggests that American audiences could have seen *three* comic performances, all of which relied on blackface as a critical element. Blackface performance became a staple of the American stage, particularly with the development of minstrelsy in the 1830s, yet it appears in numerous other comedies on the American stage in the colonial and early national periods.

British playwright George Colman's *Inkle and Yarico* (1787) centers on the interracial love story between the beautiful maiden, Yarico, native of the West Indies, and the fickle captain Inkle, whom she rescues from a shipwreck. He woos her, only to try to sell her into slavery later in the play. The play also features a parallel plot between Yarico's black servant, Wowski, and Wowski's white suitor, Trudge. Wowski's blackness stands in sharp contrast to Yarico's lighter-skinned beauty. Trudge describes her as "a nice, little plump bit ... an angel of rather a darker sort."[32] She presents in a kind of linguistic blackface as well, unlike her mistress's more poetic style. Wowski's behavior seems comically endearing while she remains on her home island, but when Trudge takes her to Barbados, the comedy of contrasts and her outsider status as a person of color become apparent. As Wowski strolls down the street with Trudge, a white

American audience can laugh at her naivete as she mistakes a prisoner for a prince and a fish seller for a fine lady.

Wows. Who be that fine man? He great prince?
Trudge. A prince – Ha! ha! – – No, not quite a prince – but he belongs to the Crown. But how do you like this, Wows? Isn't it fine?
Wows. Wonder!
Trudge. Fine men, eh?
Wows. Iss! all white; like you.
Trudge. Yes, all the fine men are like me. As different from your people as powder and ink, or paper and blacking.
Wows. And fine lady – Face like snow.
Trudge. What! the fine lady's complexions?... But did you mind the women? All here – and there; [*Pointing before and behind.*] they have it all from us in England. – And then the fine things they carry on their heads, Wowski.
Wows. Iss. One lady carry good fish – – so fine, she call everybody to look at her.
Trudge. Pshaw! an old woman bawling flounders.[33]

Like *The Beaux' Stratagem*, Colman's *Inkle and Yarico* relies on the comic juxtaposition of cosmopolitan and rustic characters. However, *Inkle and Yarico* adds the complication of racial bias that would have been particularly resonant for American theater audiences in the post-Revolutionary period, as the nation struggled to reconcile its rhetoric of liberty with its continuation (and expansion) of its slave system.[34]

Inkle and Yarico appeared on US stages within two years of its British debut. The earliest mention of it in a New York newspaper announces a performance on July 4, 1789. The advertisement describes the production as a "farce taken from Mr. Colman's opera of *Inkle and Yarico.*" The farcical adaptation bears the title *Inkle and Yarico, or A School for Avarice.*[35] That title and designation remained popular in US papers for roughly a decade, making it challenging to determine exactly what American audiences would have encountered when seeing *Inkle and Yarico* and how it might have been altered so that it could be safely designated a "farce." Was Inkle's capricious behavior the source of the absurdity? Or was it the prospect of the interracial relationships being taken seriously in the context of a nation committed to continuing chattel slavery (and in which interracial liaisons[36] were widely acknowledged to take place, but not publicly or legally sanctioned)?[37]

Early versions drew heavily on the more openly comic aspects of the play. For example, a 1791 Philadelphia paper applauded the "great truth and real humor" of Mrs. Wilson's performance as Wowski in the Southwark Theatre production. Interestingly, the paper critiqued her

appearance as "too hideous" to meet with audience approval, suggesting
that her dress had not been "proper" and "her complexion [was] too
dark."[38] The use of the phrases "too hideous" and "too dark" imply that
the critic viewing the production imagined an aesthetic line between
comical and grotesque blackness and that Mrs. Wilson had failed to
observe that nuance in her performance. By the mid-1790s, the part of
Wowski had become sufficiently popular that actresses used it for their
benefit night performances (special performances for which designated
actors received the box office proceeds), as in the case of Mrs. Abbott,
who played the role for her June 18, 1794, benefit night at Boston's
Federal Street Theatre.[39]

In 1792 (only five years after the play's British debut), American
audiences could also have encountered *Inkle and Yarico* as a "Historic
Pantomime in Three Acts," called *The Indian Heroine, or Inkle and
Yarico*.[40] This version appeared courtesy of Alexander Placide, the
French leader of a troupe of dancers and acrobats who had fled the slave
uprising in Saint Domingue for the safety of the United States. He
brought the production to Charleston, South Carolina, in 1794, with
the slightly altered title of *Inkle and Yarico, or The American Heroine*.[41]
Placide's reimagining of the play as one connected to indigenous characters
seems particularly significant – particularly in 1793 when the United States
passed a new Fugitive Slave Act that empowered local governments to
pursue escaped slaves *and* to penalize those who aided their escape or
harbored fugitives. It might have been important for some white audiences
to distance the "comedy" of *Inkle and Yarico* from a connection with
African American slavery.

Despite these efforts, British author Elizbeth Inchbald (and others)
would claim *Inkle and Yarico* as an antislavery play by the early nineteenth
century. Inchbald even argued that the play could convert William
Wilberforce himself to theater's usefulness in the abolitionist cause.[42]
However, some of the comic characters in the play – particularly
Wowski – seemed to present an obstacle to taking the play's antislavery
message seriously. Indeed, an 1816 Boston newspaper invoked the character as an example of the extent to which Blacks were "unprepared for
freedom," claiming that free Blacks would "repose under the soft shade of
the plantain," while "The yam, the plantain, the pepper-pot; the banjar
[banjo], the merry dance, and their beloved Wowski would gratify all their
wishes and crown their highest ambition."[43] Occasionally, male performers undertook the role of Wowski, further emphasizing the interpretation of the Black woman as unfit for assimilation into genteel white

American culture (and presenting a clear forerunner to the "wench" character that would become so popular in the minstrel show).

By 1820, at least a portion of the American public seemed to find the Black characters in *Inkle and Yarico* more deserving of pity than ridicule. An essay excerpted in *The Providence Gazette* (a city that had hosted numerous productions of the play over the years) described the plight of an enslaved "group of human beings," drawing particular attention to the "captain of a Dutch Guinea vessel" who routinely raped his female captives in the hopes of impregnating them and earning more money in their sale. As the author exclaimed in disgust, the captain displayed "a brutality scarcely credited in the story of Inkle and Yarico."[44] And by 1832, one year after Nat Turner's uprising ignited new debates about slavery, a speaker in the Virginia Legislature drew on the power of *Inkle and Yarico*. The speaker contended that traders in Liverpool had once banned the work because of the danger of presenting an antislavery play in a port known for trafficking slaves.[45] By 1836, a year into the infamous "Gag Rule" that attempted to quash debates over slavery, papers such as *The New-York Evangelist* identified the play as "an affecting story" that "held up the slave trade to abhorrence."[46]

Many of the comedies described above cast long shadows – comic and otherwise – on the US stage. For example, Jeffrey Richards has pointed to the influence of the Trudge and Wowski subplot in *Inkle and Yarico* on James Nelson Barker's comic opera, *The Indian Princess* (1808), which recounts the interracial Pocahontas love story with a parallel subplot between Pocahontas's attendant Nima and one of the British colonists, Robin. In their first encounter, Nima calls Robin a raccoon (because he scampers up a tree when she aims her bow at him), and he refers to her as his "dark Diana" and "dusky dear." When she questions the meaning of his nicknames, he declares them, "A pretty title that we lords of the creation bestow upon our playthings."[47]

Echoes of *The Contrast*, as well as Durang's popular Tammany redface dances, *The Indian Princess*, and even *The Beaux' Stratagem*, thread through works like playwright Mordecai Manuel Noah's 1819 comedy *She Would Be a Soldier*. Like many of its predecessors, Noah's comedy draws on the contrast among different styles of manners as well as different national and ethnic allegiances. The comic Yankee resurfaces in the guise of the braggart Jerry Mayflower, a wealthy yet uncouth farmer. He seeks a wife who can " teach me to parlyvoo, and dance solos and duets, and such elegant things, when I've done ploughing." His own accomplishments include opossum hunting, partridge snaring, and apple paring.[48] The

dilettante British character mocking the Americans appears in Captain
Pendragon, who dresses in the "height of fashion" and rebels when offered
bear meat at an American inn. He exclaims with disgust, "Bear meat! the
honourable captain Pendragon, who never ate anything more gross than a
cutlet at Molly's chop-house, and who lived on pigeons' livers at Very's, in
Paris, offered bear meat in North America!"[49] Interestingly, Noah's redface
character, known simply as the Indian Chief, does *not* become a source of
comedy in the play. He mocks others (such as Pendragon and his French
servant La Role) for their cowardice – particularly when *they* dress up in
redface to avoid capture. But, as Rachel Rubenstein has argued, Jewish
American playwright Noah identified strongly with indigenous peoples as
the possible "lost tribe" of Israel, and so his native characters speak
movingly of stolen homelands.[50] Most critics offered warm praise for
Noah's work, saying it produced "unmingled pleasure and satisfaction"
in the audience.[51]

Eventually, however, Noah's comedy would be turned against him in
an unexpected way. In the early 1820s Noah proved a persistent foe to
New York's first Black theater troupe, the African Grove Theatre. Using
his power as theater critic, newspaper editor, and sheriff of New York,
he waged a campaign against the company through both ridicule in his
paper and legal harassment. However, the performers of the African
Grove knew how to fight back, appropriating Noah's plays and staging
them in their own performance spaces, proving that they could defy his
attacks – at least temporarily. Their subtle retaliation against Noah's
persecution did not go unnoticed. On November 30, 1821, the *Evening
Gazette* announced an "Encouragement to American genius," with the
proclamation that "a company of colored gentlemen and ladies" would
be performing *She Would Be a Soldier* that evening. The author added
somewhat cryptically, "I presume 2436 spectators will attend and no
questions asked."[52] The *Evening Gazette*'s comments are exactly the
kind of inside joke that make no sense to a contemporary scholar,
unless they knew that the *Evening Gazette* opposed Noah's social and
political ambitions, and that the paper was using Noah's well-known
bias against the African Grove to poke fun at Noah's own pretensions.
The number 2436 refers to a claim Noah made in his paper, *The
National Advocate*, concerning his friend Stephen Price's Park Street
Theatre (which also featured Noah's work). One week before the
Evening Gazette jibe, Noah's *National Advocate* had claimed a record
audience of 2,436 patrons at the Park Street Theatre, displaying "a fine
trial of strength" and an event "never before known."[53] The African

Grove space, by comparison, held only a few hundred at most. While this "joke" requires layers of unpacking to become legible to a modern scholar, it may suggest the nuanced layers of irony, jest, and counter-jest peppering early national comedy.

Epilogue: "Dick the Gentleman"

On April 27, 1827, the African American newspaper *Freedom's Journal* published a short comical piece entitled "Dick the Gentleman." It recounts the tale of one "Dicky," born in the country where there were "plenty of potatoes, cabbage and corn – but no gentlemen."[54] Dick proclaims himself a gentleman and leaves his home in quest of more congenial company. He travels to New York City where he quickly became a "gentleman clerk in a splendid store for the ladies in Broadway." However, as the story notes, Dick remained discontented. He stood outside a theater observing the enticing advertisements for the plays inside. He watched horse races and lamented that he could not afford to run a horse. By dint of wheedling money out of various sources, Dick finally sets himself up as a gentleman storekeeper. As the storyteller observes,

> Now was the time for Dick to show off the gentleman and show it off he did with a vengeance. He got a horse – then a saddle – then went to the races. He pepped into the theatre – lolled at the opera – subscribed to a concert, and shook his heels at a cotillion party; the girls smiled upon him, the old maids praised him, the mothers chatted with him, and the fathers shook him by the hand and said "how do you do Mr. Dick?" Now Dicky Dash was a gentleman.[55]

The tale of Dicky Dash awakens echoes of many of the comic tropes I have described throughout this chapter. Like Jonathan the Yankee or Jerry Mayflower, Dash appears as the humble farmer who envisions the glamour and social mobility of the big city. Once there, Dash falls into dissipated habits like Little Pert in *Sans Souci*, Dimple in *The Contrast*, or Pendragon in *She Would Be a Soldier*. However, there also appears a subtext of "respectability politics" threading through the *Freedom's Journal* anecdote. Though his race is never specified, nevertheless, the comical tale of Dicky Dash illustrates the very real dangers Black Americans faced in establishing themselves as equals in white American culture. Thus, the newspaper cautions readers to *avoid* Dick's dissipated habits and pretensions, lest Black citizens become targets of ridicule. Just a few years before the publication of this story, Mordecai Noah had forced the closure of William Alexander Brown's African Grove Theatre. He had decried

Figure 6.1　"A Black Tea Party" ("Life in Philadelphia" series).
Courtesy of the Library Company of Philadelphia.

Black Americans who aspired to white culture, to the right to vote, or even to the right to walk on the sidewalks of the city alongside whites. In the late 1820s, cartoonist Edward Clay launched a series entitled "Life in Philadelphia" (based on a series of British cartoons) that brutally mocked Black Americans for aspiring to middle-class gentility in dress, speech, occupation, and entertainments. It burlesqued Black men and women wearing fine clothes, taking music lessons, promenading the streets, drinking, and gambling – many of the activities described in the cautionary story of Dick Dash (see Figure 6.1). Did the authors of the comical story in *Freedom's Journal* imagine that it might ultimately spare its Black readers pain if it reminded them to avoid attracting undue attention from white spectators?

On April 18, 1828, *Freedom's Journal* quizzed its readers: "Why is a Tragedy a more natural performance in a *Theatre* than a *Comedy*? – Because the boxes are always in Tiers."[56] Though a lamentable pun, the quip highlights the challenge of reconciling comedy with what might seem "natural" in a playhouse. As American audiences jockeyed for position in the emerging social, political, racial, and cultural hierarchies, comedy became a formidable tool to offer access or bar admission to those realms of power.

Notes

1 George Washington Parke Custis, *Pocahontas, or The Settlers of Virginia* (Philadelphia, 1830), 45.
2 "Advertisement," *Evening Post* (New York), no. 8851, December 24, 1830: [2]. Also see the *Southern Patriot* (Charleston, SC), November 17, 1830.
3 The quote in the heading is from George Farquhar, *The Beaux' Stratagem: A Comedy* (London: J. M. Dent and Co., 1898), 11.
4 *The New-York Gazette*, September 6, 1773.
5 Farquhar, *The Beaux' Stratagem*, 11.
6 *New-York Mercury*, March 22, 1762.
7 In 1774, Congress issued a ban on theatrical entertainments (along with cock-fighting, horse-racing, gambling, and other entertainments deemed inconsistent with the gravity of a wartime government). As a result, many professional theater troupes left the United States, settling in Jamaica, Canada, Britain, and elsewhere. The congressional ban did not stop amateur performances *or* festivities staged by British officers and Tory loyalists, bored during the lengthy British occupation of cities such as Boston and New York. Additionally, some American officers, including George Washington, staged amateur performances to inspire their troops. The Continental Congress reissued the anti-theater ban in 1778, decreeing that any officer participating in illicit entertainments would be stripped of his rank. For more on this topic, see Heather S. Nathans, *Early American Theatre from the Revolution to Thomas Jefferson: Into the Hands of the People* (Cambridge: Cambridge University Press, 2003).
8 *The New-York Packet*, March 2, 1787.
9 The quote in the heading is from Royall Tyler, *The Contrast*, in Jeffrey H. Richards, ed., *Early American Drama* (New York: Penguin Classics, 1997), 32.
10 *Sans Souci. Alias Free and Easy; or, An Evening's Peep into a Polite Circle* (Boston: Warden and Russell, 1785), 5–6. Note that the play is often attributed to Mercy Otis Warren, but she denied authorship. Scholar Jeffrey H. Richards, an authority on Warren, suggests that she was probably *not* the author. However, some databases do assign the play to her.
11 *Sans Souci*, 11
12 "Falmouth, January 22." *Falmouth Gazette and Weekly Advertiser* (Falmouth, ME), 1, no. 4, January 22, 1785: [3].
13 *Fowle's New-Hampshire Gazette, and the General Advertiser* (Portsmouth, NH) 29, no. 1473, January 21, 1785: [3].

14 David Shields, *Civil Tongues and Polite Letters in British America* (Chapel Hill: University of North Carolina Press, 1997), 315.

15 Ibid., 315.

16 Christopher S. Lukasik, *Discerning Characters: The Culture of Appearance in Early America* (Philadelphia: University of Pennsylvania Press, 2011), 63–64.

17 Ibid., 64.

18 "New-York, May 5," *Massachusetts Gazette* (Boston) 6, no. 329, May 11, 1787: [3].

19 Tyler, *The Contrast*, 57.

20 Ibid., 32.

21 Ibid., 23.

22 "Natural" also had numerous complex connotations during the post-Revolutionary period, including its associations with "natural law," with the status of enslaved peoples or Native Americans, and with illegitimacy in birth (to be the "natural" son or daughter of someone without the benefit of wedlock).

23 Lynn Matluck Brooks, "Staged Ethnicity: Perspectives on the Work of John Durang," *Dance Chronicle* 24, no. 2 (2001): 193–222.

24 Later performers such as Charles Matthews, the British comedian, would use a similar style of impersonating multiple stage stereotypes within the course of one performance, presenting an evening of monologues that surveyed characters from all different social, racial, and ethnic groups.

25 *La Fôret Noire* (Boston: John and Jos. Russell, 1795).

26 "Diary of Dr. Alexander Anderson," included in W. W. Pasko, ed., *Old New York: A Journal Related to the History and Antiquities of New York City*, vol. 1 (New York: W. W. Pasko, 1890), 246.

27 *Telegraphe and Daily Advertiser* (Baltimore), July 2, 1804: 3.

28 "Advertisement," *American and Commercial Daily Advertiser* (Baltimore) 13, no. 2264, August 6, 1806: [3].

29 Michael Ragussis, *Theatrical Nation: Jews and Other Outlandish Englishmen in Georgian Britain* (Philadelphia: University of Pennsylvania Press, 2010).

30 "Advertisement," *Massachusetts Mercury* (Boston) 7, no. 2, January 5, 1796: [3].

31 Jeffrey Ravel, *The Contested Parterre: Public Theater and French Political Culture, 1680–1791* (Ithaca, NY: Cornell University Press, 1999).

32 George Colman, *Inkle and Yarico* (London: G. G. J. and J. Robinson Printers, 1787), I, iii.

33 Ibid., 34–35.

34 This contradiction drew passionate criticism both within the United States and beyond, as British, French, and other European powers decried white Americans' hypocrisy in preserving the institution of slavery through the Constitution.

35 "Advertisement," *Daily Advertiser* (New York) 5, no. 1363, July 3, 1789: [2].

36 I acknowledge the problematic use of the term "relationship" here when so many liaisons between white men and enslaved Black women were

nonconsensual. However, in *Inkle and Yarico*, Yarico begins the story in a position of power.

37 Some advertisements for the play, such as one in a 1792 Norfolk, VA, paper, appeared alongside advertisements for runaway slaves. *Norfolk and Portsmouth Chronicle* (Norfolk, VA) 3, no. 131, February 25, 1792: [3].

38 "Inkle and Yarico," *General Advertiser* (Philadelphia), no. 182, April 30, 1791: [3].

39 "Advertisement," *Columbian Centinel* (Boston) 21, no. 29, June 18, 1794: [3].

40 "Advertisement," *Pennsylvania Journal, or, Weekly Advertiser* (Philadelphia), no. 3561, June 27, 1792: [3]. This production may have been based on a version of the *Inkle and Yarico* story published in *The Spectator*, which claimed that Yarico was "Indian," rather than Black, and also that Inkle tried to sell her when she was pregnant with his child.

41 *The City Gazette & Daily Advertiser* (Charleston, SC) 12, no. 2268, October 28, 1794: [3].

42 Remarks by Elizabeth Inchbald included in the 1816 edition of *Inkle and Yarico*, available on Project Gutenberg: www.gutenberg.org/files/36621/36621-h/36621-h.htm.

43 *Boston Intelligencer* (Boston, MA), June 8, 1816: [2].

44 "Description," *Providence Gazette* (Providence, RI) 1, no. 4, January 13, 1820: [1].

45 "Legislative Acts/Legal Proceedings," *National Gazette* (Philadelphia), February 21, 1832: 4.

46 *New York Evangelist* (New York), April 9, 1836: 4.

47 James Nelson Barker, *The Indian Princess*, in Jeffrey H. Richards, ed., *Early American Drama* (New York: Penguin Classics, 1994).

48 Mordecai Manuel Noah, *She Would Be a Soldier* (New York: Longworth's Dramatic Repertory, 1819), 19.

49 Ibid., 37.

50 Rachel Rubenstein, *Members of the Tribe: Native America in the Jewish Imagination* (Detroit, MI: Wayne State University Press, 2010).

51 "Theatrical Communication," *Boston Commercial Gazette* (Boston, MA), 53, no. 6, January 3, 1820: [2].

52 "Encouragement to American Genius," *Evening Post* (New York), no. 6063, November 30, 1821: [2].

53 "[Theatre; Monday; Sustain; Character; Departments]," *National Advocate* (New York) 9, no. 2556, November 28, 1821: [2]. Danielle Rosvally has done groundbreaking work on the physical layout of the African Grove performance space as part of her investigation into Price's allegations against the company. I am indebted to her for our many conversations about this topic.

54 *Freedom's Journal*, April 27, 1827.

55 *Freedom's Journal*, April 27, 1827.

56 *Freedom's Journal*, April 18, 1828.

CHAPTER 7

"To assume her Language as my own"
The Revival Hymn and the Evangelical Poetess in the Early Republic

Wendy Raphael Roberts

In 1791, the Boston poet and pious Baptist Jenny Fenno published *Original Compositions*, which the title page described as a work of both "Verse and Prose, Moral and Religious." This work, as well as her subsequent publications, participated in an established evangelical poetic culture that awakened and reimagined the role of the woman poet for the extraordinary works of God expected in the last days of Christian history. Fenno signals this history by closing her book with the verse of early evangelicalism's first idealized transatlantic poetess, Elizabeth Singer Rowe: "What can I add, for all my words are faint? / Celestial love no eloquence can paint; / No more can be in mortal sounds express'd, / But vast eternity shall tell the rest."[1] By closing with the English poet's well-known lines, Fenno placed herself within a tradition of women poets who drew their spiritual authority from the persona of the evangelical muse Rowe epitomized. These particular lines gesture to central aspects of this potent tradition – the limits of eloquence, the primacy of heavenly sounds, the future of eternal verse, and the prolific and ever-present poetess even as she performs ephemerality. By the time Fenno published her book, the woman poet-minister role in early evangelicalism had been flourishing for over half a century.

To begin an essay on revival hymns in the early American republic with a barely-known woman poet and her "original compositions" of verse and prose, rather than a hymnbook or a famous hymn by Isaac Watts or Charles Wesley, may seem curious. My purpose in doing so is to reposition the expected relationship of evangelicalism to something called hymn and something called poetry in early America and to emphasize the centrality of evangelical women poets to the culture and development of early American poetics, which had lasting effects well into the nineteenth century. This essay will move quickly through three related claims. First, early evangelical poetry was a capacious lived literature that constituted one of the major aesthetic developments of the eighteenth century. Second, one of the momentous outgrowths of this eighteenth-century experiential Christian poetics was an early form of the Poetess, a trope scholars predominantly discuss as a nineteenth-century cultural form. And third, recognizing this longer development of the evangelical poetess resituates the poetics of Phillis Wheatley Peters[2] within an anti-white supremacist tradition produced by free and enslaved Black people. Together, the essay argues for the necessity of broader and deeper engagement with various eighteenth-century religious poetics in order to braid them back together with the social forms and histories within which they arose and remained entangled.[3]

A Brief Introduction to Early Evangelical Verse

Though one would not know it by perusing American literature anthologies or even most scholarly books on early American history and culture, the most prolific new verse form in the eighteenth century was the Protestant hymn, which quickly became a primary feature of the transatlantic evangelical movement in its various manifestations. Stephen Marini writes that "hymns of evangelical Protestantism are the most widely used spiritual texts in American history."[4] I would emphasize that, taken as a whole, revival poetry – both hymnal and nonhymnal forms – was the most widely used verse in British North America and the early republic. The sheer breadth of the hymn and its mutability across diverse contexts surely makes it one of the most complex and important literary forms.[5]

Attending to revival verse undermines narratives of national literary history that have traditionally depended on the decline of religion as well as on the unfounded idea that British North Americans did not produce a vibrant poetic culture. Though a national literature became an urgent project in the early decades of the United States, a significant culture of verse produced by an aesthetic movement that began in the first part of the eighteenth century – what is now called evangelicalism – already saturated the colonies. In fact, some of the largest verse coteries formed in the middle and second half of the eighteenth century and only expanded in the early nineteenth century; one of the most extensive consisted of Methodist circuit riders who sung, recited, exchanged, and sold verse as well as local Methodist meeting leaders, many of whom were women. That these have not been considered poetic coteries speaks to the strange work the label "religion" can do to separate cultural practices from the literary.

Regardless of its tepid reception by those invested in elite, national literatures, revival verse appears to have mapped on to the reality of many people's lives in transatlantic early America; that is, it was a lived genre that felt right. And just as revival verse is necessary to understand the full impact of poetry in early America and its contours into the nineteenth century, the impossibility of separating poetics from early evangelicalism should be quite clear. There has been a long historiographic tradition that emphasizes theological tenets to define and study evangelicalism. While theology was (and continues to be) important to evangelicals, changes in theology alone cannot adequately describe the shifts in Protestant Pietistic religion that occurred in the eighteenth century. And it certainly cannot when evangelicalism is continually set against aesthetics, a body of philosophical inquiry with which it coterminously emerged. Early evangelicalism can best be defined, described, and accounted for as a religio-aesthetic movement that centered a felt way of experiencing God and one's Christianity as more authentic than others.[6] Revival verse, like the kind of conversion experiences it promoted and facilitated, created felt religious authenticity.

While religious experience, and especially religious poetry, could once appear marginal to the predominant understandings of the eighteenth century as the age of enlightenment, scholars have come to see how central feeling, affect, and religion were to the period. Evangelicalism does not stand adjacent to or outside the major developments and trajectories of modernity, but is intimately bound up with enlightenment. This appears not only in its emphasis on an authentic knowledge of God through sensory and bodily experiences of God's sublimity, beauty, and holiness, but also in its preoccupation with documenting God's acts in history. Popular religious knowledge, or experiential conversion, became grounded in sense experience, time, and documentation. Evangelical conversion and awakenings were instantaneous experiences of God, or what is called punctiliar conversion, confirmed through retelling – whether orally or in writing. Conversion experiences – retold, written in narrative and poetry, and referred to in sermons – propelled a new archival drive, which also drove more conversion experiences. At least from a genre perspective, conversion narratives overtook formal creeds and became a new major literary output of Protestant Christianity.[7] Hymns and revival poetry were even more prolific than conversion narratives; yet these new verse forms were also intimately tied to conversion – either inducing it, memorializing it, or rekindling it. In this sense, evangelical verse is a crucial part of the vast archive produced by punctiliar conversion. Even further, the poetics of evangelical conversion was part of a larger archival accumulation in the eighteenth century that included the development of natural science, colonization, and nation building. These entanglements underscore how important it is not to separate evangelicalism and its literatures from other social developments.

While poetry seems to be optional for many historians of early America, understanding early evangelical culture without attention to verse is akin to explaining changes in American politics in the twenty-first century with no attention to social media platforms. While contemporary historians may view verse as inconsequential or banal, eighteenth-century evangelicals did not. Rather, as the Reverend Samuel Davies declared, verse – both hymnal and nonhymnal – was the language of heaven that would *"diffuse celestial Fervour through the World!"*[8] Though God dispersed poetic talent on this earth, in heaven all the saints would inhabit a poetic tongue. Poetry, considered the essence of the Bible's language and central to the workings of the Holy Spirit, was responsible for fanning the flames of revival. If, as Jonathan Edwards argued, to know God one had to have a direct experience of God's beauty and sweetness, that is, have an aesthetic experience of God, poetry was the vessel and the language of that experiential awakening.[9] Because God created and could save all people, evangelicals promoted a common aesthetics basic to all humanity. In a century that invented the modern field of study known as aesthetics, which often treated this inquiry as a matter of discerning, organizing, and prioritizing elevated and exclusive taste, the early evangelical religio-aesthetic movement worked in the opposite direction. It is also worth noting that evangelical aesthetics entailed a specific anthropology (i.e., theological understanding of humankind) that was entwined with an emerging natural science and comparative anthropology in the eighteenth century.

When Asahel Nettleton published his *Village Hymns* (1824) for the sole purpose of literary respectability, he proclaimed the majority of revival hymns "entirely destitute of poetic merit."[10] This was certainly declaring the obvious. From the genesis of the evangelical hymn, its practitioners proclaimed and celebrated it as separate from the elite literary world of distinguished taste. Nettleton's collection of hymns was part of a metamorphosis that began to occur within evangelicalism in the early national period as white mainline churches attempted to absorb the energy of revivalism and some revivalist denominations clamored to gain middle-class respectability. Yet it would be a mistake to think that designating some Protestant hymns respectable and others degraded was something new. In fact, Watts, the father of evangelical hymnody, who reinvented the Protestant hymn and spurred its increased use for personal devotion, liturgy, and homiletics, relied on this distinction to create appropriate verse genres for different intellectual and aesthetic capacities. He relished respectable verse and coteries of taste at the same time that he argued for the necessity of a common Christian poetics.

When Watts and others wrote and promoted hymnal and nonhymnal evangelical verse for everyone, its inclusivity and leveling qualities also embedded a schema of authority tied to class, gender, and emerging ideas of race. One of the clearest places to see this is within Watts's formulation of the revival hymn as verse for the "plainest capacity."[11] Those with refined capacities in eighteenth-century emerging aesthetic thought were of the elite social class, white, and predominantly male. True Christians, Watts and others argued, needed to write verse for the most humble. When white missionaries asked for Watts's hymns for enslaved Africans and Native Americans, they often idealized their targets as more naturally musical and attuned to heavenly sounds at the same time that this confirmed their putatively low intellectual capacity. Though evangelicalism has often been considered part of a democratization process in America, it was never quite that simple. In fact, the increased attempts to convert enslaved Africans indicates the solidification of white supremacy in evangelicalism, not its diminishment.[12]

The operation of authority in and through a popular genre can be particularly vexed. Hymns are often compared to anonymous poems, ballads, or folk songs in terms of their classed and raced status.[13] While authorship of hymns functioned differently than other genres, it still produced religious and poetic authority through a person, a persona, or an institution. For instance, Richard Allen's *A Collection of Hymns and Spiritual Songs* (1801) accompanied the new African Methodist Episcopal Church's formation, which arose as a direct response to white supremacy, to confer authority as a church. Or, for example, sectarian hymnals appeared in the late 1820s to undermine the stated ecumenical mission of earlier hymnbooks. Certain hymn writers were famous and authorized the form and spirit of the revival hymn. And being known as a hymn writer buttressed one's spiritual authority in other realms. Authority was also vested in the user through tangible effects on, in, and through that person, such as falling down, crying, trembling, or simply a deep, holy gaze. The different spaces and uses of hymns and other verse forms meant that authorship was more expansive and malleable than a name on a title page. This is especially true in the case of the emerging early evangelical poetess in which authorship and authority aspired to hover spirit-like over the poetic experience. It is to this aspect of evangelical poetry that I turn to next.

The Early Evangelical Poetess

The figure of the nineteenth-century Poetess and her function in the development of the lyric has transformed the fields of historical poetics and women's poetry. Virginia Jackson has persuasively argued that the Poetess is the emerging lyric, which became synonymous with modern poetry.[14] Central to this discussion is the recognition that, as Yopie Prins succinctly writes, the Poetess is "the personification of an empty figure," "a trope, 'available for occupancy,' yet also advertising its vacancy."[15] As Jackson and Prins write, the Poetess is "not the content of her own generic representation; not a speaker, not an 'I,' not a consciousness, not a subjectivity, not a voice, not a persona, not a self."[16] Rather, the Poetess is a trope who performs "lyrical reflections on the conventions of subjectivity attributed to persons and poems." Though the Poetess has always been political, she has helped structure separate spheres and white domesticity. Tricia Lootens writes that study of the Poetess and of Poetess performance remains salient today because they "invite us, precisely through their mythic absolute identification with 'separate spheres,' into the vulnerable, violently structured, racially haunted hearts of our own inherited dreams of private innocence."[17]

The scholarship on the trope of the Poetess has proliferated over the last several decades, and I cannot do justice here to its various contours. My argument is simply that scholars have shortchanged its genesis. Scholars often place the nineteenth century as the time of the Poetess in American culture, but her widespread emergence can be traced to early eighteenth-century evangelical poetics, which braided together aesthetic experience, conversion, and espousal piety. Though revivals could be unruly, populist spaces with a degree of sensuousness seemingly far from the ideals of white domesticity, the Poetess's devotional intensity, pious domesticity, and generic presence actually stems from this revival culture's reliance on espousal piety, which infused revivalism and its sensuous religious grounding from its earliest stirrings. Many Pietists, including evangelicals, understood their relationship to Christ primarily through the metaphor of espousal – that is, the believer's marriage to Christ. This was a Christian reinterpretation of the poetry of *Song of Songs* as individual and personal salvation based in aesthetic experience. When I refer to espousal piety, I mean to stress not only the personal piety and intense religious feeling connected to the larger transatlantic emergence of Pietism, but also this significant metaphor through which evangelicals daily experienced their connection to "true" religion. That is, to feel one's self as an authentic

Christian who had found "real" religion one entered into this sacred metaphor of Christ's beloved and then lived it out. Neither poetry nor religion was something that early evangelicals thought one could pick up and put down at will; rather, they were mutually imbricated aesthetic experiences through which one found authenticity via an affective and ongoing relationship with Christ. In other words, their poetry, like their religion, was lived – and this most often through the espousal metaphor.

This can be readily documented not only through the bestselling evangelical poems, including Ralph Erskine's *Gospel Sonnets*, which shows just how widespread the expressed idea of espousal to Christ was in early evangelicalism, but also through the development of the evangelical idealized muse – or poetess – that proliferated with Watts and Rowe's verse. Rowe's influence on evangelical poetics rivals Watts not only in terms of the number of reprintings of her devotional works throughout the eighteenth century (there were upward of fifty reprintings in British North America alone), but also because her devotional persona became attached to heavenly language itself. Known as "The Heavenly Singer," Rowe was Watts's declared muse whose language he abstracted into the very essence of Christian worship. In his forward to her *Devout Exercises of the Heart* (1738), he urged readers to do as he had done – "to assume her Language as [his] own":

> LET me persuade all that peruse this Book, to make the same Experiment that I have done; and when they have shut out the World, and are reading in their Retirements, let them try how far they can speak this Language, and assume these Sentiments as their own: And by aspiring to follow them, may they find the same Satisfaction and Delight, or at least learn the profitable Lessons of Self-Abasement and holy Shame. And may a noble and glorious Ambition excite in their Breasts a sacred Zeal to emulate so illustrious an Example.[18]

That the vast influence of Rowe has been overlooked in accounts of early evangelical verse speaks to the success of this enterprise.[19] Her persona appears nearly invisible because it dispersed everywhere as she became synonymous with espousal piety and evangelical verse itself. Rowe's poetry was heavenly verse in the same breath that it became an idealized example of how to read (i.e., perform piety) as an authentic Christian.

This clearly has implications for how we understand the historic development of both the Poetess and the lyric, a history that Jackson argues subsumed social relations and genres into a reading practice.[20] I have intentionally not capitalized the word "poetess" in reference to the eighteenth-century evangelical persona emerging within espousal piety to underscore the historical distance and nuanced development that is necessarily part of such a trajectory. And this genealogy takes several avenues – Rowe's neoclassical and elite poetics were one aspect of her oeuvre while evangelicalism's uses for her devotional persona within the common poetics of revivalism were another. But the point remains: scholars lose too much essential context when they look to the late eighteenth century as the genesis of the trope of the Poetess in American poetry. Instead, they should look to the late eighteenth century for its most successful antiwhite supremacist critic. Phillis Wheatley Peters, who is sometimes named as the first American Poetess, rejected the early evangelical poetess as an exclusionary and anti-Black persona unfit for Christian and abolitionist poetics.

Phillis Wheatley Peters and the Revival Hymn

"Who has put Phillis Wheatley's poems to heart, or thinks to use any of her lines to describe a situation that is not Phillis Wheatley's situation?" asks Rowen Ricardo Phillips when reflecting on Wheatley's place within African American literary history.[21] In the immediate context of the idealized eighteenth-century evangelical poetess, this question takes on a particular significance. In Watts's phrasing: Who assumes Wheatley's language as her own, as one would the idealized Rowe? And how might Wheatley's poetics resist such a use for her poetry? One place to begin is with the overlooked fact that Wheatley never published a revival hymn. Wheatley made one of the most important interventions in early American evangelical hymnody through her refusal to write revival hymns. It has in large part been missed because of broad inattention to the history of revival poetics. But as soon as the ubiquity of hymns and other revival poetries becomes visible, her refusal to publish revival hymns becomes meaningful. Arguably the most important poet in the early American nation, Wheatley's rejection of revival hymns unravels the well-trod story of American Christianity's democratization.

We can start where most readers of Wheatley begin: with the frontispiece that accompanied her book *Poems on Various Subjects, Religious and Moral* (1773).[22] Fashioned after the Countess of Huntingdon's own portrait, who insisted on the inclusion of the image, Wheatley appears as a pious, early evangelical poised to write her poetry. And just as in the Countess's portrait, which also features similar clothing and a posed hand against the chin with slightly lifted index finger, the same small book with the same binding sits close by.[23] In the Countess's portrait, the book is clearly a hymnbook, and it functions to identify her Methodism and

accentuate her pious leadership and authority in the transatlantic evangelical community. Read in tandem with the Countess's portrait, Wheatley's
frontispiece claims her as a part of the transatlantic evangelical community
in which publicly displaying hymnbooks worked to announce one's
Methodist or Dissenter allegiances.[24] However, Wheatley's book of poems
is curiously at odds with this presentation. While the imaginary hymnbook
might flag her identity as a Methodist, the actual book of poems contains
no evangelical hymns. For Wheatley–the famed elegist of the transatlantic
celebrity preacher George Whitefield, sponsored by the Huntingdon
Connexion, and enslaved by a revival-supporting family fluent in revival
practices– this is quite remarkable.

Rather than publish revival hymns, Wheatley penned neoclassical
hymns. Several scholars have shown how writing neoclassical poetry
directly engaged the politics of the forming nation and its relationship to
slavery.[25] Wheatley's poetry insisted on her own intellect – her expansive
imagination, cultivated poetic taste, and participation in classical literary
tradition, which, she continually pointed out, included Africans. Intellect,
especially exhibited through aesthetic refinement, as early American
scholars have shown, was essential for rights-bearing liberal subjects.
That Wheatley exhibited her genius to promote abolition was not a secret.
Others, including those in her poetic coterie, pointed to her poetry as
proof of elevated emotional and intellectual capacity that proved her
bondage was unjust.[26] The plainest capacity associated with the revival
hymn could not boost such an argument. Even more, to write as one
immersed in revival culture yet to leave out its most vital verse form
critiqued the entire enterprise of evangelical poetics and its relationship
to Blackness and the plainest capacity. It skewed the rubric of capacities
that organized verse genres and the proliferating archive of punctiliar
conversion that supported evangelical anthropology, which depended on
a common aesthetic ability to experience God.

Wheatley's refusal to publish revival hymns not only exploited verse
form to display her intellectual capacity and to question received notions of
raced capacities; it also actively exposed the invented whiteness of the
evangelical poetess. The absence of evangelical hymns in her book of
poetry poignantly gestures toward her exclusion from the white
domesticity from which the heavenly song of the poetess arose. To read
past this absence is to miss Wheatley's refusal to acquiesce to the notion
that white womanhood should be at the center of evangelicalism.

Wheatley strategically refused sentimental kinship with white women
and instead practiced a speculative kinship through her prophetic speech.

Britt Rusert positions speculative kinship, which is "an imaginative project of mapping descent . . . across the African diaspora that did not hinge upon the Atlantic slave trade," as a precursor to the Black ethnographic work, or "fugitive science," of the nineteenth century.[27] Wheatley's sustained critique of sentimental kinship and her practice of speculative kinship starkly appears when comparing two coterie poems produced in response to the same prompt. According to the London magazine, on January 1, 1772, a coterie of Boston women challenged each other to write a poem on a subject they could not recall having seen before – ironically, of course, that subject was "recollection." Wheatley took up this challenge. So also did the white poet Deborah How Cottnam, whose poem "On Recollection" Jane Tyler copied in her own commonplace book – a book that was given to Tyler for such purposes by Ruth Barrell Andrews, who wrote the first known poem about Wheatley's soon-to-be-published book.[28]

The two poems written on the same prompt could not be more different. Cottnam, who wrote under the cognomen Portia, performs heightened female sentiment from the first line, which bolsters a universalized soul equated with reason. In comparison to Portia's first phrase "What reccollection is, oh!," Wheatley's first phrase appears entirely devoid of emotion: "Mneme, begin."[29] The understated power of the first phrase places Mneme as the genesis of poetics, history, and justice, who inspires the "sacred Nine" and in turn their "vent'rous *Afric* in her great design." Mneme, unmotivated by sentimental affect, assists the poet to "trace [Mneme's] springs" to the eventual "race" who will face her judgment for "scorn[ing] her warnings," "despis[ing] her grace," and persisting in "their horrid crime[s]." In other words, Wheatley's poem provides a sweeping account and condemnation of slavery in the traditions of African, classical, and Christian prophecy. On the contrary, Portia emphasizes familial relationships both in this life and in the one to come as the basis of morality. Importantly, she declares memory (associated with women) to be "the minds perfection, and the stamp of Heaven," and underscores "In this *alone*, the strength of reason" (associated with men) "lies." Her argument comes down to a grand defense of the family and separate spheres that undergirds both society and heaven. White espousal piety projects a history and a future much different than the "vent'rous *Afric*."

To trace Mneme's springs embarks upon a speculative kinship that enables Wheatley to insert Africa at the center of evangelical poetics by remaking the Calvinist couplet. The Calvinist couplet was a verse practice of early evangelicals that embedded espousal poetry into the rhymed couplet.[30] The verse form, which looked exactly like the prototypical Popian couplet, expressed the marriage of the believer and Christ through the wedding of two lines of verse via rhyme. In this way, rhyme became an embodied practice of evangelicalism in which believers experienced at the level of affect the holy metaphor of espousal in the everyday. The Calvinist couplet helped acclimate believers to particular theological tensions that were internalized at the level of affect: tensions such as those between law and grace, God's sovereignty and man and 's will, spiritual freedom and slavery to sin could feel right in the same way that a rhymed couplet did.

Wheatley knew this tradition well; and in her hands, the couplet became an opportunity not only to perform her intellect through the neoclassical couplet but also to put pressure on the Calvinist couplet. We can see this most easily in her poem "To the University at Cambridge" in which she takes up the revival poet-minister role and audaciously declares herself the Ethiop. For a revival audience whose affective piety was intimately bound up with the *Song of Songs'* metaphor of espousal, the Ethiop bespoke the original Bride of the biblical text: "I am black, but comely, O ye daughters of Jerusalem" (1:5). Nowhere else in her poetic oeuvre does Wheatley utilize espousal imagery. She grounds her authority in an original, rather than a recursive, relationship to the biblical text that bypasses white womanhood and its attendant affect and sentimentality.

The stakes of this declaration become clear in the context of her demand "to scan" the poem, which has been evacuated of both her usual neoclassical heroic couplets and the Calvinist couplet, and replaced by blank verse. Revivalist soteriology had been infused with espousal piety via the couplet since its inception. In light of New England's recent investment in revitalizing Calvinism through a benevolent Christianity that promoted abolition, Wheatley's suspension of the couplet in the same poem in which she claims the title of the original Bride of Christ announces her political project. The poem recasts the paradoxes of living out Calvinism not just in terms of law and grace, God's sovereignty and man's will, spiritual freedom and slavery, but most importantly political freedom and slavery. In the context of evangelical espousal poetics and the Calvinist couplet, Wheatley's poem clearly remade the spouse of Christ and inserted Africa into the foundation of the evangelical structure of affect, theology, and poetics. In her very poetic forms, which Wheatley understood to be at the heart of evangelical practice, she demands that readers shun the evil of slavery, "the deadly serpent in its egg," at the center of an unfolding Christian history.[31]

Wheatley's critique remains salient for scholars of early America today for many reasons, including that it offers new ways of understanding both the revival hymn and the Poetess in the nineteenth century. Evangelical archives – and especially the writing forms that accompanied punctiliar conversion, namely, conversion narratives and revival verse – were part of the larger accumulation of eighteenth-century archives associated with natural history and nascent race science, colonization, and nation building. Hymns and revival poetry, specifically, were charged sites for Black and white femininity; and the capacities that attended each of these formations were part of what would later enable sentimentalism to prop up race science.[32] In particular, Wheatley's poetics foregrounds and critiques how the very form of the eighteenth-century evangelical poetess was bound up in whiteness. Specifically, the absence of revival hymns in Wheatley's published works challenges the ephemeral and white evangelical poetess who underwrote early evangelical affect and its relation to domesticity and instead centers Black femininity and prophetic speech in Christian history.

To Phillips's provocative observation (who thinks to treat Wheatley's words as their own?), Wheatley's poetics answers by refusing the "vacancy" sign of the Poetess. As Wheatley points out, it took work to turn the *Song of Songs'* bride white. Espousal poetics was not an innocuous aesthetic and religious practice; it constituted a social imaginary that enabled white supremacy through the fiction of capacities that defined the white liberal rights-bearing subject. Wheatley's claim to the Ethiop, the original Spouse of Christ, shook this ground. We might interpret the proliferation of the white evangelical Poetess in the nineteenth century as a reactionary and constant reassertion of evangelicalism's supposed whiteness. Laura Mandell pointed out some time ago that Wheatley's political poetry corresponds to the first critical emergence of the "Poetess" as a category within the United States that was "profoundly concerned with the indeterminacy of nationality."[33] Lootens rhetorically asks, "Who made the Poetess white? No one; not ever," to emphasize the failed attempts to privatize and apoliticize the figure of the Poetess.[34] Wheatley's claim to be the Ethiop, to be the central figure of evangelical piety and poetics, to sign a name that though not her own emphatically demanded a there there, to write with words that could not be assumed by another, can and should continue to disrupt the racialized and gendered separate spheres that undergird white supremacist visions of aesthetics, religion, and the nation.

This essay provides a brief window into a prolific early American verse world invested in popular aesthetic experience that formed the basis for what would become the default understanding of authentic religion and spirituality in American culture from the eighteenth century to today – personal affective experience. Personal experience (or felt religious authenticity) came to define scholarly and lay ideas of religion against social and institutional formations; it also came to define with various contours poetry as a genre. The nuances of these entwined histories call out for more scholarly attention. Though the modern, lyric poet has been said to proclaim alone to a largely uninterested universe and audience, early evangelical poets created rich poetic social networks that exchanged highly impactful verse forms to create and sustain multiple communities, and in the process influenced the trajectory of American history and culture. Poetry and early evangelicalism wed from the start, and that fact matters to the literary and cultural histories that scholars write. I have shown one way in which it does. New scholars who chose to follow such trajectories will find ample poets writing in eighteenth-century America, both in print and in manuscript, many of them religious, in archives across the country and in the most popular electronic databases. Their writings are waiting to be taken up and theorized by new scholars who might ask how these productions help us understand not only the development of something called American poetry and something called religion, but also how these evolutions can impede our understanding of the texts and pasts we study.

Notes

1 Jenny Fenno, *Original Compositions, Prose and Verse. On Subjects Moral and Religious* (Boston: Joseph Bumstead, 1791), 125.

2 I refer here to the full name of Phillis Wheatley Peters following poet and scholar Honorée Fanonne Jeffers's critique that scholars should use the name the poet herself chose to take when she married John Peters rather than the name her enslavers forced her to take. Jeffers, *The Age of Phillis* (Middleton, CT: Wesleyan University Press, 2020), 179. I retain the use of the name Wheatley throughout most of the essay because I am implicitly addressing the power of the author function, which has resided within the name Wheatley and the reading of her poetry.

3 A longer version of these arguments appear in Wendy Raphael Roberts, *Awakening Verse: The Poetics of Early American Evangelicalism* (Oxford: Oxford University Press, 2020).

4 Stephen Marini, "Hymnody as History: Early Evangelical Hymns and the Recovery of American Popular Religion," *Church History* 71.2 (2002): 273.

5 John Knapp, "Isaac Watts's Unfixed Hymn Genre," *Modern Philology* 109.4 (2012): 463–482. Important recent work on the culture and function of early American hymns includes Christopher N. Phillips, *The Hymnal: A Reading History* (Baltimore, MD: Johns Hopkins University Press, 2018); Claudia Stokes, *The Altar at Home: Sentimental Literature and Nineteenth-Century*

American Religion (Philadelphia: University of Pennsylvania Press, 2014); Mark A. Noll and Edith L. Blumhofer, eds., *Sing Them over Again to Me: Hymns and Hymnbooks in America* (Tuscaloosa: University of Alabama Press, 2006); and Mark A. Noll and Edith L. Blumhofer, eds., *Sing the Lord's Song in a Strange Land: Hymnody in the History of North American Protestantism* (Tuscaloosa: University of Alabama Press, 2004). On British hymns, see Isobel Rivers and David L. Wykes, eds., *Dissenting Praise: Religious Dissent and the Hymn in England and Wales* (Oxford: Oxford University Press, 2011).

6 Linford Fisher, "Evangelicals and Unevangelicals: The Contested History of a Word, 1500–1950," *Religion and American Culture* 26.2 (2016): 184–226.

7 W. R. Ward, *The Protestant Evangelical Awakening* (Cambridge: Cambridge University Press, 1992), 2; D. Bruce Hindmarsh, *The Evangelical Conversion Narrative: Spiritual Autobiography in Early Modern England* (Oxford: Oxford University Press, 2005); and Gordon T. Smith, *Transforming Conversion: Rethinking the Language and Contours of Christian Initiation* (Grand Rapids, MI: Baker, 2010), 5.

8 Samuel Davies, *Miscellaneous Poems* (Williamsburg, VA: William Hunter, 1752).

9 Jonathan Edwards, "A Divine and Supernatural Light," in *The Works of Jonathan Edwards, vol. 17: Sermons and Discourses, 1730–1733*, ed. Mark Valeri (New Haven, CT: Yale University Press, 1733), 415.

10 Asahel Nettleton, *Village Hymns for Social Worship: Selected and Original: Designed as a Supplement to Watts's Psalms and Hymns*, 2nd ed. (Hartford, CT: Goodwin, 1824), v–vi.

11 Isaac Watts, "Preface," in *Horae Lyricae, Poems, Chiefly of the Lyric Kind* (London: S and D. Bridge, 1706), viii.

12 Katharine Garbner, *Christian Slavery: Conversion and Race in the Protestant Atlantic World* (Philadelphia: University of Pennsylvania Press, 2018).

13 For the most comprehensive treatment of American ballads as a classed and raced genre, see Michael C. Cohen, *The Social Lives of Poems in Nineteenth-Century America* (Philadelphia: University of Pennsylvania Press, 2015).

14 Virginia Jackson, *Dickinson's Misery: A Theory of Lyric Reading* (Princeton, NJ: Princeton University Press, 2005).

15 Yopie Prins, *Victorian Sappho* (Princeton, NJ: Princeton University Press, 1999), 180, 184.

16 Virginian Jackson and Yopie Prins, "Lyrical Studies," *Victorian Literature and Culture* 27.2 (1999): 523.

17 Tricia A. Lootens, *Political Poetess: Victorian Femininity, Race, and the Legacy of Separate Spheres* (Princeton, NJ: Princeton University Press, 2016), 1.

18 Isaac Watts, "Preface," in Elizabeth Singer Rowe, *Devout Exercises of the Heart in Meditation and Soliloquy, Prayer and Praise*, 3rd ed. (London: R. Hett and Brackstone, 1738), 15–16.

19 Recent work on Rowe includes Sarah Prescott, *Women, Authorship and Literary Culture, 1690–1740* (Basingstoke: Palgrave Macmillan, 2003); Melanie Bigold, *Women of Letters, Manuscript Circulation, and Print*

Afterlives in the Eighteenth Century: Elizabeth Rowe, Catherine Cockburn and Elizabeth Carter (Basingstoke: Palgrave Macmillan, 2013); Paula Backscheider, *Elizabeth Singer Rowe and the Development of the English Novel* (Baltimore, MD: Johns Hopkins University Press, 2013); and Deborah Plymouth Kennedy, *Poetic Sisters: Early Eighteenth-Century Women Poets* (Lewisburg, PA: Bucknell University Press, 2013).

20 Virginia Jackson, "The Poet as Poetess," in *The Cambridge Companion to Nineteenth-Century American Poetry* (Cambridge: Cambridge University Press, 2011), 54–75.

21 Rowen Ricardo Phillips, *When Blackness Rhymes with Blackness* (Champaign, IL: Dalkey Archive Press, 2010), 22.

22 Phillis Wheatley, *Poems on Various Subjects, Religious and Moral* (London: A. Bell, 1773).

23 At the National Portrait Gallery, www.npg.org.uk/collections/search/portrait Extended/mw03325.

24 Phillips, *The Hymnal*, 33.

25 John Levi Barnard, *Empire of Ruin: Black Classicism and American Imperial Culture* (Oxford: Oxford University Press, 2018; David Waldstreicher, "Ancients, Moderns, and Africans: Phillis Wheatley and the Politics of Empire and Slavery in the American Revolution," *Journal of the Early Republic* 37.4 (Winter 2017); Eric Slauter, "Neoclassical Culture in a Society with Slaves: Race and Rights in the Age of Wheatley," *Early American Studies* 2.1 (2004): 81–122; Edward Cahill, *Liberty of the Imagination: Aesthetic Theory, Literary Form, and Politics in the Early United States* (Philadelphia: University of Pennsylvania Press, 2012). Specific to emerging racialized science and Wheatley, see especially Katy Chiles, *Transformable Race: Surprising Metamorphoses in the Literature of Early America* (Oxford: Oxford University Press, 2014).

26 For instance, see Ruth Barrell Andrews's poem "Slavery," published in full in Wendy Raphael Roberts, "'Slavery' and 'To Mrs. Eliot on the Death of Her Child': Two New Manuscript Poems Connected to Phillis Wheatley by the Bostonian Poet Ruth Barrell Andrews," *Early American Literature* 51.3 (2016): 665–681.

27 Britt Rusert, *Fugitive Science: Empiricism and Freedom in Early African American Culture* (New York: New York University Press, 2017), 74, 67.

28 Jane Tyler Book, Royall Tyler Family Collection, Vermont Historical Society.

29 Tyler Book; Phillis Wheatley, "On Recollection," in *Poems on Various Subjects, Moral and Religious* (London: Printed for A. Bell, 1773), 62.

30 For a full explanation of the Calvinist Couplet, see Roberts, *Awakening Verse*.

31 Wheatley, "On Recollection," 15–16.

32 Kyla Schuller, *The Biopolitics of Feeling: Race, Sex, and Science in the Nineteenth Century* (Durham, NC: Duke University Press, 2017).

33 Laura Mandell, "Introduction: The Poetess Tradition," *The Transatlantic Poetess in Romanticism on the Net* (2003), para. 5.

34 Lootens, *Political Poetess*, 7.

CHAPTER 8

"Ambiguities and Little Secrets"
Taste-Making and the Rise of the American Cookbook
Elizabeth Hopwood

Two Ounces of Ginger

In *American Cookery*, the first American-authored cookbook (1796), Amelia Simmons offers the following recipe for gingerbread cake:

> Three pounds of flour, a grated nutmeg, two ounces ginger, one pound sugar, three small spoons pearl ash dissolved in cream, one pound butter, four eggs, knead it stiff, shape it to your fancy, bake 15 minutes.[1]

This recipe may be difficult for the modern home cook to parse: besides employing the now-unfamiliar pearl ash as a leavener, the recipe provides no instruction regarding the amount of cream to use, the temperature at which the cake should be baked, nor how to determine the doneness of the final product. Written, however, "for the improvement of the rising generation of *Females* in America," such a recipe would have been practical for cooks and domestic help in the kitchens of the early republic. Nearly 200 years later, preeminent American food writer M. F. K. Fisher would declare: "A recipe is supposed to be a formula, a means prescribed for producing a desired result, whether that be an atomic weapon, a well-trained Pekingese, or an omelet. There can be no frills about it, no ambiguities . . . and above all no 'little secrets.'"[2] This essay will contend that Simmons's cookbook, and indeed the many cookbooks and domestic management texts that circulated in the early republic, were in fact immensely ambiguous and full of "little secrets." These are not necessarily "secrets" of measurements or preparation methods, but instead mystifications of a long history of Atlantic production that enabled these dishes to be consumed and celebrated in the space of the United States.

As a textual object, the purpose of the cookbook appears prescriptive, a genre that is objective, neutral, and even scientific. Instructions, when precisely followed, promise to produce consistent results. For Simmons, such results – a dessert, an appetizer, an entrée – are dishes that taste good and, perhaps even more importantly, are of *good taste*, meaning that they uphold particular American values and judgments. What I suggest here extends this research to explore the means by which early American recipes and cookbooks rely on commodities – and labor – that are products of a transatlantic framework. Early American cookbooks help to create the idea of an America built on and sustained by values of frugality, simplicity, wholesomeness, and pastoral sufficiency: all values that would equate to a notion of what is considered "good taste." Positioning the genre within a broader Atlantic economic and cultural framework, however, reveals some of the hidden ways raw materials and commodities came to be shipped, stirred, baked, and served. These are complicated and often invisible stories of how the production of good taste is predicated on suppressing the violence inherent in the system of food production. Reading recipes against the grain can help us see slavery, Atlantic commodity production, and household kitchen labor as secret ingredients within the larger recipe for how to create an American home.

What ambiguities or secrets does Simmons's seemingly simple recipe for gingerbread cake conceal and reveal? Glynnis Ridley offers a reading of Simmons's text as a political affirmation that uses the language of food to assert a newly American cultural identity. Simmons's title page describes herself as "an American orphan." By offering a self-representation as an orphan, she draws a parallel between her familial circumstances and that of the United States, a newly emancipated and parentless child of Britain.[3] The cookbook becomes more than a series of instructions – it is an object through which both author and reader might use to self-fashion as an American. The preface of *American Cookery* also positions itself as a distinctly American manual through its emphasis on local, easily accessible ingredients to support and grow the domestic economy. Simmons highlights the relationship between food, cooking, and morality, particularly for the orphan subject, who, she writes, "must depend solely upon *character*. How immensely important, therefore, that every action, every word, every thought, be regulated by the strictest purity, and that every movement meet the approbation of the good and wise."[4] Simmons's expectations for how food serves as a means by which to demonstrate "good" or "wise" character anticipates Jean Anthelme Brillat-Savarin's 1825 adage: "Tell me what you eat and I'll tell you what you are." She echoes the traces of earlier humoralism, theories of medicine that associate digestion with the four humors; food is a way of balancing one's humors and, thus, monitoring and adjusting one's personality.[5] If who you are is based on what you eat, then choosing to eat in an American fashion offers the potential to imbue yourself with the values associated with those foods. Simmons emphasizes the use of American-produced corn as a main staple and regularly employs regional ingredients such as pumpkins, corn, apples, and cranberries, showing how an American appetite and cuisine might be built and sustained through local agriculture. My argument is that although the ingredients of a recipe may seem inconsequential (after all, what is noteworthy about a pinch of salt or cup of sugar?), close attention to recipe structure and ingredient lists can bely the rhetoric of homeliness and character- and nation-building that the cookbook ostensibly fore-grounds. Going back to Amelia Simmons's recipe with which this essay opens, we encounter flour, pearl ash, sugar, butter, nutmeg, eggs, and ginger. I want to pause on the use of ginger to unpack and split open our received notion of what these recipes might tell us about the extranational in American recipes. In an American recipe for gingerbread cake, what might two ounces of ginger reveal?

Two ounces of a spice is, on the one hand, minor. But how did ginger – a spice cultivated in the West Indies – end up in the first American cookbook? And what might a focus on this minor ingredient illuminate about the study of the cookbook as a textual object? Ginger and its familial rhizomes, turmeric and cardamom, are native to tropical climates and prevalent in Southeast Asia. Like sugarcane, it was introduced to Europeans via the spice trade when it was brought to the New World and planted and harvested in the Caribbean. Jamaican ginger, in particular, was used medicinally and for brewing beers, but was also sold locally and exported to Europe and the American colonies. Its use in the Caribbean, specifically Barbados, is recorded and described in Richard Ligon's plantation manual, *A True and Exact History of the Island of Barbados* (1673), where he suggests that for a plantation of 500 acres of land, 200 acres be allotted for sugar production, 80 for pasture, 120 for wood, 30 for tobacco, and five for ginger (the rest allocated for cotton, corn, potatoes, plantains, cassava, and a few acres for fruits like pineapple, lemons, and limes). Ligon describes the harvest of ginger as follows:

> When 'tis ripe, we dig up the roots, (cutting off the blades) and put them into the hands of an Overseer, who sets many of the young Negroes to scrape them with little knives, or small Iron spuds, ground to an edge. They are to scrape all the outward skin off, to kill the spirit, for, without that, it will perpetually grow. Those that have Ginger, and not hands to dress it thus, are compelled to scald it, to kill the spirit; and that Ginger is nothing so good as the other, for it will be hard as wood, black, whereas the scrapt Ginger is white and soft, and hath a cleaner and quicker taste.[6]

The production of ginger is thus reliant on the stolen labor and skill of enslaved people, whose painstaking work of scraping the skin off the plant to "kill the spirit" enabled the spice to be exported and used in the recipes like the ones Simmons describes. "Killing the spirit" is a method by which the root becomes usable and controlled but it also echoes rhetoric of the control of enslaved individuals. Ligon employs language of an agricultural and culinary threat not only in the production of ginger but in its consumption: he describes the taste of ginger as "violently strong" and, when cut, "sends out such a vapour into our Lungs, as we fall all a coughing, which lasts a quarter of an hour after the fruit is removed."[7] I begin my reading of cookbooks by turning to Ligon's plantation manual for two reasons: first, to consider how an agricultural substance may be dependent on enslaved labor in order to be harvested and then transported from the West Indies to the colonies. The language used to describe the production and consumption of the crop stands in stark contrast to Simmons's imagining of gingerbread as part of the cuisine that affords virtue and character to an orphan. In order to transform an unruly root in to an item of good taste that can be mixed with flour and butter, the spirit must first be killed. Connecting Ligon's manual to Simmons's cookbook illuminates how genres of food and eating culture have a long tradition that disavows or otherwise ignores the source and labor of production. Read this way, the recipe becomes a print technology for masking or sublimating labor – especially exploitative labor. The tedious and back-breaking labor Ligon describes is absent from accounts of using the end product.

On the one hand, this absence is not surprising: it is, after all, neither the aim nor the project of the cookbook to account for or offer a history of each ingredient. But centering our reading of the recipe around such issues reveals a broader story of how slave labor in the Caribbean contributes to an early American culinary and cultural identity. In withholding the larger story of the labor and production of ingredients, the cookbook reads as an instructional manual: follow these steps to put dinner on the table. But the cookbook is *not* merely an instructional manual; it purports to have a larger purpose in shaping and ordering domesticity within an American frame-work – with shaping "good wives, and useful members of society."[8] That Simmons's purpose is to teach women how to be economical, resourceful, and virtuous Americans is not unique to her: this rhetoric is everywhere in cookbooks published in the early republic, in the long nineteenth century, and beyond. So too is the rhetoric that good cooking and morality are distinctly linked. My reading of the cookbook situates its rhetoric of nation-building against stories of production and labor that enable not only meals, but entire cultures of taste. In the rest of this essay, I will trace how the modern cookbook and recipe structure as we know it today emerges from its adolescent form in the early republic and suggest that American notions of "good taste" are foregrounded in an exploitative transatlantic system.

From Almanacs and Receipts to the Modern Cookbook

If we understand domesticity as a means through which to catalog and order one's family unit to best fit the value system of the nation, how better to accomplish this work than with a text that purports to do exactly that – the cookbook?[9] Although versions of cookbooks and written recipes (or "receipts") have existed for centuries, the material conditions of the cookbook and the format we recognize today began to take shape only in the mid-nineteenth century. Prior to that period, recipes could have been found in private family collections, in locally circulated books, attached to product advertisements, and in conduct manuals and domestic management texts. Cookery books were always influenced by British publications, but in the early republic, the almanac is likely the closest precursor to the American version of the genre, in both format and rhetoric.

Thomas's Almanack, for instance, printed in February 1789 in Massachusetts by Isaiah Thomas, includes proverbs for every day of the year and describes the publication as containing "a selection of matters curious and useful."[10] Such curious matters include an essay on eclipses, a remedy for foot corns, a short history of potatoes, and a catch-all section called "Recipes," such as Thomas's recipes for mead and molasses made of apples. By following the instructions, he promises that "you will have a fine family molasses preferable to that imported," echoing Amelia Simmons's appeal to choose local ingredients for the betterment of one's family and region. Thomas concludes this issue with a list of excise duties in Massachusetts on popular imported items like wine, rum, tea, coffee, cocoa, chocolate, sugar, lemons, and raisins, showing that, like Simmons's cookbook, choosing local ingredients may be virtuous, but is not always practical or economical, and that the wealthier households of 1789 would likely rely a great deal on raw materials coming from across the Atlantic. The development of good taste and American culinary identity cannot be divorced from labor, but it also cannot be divorced from transactions in capital. *The Farmer's Almanac,* printed in March 1831, also echoes this rhetoric: included is an ode to corn as the basis for the best

hasty pudding. Here, the virtue inherent in supporting a domestic economy is extolled through the endorsement of local grains as a dietary
staple.[11] Mark McWilliams has categorized such choices of what to eat
in the early republic as a means through which to practice and perform
what he calls "republican simplicity." This concept is rehearsed throughout
domestic management texts and recipes of the early republic (and, as
McWilliams highlights, in early American novels as well). Performing
republican simplicity meant that cooking and eating choices should promote agrarianism, local economy, wholesomeness, and a rejection of
luxury (particularly the richness of French cuisine). Of course, such tenets
seem utterly preposterous when practiced in the background of a nation
dependent on slavery. To read early American texts as supporting simple,
wholesome eating styles and cultural practices occludes the very real
contributions that an enslaved labor force was making, not only in terms
of labor but in terms of contributions of culinary practice and knowledge.

   A cookbook's premise of teaching the practice and management of
American good taste necessarily takes up broader conversations of aesthetics. Such an understanding would have excluded an enslaved and
nonwhite population in the adolescent republic as tasteful "consumers."
In his 1825 treatise on taste-making and gastronomy, French gastronome
and writer Jean Anthelme Brillat-Savarin celebrates the exploration and
discovery of new food items that widen one's horizons: "The last few
centuries have also seen important advances in the sphere of taste; the
discovery of sugar and its uses, alcohol, ices, vanilla, tea, and coffee have
provided our palate with hitherto unknown sensations."[12] Employing the
language of empire, Brillat-Savarin argues for not only the "discovery" of
an otherwise "unknown" sense but a possible new sensibility: an expanded,
sophisticated palate. In so doing, Brillat-Savarin echoes an understanding
of taste that relies just as much on one's ability to experience it as it does
one's ability to then make sense of it. The entrance of cane sugar and its
offshoots – rum, molasses – into the culinary milieu and cultural aesthetic
is framed not merely as a fleeting sensation of the tongue but as an
"important advance" within a presumably already-existing "sphere of
taste." But Brillat-Savarin's assertion points to a paradox of how aesthetics
operated in the nineteenth-century Atlantic world: even as skilled enslaved
laborers produced objects that would become paragons of taste, their skills
and knowledges were publicly excluded from the aesthetic outcomes such
an inhumane system enabled. Enlightenment philosophers such as Lord
Kames, Archibald Allison, and Adam Smith emphasized that aesthetics

must involve both a sensory experience and the ability to reflect on and assess that experience. The "sphere of taste" Brillat-Savarin proposes rehearses this account as it is composed of both objects that are tasted, judged, and valued (sugar, alcohol, vanilla) and human subjects who have the ability to participate in the act of tasting and judging. Who is the "our" of "our palate"? Who is included in the sphere of sense and sensibility? In other words, who is deemed as being able to sense and who is not, and for what reasons?[13] Notably absent from this sphere and excluded from participation in these Western notions of aesthetic experience and judgment are African and non-Anglo subjects whose lives and limbs were destroyed in the production of sugar and other commodities that traveled the Atlantic. I use Brillat-Savarin's understanding of senses and taste to argue that while cookbooks like Simmons's purport to create the idea of America – a vision of local, simple ingredients from the land – as a textual object the genre provides opportunities to decode and unravel tensions embedded in the ingredient lists.

Structures and Systems of Taste-Making

Almanacs that prescribed household order and espoused values of simplicity while foreclosing stolen labor and production laid the groundwork for modern cookbooks to thrive. In tracing the rise of the modern cookbook, we see remnants of the household tips and recipes that made almanacs so useful and popular toward the development of the home. Whereas almanacs compiled tips on growing and harvesting, the cookbook – likely because of its expected white female audience – turns inward toward the domicile. The recipes contained in these cookbooks would have looked similar to Simmons's recipe for gingerbread cake: a short passage with approximate (sometimes nonexistent) measurements. For instance, Simmons's full recipe for apple pie instructs the reader thusly: "Stew and strain the apples, to every three pints, grate the peal of a fresh lemon, add cinnamon, mace, rose-water and sugar to your taste – and bake in paste." No structured list of ingredients is provided, and no further instructions are given regarding measurements; the ability to make pastry dough ("paste") is presumed knowledge, delivered without remark. The origins of the recipe structure familiar to modern readers can be traced to 1816 England with Dr. William Kitchiner's *The Cook's Oracle*, where he provided exact measurements and order of use, instead of relying on cooking by sight or feel. M. F. K. Fisher, in her belief that recipes contain "no ambiguities or little secrets," credits Dr. Kitchiner's methodology as a solution to the previous "irksome" lack of time, method, and order so prevalent in recipes from the eighteenth and early nineteenth century. Kitchiner's ideas did not take hold within the public print sphere until 1861, when Isabella Beeton published *Mrs. Beeton's Book of Household Management*. This influential text (and ensuing editions) listed correct cooking times, the time needed for preparation, and even approximate costs. It was written with white middle-class British households in mind, for women with minimal household staff.

Attending to the structure of the recipe that Kitchiner first promoted can help readers locate the rhetorical project of the recipe – as promoting so-called concepts of republican simplicity, for instance. But it is also a useful methodology for teasing out those "minor" moments: of obscured production, invisible labor, or the reliance on Atlantic world production in order to construct an ideal American home. Like Simmons, Mary Randolph, author of *The Virginia Housewife, or Methodical Cook* (1824) associates individual virtue with eating. Her preface emphasizes consistency and economy: she claims, "The prosperity and happiness of a family depend greatly on the order and regularity established in it."[14] Her preface further links eating not only with individual character but with a responsibility to the nation.

> The government of a family, bears a Lilliputian resemblance to the government of a nation. The contents of the Treasury must be known, and great care taken to keep the expenditures from being equal to the receipts. A regular system must be introduced into each department, which may be modified until matured, and should then pass into an inviolable law.

The values that are expressed here constitute the tenets of "good taste": the ability to perform one's assigned role in the nation and to uphold values of morality, economy, frugalness, order, and control.

Such values are also espoused in what is considered to be the first Black-authored domestic management text. Robert Roberts's *The House Servant's Directory* (1827) was a collection of household knowledge that includes cleaning and repair instruction, behavioral and managerial recommendations, and recipes for items like beer, jams, and syrups. The preface from the publishers reinforces the language of morality, order, and control, referencing Kitchiner's success in standardizing the recipe:

> If the public have applauded Dr. Kitchener for improving the minutiae and economy of the larder, what praise is not due to an humble attempt to amend the morals and awkwardness of domestics?... To borrow a phrase

from the kitchen, our aboriginal servants need *grilling*; they require much instruction, and an apprenticeship to the art and faculty of *unbending*.[15]

Later Black-authored cookbooks would not appear until 1866, with Malinda Russell's *A Domestic Cookbook: Containing a Careful Selection of Useful Receipts for the Kitchen*. In 1881, Abby Fisher, formerly enslaved, would publish *What Mrs. Fisher Knows about Old Southern Cooking*.[16] The lack of early American Black-authored cookbooks should not be taken to mean that the contributions of Black cooks were any less than those of white cooks. In many cases, the contributions and knowledge systems of enslaved cooks were not codified within printed recipe books but were instead passed down from generation and then incorporated – often without credit – into the larger American milieu of what was considered "good taste." Danya Pilgrim, for instance, illuminates the role of service within the larger topic of foodways to argue that the lives, skills, and trades of Black waiters in Philadelphia contributed much to the broader land-scape of eating culture.[17] Black subjectivity has always informed and shaped cooking and eating practices throughout the space of the United States and the Atlantic, even as this work occurred outside the textual medium of the cookbook. As much as cookbooks can reveal about the stories of domestic labor and culinary craft, they are also a limited means through which to understand how culinary and cultural practices are shaped and codified outside a middle-class white subjectivity.

Sugar: A "Test of Civilization" and "Necessary of Life"

One place we see this shaping of culinary practices is in Mary Peabody Mann's 1857 cookbook, *Christianity in the Kitchen: A Physiological Cookbook*. This cookbook is an extensive collection of recipes that advises cooks in simple, healthy meals that espouse Christian values by avoiding "injurious ingredients," notably, sweets, adulterated flours, meat, and alcohol.[18] Echoing Amelia Simmons and Mary Randolph, Mann also incorporates Sylvester Graham's understandings of how health can influence virtue, not only for one's individual body but for the sake of the nation at large. Mann is particularly invested with how food might mirror or effect one's Christian sensibilities, insisting that "health is one of the indispensable conditions of the highest morality and beneficence." One of the first foods she finds fault with is wedding cake, which, along with "compounds" such as suet plum-pudding, "should never find [its] way to any Christian table" because "it looks ominous to see a bridal party celebrating nuptials by taking poison." She takes issue with flour and leavening agents that are adulterated by impure ingredients and metals (and the "dishonest bakers" who peddle them), as well as the havoc that fatty, heavy foods can wreak on the digestive system. There is another poison implicated that I wish to examine more closely: sugar.

Sugar, of course, was a driving force behind the Atlantic slave trade and, as scholars such as Kyla Wazana Tompkins have argued, a driving force behind our understanding of racial modernity.[19] Christopher Columbus brought sugarcane seedlings to the New World in 1493, where it flourished in the Caribbean soil. The art and technology of planting and manufacturing sugar was learned from the Portuguese (who maintained numerous plantations in Brazil) and the Dutch; numerous would-be planters traveled from England to Barbados in the seventeenth century to make their fortune in sugar. Sidney Mintz has most famously identified the demand for sugar rising as tea and coffee consumption increased by the eighteenth century, and points out the strangeness that two crops from opposite sides of the globe should be consumed together, noting how capital drives the production of crops that enable culinary appetites. Nineteenth-century American cookbooks continued to celebrate sweetness. *The American Practical Cookery-Book, or, Housekeeping Made Easy, Pleasant, and Economical in All Its Departments* (1859), authored by "a practical housekeeper," states that "Cooking is often much improved by a judicious use of sugar and molasses."[20] And Caroline Gilman, author of *The Lady's Annual Register: Housewife's Memorandum-Book for 1838*, suggests that the American appetite for sugar was only increasing, particularly compared with European nations. Curiously, she posits this as a marker of civilization, as if the rate of sugar consumption will return an advanced and well-mannered citizen: "Sugar[,] a test of civilization. Political economists consider the amounts of *sugar* used in any two countries as a test of the relative degrees of comfort which they enjoy. Ireland consumes in the proportion of five pounds a head; France, seven; Spain, seven and a half; the United States eighteen, and Great Britain twenty-five. But the molasses and maple sugar of the United States will probably place them on an equal footing with Britain." Mintz identifies sugar as reframing the British and colonial appetite, effectively restructuring meals and, with it, social structure, order, and class.[21]

Consuming sugar – or boycotting it – could be read as a political move for early Americans, particularly following the Sugar Act of 1764, which taxed sugar for the benefit of the British. It was also an economic issue, as Gilman's inclusion of molasses and maple sugar suggest. *The Farmer's*

Dictionary (1846) suggests that European and North American reliance on sugar is a necessity and "certainly one of the most important acquisitions which the agriculture of tropical countries owes to the voyages of naturalists."[22] The manual provides an account of sugarcane production in the West Indies and Central America where three varieties (the Creole, the Batavian, and the Otaheitan) are cultivated, with the Otaheite cane being more prevalent. The use of enslaved labor, such as the digging performed by "a negro," is referenced but dismissed as labor that is "easily performed, both in regard to field-work and the manufacture of sugar."[23] *The Dictionary* catalogs attempts to cultivate sugar on American soil using American crops such as beets, corn, and sorghum, a practice that began in the early republic.[24] In an entry on corn sugar, for instance, the editor notes that "The sweetness of the corn-stalk is a matter of universal observation. Our forefathers, in the revolutionary struggle, resorted to it as a means to furnish a substitute for West India sugar" before concluding that there is "no account of any successful operation of the kind."[25] Although ostensibly important for the health of its citizens, as an import sugar was costly:

> It is said that the general use of sugar in Europe has had the effect to extinguish the scurvy and many other diseases formerly epidemical. It may be doubted whether a tropical country can ever furnish a great amount of exports, except through the means of compulsory labour. It appears, then, highly probable, that if the inhabitants of temperate countries wish to continue the use of sugar, they must find some means to produce it themselves. (185)[26]

Native sugar crops promised both to become "an article of profitable export," while enabling families to "thus save a considerable bill of expense yearly paid for foreign sugars."[27]

Setting Mann's cookbook and her critique of sugar against the backdrop of the Sugar Revolution and America's scramble to produce its own sugar products reveal a much more complicated story of how an ingredient contributes to or even clashes with the nation's notions of taste in the mid-nineteenth century. Mann's cookbook rhetorically aligns with that of Amelia Simmons's first American cookbook by suggesting that pure, unadulterated foods can promote Christianity, civic order, domesticity, and, thus, moral citizens. But wherein Simmons's text constructs and reifies ideals of the nation, Mann takes up a discourse that puts the state of Christianity and morality as the central concern and health outcome. Mann argues that wedding cakes and other heavy, sugary items are unchristian because "health is one of the indispensable conditions of the highest morality and beneficence" and therefore a threat not only to public health but to public morality. This is instantiated within a nationalist discourse as she says that dyspepsia and other health-related maladies will be "banished from good society" as soon as the "gospel of the body is fully understood."[28] Echoing Sylvester Graham and other health reformers of the mid-nineteenth century, Mann asserts that her cookbook "will differ from all other cookery books, in leaving out from the composition of breads, cakes, pies and puddings."[29] Mann encourages one to pay attention to time of eating, quality of eating, and quantity of eating. She advocates quality foods that are simply cooked and the use of garden-grown vegetables over those "which have been picked, and kept for market *even one night*."[30] She also pays particular attention to the habits of food preparation, noting, for instance, that "spices were undoubtedly made for use in those climates where they grow, but the natives of those climates use them much more sparingly than we do" and are naturally predisposed to be able to tolerate them, suggesting that one's national belonging and identity should be heeded in order to attend to proper health and digestion. "Science," she writes, "may at last bring us to the conclusion, – and there are already some indications that it will do – that each climate and region produces those articles of food which it is most healthful to eat in their respective localities."[31] In advocating certain location-bound modes of eating in order to improve a uniquely American and Christian appetite and body, Mann's cookbook demarcates boundaries between the national and the foreign and insists that such boundaries exist (by nature and science) at the site of the stomach. Mann is perhaps somewhat prescient in advocating the use of seasonal, local produce (and her critique of gluten): "The plantain, fig, and banana – delicious fruits in their localities, – are nearly tasteless when imported half ripe," she writes. But her text is also an attempt to self-fashion the nation to better adhere to Christian morality and appeal to shared understandings of good taste. In co-implicating virtue, health, and religion, the text refuses the idea of American good taste is necessarily divorced from a transatlantic cultural and economic framework.

Despite her initial appeal to her readership, Mann includes sugar as an ingredient in well over fifty recipes in the collection.

Conclusion

In H. I. Harwell's 1816 *The Domestic Manual, or Family Directory*, the author promises a manual that is simply written and might fulfill Fisher's later call for no ambiguities and no little secrets: "In general, every receipt in the arts has been so wrapt up in mystery, that in reading a receipt, the man of plain good sense is often. . .bewildered." Hartwell's proposes to be a manual anyone could understand and benefit from. Within the opening pages, in between a recipe for getting rid of moths and a varnish for brass, readers find a recipe for ginger wine:

> To each gallon of water, put two pounds of lump, or best Havanna white sugar, and one ounce and a half of coarsely powdered ginger, tied up in a coarse linen bag; boil these together for half an hour.

The result is a "most excellent cordial liquor, and very cheap."[32] Whether or not this recipe succeeds in promoting a simple, virtuous collation depends on how we read it: divorced from considerations of minor ingredients and their origins, of Atlantic production, and of the project of determining "good taste" – and who was included in that project – we might read a straightforward recipe and, after a month's fermentation, enjoy a tasty cordial. But in this essay I have begun to open up other methodologies for reading cookbooks that foreground their textual ambiguities: the Havana white sugar harvested by an enslaved and skilled population, the ginger being transported from across the Atlantic. These two ingredients disrupt the homeyness of the home that the text purports to manage. Cookbooks invoke a sense of imagination, an allure and promise that is part aspirational ("here's what you could do") and part formulaic ("here's how to do it"). Readers are given a means to enjoy and experience domestic tranquility – an aesthetic built around steps, instructions, and order. We might instead read cookbooks to understand formations of aesthetics and cultures of taste. Food engenders rituals and traditions that continue to have contemporary resonances – sugarcane became part of an Atlantic world appetite and culture in Europe, while its production depended on the back-breaking labor of enslaved individuals in the Caribbean. Food practices and the constellation of texts that describe them – the travel and plantation narrative, the almanac, the recipe, the cookbook – recentered aesthetic values as occurring within the home, changed cultural appetites and commodity relations, and have ultimately become part of national and transnational identity formations that remain to this day. Perhaps more than any other genre, the objective of the cookbook is to construct a fantasy of home. However, close attention to the narratives within its pages, as well as the commodities used in recipes, reveal anxieties about how communities form and function in the wake of (and face of) invisible labor and a colonial economy. In order to construct a home, one must necessarily foreclose that which is not "the home": namely, the labor, the ingredients, the scenes of production involved. Read this way, Simmons's two ounces of ginger are the material end product – and beginning – of a vast and complex story.

Notes

1 Amelia Simmons, *American Cookery: The Art of Dressing Viands, Fish, Poultry, and Vegetables* (Hartford, CT: Hudson and Goodwin, 1796).
2 M. F. K. Fisher, "The Anatomy of a Recipe," in *With Bold Knife and Fork* (New York: Paragon, 1983), 20.
3 See Glynis Ridley, "The First American Cookbook," *Eighteenth-Century Life* 23, no. 2 (1999): 114–123. www.muse.jhu.edu/article/10494. Ridley has pointed to this recipe, and the cookbook as a whole, as a political narrative that echoes anxieties of the young nation.
4 Simmons, *American Cookery*, 3.
5 Jean Anthelme Brillat-Savarin, *The Physiology of Taste; or, Meditations on Transcendental Gastronomy* [1825] (New York: Vintage, 2011).
6 Richard Ligon, *A True and Exact History of the Island of Barbados* (London: Printed for Humphrey Moseley, 1657). HathiTrust Digital Library.
7 Ibid., 84.
8 Simmons, *American Cookery*, 3.
9 Literary scholars such as Gillian Brown have pushed on the ideals of domesticity espoused by mid-nineteenth century writers like Catherine Beecher and Harriet Beecher Stowe by considering how a domestic ideology is never just about the private space of the home, but instead invokes anxieties about the shape and boundaries of the nation and role of race and slavery in supporting it.
10 From Karen M. Bloom, *Almanac &c.: A Collection of Early American Almanacs* ([New York?]: privately printed by Westvaco, 1985).
11 Ibid.
12 Brillat-Savarin, *The Physiology of Taste*, 33.
13 See Kyla Schuller, *The Biopolitics of Feeling: Race, Sex, and Science in the Nineteenth Century* (Durham, NC: Duke University Press, 2017).
14 Mary Randolph, and Elizabeth Robins Pennell Collection, *The Virginia House-wife* (Washington, DC: Printed by Davis and Force, 1824). www.loc .gov/item/73217897/.
15 *Robert Robert's The House Servant's Directory* (Boston: Munroe and Francis, 1827).
16 See Doris Witt, "In Search of Our Mothers' Cookbooks: Gathering African-American Culinary Traditions." *Iris: A Journal About Women* 12 (Fall/Winter 1991): 22–27; Rafia Zafar, "The Signifying Dish: Autobiography and History

in Two Black Women's Cookbooks." *Feminist Studies* 25:2 (Summer 1999): 449–469; Rafia Zafar, "What Mrs. Fisher Knows about Old Southern Cooking," *Gastronomica* 1:4 (2001): 88–90; and Rafia Zafar, "Elegy and Rembrance in the Cookbooks of Alice B. Toklas and Edna Lewis," *MELUS* 38:4 (December 2013): 32–51; Jan Longone, "Early Black-Authored American Cookbooks," *Gastronomica* 1:1 (2001): 96–99; and Christina Bolzman, "The Legacy of Malinda Russell," *Michigan History Magazine* 96:4 (July/August 2012): 22–25.

17 Danya M. Pilgrim, "Masters of a Craft: Philadelphia's Black Public Waiters, 1820–50," *The Pennsylvania Magazine of History and Biography* 142, no. 3 (2018): 269–293.

18 Mary Peabody Mann, *Christianity in the Kitchen: A Physiological Cookbook* (Boston: Ticknor and Fields, 1857).

19 Kyla Wazana Tompkins, "Sweetness, Capacity, Energy," *American Quarterly* 71, no. 3 (2019): 849–856. doi:10.1353/aq.2019.0058.

20 A Practical Housekeeper, *The American Practical Cookery-Book; or, Housekeeping Made Easy, Pleasant, and Economical in All Its Departments. To Which Are Added Directions for Setting out Tables and Giving Entertainments; Directions for Jointing, Trussing, and Carving; and Several Hundred Additional Receipts* (Philadelphia: J. W. Bradley, 1859).

21 See also Mimi Sheller, *Consuming the Caribbean: From Arawaks to Zombies* (London: Routledge, 2003), and Matthew Parker, *Sugar Barons: Family, Corruption, Empire, and War in the West Indies* (New York: Walker, 2011). By 1770, Parker explains, "sugar had achieved a revolution in eating habits in England. Along with coffee, tea, and cocoa, jams, processed foods, chocolate and confectionery were now being consumed in much greater quantities. Treacle was spread on bread and put on porridge. Breakfast became sweet, rather than savoury. Pudding, hitherto made of fish or light meat, now embarked on its unhealthy history as a separate sweet course" (296). The effect this had on the slave trade was enormous: "From 1701 to 1810 Barbados, a mere 166 square miles in area, received 252,500 African slaves. Jamaica, which in 1655 had been invaded by the British, followed the same pattern of 'economic development'; in the same 109 years, it received 662,400 slaves" (53). See also Stuart B. Schwartz, *Tropical Babylons: Sugar and the Making of the Atlantic World, 1450–1680* (Chapel Hill, NC: University of North Carolina Press, 2004); Arthur L. Stinchombe, *Sugar Island Slavery in the Age of Enlightenment: The Political Economy of the Caribbean World* (Princeton: Princeton University Press, 1995); Richard Follett, *The Sugar Masters: Planters and Slaves in Louisiana's Cane World, 1820–1860* (Baton Rouge: Louisiana State University Press, 2005); and Vera M. Kutzinski, *Sugar's Secrets: Race and the Erotics of Cuban Nationalism* (Charlottesville: University of Virginia Press, 1993).

22 *The Farmer's Dictionary: A Vocabulary of the Technical Terms Recently Introduced into Agriculture and Horticulture from Various Sciences*, ed. D. P. Gardner (New York: Harper & Brothers, 1846), 185–188.

23 Ibid., 764–765.

24 Cane sugar was also cultivated in Louisiana, although not at the scale of Caribbean production. *The Farmer's Dictionary* notes that beet sugar, common in France and Germany, may be produced by households but likely will not become profitable (91). An 1859 manual called *Experiments with Sorghum Sugar Cane* erroneously predicted that "within less ten years [sorghum] sugar will be produced in quantity sufficent for home consumption, if not for export, in most of the Middle, and perhaps some of the Northern stages. Hedges, Free & Co., *Experiments with Sorghum Sugar Cane: Including Treatise on Sugar Making; also, a Descriptive Catalogue of Sugar Making Apparatus, Farm Implements, Etc.* (Cincinnati, OH: The Company, 1859), 10. See also Wendy A. Woloson, *Refined Tastes: Sugar, Confectionery, and Consumers in Nineteenth-Century America* (Baltimore: Johns Hopkins University Press, 2002).

25 *The Farmer's Dictionary*, 184–185.

26 Ibid., 185.

27 Ibid., 185.

28 Mann, *Christianity in the Kitchen*, 2.

29 Ibid., 3.

30 Ibid., 12.

31 Ibid., 12

32 H. I. Harwell, *The Domestic Manual; or, Family Directory. Containing Receipts in Arts, Trades and Domestic Oeconomy; Selected from the Best Authors, and Practical Artists; and Containing Many Processes, Never before Published* (New London, 1816).

PART II

Networks

CHAPTER 9

Modern Bigotry
The War for the Ohio, the Whiskey Rebellion, and the Settler Colonial Imagination of the Early Republic

John Mac Kilgore

The nation-building project of the United States was not an inevitable success. Geopolitical instability, regional division, Indigenous resistance, and economic precarity threatened to undermine the fledgling republic as soon as it was born. Although he celebrated the victorious outcome of the Revolutionary War as "little short of a standing miracle,"[1] George Washington knew that only a standing army could accomplish the unmiraculous work of creating, securing, and extending a "fiscal-military state" to rival the imperial superpowers surrounding the United States on all sides.[2] The prosperity and progress of the debt-ridden nation, suffering from deep financial crisis, hinged on the sale of land (i.e., the acquisition of "Indian country") and the ability to raise revenue and regulate commerce. However, the state economy met two main lines of resistance to those objectives: *externally*, the effort of Indigenous nations to preserve their territorial sovereignty and curb frontier settlement; and *internally*, the effort of regional polities (especially in the backcountry) to defend their right to socioeconomic autonomy from federal imposition.

In 1794, George Washington successfully addressed both domestic and foreign threats to fiscal-military empire by exhibiting the powers he helped to constitutionalize in 1787. First, he received congressional approval to raise an army and "declare War" on the United Indian Nations resisting colonization of the Ohio Country, culminating in the August 20, 1794, Battle of Fallen Timbers, led by Major General Anthony Wayne. Then, a month later, he formally claimed the power to "suppress Insurrections," stamping out popular revolt in western Pennsylvania against unequal taxes and government for the wealthy, the 1794 uprising we now know as "the Whiskey Rebellion." In his November 19, 1794, Message to Congress, Washington emphasizes that recent military operations to subdue the "enemies of order"[3] in the West and the "hostile Indians north of the Ohio"[4] equally prove the necessity of having a permanent "army of the constitution"[5] to secure the interests of the United States. These two events, then, considered minor episodes in popular memory of the early republic, mark a major turning point in the US nation-state, one that tells the origin story of the US military complex and how the US claimed the western frontier *as* national-colonial space.

But there is an important subtext to the plot of 1794 that further links the war against the United Indian Nations to the Whiskey Rebellion: the struggle to define not only the geopolitical but also the racial-ethnic boundaries of the United States. In the literature that justified and finessed the military actions of 1794, Anglo-Americans often lumped Native peoples and backcountry immigrants together as "savages" living outside the law of Anglo-Saxon civilization, a fact that frontier settlers, predominantly from Ireland and German-speaking Europe, resented as they coalesced into a new body of "white people" through a shared history of war with Indigenous nations.[6] If Ed White is correct that the "origins of [US] nationalism" lie in "Indian war" and settler sovereignty – "group violence" organized around "racialized fusion"[7] – then the colonial war for the Ohio and the Whiskey Rebellion represent a project not only to control the frontier but also to stabilize the boundaries of national whiteness in an era that equated republican citizenship with white sovereignty.[8]

Conditioned by the "fears and realities of Indian warfare," literature of the early republic helped to mold and consolidate a "white American consciousness"[9] by generating a language of US nativism designed, in the words of Gina Caison about a different context, "to maintain land claims under more romantic notions of race, place, and economy."[10] Thus, a settler-colonial structure of national reading, writing, and feeling doubles US nation-building and the violence it occasions on the frontier. This is no minor war, no minor literature. Taking my inspiration from recent historical works by Roxanne Dunbar-Ortiz, Nick Estes, Jeffrey Ostler,[11] and others who center Native sovereignty and settler violence in early US history, to downplay the significance of the incredible revolutionary struggle for independence waged by the United Indian Nations in the Ohio Country opposite the outrageous genocidal campaign pursued by the United States is to reproduce a colonial narrative that trivializes Indigenous resistance and settler-colonial catastrophe, yesterday and today.[12] Moreover, it is my contention that, read through the lens of settler colonialism, the Whiskey Rebellion and its literature become doubly significant, not merely as "a frontier epilogue to the American Revolution"[13] but as a major political crisis over the future composition of fiscal-military empire in North America.

My shorthand for the literary production of settler-colonial nationalism is "modern bigotry," a pun on the central text around which this chapter orbits, Hugh Henry Brackenridge's magnum opus, *Modern Chivalry* (1792–1815), one of the first US novels.[14] I do not foreground Brackenridge arbitrarily. As an influential author, lawyer, politician – and bigot – who settled in the frontier outpost of Pittsburgh in 1781, Brackenridge played a special role in shaping the literary genre of the "anti-Indian sublime,"[15] specifically in response to the US war against the Indigenous people of the Ohio and the Whiskey Rebellion. Politically, his sympathies lay with bourgeois professionals like himself, neither "opulent" nor "indigent,"[16] men of talent and industry who establish liberal institutions for deliberative democracy in education, law, journalism. And *literature*. Since at least his college days, when he and his friend Philip Freneau penned and recited one of the first odes of American manifest destiny, *A Poem, on the Rising Glory of America* (1772),[17] Brackenridge believed that liberty and literature are mutually constitutive in a healthy republican civilization. His sprawling mock-epic satire *Modern Chivalry* – an American *Don Quixote* published in seven installments between 1792 and 1815 – inculcates the same lesson. Brackenridge, as the authorial voice who punctuates the picaresque narrative with short essays and critical remarks, says about the social function of literature: "There is a natural alliance between liberty and letters. Men of letters, are seldom men of wealth, and these naturally ally themselves with the *democratic interest* in a commonwealth. These form a balance with the bulk of the people, against power, springing from family interest, and large estates."[18] However, in forming that balance, men of letters still have a privileged social authority; it is their duty to educate the common people – "Tom, Dick, and Harry, in the woods"[19] – on the rational foundations of a republic devoted to truth and justice.[20]

And yet in the terms of *On the Rising Glory of America*, the democratic interest of men of letters does share at least one commitment with both men of wealth and average settlers: the right of a white commonwealth to colonize land and bring the light of civilization – a "new Jerusalem"[21] – to the "desart plain or frowning wilderness."[22] There was only one problem, of course: Native America. For Freneau and Brackenridge, the "fierce Indian tribes / With deadly malice arm'd and black design"[23] stand in the way of all the "wealth and pleasure agriculture brings," and with it "palaces, / Puisant states and crowded realms."[24] By the time Brackenridge moved to Pittsburgh, what was once the multiethnic home of diasporic Native communities – primarily Shawnees, Delawares, and Mingoes – had been transformed through illegal settlement and anti-Indian violence into a multiethnic colony of Europeans. But the town still occupied a border with "Indian country" on the Allegheny River. Seemingly locked into a permanent if informal war with the Tribal nations of the Ohio (who were still reeling from the effects of the Seven Years' War and the American Revolution), western Pennsylvanians experienced and aggravated conflict with Indigenous peoples like white communities all across the trans-Appalachian region.[25] Brackenridge heard the stories from his neighbors. And he hated Indians. As soon as he settled in Pittsburgh, he worked to translate that hatred into policy by writing sensational accounts of "Indian atrocities." In 1783, for example, Francis Bailey published Brackenridge's *Narratives of a Late Expedition against the Indians*,[26] a pamphlet version of articles he had written for the *Freeman's Journal* consisting of two captivity narratives related to the 1782 Crawford expedition. Bailey's preface "To the Public" makes the intentions of the work all too clear. He hopes it will convince the government "that an extirpation of them [the "fierce and cruel" Indians] would be useful to the world, and honourable to those who can effect it."

A decade later, when Brackenridge published the first volume of *Modern Chivalry*, the northwestern campaign against the Indigenous people of the Ohio Valley not only had not ended; it had escalated into a national crisis. Now Indigenous nations were formally uniting, coordinating an international front against US imperialism. Outraged by American aggression and forced land cessions during and after the Revolutionary War, delegates from across Native America, including Shawnees, Wyandots, Delawares, Ottawas, Ojibwes, Potawatomis, Creeks, Chickamauga Cherokees, Haudenosaunees, Miamis, Weas, Piankashaws, and Kickapoos, organized a confederacy in the 1780s that would put a stop to illegal treaties and settlement, and insist on the Ohio River as the national boundary line. They called themselves the United Indian Nations. And they would lead the Native American campaign for political independence in the Old Northwest and Old Southwest over the course of the next decade.[27] Meanwhile, the first US Secretary of War, Henry Knox, vowed to annihilate the Ohio Natives. But he underestimated his foe. Under the military leadership of Blue Jacket (Shawnee) and Little Turtle (Miami), the United Indian Nations humiliated the militias of the United States twice, in Harmar's defeat of 1790 and St. Clair's defeat of 1791.[28]

This context is crucial for reading the early volumes of *Modern Chivalry*. In volume 1, book 5, chapter 1, the genteel protagonist, Captain Farrago, and his "bog-trotter" Irish servant, Teague O'Regan, encounter a confidence man who wants to hire Teague to masquerade as an Indian chief, a "king of the Kickapoos."[29] US commissioners, the man explains, pay large sums for Indian treaties and so he fabricates them. Because Teague "talks Irish," his "unknown gibberish" will easily "pass for an Indian language" and successfully pull off the fraud.[30] When the dubious Farrago expresses his astonishment that the government does not perceive the farce, the treaty man echoes views that Brackenridge published the same year (1792) in an article for the *National Gazette*, "Thoughts on the Present Indian War," namely, that federal officials, working at a great distance from the frontier, know nothing about actual American Indians. The treaty-maker remarks, "The legislature, hears of wars and rumours of wars, and supports the executive in forming treaties. How is it possible for men who live remote from the scene of action, to have adequate ideas of the nature of Indians[?]. . . Do you think the one half of those savages that come to treat, are real representatives of the nation[?]"[31] Treating with Indians is useless, anyway, the treaty man goes on to say in justifying his trade, for it always leads to "fresh war," and thus "it can be no harm to make a farce of the whole matter; or rather a profit of it."[32] Besides, profiting from illegal land deals is the American way *par excellence*: "it is a very common thing for men to speculate, now a-days."[33]

In the "Containing Observations" chapter following this scene, Brackenridge summarizes his satire of Teague "in an Indian dress" by repeating the joke that it "would be necessary for him only to talk Irish, which he might pass for the Shawanee, or other language,"[34] to conduct as legitimate a business as any putatively authentic Indian treaty. After all, Indians are only "sort of human creatures."[35] It makes no sense to deliberate with them. By the same logic, Brackenridge wonders why "the agricultural societies, have not proposed treaties with the wolves and bears, that they might not clandestinely invade our sheep and pig folds. This might be done by sending messages to several ursine and vulpine nations, and calling them to a council fire."[36] Brackenridge's horrifying views are a pretext, first, to justify his position that Indigenous peoples have no right to the lands they inhabit and, second, to justify his support of racial genocide in the face of Indigenous opposition. What he wants is for the United States to move away from a contract of sale and toward military occupation, establishing a permanent army on the frontier. In "Thoughts on the Present Indian War," for example, Brackenridge lobbies for the military to teach the United Indian Nations a lesson once and for all: "The question is, whether we shall submit ourselves to the savages, or they to us? I say, let us conquer because we cannot depend upon them."[37] Or, as he writes in his 1792 poem, "Thoughts on Indian Treaties," the United States would do better to send in a "veteran army" than pursue diplomacy:

> To drive them from the infested borders,
> And put a period to their murders,
> Exterminating race at once,
> For their own happiness and man's.[38]

From essay to poem to novel, Brackenridge's 1792 writings are published not in a vacuum but in the context of a fierce national debate, played out in literary journals, over the government's American Indian policy. As Colin Wells's *Poetry Wars*[39] convincingly shows, poetry in the early republic – and I would extend this point to literature as such – functioned as a persuasive form of public discourse participating in a "series of literary wars" to determine "the political course of the new nation."[40] To name only one germane example, a 1792 verse satire, published in the *American Mercury* as part of a series called "The Echo" by the "minor" Connecticut Wits (Lemuel Hopkins, Richard Alsop, Theodore Dwight, Elihu Hubbard Smith),[41] directly attacks Brackenridge's "Thoughts on the Present Indian War" in what amounts to an ideological critique of his apology for brute violence and the dehumanization of Native Americans. The barbed parody turns Brackenridge's description of urban easterners as sentimental and idealistic Indian sympathizers, a "dreaming clan,"[42] against itself by underscoring the fictive strategies – the storybook stereotyping and racial romanticism – required to reduce Native peoples to a group of animals and glorify settler colonial force. In Brackenridge's political landscape, a Manichean war is being waged between the "LAMBS" of "Kentucky,"[43] so "mild and good," and the evil Indians, those "savage Wolves."[44] The poem also uses the occasion to mock Henry Knox over the impolitic military campaigns he led against the Ohio Natives by satirically offering that the heavy loss of life, the "sacrifice of two armies," must surely be part of his ingenious strategy "to lull the savages into such perfect security as to render them an easy conquest to General Scott, and the brave Kentucky Militia."[45]

While white Americans fought over US-American Indian relations in the public sphere, Indigenous nations were busy deliberating over strategies of resistance to US imperialism, knowing full well that "exterminating the race at once" was the underlying purpose of frontier settlement. In 1792, the same year that Brackenridge satirizes Indian treaties and advocates for genocidal war, an international council of Indigenous peoples took place at the new headquarters of the Northwestern Confederacy, "The Glaize." The goal was to broaden and strengthen the ties of unity such that the United States would be forced to deal with Indigenous nations as one body – what Mohawk leader Joseph Brant invoked as "the Dish with One Spoon."[46] We are privileged to have a record of this assembly in "A Short Narration of My Last Journey to the Western Country" (1792–93), written by Hendrick Aupaumut,[47] a Mahican diplomat from the Stockbridge community whom the Washington administration sent as a US envoy to negotiate for peace. "Short Narration" ought to be canonical reading for early Americanists. It provides a powerful Native-centered view on US settler colonialism, speaking both to the deep kinship networks and national compacts underwriting a shared system of Indigenous sovereignty and to the competing allegiances and divided response of Native nations confronted with the demands of rival Euro-American empires.[48] As a work of literature, Aupaumut's council record introduces "Native communicative practices into European and Euro-American cultural and political institutions,"[49] including condolence rituals, written speeches, oratory, wampum, pipes, and news reports.

One of the central problems around which "Short Narration" revolves is the hostile presence of white settler-soldiers, or the "Big Knives," across the frontier. Should the nations insist that American forts and settlers first be removed from Indigenous lands as a condition for making peace with the United States? This fraught question leads to serious and heated debate among council delegates. Ultimately, the Northwestern Confederacy stands behind the position of Shawnee leadership, that the "United States have laid these troubles, and they can remove these troubles. And if they take away all their forts and move back to the ancient line, then we will believe that they mean to have peace, and that Washington is a great man,"[50] a declaration that de facto means war with the next-mustered US army, to the chagrin of Aupaumut and other Native leaders. One such leader, the Delaware sachem Big Cat, delivers a speech to the US government (dictated by Aupaumut) in which he asks his "Brothers," the Americans, not to blame and punish all Western Natives for the actions of Native militants just as he does not blame the United States for all of the actions committed by the Big Knives. However, Big Cat wants it to be clear that peace negotiations broke down after the council received word that the Big Knives had occupied Fort Jefferson and were preparing for war, among other concerns. He then makes a request: "if you will lengthen your patience, and manifest your power in withdrawing the Big knifes from the forts which stands on our land – then repeat your Message of peace to us."[51] Subsequently, in a key passage, Aupaumut details his effort to disambiguate the aims of the United States and the aims of frontier settlers by emphasizing that the latter are not truly American *citizens*;

indeed, they are "so bad ... because they have run away from their own country of different States ... [and] become lawless. They have lived such a distance from the United States, that in these several years the Law could not reach them."[52] While Aupaumut goes on to assure the delegation that, since the termination of the Revolutionary War, the law now *does* bind the Big Knives, his argument is less than convincing given the repeated hostilities of frontiersmen up until the present hour.

That Aupaumut rhetorically positions the backcountry as a border terri-tory both inside and outside the jurisdiction of the United States highlights the ambiguous, quasi-autonomous, counternational position of settler col-onies across the western frontier. This problem plagued the Washington administration. To be sure, the war to vanquish Indigenous resistance in the West was simultaneously a war to exert federal control over the trans-Appalachian area as anti-federal separatist movements began to develop out of the doctrine of "sovereignty through popular conquest" – the conquest of "Indian country."[53] Federalist literature entered the political fray for the same purpose, to advocate for nationally managed settler colonialism. To return to the Connecticut Wits, for example, their verse satire of Brackenridge may seem surprisingly progressive as a critique of American militarism and anti-Indian racism,[54] but a broad examination of their literary output reveals that, per mainstream Federalism and the Washington administration's stated American Indian policy as articulated by the Northwest Ordinance, the Wits were not so much opposed to fiscal-military empire as they were to the unregulated (immigrant) settlement of the frontier and the popular jingoism that preferred violence to diplomacy. Appalled by "a borderland forever afire with tax revolt, separatism, and war,"[55] putatively liberal elites like the Wits superimposed a pronational, class-based xenophobia on an otherwise laudable if paternalistic argument for the human and political rights of Native Americans. Take the 1795 New Year's verse by Dr. Lemuel Hopkins, published in the *Connecticut Courant*. After painting a picture of the chilling horrors emerging out of the French Revolution, Hopkins worries that Jacobin terrorism will spread to the United States, especially given the social complex of the western frontier where "men of sans-culotte condition"[56] celebrate and practice anarchy:

> And see yon western rebel band,
> A medly mix'd from ev'ry land;
> Scotch, Irish, renegadoes rude,
> From Faction's dregs fermenting brew'd;
> Misguided tools of antifeds,
> With clubs anarchial for your heads.[57]

By contrast, the poem then champions the first true army of the United States raised by George Washington under the leadership of "Mad" Anthony Wayne (or the "Black Snake" to Native Confederation members), who defeated the United Indian Nations in the 1794 Battle of Fallen Timbers.[58] This military incursion resulted in the cession of the Ohio via the 1795 Treaty of Greenville, an event praised by Hopkins for opening up the Ohio territory to "civilized" settlement:

> See next the veteran troops of Wayne,
> March o'er the savage bands of slain,
> And scatter far, like noxious air,
> Those victors of the fam'd St. Clair;
>
> . . .
>
> Here then Columbians seek your farms,
> When warlike Wayne shall quell alarms.[59]

Insofar as "Wayne barricades the west frontiers" in order to convert them into a "land of peace,"[60] the Wits find common cause with their literary enemy, Hugh Henry Brackenridge, who admonished the federal government in *Modern Chivalry* to "increase, or at least fill up, the establishment of troops, under the command of General Wayne. Let him have an opportunity of giving them [the United Indian Nations] at least one blow."[61] Washington finally listened to him. And when Wayne died a few months after dealing that blow, Brackenridge penned a eulogy to the "Brave honest soldier" who "Gives a celebrity to spots of earth"[62] taken by force and drenched in blood.

By winning the war for the Ohio area, the Washington administration addressed one of the major grievances of the backcountry – that the federal government did not protect the farms and families of settlers from "Indian raids." Instead, it treated frontier communities as if *they* were savages. As the New Year's verse above underscores, there was some truth to that accusation. Timothy Pickering spoke for many powerful politicians when he proclaimed that "savage emigrants" on the frontier, being the "least worthy subjects of the United States," "little less savage than the Indians,"[63] pose a threat to civilized development matched only by the Indians themselves. These "Indianized" whites of the West, whom Benjamin Franklin called "Christian white Savages"[64] and George Washington dubbed a "parcel of barbarians,"[65] were in fact seasoned settler-soldiers who made the "killing of Indian men, women, and children a defining element of their first military tradition and thereby part of a shared American identity."[66] Ed White explains that, while white settlers "fuse as a counternation, as killers of Indians," they "fuse, too, as antagonists of the Philadelphia elites, because they see, with some accuracy, that their situation is similar to that of the dispersed Indians: they are second-class resources administered by a centralized imperial system."[67] Not only do the "political entrepreneurs"[68] who run the government fail to protect and serve frontier communities; these same wealthy capitalists, landowners, and speculators (including George Washington himself) buy up all the land in the region, pass legislation rewarding local elites and corporate businesses, and push backcountry settlers into debt, dependency, destitution.

Herein lies the settler-colonial context for the Whiskey Rebellion, a three-year protest that extended across the entire trans-Appalachian region in the wake of the 1791 Hamiltonian tax bill, but that the government deemed most dangerous – and singled out – in western Pennsylvania. While the excise was in the most superficial sense a "whiskey tax," poor Westerners, for whom distilled spirits operated as a form of currency, experienced the law as an oppressive internal tax by wealthy elites on direct income that disproportionately affected those with no income to spare.[69] Nine thousand men don't march on Pittsburgh, prepared for war with the national government, over mere whiskey. As Terry Bouton clarifies, participants (correctly) believed that the Federalist financial revolution rewarded "bankers and war debt speculators" while "punishing ordinary people by limiting currency and credit and enacting new taxes, including an excise tax on distilled spirits."[70] In defying the excise, they articulated concrete demands for economic reform, putting pressure on political leaders to have "Hamilton's entire program rolled back and new policies put in place that limited speculation, taxed the wealthy, and made it easier for ordinary people to acquire the money and credit they needed to run their farms and businesses."[71]

One need only read the pamphlet-sermons of Herman Husband, the self-titled "Philosopher of the Allegheny," and an important figure in the Whiskey Rebellion, to see the falsehood of the charge leveled by federal officials that backcountry rebels were enemies of order, an antigovernment mob. In *Proposals to Amend and Perfect the Policy of the Government of the United States of America* (1782) and *A Sermon to the Bucks and Hinds of America* (1788),[72] Husband puts forward his utopian vision of a rationally managed federal system and agrarian labor democracy where the most power and authority rests in local townships of equal size, and higher levels of representative government work as administrative units to coordinate and oversee the combined interests of towns, districts, counties, states, and (in Husband's plan) regional empires. An enthusiastic proponent of

American manifest destiny, Husband does not question settler-colonial empire but radicalizes equality for white men "by making laws, prohibiting the monopolizing of lands,"[73] stipulating that everybody owns a share of the land (and the country's wealth), and proposing a tax "equal with Property,"[74] among other measures. To Husband, the architects of the despotic and ungodly US Constitution enshrined the power of government to "draw a revenue and lay taxes to the ends of our continent, to the oppression of the people,"[75] leading him to prophecy a political millennium when, "in the last days, the labouring, industrious people, the militia of freemen, shall prevail over the standing armies of kings and tyrants, that only rob them, and live upon their labour, in idleness and luxury."[76] Ideas like these made Husband popular with the Whiskey Rebels, who elected him to negotiate with the federal commission, but unpopular with the Washington administration, which arrested and tried him for sedition (he was ultimately pardoned).[77]

Rewriting the Whiskey Rebellion from the standpoint of its participants, it would be more apropos to call the event the "Tinker's Rebellion" after its symbolic leader "Tom the Tinker," the name deployed by insurgents as a figure of their collective identity and protest. According to Brackenridge, the appellation "Tinker" was a witty pun for *mending a still* – that is, destroying (tinkering with) the distilleries of individuals who complied with the whiskey tax.[78] There's an underlying political statement here, too: the tinkers, as a class of manual laborers, are fixing the problem of taxes themselves, providing a *material solution* to Hamiltonian tyranny by undermining the political machinery's ability to work. Tom the Tinker repairs a broken government. But Tom is also an author and publisher. He posts notices in local newspapers and public spaces warning compliant distillers that he will tinker with their property if they do not join the anti-excise revolution.

Accordingly, in *Modern Chivalry*, Brackenridge introduces Tom the Tinker as a literary character, calling him the "chief of the insurrection, in the western parts of Pennsylvania, in the year 1794,"[79] but the novel does not portray Tom sympathetically. He is a caricatured symbol of populist anarchy that Brackenridge associates with the Irish underclass of the "mad-cap country,"[80] satirized as white savages opposed to law and order. The aforementioned treaty-maker scene already makes explicit the way that Teague O'Regan's Irish brogue qualifies him to masquerade as an American Indian, although it should be noted that Brackenridge also intends to mock ignorant eastern elites who do not recognize the difference between immigrants and Natives, which reflects his double-edged satire leveled against the anti-democratic "tendency to extremes"[81] – both the "aristocrats endeavouring to detrude the people, and the people contending to obtrude themselves."[82] In another scene, Captain Farrago, as an ironized voice of the aristocracy himself, argues that Teague cannot join the American Philosophical Society because he is illiterate, "his language being that spoken by the aborigines of his country,"[83] thus marking him as an Irish indigenous man, a "white Indian." Brackenridge's caricature of the Whiskey Rebellion follows from the same notion. Helping Teague to assimilate into the project of white nationalism, Captain Farrago agrees with George Washington to have his Irish servant appointed a federal excise officer. It's a short-lived job, however. An anti-excise mob tars and feathers Teague, but not before he tries to renounce his post, declaring that he would prefer to join the protestors if only out of ethnic solidarity: "if dere are any Irish boys amongst dem I would rather join wid dem." After the crowd cries, "*Liberty and no excise, liberty and no excise; down with all excise officers*," Teague exclaims, "dey are like de savages, dey have deir eyes upon me, I shall be scalped,"[84] as Brackenridge once again points up the association of rebellious backcountry settlers with hostile Indians, simultaneously poking fun at the contradiction of popular cries for liberty enacted through "savage" violence and the hysterical response of federal officials who can read antitax protest only as a kind of "Indian war." All the same, when Captain Farrago attempts to negotiate with the mob to no avail, the point is clear: if you cannot reason with Indians, neither can you reason with the frenzied rabble.

It turns out that, at the intersection of fiction and reality, literature and life, Brackenridge scripted himself as a Captain Farrago in the flesh during the actual Whiskey Rebellion, which we learn from his quasi-novelistic, highly entertaining account of the event, *Incidents of the Insurrection in the Western Parts of Pennsylvania* (1795).[85] Therein, Brackenridge, in order to refute the popular accusation that he was a friend of the rebellion, congratulates himself for surreptitiously leading Tom the Tinker away from out-and-out violent revolution while also explaining that he was forced to play the role of a pretended ally, to "put on a mask of being with the people"[86] – elsewhere he calls his performance a "burlesque" of "being for Tom the Tinker"[87] – both to avoid becoming the victim of mob violence and to "repair the mischief," to save his community "from error of conduct, and danger of life."[88] He does so first and foremost by employing his literary wit and rhetorical savvy to soften people's anger, and the ongoing war against the United Indian Nations plays a key role in this. For example, at the Mingo Creek church meeting subsequent to the attack on federal tax inspector and wealthy land speculator John Neville, at his home of Bower Hill, Brackenridge humors the rebels with his familiar set piece from *Modern Chivalry*, indulging in "a good deal of pleasantry at the expence of the executive, on the subject of Indian treaties."[89] This includes a mock performance of speeches between General Knox and the Seneca leader Cornplanter, after which Brackenridge queries his audience: "Now, said I, if Indians can have treaties, why cannot we have one two [*sic*]?"[90] While Brackenridge plays this scene off as a comedic diversion, western dissidents did in fact rhetorically and ritually "play Indian" as a means of protest against their treatment by the government, some of them painting themselves "as the warriors amongst the Indians do, when they go to war,"[91] and yet not out of sympathetic identification with the plight of Indigenous peoples but out of invidious resentment toward them. Significantly, when the rebels decide to target Major Isaac Craig as a friend of the excise law, Brackenridge convinces them not to in part because Craig "had the care of the military stores that were sent forward occasionally, and intended for the campaign at that time carrying on against the Indians; that it might derange these operations, and give offence to the people of Kentucky, who were also against the excise law."[92] The war against the United Indian Nations, then, even trumps Tom the Tinker's revolution.

Perhaps the most illuminating piece of literature to emerge from the Whiskey Rebellion that explicitly ties the event to settler-colonial politics is an anonymously authored satire titled "An Indian Treaty," published on August 23, 1794, in the *Pittsburgh Gazette* by printer John Gaston at the behest of Tom the Tinker. Included in *Incidents of the Insurrection*, "An Indian Treaty" consists of four speeches by members of the "Six United Nations of White Indians, settled on the Heads of the Ohio"[93] for negotiations with the federal government, speeches that offensively parody features of Native diplomacy – for instance, a wampum belt "on which is inscribed, 'Plenty of whiskey without excise.'"[94] The first speaker, "Captain Blanket, an Indian chief," holds forth that if the "great council at Philadelphia" wants to negotiate terms with the western counties, then it should follow the "custom" of the government "to pay Indians well for coming to treaties" and work to "satisfy all our demands."[95] If the commissioners refuse to do so, the third speaker, "Captain Alliance," threatens that the "White Indians" might form an alliance with Kentucky, separate from the Union, and seek the support of the British, who would be only too happy to unleash "numerous legions of white and yellow savages"[96] and annihilate "your good old warrior Wayne" so that "your great council might for ever bid adieu to their territory west of the mountains."[97] The second speaker, "Captain Whiskey," bristles that the Washington administration has chosen to raise an army to enforce tax collection instead of deploying the nation's military power to subdue the true western enemies: "It is a pity that this army had not been employed long ago, in assisting your old warrior, general Wayne; or chastising the British about the lakes. However, I presume it is the present policy, to guard against offending a nation with a king at their head. But remember, brothers, if we have not a king at our head, we have that powerful monarch, captain Whiskey, to command us."[98] Do not forget either that the Captain is Irish, has "peopled three-fourths of this western world with his own hand," and will prove capable, with the intrepid "sons of St. Patrick," of defending his "principles and passions – that is, a love of whiskey,"[99] despite inferior numbers. The Ohio Natives have shown it can be done: "It is a common thing for Indians, to fight your best armies at the proportion of one to five; therefore, we would not hesitate a moment to attack this army at the rate of one to ten."[100] But war is not what the "White Indians" want. "Captain Pacificus" concludes the treaty negotiations by offering terms of peace that echo the position of the United Indian Nations in 1792: "if you are the messengers of peace, and come to offer us a treaty, why attempt to deliver it at the point of the bayonet[?]"[101]

All satire aside, "An Indian Treaty" exhibits how backcountry insurgents marked their status as unassimilated citizens of the United States along ethnic lines. Even while identifying as white, they recognize that, in an Anglo-American hierarchy of white races, their communities are considered inferior, lawless, degraded, occupying a "savage" *frontier of whiteness*. However, frustrated by their political marginalization and second-class treatment, backcountry settlers also appeal to a shared white national consciousness that *ought* to be acknowledged by the government, and this is predicated on anti-Indian racism, on the offense of being linked to Native Americans. That is why Hugh Henry Brackenridge, after peace has been restored to western Pennsylvania, encourages his "fellow citizens" to sympathize with the Whiskey Rebels, notwithstanding their excesses and errors, for "they are yourselves; you have them for your compatriots against a common foe; and I will pledge myself, they will not disgrace you in any enterprise it may be necessary to undertake, for the glory of our republic, however daring and hazardous it may be."[102]

By the time Brackenridge publishes the final volume (and entire revised version) of *Modern Chivalry* in 1815, his desire to see western Pennsylvania absorbed into the American mainstream may have come true, but so had his worst fear – that Tom the Tinker might rise to power and the popular rebellion *against* the state would become the popular rebellion *of* the state. Despite joining the Democratic-Republican party, Brackenridge updates *Modern Chivalry* to criticize Thomas Jefferson for choosing (like a veritable Tinker's man) to "break judges, abolish taxes, dismantle navies" and "depress armies,"[103] among other evils. Thank goodness, the recent War of 1812 required renewed investment in the fiscal-military state, for "without an army and a navy, are you safe within or without? Not while you live in a country where there is a *water on one side* and *savages on the other*. John Bull will come by the water, and Tecumseh by the wilderness."[104] That is what the War of 1812 proved. The Madison administration had to build up the US armed forces in order to defeat British neocolonialism at sea and defend American neocolonialism on the frontier, once again meeting the resistance of the latest organization of the United Indian Nations (reduced by Brackenridge to Tecumseh's War). If the army came into existence in 1792 to dispossess the Ohio Natives, the United States finally achieved that aim by 1815, having created a full-fledged peacetime military establishment and completed a forty-year project to consolidate a settler-colonial nation-state. As Alan Taylor states in *The Civil War of 1812*, "Although the Americans lost the northern war to conquer Canada, they won the western war to subdue Indian resistance."[105] Taylor also highlights that it was the War of 1812, not the American Revolution, that produced a more cohesive American nationalism, that, in fact, a "fluid uncertainty" defined the early republic, "precarious" and "embattled," full of divided loyalties, on the brink of sectional dismemberment, still suffering from an Anglo-American identity crisis.[106] The War of 1812 largely changed that. And as Brackenridge predicted, frontier Americans would prove themselves compatriots against a common foe for the glory of the republic. The "passions of patriotism"[107] that arose from the war also found expression in an outpouring of distinctly national US literature, but a transformation occurred in the process. In the popular frontier romance, for example, a genre designed to naturalize, celebrate, and project forward the colonization of Indigenous lands, coding US settler supremacy as alternately heroic or tragically necessary and Indigenous resistance as alternately vanishing or demonic thematically unites otherwise very different works of fiction such as Samuel Woodworth's *The Champions of Freedom* (1816), James Fenimore Cooper's *Last of the Mohicans* (1826), and Robert Montgomery Bird's *Nick of the Woods* (1837). No longer the subject of satire, no longer an ignoble savage, now the backcountry settler-soldier – the "white Indian" – has become the paragon of the American patriot, a new literary hero for the Jacksonian Age.

Notes

1 George Washington, "Farewell Address to the Armies of the United States, *November 2, 1783*," in *George Washington: Writings*, ed. John Rhodehamel (New York: Library of America, 1997), 542–46, here 543.

2 Typically used to refer to modern European empires, especially the British empire of the eighteenth century, a fiscal-military state is one that finances its imperial military operations through taxation, funded debt, and banking and credit institutions. While the early republic may not be considered a fiscal-military state in a strong sense, the Constitution and Federalist policy enshrined the fiscal-military powers – and ambitions – of the state, as Gordon Wood and Max Edling have noted. See Gordon S. Wood, *Empire of Liberty: A History of the Early Republic, 1789–1815* (New York and Oxford: Oxford University Press, 2009), 93–94; Max M. Edling, *A Revolution in Favor of Government: Origins of the U.S. Constitution and the Making of the American State* (New York and Oxford: Oxford University Press, 2003), 220–27, and *A Hercules in the Cradle: War, Money, and the American State, 1783–1867* (Chicago: University of Chicago Press, 2014).

3 George Washington, "Sixth Annual Message to Congress, November 19, 1794," in Rhodehamel, ed., *George Washington: Writings*, 887–95, here 888.

4 Ibid., 893.

5 Ibid., 892.

6 Peter Silver, *Our Savage Neighbors: How Indian War Transformed Early America* (New York: W. W. Norton & Co., 2008), xix–xx.

7 Ed White, *The Backcountry and the City: Colonization and Conflict in Early America* (Minneapolis: University of Minnesota Press, 2005), 121.

8 Matthew Frye Jacobson, *Whiteness of a Different Color: European Immigrants and the Alchemy of Race* (Cambridge, MA: Harvard University Press, 1998), 15–38.

9 Colin G. Calloway, *The Indian World of George Washington: The First President, the First Americans, and the Birth of the Nation* (New York and Oxford: Oxford University Press, 2018), 285.

10 Gina Caison, *Red States: Indigeneity, Settler Colonialism, and Southern Studies* (Athens, GA: University of Georgia Press, 2018), 31.

11 Roxanne Dunbar-Ortiz, *An Indigenous Peoples' History of the United States* (Boston: Beacon Press, 2014); Nick Estes, *Our History Is the Future: Standing Rock versus the Dakota Access Pipeline, and the Long Tradition of Indigenous Resistance* (London and New York: Verso, 2019); Jeffrey Ostler, *Surviving Genocide: Native Nations and the United States from the American Revolution to Bleeding Kansas* (New Haven: Yale University Press, 2019).

12 See Adam Dahl, *Empire of the People: Settler Colonialism and the Foundations of Modern Democratic Thought* (Lawrence: University Press of Kansas, 2018); Dunbar-Ortiz, *An Indigenous Peoples' History*; Walter L. Hixson, *American Settler Colonialism: A History* (New York: Palgrave Macmillan, 2013); Ostler, *Surviving Genocide*.

13 Thomas P. Slaughter, *The Whiskey Rebellion: Frontier Epilogue to the American Revolution* (New York and Oxford: Oxford University Press, 1986).

14 Hugh Henry Brackenridge, *Modern Chivalry*, ed. Ed White (Indianapolis: Hackett, 2009).

15 Silver, *Our Savage Neighbors*, xix–xx, 282–85.

16 Brackenridge, *Modern Chivalry*, 13.

17 *A Poem, on the Rising Glory of America; Being an Exercise Delivered at the Public Commencement at Nassau-Hall, September 25, 1771* (Philadelphia, 1772).

18 Brackenridge, *Modern Chivalry*, 281.

19 Ibid., 331.

20 On Brackenridge's "democratic middle way" and *Modern Chivalry*, see Dana D. Nelson, *Commons Democracy: Reading the Politics of Participation in the Early United States* (New York: Fordham University Press, 2016), 67–83.

21 Brackenridge, *A Poem*, 25

22 Ibid., 15.

23 Ibid., 11.

24 Ibid., 15.

25 Daniel K. Richter, *Facing East from Indian Country: A Native History of Early America* (Cambridge, MA: Harvard University Press, 2001), 168, 184–87, 211–14, 221–25.

26 Hugh Henry Brackenridge, *Narratives of a Late Expedition against the Indians; with an Account of the Barbarous Execution of Col. Crawford; and the Wonderful Escape of Dr. Knight and John Slover from Captivity, in 1782* (1783).

27 For source material on the United Indian Nations, see Lisa Brooks, *The Common Pot: The Recovery of Native Space in the Northeast* (Minneapolis: University of Minnesota Press, 2008); Gregory Evans Dowd, *A Spirited Resistance: The North American Indian Struggle for Unity, 1745–1815* (Baltimore: Johns Hopkins University Press, 1992); John Heckewelder, *A Narrative of the Mission of the United Brethren among the Delaware and Mohegan Indians, from Its Commencement in the Year 1740, to the Close of the Year 1808* (1820); Isabel Thompson Kelsay, *Joseph Brant, 1743–1807: Man of Two Worlds* (Syracuse: Syracuse University Press, 1984); "Speech of the United Indian Nations, at Their Confederate Council, Held Near the Mouth of the Detroit River, the 28th November and 18th December, 1786," *American State Papers: Indian Affairs*, 1, 8–9 (1832); and Richard White, *The Middle Ground: Indians, Empires, and Republics in the Great Lakes Region, 1650–1815, Twentieth Anniversary Edition* (Cambridge, UK: Cambridge University Press, 1991/2011).

28 Ostler, *Surviving Genocide*, 91–104.

29 Brackenridge, *Modern Chivalry*, 34.

30 Ibid., 34.

31 Ibid., 35.

32 Ibid., 35.

33 Ibid., 35.

34 Ibid., 38.

35 Ibid., 38.

36 Ibid., 38.

37 Hugh Henry Brackenridge, *Gazette Publications* (1806), 102.

38 Ibid., 105.

39 Colin Wells, *Poetry Wars: Verse and Politics in the American Revolution and Early Republic* (Philadelphia: University of Pennsylvania Press, 2017).

40 Ibid., 1.

41 An association of poets and professionals centered around Yale College, the first generation of Connecticut (or Hartford) Wits – John Trumbull, Joel Barlow, David Humphreys, and Timothy Dwight – made their name writing highbrow epic and mock epic verse, glorifying the rise of the American republic and satirizing anyone they viewed as that republic's enemy.

42 *The Echo, with Other Poems* (1807), 32.

43 Ibid., 34.

44 Ibid., 35.

45 Ibid., 33.

46 Ostler, *Surviving Genocide*, 104–6; Brooks, *The Common Pot*, 121–24.

47 Hendrick Aupaumut, "A Short Narration of My Last Journey to the Western Country" (1827), ed. Benjamin Coates, in *Memoirs of the Historical Society of Pennsylvania*, vol. 2: 76–131. "Short Narration" was first published (and can be easily accessed) in the 1827 *Memoirs of the Historical Society of Pennsylvania*, vol. 2.

48 See Mark Rifkin, *When Did Indians Become Straight?: Kinship, the History of Sexuality, and Native Sovereignty* (New York and Oxford: Oxford University Press, 2011), 127–37; Brooks, *The Common Pot*, 127–41.

49 Sandra M. Gustafson, "Hendrick Aupaumut and the Cultural Middle Ground," in *Early Native Literacies in New England: A Documentary and Critical Anthology*, ed. Kristina Bross and Hilary E. Wyss (Amherst: University of Massachusetts Press, 2008), 242–50, here 242.

50 Aupaumut, *A Short Narration*, 121.

51 Ibid., 125.

52 Ibid., 128.

53 See Andrew R. L. Cayton, "Radicals in the 'Western World': The Federalist Conquest of Trans-Appalachian North America," in *Federalists Reconsidered*, ed. Doron Ben-Atar and Barbara B. Oberg (Charlottesville: University Press of Virginia, 1998), 77–96; Silver, *Our Savage Neighbors*, 285.

54 See Wells, *Poetry Wars*, 152–65, on the Wits' treatment of race and racism, including his reading of the Brackenridge satire.

55 Silver, *Our Savage Neighbors*, 292.

56 *Echo*, 213.

57 Ibid., 213.

58 See William Hogeland, *Autumn of the Black Snake: George Washington, Mad Anthony Wayne, and the Invasion That Opened the West* (Farrar, Straus and Giroux, 2017).

59 *Echo*, 213–14.

60 Ibid., 231.

61 Brackenridge, *Modern Chivalry*, 176.

62 Brackenridge, *Gazette*, 108.

63 "Timothy Pickering to Rufus King" (June 4, 1785), in *The Life and Correspondence of Rufus King*, vol. 1, ed. Charles R. King (New York: G. P. Putnam's Sons, 1894), 106–7, here 107.

64 Benjamin Franklin, *The Political Thought of Benjamin Franklin*, ed. Ralph L. Ketcham (Indianapolis: Hackett, 2003), 161.

65 George Washington, "To — [Richard]" (1748), in *The Writings of George Washington, vol. 1: 1748–1757*, ed. Worthington Chauncey Ford (New York: G. P. Putnam's Sons, 1889), 7.

66 John Grenier, *The First Way of War: American War Making on the Frontier, 1607–1814* (Cambridge, UK: Cambridge University Press, 2005), 12.

67 White, *The Backcountry*, 112.

68 Brian Phillips Murphy, *Building the Empire State: Political Economy in the Early Republic* (Philadelphia: University of Pennsylvania Press, 2015), 2.

69 Hogeland, *Autumn of the Black Snake*, 67–68. On the working-class roots of the rebellion, see Wythe Holt, "The Whiskey Rebellion of 1794: A Democratic Working-Class Insurrection," paper presented at the Georgia Workshop in Early American History, January 23, 2004.

70 Terry Bouton, "William Findley, David Bradford, and the Pennsylvania Regulation of 1794," in *Revolutionary Founders: Rebels, Radicals, and Reformers in the Making of the Nation*, ed. Alfred F. Young, Gary B. Nash, and Ray Raphael (New York: Alfred A. Knopf, 2011), 233–51.

71 Ibid., 234.

72 [Herman Husband], *Proposals to Amend and Perfect the Policy of the Government of the United States of America* (1782), *A Sermon to the Bucks and Hinds of America* (1788).

73 [Herman Husband], *XIV Sermons on the Characters of Jacob's Fourteen Sons* (1789), 32.

74 Husband, *Proposals*, 22.

75 Husband, *Sermon*, 14.

76 Husband, *XIV Sermons*, 21.

77 On Husband, see Wythe Holt, "The New Jerusalem: Herman Husband's Egalitarian Alternative to the United States Constitution," in *Revolutionary Founders: Rebels, Radicals, and Reformers in the Making of the Nation*, 253–72, and William Hogeland, *The Whiskey Rebellion: George Washington, Alexander Hamilton, and the Frontier Rebels Who Challenged America's Newfound Sovereignty* (Simon & Schuster, 2006).

78 Hugh Henry Brackenridge, *Incidents of the Insurrection in the Western Parts of Pennsylvania, in the Year 1794* (1795), I: 79.

79 Brackenridge. *Modern Chivalry*, 292.

80 Ibid., 371.

81 Ibid., 297.

82 Ibid., 12.

83 Ibid., 15.

84 Ibid., 213.

85 Brackenridge, *Incidents.*
86 Ibid., I: 46.
87 Ibid., I: 82.
88 Ibid., I: 115.
89 Ibid., I: 34.
90 Ibid., I: 34.
91 Ibid., I: 54.
92 Ibid., I: 61.
93 Ibid., II: 6.
94 Ibid., II: 8.
95 Ibid., II: 6.
96 In context, the author appears to use "yellow" as a racial marker for Indigenous people.
97 Brackenridge, *Incidents*, II: 8.
98 Ibid., II: 7.
99 Ibid., II: 7.
100 Ibid., II: 7.
101 Ibid., II: 8.
102 Ibid., II: 84.
103 Brackenridge, *Modern Chivalry*, 423.
104 Ibid., 518.
105 Alan Taylor, *The Civil War of 1812: American Citizens, British Subjects, Irish Rebels, & Indian Allies* (New York: Alfred A. Knopf, 2010), 428.
106 Ibid., 8.
107 Nicole Eustace, *1812: War and the Passions of Patriotism* (New York: University of Pennsylvania Press, 2012).

CHAPTER 10

"This Politick Salvage"
Defining an Early Native American Literary Aesthetics

Drew Lopenzina

A good mind working well will always choose peace.

—Paul Williams

Sometime in the winter of 1607/1608 the English settler and soldier of fortune John Smith engaged in a prolonged dialogue with Wahunsunacook (known to most of us today as Powhatan), leader of the Powhatan Confederacy and father to Pocahontas. Their conversation covered many topics, ranging from land, corn, trade, and war to, perhaps surprisingly, notions of kinship. Although their acquaintance with one another up to this point was brief, the idea of "kinship" manifested itself in the fact that both had already adopted diplomatic protocols in which Powhatan was referred to as "father" and Smith regarded as a "sonne." When Powhatan reminded him of these protocols, as related in Smith's 1624 *Generall Historie of Virginia and the Summer Isles*, Smith replied, "I call you father indeed, and as a father you shall see I will love you," but, he felt compelled to add, "the small care you have of such a childe caused ... me to looke to my selfe."[1] The implication was that the agreed-on terms of diplomatic kinship had failed to foster in Smith an increased sense of trust or intimacy. Sensing some kind of devious design behind Powhatan's offers of peaceful accord, Smith was inclined to take an ever more aggressive stance, hoping to expose the true intent of "this politick salvage."[2]

The exchange is fascinating, as much for what it reveals concerning Smith's fraught attempts to negotiate a position of strength from weakness as for what it suggests about indigenous diplomacy in the seventeenth century and, for our purposes here, how such traditions extend into the nineteenth century and, indeed, to present times. When Smith refers to Wahunsunacook as "this politick salvage," it is not meant as a compliment. Smith was highly motivated to denigrate the "politick" side of Powhatan culture and to emphasize the "salvage." As literary historian Rachel Bryant observes, "Smith actively obscured Powhatan diplomatic activity and political agency" placing in its stead "an early drama of English exceptionalism" that has since been "internalized by generations of settlers desperate to view themselves and their societies as the rightful and natural inheritors" of North America.[3] Still, the phrase "politick salvage" registers something of the collective surprise and frustration English colonists experienced on realizing that Natives of Tsenacomaca (what we today call southeastern Virginia) would not simply bend to settler colonial will, but rather were clever and pointed negotiators whose diplomatic goals proved more layered and complex than any had anticipated.

And herein I locate an opening into what might seem the rather opaque task of defining an early indigenous literary aesthetic. This essay proposes to take seriously the "politick" side of Smith's offered binary and to suggest, in fact, that politics, diplomacy, and a desire for peace were defining markers of indigenous cultural and literary engagements. Indigenous peoples in the period of colonization were as capable of, and prepared for, violent encounter as humans have ever been in all places and times. The specific effect of colonial reporting, however, is always to reduce indigenous nature to just such a narrow set of cultural responses, meant to justify and ameliorate acts of settler violence intended either to destroy or to remove indigenous presence on the land. The archival record, imprinted in the service of settler colonialism, has operated in such a way as to make this history of violence seem inevitable. European settlers arriving on this continent with an eye toward possessing it wrote off Native peoples as unqualified stakeholders. History has done them the favor of endlessly echoing that claim.

As Alyssa Mt. Pleasant, Caroline Wigginton, and Kelly Wisecup have recently noted, many scholars have yet to fully grapple with "the consequences of uncritically reproducing methodologies grounded in colonial perspectives." Scholars necessarily rely "on materials in archives created by and for colonists," thereby "transmitting the biases and assumptions encoded in colonists' language and worldviews."[4] The abovementioned scholars call for a more active engagement with indigenous materials and cultural frameworks to counter such biases – an interpretive methodology I fully embrace here. A mindful reading of the colonial archive, however, can nevertheless yield aspects of Indigenous tradition of which settler reporters were themselves unaware. I contend that these traditions not only can be teased out from the colonial record, but, when taken together, they begin to inform the outlines of an indigenous literary aesthetic. The colonial archive, almost in spite of itself, turns up repeated instances of indigenous overtures of peace, presented in traditional frameworks, that can be effectively traced in recognizable patterns from the earliest recorded encounters of the colonial period through to the first major indigenous literary productions of the late eighteenth and early nineteenth centuries. When indigenous authors such as Samson Occom and William Apess begin appearing in print they carried forward these traditions, confounding colonial notions of what it means to be a "politick salvage."

The record of colonial exploits in North America has in common a set of ready signifiers meant to cast indigenous peoples in the most dehumanizing light. The term "savage," in particular, was not simply a marker of inferiority, but was meant to situate Native peoples among the brute animals of the fields and forests. A "savage" people were thought to exist outside the restraints of community, law, order, religion, and culture. Lacking the refinement of European writing, a "savage" people were presumed to have no literature to preserve, no history to recall, no word of God to pass forward from one generation to the next. Edward Johnson, a chronicler of the Puritan's early settlement in Massachusetts, offers a perfect encapsulation of this trope when he writes in his 1653 *Wonder-Working Providence* that, "as for any religious observation, they [the Natives of New England] were the most destitute of any people yet heard of."[5] In Johnson's estimation, any English soul wishing to settle New England must expect to "be Landed among barbarous Indians famous for nothing but cruelty" and, furthermore, encounter a "Wildernesse" described in various instances as "vast,"[6] "desart,"[7] "howling," and "untilled."[8] Such claims were readily translated into the productions of white nineteenth-century historians, as was the case with the famous politician and orator Daniel Webster, who noted at an event celebrating the 200th anniversary of the Plymouth landing that, prior to settler occupation, "the whole soil was unreclaimed from barbarism."[9]

This language continues to shape settler characterizations of both indigenous peoples and the land itself, so that even thriving communities replete with villages, temples, trade, agriculture, and bustling human activity can be cognitively erased for future generations by the simple deployment of the word "wilderness." It didn't matter that every colonial reporter, at some point or other, would also feel compelled to gape in wonder at the actual productivity of indigenous agricultural practices. In practically the same breath that Johnson calls New England a "desart," he observes the practice of the local Natives who place "alewives" or small herring "under their Indian Corne, which they plant in Hills five foote asunder, and assuredly when the Lord created this Corne, hee had a speciall eye to supply these his peoples' wants with it, for ordinarily five or six grains doth produce six hundred" (114). The *fertile desert*, it turns out, is the agricultural equivalent of the "politick salvage." Such brief acknowledgments of indigenous civilization, however, are quickly made to vanish, replaced by a language of brute waste. Indigenous presence on the land was conceived as *vacuum domicilium* – empty space, devoid of value until occupied, colonized, and, in the eyes of the settler state, improved on and commoditized. Within this illusory framework, Native civilization was ranked lower even than natural features of the landscape such as trees, "goodly meadows," and other mineral resources so coveted by the colonizing regime.[10]

The illusion, however, proved difficult to maintain, and nearly every author of the colonial era wrestled at some time or other with this confused settler syntax. Having thoroughly internalized its narrative structure, chroniclers of the period were often compelled to strain beyond its parameters to justify events and outcomes failing to conform to their rhetorical models. As Johnson notes of a 1637 diplomatic council with the Narragansett, "it was matter of much wonderment to the English, to see how solidly and wisely these savage people did consider of the weighty undertaking of a war." The sachem Canonicus, surrounded by his "nobility," impressed the English with the gravity of his speech as he cautioned them concerning the tragic "effects of war," which sometimes might prove "sad and mournfull for the victors themselves."[11] Smith, too, in the presence of Wahunsunacook, noted how the Powhatan leader sat in state "upon a Throne ... with such a Majestie as I cannot expresse, [nor] yet have often seene, wither in Pagan or Christian." As Smith relates, "with a kind countenance hee bad me welcome." Gifts were exchanged and a "great oration" was made "by three of his Nobles, if there be any amongst Salvages."[12]

The impressions conveyed in such passages perfectly capture the tension of colonial reporting. Johnson is compelled to admire the peaceful overtures of a people whose very humanity he has repeatedly denigrated in the most appalling terms. And Smith is forced to recognize the impressive qualities of his indigenous rivals while still laboring to maintain their delegitimized status. If "noble" attributes present themselves in his "salvage" hosts, Smith must drape the title in irony, effectively retracting it even as he acknowledges its presence. I refer to this effect of colonial reporting, and the cognitive dissonance it forwards, as *unwitnessing*, a rhetorical mode in which the very thing being commented on for some pragmatic purpose of exposition must then be repeatedly and forcefully retracted to serve prevailing colonial ideologies of conquest.[13] This reflexive strategy troubles all of Smith's interactions with Wahunsunacook, whose "politick" nature cannot help but appear as an oxymoron given the persistent presumption that "salvages" are not supposed to be political. Smith's encounter with Wahunsunacook proved so significant for him, in fact, that between 1608 and 1624 he penned three separate versions of it, each time offering a more expanded transcript of the dialogue in question as if still struggling to properly situate the exchange.[14] In each version, Smith conveys something of the ceremony and order with which the Powhatans conducted themselves in diplomacy, including the kinship relation of son to father that he bears with Wahunsunacook. At one point, Smith even makes it clear that Wahunsunacook has ceremonially adopted him into the confederacy, stating that Powhatan would "for ever esteeme him [Smith] as his sonne Nantaquoud."[15]

It is not surprising that Wahunsunacook was determined to remind Smith of the kinship relations he had taken pains to establish during Smith's famous captivity and subsequent "rescue" by Pocahontas only a few weeks earlier. Up until this point the various tribes of the Powhatan Confederacy had been cautiously open to trading for beads, trinkets, cloth, and other items the English had brought with them. More than once, however, Smith resorted to a display of firearms and, as often as not, outright violence, to supply the new colony's wants. From a Powhatan perspective, parties who have established ties of kinship did not threaten one another or meet in council fully armed as Smith insisted on doing. Wahunsunacook observes, "What will it availe you to take that by force you may quickly have by love, or to destroy them that provide you food."[16] He decrees that rather than think of the English as strangers, they should all be regarded as one "and that the Corne, weomen and Country, should be to us as to his owne people."[17]

Bryant notes that "instead of eradicating the English ... the Powhatans decided that they would teach the English how to belong – how to participate and thrive within the established networks that comprised Tsenacomoca."[18] This was in keeping with indigenous frameworks of diplomacy that predate European colonization. Abenaki historian Lisa Brooks emphasizes this dynamic in her recent history of King Philip's War, *Our Beloved Kin*. In relation to Native peoples of the Northeast, she observes that "in this world, one could not inhabit a place without belonging to a particular family." To enter into Native space meant "to enter into its network of people, diplomatic practices, and reciprocal relations."[19] Such networks, referred to by many indigenous critics today as "kinship networks," transcended immediate familial bonds to form a more comprehensive metaphorical set of relations between peoples sharing space. The Dakota ethnographer and novelist Ella Deloria emphasized the centrality of kinship in her 1944 study, *Speaking of Indians*, stating that beyond all other personal objectives or claims,

> one must obey kinship rules; one must be a good relative. No Dakota who has participated in that life will dispute that ... without that aim and the constant struggle to attain it, the people would no longer be Dakotas in truth. They would no longer even be human.... [T]o be civilized was to keep the rules imposed by kinship for achieving civility, good manners, and a sense of responsibility toward every individual dealt with. Thus only was it possible to live communally with success.[20]

Understanding these bonds of civility, and the diplomatic protocols by which they were held in place, is essential to understanding indigenous community and the ways indigenous peoples would work to represent that community in later writings. This indigenous land was no wilderness, as the Europeans defined it, but instead a sustaining space that nourished the countless villages and communities inhabiting it. As Brooks notes, this space was often referred to in the diplomatic speeches of indigenous orators as "the common pot," or the bowl from which everyone sharing that space must eat.[21]

Wahunsunacook's words (however imperfectly translated) reflect the values of the common pot. Smith, however, did not soften to such appeals of hospitality, but rather perceived them as a transparently laid trap. He blustered that it was English custom to "weare our armes as our apparel [and] as for the danger of our enemies, in such warres consist our chiefest pleasure."[22] Bryant has usefully referred to Smith's response in this moment as "kinshipwrecking," or "a conventional mode of storytelling that moves to destroy and supplant traditional indigenous kinship structures and obligations."[23] Settlers like Smith not only rejected offers of kinship, but actively worked to disrupt the existing kinship networks holding indigenous communities together. Cherokee scholar Daniel Heath Justice echoes this sentiment precisely when he asserts that kinship "was *specifically* targeted by colonial authorities in their efforts to destroy Indigenous communities; indeed kinship was the primary target."[24]

Although Smith designed his encounter in print to elevate his own standing as a colonial powerbroker, inadvertently or not, he offers readers a glimpse into forms of eastern indigenous diplomacy as well as into the mind of Wahunsunacook, who almost certainly comes across, with some 400 years of hindsight, as the more prudent and skilled negotiator of the two. For Smith, the words "politick" and "subtill" are synonyms for "treacherous." He would have us believe that to take the Powhatan chief at his word would be a death sentence for he and his men. But our historical remove affords us perspective to reconsider Smith's hard-line stance (he would not be the first historical leader to tragically misread an overture of peace).

What if we peeled away all the layers of colonial rhetoric surrounding not just this one exchange, but the entire settler colonial enterprise, stripping the word "politick" of its implied irony and erasing the misnomer of "wilderness" when describing indigenous space? Although it may be difficult to decolonize our own collective thinking on such matters, I operate from the assumption that such interactions did not take place in dark, primeval forests, but rather in cleared village spaces. I do not assume that Native leaders were fixated on laying deadly traps, but rather that they were skilled at diplomatic encounters, and in many if not most cases, exceeded Europeans in their attempts to seek peaceful resolution. Mattaponi historians, directly descended from the Powhatan Confederacy, affirm this in their oral history, which relates that the "cultural foundations of Powhatan society included respect for life, seeking the good of the tribe, and appeasing evil ... It involves attempting to strike a balance between submitting to unwanted demands and preventing the loss of life."[25] As Bryant and others have argued, Wahunsunacook received Smith in a posture of peace, using the opportunity of Smith's short captivity to enact diplomatic protocols designed to restore balance to a potentially volatile situation.[26] In fact, directly following the dialogic encounter related above, Smith and his men were approached by an "ancient Oratour" who presented Smith with "a great bracelet and a chaine of pearle" accompanied by a ceremonial speech that Smith failed to understand but which, in all likelihood, was meant to seal the diplomatic agreements established in the preceding council. Smith constantly attempts to denigrate the Powhatan leader's intentions, telling us he is a "subtill Savage" who merely "trifled the time to cut his [Smith's] throat," but Smith cannot fully shed the account of its "politick" qualities or the ceremonial structure of Wahunsunacook's council.[27] The series of cognitive disconnects become a rupture disturbing the very integrity of Smith's account, as he deals with people who are in every way his equal but labors, beyond his own eyewitness, to render them rhetorically inferior. At any point, the Powhatan people might have used overwhelming force to exterminate the Jamestown settlers or at least make it too difficult for them to remain in Native space. Instead, however, they deliberately chose a peaceful tack.

So permit me to say it again. "*Salvages*" are not *supposed* to be "*politick.*" Aristotle, in his *Politics*, attempts to give definition to the term, observing that "He who is without a state is either above humanity or a beast, so that he is contemptuously denounced by Homer as 'the tribeless, lawless, homeless one'; for he is so by nature, craving war like one who is not restrained by any yoke."[28] Settler colonialism projected such definitions on the indigenous peoples they encountered – although it requires feats of mental gymnastics for contemporary readers to ignore the hypocrisy inherent in such rhetorical stances. Nevertheless, the politics of settler colonialism were such that Native identity had to endure a complete systemic devaluation. The belief was routinely entertained that Natives worshipped the devil, practiced child sacrifice, and cannibalized one another, notwithstanding evidence for such claims was largely anecdotal or subject to gross misinterpretation.[29] The language and signifiers brought into the service of denigrating Native peoples allowed settler-colonial intruders and their heirs to, in fact, *unwitness* the complexity of indigenous civil structures and rhetorically dismantle their diplomatic outreaches, to the extent that when a Native person was caught engaging in politics, the act itself came to be perceived as an anomaly and to the detriment of his race. As Henry David Thoreau lamented on a trip to the Penobscot Indian village at Old Town, Maine, in 1846, although "a row of wigwams, with a dance of powwows, and a prisoner tortured at the stake, would be more respectable," nevertheless "Politics is all the rage with them now."[30]

It remains difficult for many today to register sustained indigenous presence – to apprehend the parameters of indigenous civilization, past or present, or locate within anything of true political substance. The indigenous form lies etched before the American public like the chalk outline of a murder victim on a TV police procedural. There is some sense that a crime has been committed, but the body has long been removed and only the outline remains – a sidewalk petroglyph of some vanished race. Nevertheless, the intricacies of indigenous diplomacy, particularly in the Northeast, are alluded to in countless historical documents recorded by settler-colonial witnesses as well as in records produced by Natives themselves. What they demonstrate is not a puerile or disinterested detachment from colonial affairs, but a fully fleshed, actively engaged body politic seeking a path to balanced coexistence in a time of great violence and upheaval.

Most scholars of indigenous studies today have embraced the words of Osage author Robert Warrior, who argues that Native peoples should focus on their own intellectual traditions, understanding that within such frameworks of belief, exchange, and resistance are critical lessons that, for too long, have failed to find "a voice in Native political processes."[31] One of the most well-documented examples of Native political engagement in the colonial era can be apprehended in the practice of wampum exchange, a tradition shared by many indigenous groups of the Northeast. Wampum consists of white and purple beads, typically fashioned from the shells of the quahog and whelk, which are woven together in strings or as belts with rich tapestried designs. Wampum is central to a number of ceremonial functions that, according to anthropologist Frank Speck, included its use as a mnemonic document "to be kept in the council house ... and read over again each recurring meeting to refresh the memories of the delegates."[32] More than just records of an agreement, however, wampum serves the ceremonial function of clearing a path for sound diplomacy, creating a space where parties in conflict might put aside their grievances and hear one another's entreaties without emotional obstruction. Abenaki anthropologist Margaret Bruchac states that wampum belts comprised "conceptual beliefs embodied in material substances, diplomatic understandings woven into tangible form, and human relationships facilitated by objects as ritual partners."[33]

The Haudenosaunee trace their own political organization as a nation to the story of how wampum was created, telling how the grieving Hiawatha, having lost his daughters to mindless warfare, was consoled at the hands of the enigmatic "Peacemaker" who used strings of wampum to wipe away Hiawatha's tears. In league with one another, Hiawatha and the Peacemaker would use the protocols enacted in their first meeting to bring peace to the warring tribes and bond them together in lasting union under the Great Law of Peace.[34] In keeping with this tradition, wampum was necessarily present at any major agreement or treaty between the colonists and Native peoples of the Northeast, even when the colonists themselves were quite unaware of the function it served. Quite possibly, Smith himself unwittingly participated in such a ceremony when in 1608, as earlier mentioned, he was greeted by an "ancient Oratour" presenting him "a great bracelet and a chaine of pearle." But the ceremonial gesture is subsequently *unwitnessed* as the diplomatic intricacies of the exchange either fail to register or are outright ignored by colonial reporters.

The protocols of indigenous diplomacy eventually became threaded into Native literary endeavors in the wake of settler colonialism. Even as power relations and modes of expression were rapidly shifting, Native peoples insisted on keeping their traditions in circulation. Brooks observes how "transformations occurred when European systems entered Native space. Birchbark messages became letters and petitions, wampum records became treaties, and journey pictographs became written journals."[35] Native people did not abandon their forms of representation and diplomacy through the onslaught of settler colonialism so much as they transitioned them, out of necessity, into newer literary frameworks.

This can be seen in the 1744 Treaty of Lancaster, when the Seneca orator Canassatego metaphorically mapped out this literary migration. Observing how, on first arriving at this land, the English "Governor" desired "to become one People with us," but saw that "the Rope which tied [their] ship to the great Mountain was only fastened with Wampum, which was liable to break and rot . . . he therefore told us he would give us a Silver Chain, which would be much stronger and last forever." The English then supplied the Seneca with "Hatchets and Guns, and other Things necessary for the Support of Life." But after repeated breaches of trust, Canassatego was quick to remind that the Natives had no need of European goods or customs and had lived as well or better, in fact, before the English ever came among them. As for now, he continued, "we are straitened, and sometimes in want of Deer, and liable to many other Inconveniences . . . and particularly from that Pen-and-Ink Work that is going on at that Table." Canassatego concluded his speech by reminding the colonial authorities of past treaties. He noted that the nations of the Haudenosaunee Longhouse were still "willing to treat with you . . . in confirmation of which we present you this belt of wampum."[36] The speech, like Powhatan's exchange with John Smith, covers land, trade, war, and kinship. But it also explicitly points to the ways that western literacy, or "pen and ink work," has intruded on traditional forms of diplomacy while simultaneously reinforcing wampum exchange, in the end, as the more trustworthy marker of agreement.

Settlers, too, found themselves weaving the protocols of wampum exchange, both witnessed and unwitnessed, into their written relations as they were forced to adapt to these diplomatic frameworks. Roughly a decade after the Treaty of Lancaster, in 1754, a twenty-two-year-old George Washington, looking to establish himself in the eyes of the British colonial gentry in Virginia, traveled into the Ohio River Valley, ostensibly to deliver a letter to the French commandant stationed at the newly constructed fort at the headwaters of the Ohio. But Washington was also sent to reinforce diplomatic ties with the loose confederation of Native peoples who either traditionally occupied this space or had been forced there by recent colonial upheavals. Both the British and the French claimed title to the Ohio Valley, the French falling on the doctrine of discovery as a means of legitimizing their ownership and the English claiming to have purchased the land (essentially everything west of Virginia) from the Six Nations of the Haudenosaunee in the aforementioned Lancaster Treaty.[37] But the indigenous peoples of this space had different ideas, hoping to keep these large forces of colonial empire at bay by forwarding notions of shared space.

The Seneca orator Tanaghrisson, most commonly referred to by historians as the "Half King," explained this position to Major Washington, working within the ceremonial protocols involved in wampum exchange. Reciting for Washington a speech he had recently delivered to the French commandant, he explained how the French had, "in former days, set a Silver Bason before us, wherein there was the Leg of a Beaver, and desir'd of all Nations to come and eat of it." By relating this speech, Tanaghrisson was recalling the treaty first struck with the French at Montreal nearly 150 years earlier. But he was also offering a reminder to both French and British authorities that, at least according to Haudenosaunee protocols, the land was a "silver bason" or common pot and they had all agreed to eat from it. Washington, particularly at this point in his career, would have had no conception of the "common pot" as a diplomatic metaphor, and yet it finds its way into his account as he attempts to faithfully record his transactions.

Stressing the kinship relations established between all parties, Tanaghrisson continues,

> I desire you may hear me in Civilness.... Both you [the French] and the English are white, we [meaning the Natives] live in a Country between; therefore the Land belongs to neither one nor t'other: But the Great Being above allow'd it to be a Place of Residence for us; so fathers I desire you to withdraw ... for I will keep you at Arms length: I lay this down as a Trial for both, to see which will have the greatest Regard to it, and that Side we will stand by, and make equal Sharers with us.[38]

Although Washington expressed little regard for the Native peoples with whom he was forced to negotiate throughout his life, in this context he was compelled to adopt the protocols of the eastern woodland tribes, exchanging strings of wampum and adhering to their ceremonial kinship structure rather than enforcing European protocols. As Tanaghrisson pointedly stated, the colonial powers were never given invitation to occupy the lands of the Ohio Valley. Their presence was tolerated as "equal sharers," but Tanaghrisson, employing the language of kinship, also reminds Washington, "Brother, as you have asked my Advice, I hope you will be ruled by it."[39]

In the long run, of course, Washington had no intention of adhering to the ideals of the shared space embodied in the metaphor of the common pot. As noted by historian Colin Calloway, his plans for "Indians' lands . . . would require their absence not their presence,"⁴⁰ and by 1779 Washington, as general of the Continental Armies, would duplicate the "kinshipwrecking" strategies of John Smith, ordering a series of invasions into Iroquois lands designed as scorched-earth campaigns intended to destroy cornfields, flatten villages, and sow terror among civilians. For his efforts, he earned the name of Conotocarious, or "Town Destroyer."⁴¹ Calloway observes how, on entering Native country as a young man, Washington "addressed Indians as brothers," having "learned and practiced the essentials of Indian diplomacy." As president, however, "he addressed them as children and mandated policy for them."⁴²

By the latter half of the eighteenth century, Native peoples had become more and more immersed in the protocols of European writing, but their textual productions continued to carry forward distinct discursive traditions that had informed earlier interactions with colonists. In 1764, a decade following George Washington's meeting with Tanaghrisson, the Mohegan preacher Samson Occom began his public career as an author by writing petitions for his tribe. Occom, an ordained Presbyterian minister, achieved a modest level of fame in the latter half of the eighteenth century for his sermons, a 1774 book of hymns, and for being a highly visible cultural contradiction – a writing, preaching, "politick salvage." Occom's career as a successful indigenous cultural broker in the world of colonial affairs stands out for its sustained engagement with literacy over a fifty-year period. It commenced when he first put pen to paper to keep a journal in December 1743 and extended to his last known correspondence in the year of his death in 1792. His life marks a transition point where Native peoples of the Northeast began seeking out pathways to represent themselves in the colonial archive, rather than being predominantly represented by others. In his 1768 autobiographical narrative Occom declared that he "was Born a Heathen and Brought up In Heathenism," but like many other indigenous individuals in the Northeast, Occom was trained in western literacy practices at a young age with the precise expectation that he would use those skills to convert other so-called heathens to Christianity.⁴³ Rather than becoming a simple proselytizer of settler-colonial values, however, Occom used his expertise, as well as the authority conferred on him by his title of ordained minister, to advocate for the people in his indigenous community.

The Mohegans, by this time, had long been subject to colonial authority, so that the metaphorical terms of kinship were effectively reversed and

Mohegans, too, now cast themselves as "helpless Children" beseeching a "tender parent." Despite this diminished status, however, Mohegans continued to maintain traditional markers of identity, requesting in their 1764 petition to Sir William Johnson that they be able to approach their colonial fathers "and make our Cries in your Ears."[44] Occom not only spoke perfect English, but was practiced in Latin and Greek (as well as fluent in Mohegan) and was more than capable of framing his letter in a standard colonial idiom. And yet, particularly when speaking in the voice of his tribe, he adhered to oral traditions of indigenous address and diplomacy that emphasized the visceral exchange of the appeal – the "cry" traveling from the mouth of the speaker to the ear of the listener.

The 1764 petition was an attempt by Mohegans to reassert tribal sovereignty by bypassing the white Overseers or "Guardians" assigned to their tribe and appealing directly to Johnson, who served as Superintendent of Indian Affairs for British North America. Their specific complaint was that the Overseers had appointed a new sachem, Ben Uncas III, against the wishes of the greater part of the tribe. As Occom pointed out in the petition, the tribe had "a Law and a Custom" to appoint their own sachems "Without the help of any People or Nation in the World, and When he makes himself unworthy of his Station we put him down – ourselves." The petition asserted the tribe's sovereign right to select its own leadership, refusing to cede such authority to the Connecticut colony or anyone else.[45] Informing their complaint was the belief that Ben Uncas was acting as a cipher for the colonial Overseers. Uncas had leveraged this power to enable English neighbors to harvest timber from Mohegan lands and make use of other tribal resources without, in any way, compensating the rest of the tribe. The Overseers themselves were positioned to profit from such machinations and rarely missed an opportunity to arrange circumstances accordingly. As Occom explained in the petition, "they want to root us out of our land, root & Branch, [and] they have already Proceeded with arbitrary power over us."[46]

Such corrupt practices by Overseers against tribal entities were ubiquitous throughout the Northeast and necessitated that "politics," in the words of Thoreau, become "all the rage" for Natives of New England. The conditions of settler colonialism were literally stealing food from Native mouths, and what was needed was an indigenous-centered politics that could operate effectively in settler spheres of influence to combat these developments. Sir William Johnson was perceived as a sympathetic dealer by many Natives. He had as his consort Molly Brant, a powerful woman of the Mohawk tribe, with whom he had several children by which he established true kinship ties with the Haudenosaunee. Occom had met with Johnson personally a few years earlier, and Johnson helped facilitate a friendship between the Mohegans and the Oneidas that was sealed by a belt of wampum. The Mohegan petition to Johnson, as penned by Occom, was meant to be a reminder that Mohegan customs of shared space and apportionment of tribal resources demanded that any income gained from Mohegan lands "ought to go to the benefit of the Whole Tribe."[47] These were the express values of sharing space in the common pot, and they were reiterated even more firmly in a Mohegan Declaration dated April 28, 1778, also written in Occom's hand, declaring that "we Shall look upon one another as one Family, and Will Call or look upon no one as a Stranger, but Will take one another as pure and True Mohegans; and so at this Time, we unanimously agreed that the Money does belong to the Whole Tribe, and it shall be dispos'd of accordingly for the Benefit of the Whole."[48]

Occom not only labored throughout his career to advocate for his tribe, but he worked within the channels of Christian faith to find a new hybrid path for indigenous survivance in the Northeast. His success at negotiating a discourse of indigenous sovereignty was not something he mastered simply through a formal education in western letters, but rather was absorbed from the traditional aspects of Mohegan discourse and belief he embodied when writing petitions and acting as the voice of the tribe. Occom was able to further these literary forms of expression through his outreach to other tribes, engaging in wampum diplomacy with the Oneida and others. His literary aesthetic is consistently informed by these goals and practices, and by the mid-1770s he was actively engaged in seeking out a new home space for the Christian Natives of New England, so they might get out from under the oppressive colonial yoke that sought to manipulate their system of government for settler gain. These efforts resulted in the 1785 founding of a new settlement for his people, called Brotherton, on Oneida territory in present-day New York State. As Brooks concludes of Occom, his

> strategy was to strengthen relationships within the larger coastal network and to reconstruct a new dish from among the surviving wampum-making nations, a village that could be moved along the waterways to a place with more abundant resources, away from colonial control. All of the people involved in the project were committed to the principles of Christianity that Occom had embraced as a young man, as well as to the ideals of the common pot.[49]

These ideals deeply inform Occom's written oeuvre and are manifest in the networks of kinship he worked to establish and maintain throughout Native space in the Northeast.

In her book *Literary Indians*, Angela Calcaterra argues that "Despite the political, social, and economic pressures of Euro-American colonialism, Native communities retained and evolved their aesthetic conventions in ways that contributed to power and resistance."[50] The literary ethos that developed out of this is one, perhaps, best described by Cherokee scholar Jace Weaver as "communitism," or a "proactive commitment to Native community" that participates "in the healing of the grief and sense of exile" Native peoples have experienced in the wake of settler-colonial violence.[51] Occom, in his life and career, was an influential voice for the ideals of communitism, but perhaps no figure of this period gave literary expression to that ethos as forcefully as William Apess, and it is in his writings where we see a Native literary aesthetic truly begin to cohere around the orbiting particles of tradition and ritual defining earlier diplomatic encounters and exchanges.

Apess, a Pequot author, activist, and minister who became a public figure in the 1830s with the publication of his memoir *A Son of the Forest*, was in every way the intellectual successor of Occom. Unlike Wahunsunacook, Canassatego, Tanaghrisson, or Occom even, Apess was not raised in a setting where he was surrounded by his own people or immersed in their traditions. Bonded out at the age of four to work for a white family in Colchester, Connecticut, Apess had only limited contact with the already fragile kinship networks through which Pequot tradition and identity were maintained. His mother was born an enslaved woman and was still legally in bondage at the time of Apess's birth in 1798. His father was forced to travel from town to town to seek employment and, due to the terms of Apess's indenture, was made to turn his son away whenever the young Apess came running to him seeking familial comfort or safety.[52] In fact, Apess's very situation as a bond servant, so typical of Native children of the Northeast in this era, was exemplary of the systemic manner in which "kinshipwrecking" had embedded itself in the very fabric of settler colonial oppression. The economic straits in which Apess's community was kept ensured that Native children were raised in isolation from their families, further fraying the bonds of generations through which indigenous identity had carried forward despite war, disease, displacement, and severe economic deprivation. Such practices would reach large-scale continental fulfillment later in the century with the establishment of Indian Boarding Schools specifically designed to separate children from their kinship networks and deprive them of the markers of culture and tradition at the foundation of indigenous identity.

For Apess, however, these circumstances, aided by his own Native genius, became the catalyst for his eventual politicization, launching him on a career of indigenous advocacy that would span two decades. His first full comprehension of kinship as an expression of indigeneity seemed to have come to him, almost as an epiphany, as he was wandering through the region of the Bay of Quinte in Ontario after having served with US troops on the Canadian border during the War of 1812. Falling in for a short time with the Tyendinaga Mohawk, Apess found himself embraced by the cohesiveness and healing power of the sovereign indigenous community still thriving there. He was suddenly at the center of a spiritual and political world he had not previously realized existed and, from that position of empowerment, "could not but admire the wisdom of God in the order, regularity, and beauty of creation." The experience seems to have awakened in Apess a new sense of possibility for his own New England tribe as he looked to the forest, finding it "alive with its sons and daughters." Far from beholding a hive of savage discord, Apess discovered harmony and order among the Tyendinaga – a community bonded by kinship that looked after and supported one another in keeping with the values of the common pot. As he noted, "there appeared to be the utmost regularity in their encampment and they held all things in common."[53]

Apess, still only in his late teens when he finally returned home to Colchester, Connecticut, exhibited a rare drive to want to rise above the marginalized condition culturally mapped out for his people by settler-colonial structures of dominance. He improved on his brief formal education, teaching himself to read and write and, with the help of his Aunt Sally George, become familiarized with the traditions of spiritual leadership practiced in his Pequot community. This would ultimately embolden him to seek out his ordination in the Methodist organization – a ten-year journey in which he managed to somehow circumvent or overcome the considerable obstacles thrown in his path due to his Native identity. In 1829, after first being turned down for ordination by the Methodist Episcopal Church, he wrote, "Look, brethren, at the natives of the forest – they come, notwithstanding you call them 'savage.'"[54] As with many of his generation, Apess felt that taking on the mantle of Christianity was a path of economic and even cultural empowerment for indigenous people. He would not be denied the Christian pulpit and received his ordination with the Protestant Methodists in 1831 even as, through his outreach to other

Native communities, he began more and more to internalize the protocols of indigenous diplomacy. As in the writings of Occom, of which Apess was surely aware, Christian discourse merged with the values of the common pot to create a space of agency and advocacy for New England Natives.

By 1833 Apess found himself among the Mashpee Wampanoags of Cape Cod and faced with a situation mirroring that of the Mohegans in 1764, when Occom began writing petitions for his tribe. For decades the Mashpees had been abused by the rule of Overseers who treated their assigned charges like feudal serfs, asserting control over every aspect of their personal lives and robbing them of their resources. Native individuals had little legal standing to combat these abuses. Their imposed status as wards of the state (literally, children) made it impossible to represent themselves through normal legal channels. When Apess arrived, he began to organize the community in innovative ways, using ties he had developed with the Boston press and his stature as a newly ordained minister to provoke action. One of these strategies was to issue public proclamations, the first of which was to resolve "That we as a tribe, will rule ourselves, and have the right to do so; for all men are born free and equal."[55] Insisting on such rights and devising rhetorical strategies to force the settler-colonial power structure to recognize them was, as always, at the heart of the indigenous literary endeavor. Like the Seneca negotiator Tanaghrisson before him, Apess recognized the manner by which Native peoples were being squeezed in "a Country between," kept in a liminal space by colonial powers that refused to acknowledge their full humanity. In his 1835 tract, *Indian Nullification*, Apess wrote that "it seems to have been usually the object to seat the Indians between two stools, in order that they might fall to the ground, by breaking up their government and forms of society." Greatly distrustful of age-old promises made to extend Christian brotherhood to people of color, he observed, "I greatly doubt that any missionary has ever thought of making the Indian or the African his equal."[56] Apess fully comprehended the meaning of the reversals in kinship relations that had taken place over the course of a century between Natives and colonists, declaring that "neither I nor any of my brethren enjoy any political rights: and I desire that I and they be treated like men, and not like children."[57] At Mashpee, politics was suddenly all the rage.

Thanks largely to Apess's rhetorical and organizational brilliance, the Mashpees were at least partially successful in wresting political autonomy from their Overseers between 1833 and 1834. But Apess himself remained fixed on the deeper problem of how to counteract the aesthetics of settler colonialism that, from the very start, had worked to partition Native peoples into a highly compromised corner of the human condition set apart from the spheres of civilization that white people claimed for themselves. In his 1836 *Eulogy on King Philip*, Apess innovated a platform for a sustained literary encounter in which he played the role of Native orator, diplomat, and instructor, forging a style of address designed to correct the false assertions of settler-colonial power. Just as Powhatan had done with John Smith over 200 years earlier, Apess used this performance in an attempt to reinscribe the values of the common pot and demonstrate to his audience how such values had always been central to Native diplomacy.

Apess' *Eulogy* is essentially an attempt to overlay the written record of settler history in New England with an indigenous interpretive framework, tethered to the colonial archive for the material substance of his oration, but finding therein the tools to dismantle the logics of settler colonialism. Recalling the initial 1621 encounter at Patuxet (also known today as Plymouth, Massachusetts) between the Puritan settlers and the Wampanoags, Apess noted, "a treaty was made by the Pilgrims and the Indians, which treaty was kept during forty years: the young chiefs during this time was [*sic*] showing the Pilgrims how to live in their country and find support for their wives and their little ones."[58] The narrative of the so-called Pilgrim fathers typically assumes it is the English, with their superior technology and more sophisticated social structures, who set the terms for occupying this contested space. While this would prove true enough in the long run, Apess understood what Edward Johnson and other Puritan writers had studiously unwitnessed – that it was the Wampanoags who made the first overtures of peace and hospitality and it was the Wampanoags who were teaching the English how to properly maintain this space if they were to share it in a cooperative and peaceful fashion. He reminds his audience that the "good old chief" of the Wampanoags, Massasoit, "exercised more Christian forebearance than any of the governors of that age or since. It might well be said he was a pattern for the Christians themselves; but by the Pilgrims he is denounced as being a savage."[59]

One might easily imagine that, when the Wampanoags and English forged that early treaty, their discussions covered many topics ranging from land, corn, trade, and war to notions of kinship. As is famously recalled in settler traditions of the first thanksgiving, Tisquantum, or Squanto, was sent to the settlers to teach them how to sow corn. The first harvest of that year resulted in a mutual celebration consisting of settler and indigenous foods. In the treaty, they promised to protect one another, to promote one another's interests, and even to lay down their arms when visiting the other – a concession John Smith had flatly refused to make some thirteen years earlier when speaking with Wahunsunacook, considering it a deadly trap laid by a "subtill" and "politick salvage."[60] And yet the Wampanoags' outreach to the Plymouth colonists helped carve out a fifty-year peace in Wampanoag country – a peace ultimately shattered, as Apess argues, by the English themselves and their endless greed for land. "It does appear that they courted war instead of peace,"[61] Apess declares of the English after laying out his historical case, and for all this, he adds, it was the Wampanoags who "were receiving the applause of being savages."[62] As Apess concludes, "in vain have I looked for the Christian to take me by the hand and bid me welcome to his cabin, as my fathers did them, before we were born."[63]

The Native literary aesthetic moving into the nineteenth century was one of diplomatic polity, drawing on forms of address and interaction that had been passed down as rhetorical extensions of oral stories and traditions that stood at the formation of cultural identity. Protocols of wampum exchange traced back to the story of Hiawatha and the peacemaker in their collaborative effort to "bury the weapons of war." And traditions of shared land and resources, voiced by Powhatan, Tanaghrisson, Occom, Apess, and so many others traced back to the idea of the common pot that metaphorically viewed the land as a single dish from which all must eat together in peaceful accord. Many Native authors emerged in the public sphere of print discourse in this period, with similar approaches to negotiating the troubled space between indigenous insistence on maintaining presence and settler attempts at removal: Joseph Johnson (Mohegan), David Cusick (Tuscarora), Peter Jones (Anishinabe), Elias Boudinot and John Ridge (Cherokee), E. Pauline Johnson (Mohawk), Sarah Winnemucca (Paiute), and others. To be "indigenous" is to be of a place, and when indigenous peoples began entering into the fields of alphabetic literacy practiced by European settlers, they transferred that understanding of kinship and place – how to live in that shared indigenous space – to their textual productions. European colonists, by and large, rejected that Native vision of space and identity, unwitnessing its stamp from their accounts. While Native peoples were able to imagine kinship networks that made space for Europeans, Europeans divided identity into racialized hierarchies and worked to privatize the land in ways that concentrated and commoditized wealth rather than distributing it equally.

The image of indigenous identity promoted by settler colonial history and tradition continues to stand at odds with the way that Native communities perceived themselves. In a sermon Occom delivered in May 1787, he declared that there is something very Remarkable among the Indian Heathen in this great Continent ... they are very Compassionate one to another, very Liberal among themselves, and also to Strangers, When there is Scarsity of Food amongst them, they will yet Divide what little they have if there is but a mouth full a Piece, and When any of us kills any Creature, they will equally divide it amongst them all ... and when anyone is destitute of a Blanket, he that has two will gladly give him one, and they are very kind to one another in Sickness, and they Weep with them that Weep – This I take to be human love or Being Neighbourly, according to our text.[64]

But he knew there was another order of being in the world who "don't care what is to become of their fellow man," who ignore the biblical commandment to "Love they [sic] Neighbor as thy Self." And this, Occom tells us, is the language of all oppressors, defrauders, extortionists, and "with holders of Corn."[65]

The European colonizers were, and remain today, "with holders of Corn," denigrating anything as "savage," or "primitive" that dares question the model of acquisitiveness and spoil that has defined their regime. As scholars grapple with how to restore a sense of Native civilization and a Native literary aesthetics to our conceptual engagement with a colonial past, they must first work to disentangle themselves from the colonial aesthetic of unwitnessing. We must begin to decolonize our own thought processes so that the term "politick" no longer operates as an ironic modifier when applied to Native people, and so that the term "wilderness" dissolves, giving way to a vision of families, villages, trade networks, and endless patches of corn, beans, and squash, beaming a wide swath of light into that darkness constructed by colonial reporting. As chief Irving Powless of the Onondaga explains, the ceremonial extension of kinship was a traditional way of showing "that we are all in the same house. We are all in the same family, all living together."[66] The Native literary aesthetic was crafted to convey this message to whomever might hear it, in a framework of ceremony, as Apess observed, hoping to teach newly arrived strangers "how to live in their country."

Notes

1 John Smith, "The Generall Historie of Virginia, New England, and the Summer Isles with the Names of the Adventurers, Planters, and Governours from Their First Beginning An. 1584 to This Present 1624," in *Captain John Smith: Writings with Other Narratives of Roanoke, Jamestown, and the First English Settlement of America* (New York: Library of America, 2007), 373.

2 John Smith, "A True Relation," in *Captain John Smith: Writings*, 21.

3 Rachel Bryant "Kinshipwrecking: John Smith's Adoption and the Pocahontas Myth in Settler Ontologies," *AlterNative* 1.9 (2018): 304 and 301.

4 Alyssa Mt. Pleasant, Caroline Wigginton, and Kelly Wisecup, "Materials and Methods in Native American and Indigenous Studies: Completing the Turn," *William and Mary Quarterly* 75.2 (2018): 216–217.

5 Edward Johnson, *Wonder Working Providence, 1628–1651*, ed. J. Franklin Jameson (New York: Charles Scribner and Sons, 1910), 263.

6 Ibid., 52.

7 Ibid., 111.

8 Ibid., 51.

9 Daniel Webster, "First Settlement of New England: A Discourse Delivered at Plymouth, on the 22nd of December, 1820," in *The Great Speeches and Orations of Daniel Webster: With an Essay on Daniel Webster as a Master of English Style*, ed. Edwin P. Whipple, 1923, www.gutenberg.org/files/12606/12606-8.txt (accessed October 24, 2020).

10 William Cronon, *Changes in the Land: Indians, Colonists, and the Ecology of New England* (New York: Hill and Wang, 1983), 58.

11 Johnson, *Wonder Working Providence*, 161.

12 Smith, "A True Relation," 22.

13 I define *unwitnessing* as the "decision to maintain a particular narrative structure by keeping undesirable aspects of cultural memory repressed or inactive." See Drew Lopenzina, *Red Ink: Native Americans Picking Up the Pen in the Colonial Period* (Albany: SUNY Press 2011), 9.

14 See Smith, "True Relation," 24–25; Smith "Generall Historie," 369–74; and Smith, "The Proceedings of the English Colonie in Virginia," in *Captain John Smith: Writings*, 83–87.

15 Smith, "General Historie," 322.

16 Ibid., 371.

17 Smith, "A True Relation," 23.

18 Bryant, "Kinshipwrecking," 4.

19 Lisa Brooks, *Our Beloved Kin: A New History of King Philip's War* (New Haven, CT: Yale University Press, 2018), 19–20.

20 Quoted in Ella Cara Deloria, "Publisher's Preface," in *Waterlily* (Lincoln: University of Nebraska Press, 1988), xxiv.

21 Lisa Brooks, *The Common Pot: The Recovery of Native Space in the Northeast* (Minneapolis: University of Minnesota Press, 2008), 3–4.

22 Smith, "Generall Historie," 372.

23 Bryant, "Kinshipwrecking," 2.

24 Daniel Heath Justice, *Why Indigenous Literature Matters* (Waterloo: Wilfrid Laurier University Press, 2018), 58.

25 Dr. Linwood "Little Bear" Custalow and Angela L. Daniel "Silver Star," in *The True Story of Pocahontas: The Other Side of History* (Golden, CO: Fulcrum Publishing, 2007), 55.

26 Ibid.; see also Helen Rountree, *Pocahontas, Powhatan, Opechancanough: Three Indian Lives Changed by Jamestown* (Charlottesville: University of Virginia

Press, 2005), 82–83; and Martin D. Gallivan, "Powhatan's Werowocomoco: Constructing Place, Polity, and Personhood in the Chesapeake C.E. 1200–C.E. 1609," *American Anthropologist*, New Series 109.1 (2007): 85–100. Many historians who are considered leading scholars of the era of Jamestown's settlement, such as James Horn, Karen Ordahl Kupperman, and others, have a tendency to continue to frame Powhatan culture as a society "organized for war," as though this were its most significant feature. Such a characterization diminishes the cultural and diplomatic protocols of peace that informed so much of indigenous lifeways and are demonstrably recorded in the colonial archive. While war was clearly a facet of indigenous society, as it is everywhere else, this singular interpretation springs largely from the written characterizations of European writers who were unlikely to view indigenous culture as anything other than adversarial to their own settler-colonial objectives. Only when we decolonize our own reading practices does this more human side of indigenous identity begin to materialize. See James Horn, *A Land as God Made It: Jamestown and the Birth of America* (New York: Basic Books, 2005), 17.

27 Smith, "Generall Historie," 370, 373.

28 Quoted in Bartolome de las Casas, *In Defense of the Indians*, trans. and ed. C. M. Stafford Poole (DeKalb: Northern Illinois University Press, 1992), 33.

29 See Edward Winslow, *Good News from New England*, ed. Kelly Wisecup (Amherst: University of Massachusetts Press, 2014), 106.

30 Henry David Thoreau, *The Maine Woods* (New York: Penguin Books, 1986), 6.

31 Robert Warrior, *Tribal Secrets: Recovering American Indian Intellectual Traditions* (Minneapolis: University of Minnesota Press, 1995), 113.

32 Quoted in *Wapapi Akonutomakaonol, the Wampum Records: Wabanaki Traditional Laws*, ed. Robert M. Leavitt and David A. Francis (Fredericton: Micmac-Maliseet Institute, 1990), 33.

33 Margaret M. Bruchac, "Broken Chains of Custody: Possessing, Dispossessing, and Repossessing Lost Wampum Belts," *Proceedings of the American Philosophical Society* 162.1 (2018): 69–70.

34 See Arthur C. Parker, "The Origin of the Longhouse," in *Seneca Myths and Folktales* (Lincoln: University of Nebraska Press, 1989), 403–6.

35 Brooks, *Common Pot*, 13.

36 James Merrell, ed., *The Lancaster Treaty of 1744: With Related Documents* (Boston: Bedford/St. Martins, 2008), 54–56.

37 See Colin G. Calloway, *The Indian World of George Washington: The First President, the First Americans, and the Birth of the Nation* (Oxford University Press, 2018), 48.

38 George Washington, *The Journal of Major George Washington (1754)*, ed. Paul Royster (Lincoln: DigitalCommons@University of Nebraska), 7.

39 Ibid., 10.

40 Calloway, *Indian World*, 161.

41 See ibid., 247–59.

42 Ibid., 483.
43 Samson Occom, "Autobiographical Narrative, Second Draft (Sept. 17, 1768)," in *The Collected Writings of Samson Occom, Mohegan: Leadership and Literature in Eighteenth-Century Native America*, ed. Joanna Brooks (New York and Oxford: Oxford University Press, 2006), 52.
44 Samson Occom, "1764 Petition by the Mohegan Tribe to Sir William Johnson," in Brooks, ed., *The Collected Writings of Samson Occom*, 144.
45 Ibid., 145.
46 Ibid., 145.
47 Ibid., 144–45.
48 Samson Occom, "Mohegan Tribe on Rents," in Brooks, ed., *The Collected Writings of Samson Occom*, 147.
49 Brooks, *Common Pot*, 102–3.
50 Angela Calcaterra, *Literary Indians: Aesthetics and Encounter in American Literature to 1920* (Chapel Hill: University of North Carolina Press, 2018), 2.
51 Jace Weaver, *That the People Might Live: Native American Literature and Native American Community* (New York: Oxford Community Press, 1997), 43.
52 See William Apess, "A Son of the Forest," in *On Our Own Ground: The Complete Writings of William Apess, Pequot*, ed. Barry O'Connell (Amherst: University of Massachusetts Press, 1992), 23.
53 William Apess, "Textual Afterword," in O'Connell, ed., *On Our Own Ground*, 318.
54 William Apess, "A Son of the Forest," in O'Connell, ed., *On Our Own Ground*, 51.
55 William Apess, "Indian Nullification," in O'Connell, ed., *On Our Own Ground*, 175.
56 Ibid., 230.
57 Ibid., 225.
58 Apess, "Eulogy on King Philip," in O'Connell, ed., *On Our Own Ground*, 281.
59 Ibid., 283.
60 For the terms of the 1621 treaty, see *Mourt's Relation: A Journal of the Pilgrim's in Plymouth*, ed. Dwight B. Heath (Bedford, MA: Applewood Books, 1962), 56–57.
61 Apess, "Eulogy," 292.
62 Ibid., 281.
63 Ibid., 310.
64 Samson Occom, "Thou Shalt Love Thy Neighbour as Thyself, Luke 10:26–27 (May 13 1787?)," in Brooks, ed., *The Collected Writings of Samson Occom*, 203–4.
65 Ibid., 202.
66 Irving Powless, "Treaty Making," in *Treaty of Canandaigua 1794: Two Hundred Years of Treaty Relations between the Iroquois Confederacy and the United States* (Santa Fe, NM: Clear Light Publishing, 2000), 18.

CHAPTER 11

Logics of Exchange and the Beginnings of US Hispanophone Literature

Emily García

Although the vast majority of the Hispanophone texts read and sold in the first decades of the United States were imported from Spain and other countries, the turn of the nineteenth century saw a dramatic rise in domestic Spanish-language publishing. Beginning in 1794, Philadelphia printers started producing Hispanophone texts for the domestic market; publishing houses in New York, Boston, and New Orleans soon followed suit. This explosion of early Hispanophone literature in the United States offers a range of useful frameworks for understanding American literary history, in both its Spanish- and English-language forms.

Few of the first Spanish-language texts published in the early nation fall within the belletristic definition of literature; nevertheless, as mostly political and economic treatises, they reflect the idea of literature at the time. Importantly, the authors of these texts challenge the category of the "Hispanophone," in both linguistic and national terms; some of the authors of these texts had only an uneven knowledge of the Spanish language and espoused a variety of cultural origins and political positions. In what follows, I focus on what are chronologically the first two of these Spanish-language texts: Santiago Puglia's *El desengaño del hombre (Man Undeceived)* (1794) and the anonymous *Reflexiones sobre el Comercio de España con sus Colonias en America, en tiempo de Guerra* (1799).[1] I read these objects as illustrative of how exchange – economic, linguistic, and cultural – provides a framework for understanding the beginnings of US Hispanophone literature. In their complexity and multiplicity, these texts reflect the uneasy (and in their own moment, primarily aspirational) transitions from colony to republic, monarchy to democracy, and agrarianism to commerce. Furthermore, they complicate categories that we too often imagine to bear some sort of analytic cohesiveness, such as *Hispanophone* or *literary*. Lingering on these complexities invites us to move beyond what Doris Sommer calls the "one-derland" of assuming monolingualism, monoculturalism, and monologism at the nation's founding.[2] Against what we might too quickly assume to be an interest in republicanism or even early cosmopolitanism – ideologies that tend to be steeped or sometimes defined against a nationalist project – these works reveal how economic thought and, in particular, what I call the "logics of exchange" inform both Hispanophone printing in the early republic and early republican literary culture more broadly.

The "Economic Turn" and the Logics of Exchange

An overlooked context for the new interest in Spanish-language publishing in the United States is what Sophus Reinert and Steven L. Kaplan refer to as the "economic turn."[3] As an all-encompassing way of organizing the known world for Europeans and European Americans, the economic turn was "simultaneously material and symbolic ... relating to the production, distribution and consumption of goods and services, but also to their organization and regulation, to the discourses that generate or are generated by these practices, and to the conflicts that are inseparable from them" (1). Put differently, where literary studies has sometimes tended to frame studies of literary aesthetics against the backdrop of economic histories of print circulation and production, the economic turn suggests that such an arrangement of the relationship between figure and ground misses the ineluctable imbrication of economics and aesthetics. Economics – trade, circulation, exchange, and the highly politicized understandings thereof – exerted aesthetic and otherwise substantive pressures on print industries (including what was printed and reprinted), reading publics, and the circulation of ideas.

Situated within the Enlightenment in the long eighteenth century, "the economic was a way of seeing and interpreting the world within one's own environment ... a sensibility and a technique of constructing oneself" (6) and, I would argue, collective or even national polities. In other words, the economic turn, as a framework, is useful insofar as it helps us identify how the project of conscious self-presentation and construction was not only a singular or invididuated Enlightenment-era concern, but also one that writers brought to questions of the consolidation of populations, nations, and empires. The economic turn, as an approach to the literature of this era, "accentuated the need to 'think' the next stage of state-making (or state-recasting)," and more importantly, it offered a "core phenomenological epistemology ... that favored the diffusion of the economic way and fostered pragmatic ways of appropriating it" (6). The economic, then, became the privileged logic for not only the propagation, management, and wielding of wealth and power, but also government, philosophy, language, and culture. It should not need to be said, of course, that economy, as an epistemology, governed thinking about material and imperial increase; in the Americas as well as Europe, these increases were also tied to the twinned developments of capitalism and colonialism.

In the earliest Hispanophone literature in the United States , the logic of exchange exhibits four characteristics: comparison, conversion, circulation, and, ultimately, what *Reflexiones sobre el Comercio de España con sus Colonias en America, en tiempo de Guerra* calls a "reciprocity of interests." In the immediate wake of what some have termed the Age of Revolutions, which rocked the Iberian empire as thoroughly as the British and French, the Hispanophone texts at the center of this essay frame exchange as the key to imagining the political future. I argue here that this thinking manifests in these texts through processes of translation – both linguistic and cultural – in the sense of the Latin *translatio* or the Spanish *trasladar*: to transfer from one location or context to another.

In the case of early US Hispanophone literature, then, recognizing how the logic of exchange operates in these works allows us to see them for the products of cross-cultural relations that they are; as I've argued elsewhere, they fruitfully challenge notions of cultural purity (and even originality) in the origins of Latinx and (more broadly) American literature.[4] If these texts offer early glimpses of later US policy toward Latin America such as the Monroe Doctrine, buttressed on the logic of exchange and undergirded by the Enlightenment European universalism that informed it, they also afford us a critical perspective on the broader shifts and transitions that inform US literature in the nineteenth century.

La Famosa Filadelfia and Early Hispanophone Literature

The majority of the earliest Hispanophone imprints in the United States from 1794 through the 1810s were published in Philadelphia, with a handful in New Orleans. This made sense, as Philadelphia served as the early nation's capital through the 1790s, and the intellectual and material frameworks needed for publication – printers, agents, access to advertising and subscribers – had been robust in the city since the 1770s. The city's role as seat of power, and its American Philosophical Society, attracted

Spanish Americans, and Spanish American writers and thinkers in particular, to the city as exiles and later as diplomats. There were also outliers, such as the Ligurian Santiago Puglia, who having never set foot in Spanish America arrived straight from imprisonment in Cádiz to become one of the country's first Spanish-language teachers and author of the first Hispanophone publication in the United States. The significance of Philadelphia for this early US Hispanophone community has been examined elsewhere, most recently by Rodrigo Lazo.[5] And early US Hispanophone writing, more broadly, has been studied for decades, with works by Kirsten Silva Gruesz, Anna Brickhouse, Raúl Coronado, and Nancy Vogeley being essential reading for any true understanding of this body of literature in all its cultural, geographical, intellectual, and aesthetic complexity.[6] Before Boston, New Orleans, and New York had become centers of Hispanophone letters, Philadelphia became for a time an off-shore capital of sorts of Latin American independence. Lazo argues that Philadelphia became a "space of liberation for revolutionary intellectuals" and "a new home for Spanish American exiles who went into exile after participating in revolutionary causes"; "if Philadelphia was the physical city, then Filadelfia was its Hispanophone imaginative potential," "a living lab for republicanism and a symbol of possible futures for the Americas."[7]

In the decades following the establishment of the US republic, Philadelphia became a nexus of Spanish American literary and political relations. The city was also the site of what Nancy Vogeley in *The Bookrunner* refers to as a "Hispanic vogue" for Spanish-language and Spanish American novels, grammars, and political and philosophical treatises (42), and what Rodrigo Lazo, following the Cuban exile José María Heredia, called "la famosa Filadelfia" (57), which refers not only to the city itself but to its "symbolic power" as a site of resistance and Enlightenment.[8] This "Filadelfia," spelled with Fs, also refers to the city's "multilingual history of hemispheric relations" (69), which "disrupt[s] the city by shifting it away from its nationalist associations."[9] Lazo's remark indicates how Filadelfia's multilingualism signals a move away from seeing the city as strictly the bedrock of Anglophone US national foundation. Philadelphia was, too, a major site of Francophone literary and political culture as well.

The emergence of this multilingual Filadelfia also coincided with the period in which the United States began seeking to exert, through multilingual and multicultural relations, greater dominance in the hemisphere, starting with its Hispanophone neighbors to the south and immigrants from the Spanish Americas who had relocated to Philadelphia in that era.

The United States' active support of Spanish American independence was for several influential US Americans, perhaps most notably Thomas Jefferson, a matter of US national interest, and a political strategy that was imagined to bear potential to effect important political and economic ends.

Emerging as they did out of Philadelphia's multilingual and republican print culture, *El desengaño del hombre* and *Reflexiones sobre el Comercio de España con sus Colonias en America, en tiempo de Guerra* show both the political motivations and material circumstances of the beginnings of Hispanophone literature in the United States, while also evidencing the significance of what in Spanish is called "un lleva y trae," a back and forth, that is characteristic of the Hispanophone writings of this era and later Latinx culture. In particular, the dialogue is driven by an appraisal and theorization of the political and economic positions that Spanish America and the United States will inhabit in the hemisphere, and the political significance of the United States to Spanish America and vice versa. This back and forth is a dialogue, of course, but insofar as it relies on comparison (between the English and Spanish), conversion (from the US to Spanish American context and vice versa), and circulation (between the US and Spanish America), all toward a framework of "reciprocity of interests," it evidences a broader logic of exchange.

The publication of these texts was at least in part a result of the fact that US Americans with political and cultural connections in Philadelphia had diplomatic and economic interests bound up in seeing Spanish America become independent. Because of these factors, the majority of these early Hispanophone texts are critical of the Spanish Crown and often advocate for a vision of political independence modeled on that of the United States. Authors who saw the United States favorably were, perhaps unsurprisingly, the ones favored by US printers for publication.

Puglia's Translation of Enlightenment

The first Hispanophone text of the United States, Puglia's *El desengaño*, reflects how early US Hispanophone literature emerges from and reflects the logics of exchange. It was published by Francis Bailey, the influential independence-era publisher of editions of Paine's *Common Sense* and the Articles of Confederation, among other works. In publishing Puglia, Bailey reallocated his social capital and material resources toward the independence of Spanish America; he was one of several important supporters of

US independence who saw nascent "brother" republics in the Spanish lands to the south. The process of arguing for independence entailed exchange not only of ideas and cultures but of material resources as well: the same printers who had published works championing the independence of the British colonies now dedicated themselves to publishing writings that sought to foment independence throughout the hemisphere. Rather than mere copies of those previous works, though, these first Spanish-language texts published by Bailey and other Philadelphia printers bore their own impressions of the nascent tradition of independence movements in the Americas.

Along with this bicultural context for the work, the author of this first Hispanophone text similarly challenges our need to find neat roots for *latinidad* in the early period. Santiago Puglia was born in Genoa of a Swedish father (nothing is known of his mother). After failed attempts at an education and business, he was imprisoned in Cádiz. It is from this experience that he draws most of his critique of the Spanish Crown: at the time of writing *El desengaño*, he had never set foot in Spanish America.[10] Instead, he had made his way to Philadelphia from Cádiz, and started to establish himself as one of the first Spanish- (and Italian-) language teachers in the early republic. Ultimately, his work in languages led him to serve Jefferson as a kind of secretary/cultural liaison, but not before a stint in the Health Department, for which he received a lot of grief from Pennsylvanians who believed such a role should not fall to a foreigner like Puglia. And though he was one of the first Spanish-language teachers in the United States, according to the Spanish Inquisition and even his own preface to *El desengaño*, Puglia's knowledge of the Spanish language was lacking and far from standard, further complicating his position as the first Hispanophone writer in the United States. Indeed, it is difficult to keep Puglia in any kind of stable category. He published under several pseudonyms, including James Philip Puglia and James Quicksilver. He regularly shifted political stances in his writings, as he did in *The Federal Politician*, published the year after *El desengaño*. Toward the end of his writing career, in 1821, he completed Spanish-language translations of both Thomas Paine's *Rights of Man* (1821) and Constantin-François de Chasseboeuf, comte de Volney's *La loi naturelle; ou, Catéchisme du citoyen français* (1821). These two works represented a culmination of Puglia's many years seeking to establish himself as a linguistic ambassador of British and French Enlightenment thought for Spanish America.[11] He published a series of newspaper articles from 1809 to 1811 in the *Democratic Press* that articulated and examined the moral and political problems of capital punishment, and also wrote many works that remained unpublished, including a comedic play, *The Embargo* (a copy of which he may have sent to Jefferson); an Italian-language tragicomedy; and a pedagogical treatise that announced new methods for teaching the Spanish language.[12]

Though his publications reach across the Atlantic and the Americas in both topic and intended audience, and though he wrote in at least three languages, Puglia remained squarely a Philadelphia author: all published editions of his work bear Philadelphia imprints. His publications are still relatively unknown; but the list of his printers reads like a who's who of the literary culture of the day, including both Anglo- and Franco-Americans: Francis Bailey, Matthew Carey, Jean-François (Juan F.) Hurtel, and Médéric Louis Élie Moreau de Saint-Méry. In terms of the political impact of his works, Puglia remained an aspirational figure in Philadelphia at the turn of the nineteenth century. In terms of a political and cultural community, though, he was able to establish himself, if only in fleeting moments over the course of his life, at the very center of the republican endeavor across the Americas.

Perhaps because of his limited (or nonexistent) knowledge of Spanish America, and perhaps because he was interested in writing to established ideas that had already been circulating, Puglia's *El desengaño* is mostly comprised of heavy borrowing from classical, biblical, English, and French sources. He likens ignorant nobility, for example, to Theristes, citing him as the "el hombre más cobarde é ignorante que jamás se conoció" ("most cowardly and ignorant man known in existence"); he notes that in the time of Adam there were no titles given to persons, further arguing that any nobility, really, should be considered against God's wishes for humanity.[13] He cites abundantly from the Book of Samuel, then Deuteronomy, while referencing Troy – all within two pages – to argue that "La simple lectura de la mencionada Biblia no da lugar á tudio ó interpretacion para sacar en limpio, de que Dios consintió á su Pueblo un Rey, ó Gefe con el solo objeto de castigar su imperteninencia, y desengañarle sobre la necedad de la demanda" ("The simple lesson from the Bible requires no deep study or interpretation to clearly see that God gave his people a King, or rather a Leader, with the sole object of punishing his impertinence, and enlighten him on the need to follow his orders").[14]

El desengaño del hombre, as the name suggests, is also informed by Enlightenment sources. Puglia's most significant frame of reference is Scottish and English political and economic philosophy, and he engages more with Adam Smith, Edmund Burke, Thomas Paine, and

"Walworth"[15] than any other modern figures. The possible, if not probable, rhetorical effects of these references is worth noting. In anchoring his argument in classical and Enlightenment references, Puglia implies and asserts that Spanish America is the next to inherit this political and rhetorical lineage, elevating contemporary revolutionary sentiment to the status of a world-systemic inevitability and grounding Spanish American independence in related movements on a global scale. He also makes the Spanish American cause legible to US Anglo-Americans, challenging the Hispanophobic bias that began with the earliest English colonial descriptions of Spanish America and is perhaps best illustrated by the "Black Legend." By following English models for discussing Spanish American independence, Puglia paints the Spanish not as antithetical to the United States, but rather as sharing common references and common cause. He puts a good deal of stock in this assertion of the shared genealogy of these independence politics, writing, "El orgullo de la Aristocracía [*sic*] despertó varios enemigos Tomás Paine Escritor modern, y Defensor glorioso de la *Ygualdad*. Burke con la eloquencia y Walworth con la teología, parecen dos perritos empeñados en sugetar con sus ladridos á un Toro valiente" ("Aristocratic pride inspired several opponents of Thomas Paine, a modern Writer and glorious defender of *Equality*. Burke with his eloquence and Walworth with his theology appear like two little dogs bent on trying to subjugate a valiant Bull with their little barking").[16]

Perhaps one of the most significant references and influences that Puglia derives from Enlightenment sources is the concept of universalism, though it appears quietly and just a few times in his work. In demonstrating the significance of his ideas to the Spanish American context, he claims that all laws "se dirigen al mismo objeto" ("are directed toward the same objects").[17] Here, then, he is both adding to the list of common references and concepts that his work shares with those of his US counterparts, reiterating the universalism that in some respects has been a central concept in the US founding, and establishing a common cause across the Americas.[18]

On the one hand, we might see Puglia's appeal to the universal as another consequence of his practice of modeling his work on English and European sources. On the other, though, this universalism also requires a kind of conversion, a reimagining of the histories, politics, and struggles of the Spanish Americas as in some sense a viable site for the importation of the political thinking central to earlier hemispheric revolutions, but without collapsing political and historical distinctions into a universalized framework that understood the Spanish and Anglophone

Americas as analogous. For example, he lingers on the abuses of the Spanish Crown, a fact that is certainly notable in light of his work's status as the first Spanish-language text published in the United States.

His argument is broadly organized around the essentially Painean conclusion that "No hay peor [*sic*] Gobierno en el Mundo que la Aristocracia" ("aristocracy is the worst government in the world"), especially because monarchical rule ignores what he considers to be this plain and natural fact: "Cada rueda trabaje [*sic*] en lo que pertenece, y verás que el Relox no tan solamente no se parará, pero irá con la orden mas exacta y apectable" ("Each gear will work in what is its rightful place, and you shall see that not only does a clock not stop, but it shall keep the most exact and appealing time") (105, 108). Here we see how Puglia's argument for Spanish American independence is adapted from other contexts, and consists of a combination of critiques of the Spanish monarchy on the Peninsula and reading antimonarchical works derived from English and French histories.

Further, he transfers the motivations for independence, and the methods of achieving it, from the English and French contexts to the Spanish. By now, we might accept this cross-/intra-European referentiality as a hallmark of Enlightenment discourse, inclusive of the notion that natural law might purport to transcend nation. But the effect of the cross-linguistic and cross-cultural conversations that informed the development of that thought is worth lingering on here to tease out the significance of cultural as well as linguistic translation for Puglia's work. The inclination to relocate, or transfer, Paine and his thought from the British North American/US context to the Spanish American cause relies on a logic of exchange that posits languages, nations, goods, services, and people as similar enough to be exchangeable while nonetheless still eschewing Enlightenment universalisms.

Exchanges of Commerce in *Reflexiones*

These same logics of exchange also shape the second Hispanophone work published in the United States, the anonymous *Reflexiones sobre el Comercio de España con sus Colonias en America, en tiempo de Guerra*, published five years after *El desengaño*, and also in Philadelphia.[19] Like Puglia's work, it draws on English- and French-language sources as inspiration, positions England and the United States as models for the Hispanophone Americas, and uses comparison and analogy more often than not to advance its argumentation. While it is critical of mercantilism and favors a free market, it locates this point within a broader dialogue between commerce, on the one hand, and manufacturing and agriculture, on the other, ultimately making the case for the latter by articulating its significance to the former.[20] As a rule, the text highlights the centrality of circulation and reciprocity as the means by which to develop the wealth of Spanish colonies (and arguably the metropole).

The polyglot form of the text echoes its argumentative content; citation requires its own logic of exchange. *Reflexiones sobre* begins with an epigraph from John Gray's *Essential Principles of the Wealth of Nations* (1797) – a scathing critique of Adam Smith – in its original English. Directly afterward, he shifts into a variation on Locke:

> Todos los Goviernos deben tener por objeto la felicidad publica. Las Monarquias como las Republicas no deben perder un instante de vista este punto importante: los pueblos como los individuos bendicen la mano que les hace felices, y es undubitable, que el amor de los Vasallos es la basa mas soilda del Trono. De esta reciprocidad de intereses debe resultar el esmero de parte de los que goviernan en fomenter la prosperidad general: su poder se consolidara por la gratitude publica, y las Naciones cogeran el fruto de su cuidado y vigilancia.

> [Public happiness ought to be the aim of every government. Monarchies, as well as republics, should not for one moment lose sight of this important object. Nations, as well as individuals, bless the hand that makes them happy: and surely the love of the subject is the most solid basis of the throne. From this reciprocity of interests must arise, on the part of those who govern, every endeavor toward the general prosperity; their power will consolidate itself by public gratitude, and nations will reap the fruit of their care and vigilance.][21]

Not long after, the anonymous author quotes a book by a well-known (albeit unnamed) French author. Or, rather, it might be better said that he "quotes": although the author uses quotation marks, he also notes that he is citing these words from memory, from a book he had read some time ago. The quotations, then, serve to locate his own argument within the authenticity of those (Frenchmen) who had come before; the citational gesture matters more than the specificity of the words or the precision of his memory.

He offers Spanish translations of this French work, paraphrasing the French "Autor" to argue that commerce is "el movimiento, o circulación de los objetos de cambio, por el que nos deshacemos de nuestros sobrantes, y adquirimos lo que nos hace falta" ("the movement or circulation of the objects of exchange, by which we get rid of our surpluses, and whereby we obtain the articles we are in want of").[22] He then elaborates, still quoting, that it is artisans and farmers who make the most contributions to commerce, because, when you look at it, merchants are merely "los corredores, los tragineros del Comercio" ("the brokers and carriers of Commerce").[23] And, in fact, when they charge too much for their "interference," they are its "greatest enemies."[24] The anonymous author of *Reflexiones* takes a starkly different approach to the question of mercantilism, however; the merchant-driven *circulation* of goods, he argues, is key to the development of wealth – just as the circulation of ideas and languages comprises the very coming into being of these early Hispanophone works. Without the movement – the *lleva y trae* – the system fails.

Of course, circulation without rational direction is not enough. "El Comercio, el comercio es el favorito de la atención publica," he acknowledges. But then comes a necessary correction:

> Las mejores cosas vienen a ser peligrosas por el abuso: un torrente los arrastra, y lo desola todo; perso sis u agua se recoge, y distribuye con inteligencia por Canales bien dispuestos, en lucar de ser peligroso, es una fuente de prosperidad, y de riqueza. El fuego es para los hombres, generalmente hablando, una cosa necesaria ... al mismo tiempo este element consolador abrasa, consume, y aniquila todo, si la prudencia y la vigilancia no lo manejan con discernimiento. Lo mismo sucede en el Comercio.[25]

> [The best of things become dangerous, when abused; a torrent sweeps and destroys all it finds in its way; but if its waters are banked up, and intelligently distributed by well-directed canals, instead of being dangerous, it is a source of prosperity and riches. Fire, generally speaking, is to man a necessary agent: it is a protection against the inclemency of winter, and extremely useful for domestic purposes, and in several operations of the Arts; when at the same time, this comforting element burns, consumes, and annihilates everything, if prudence and vigilance do not manage it with discretion. The same happens with respect to trade.][26]

The implication here is that Spain is suffering from an out-of-control mercantilist approach to the detriment of all else. The analogy to fire has double significance because he has also linked fire with the ways artisans use it to turn metal into objects of use; contained and rationalized, fire transforms raw materials into wealth; uncontained and unrationalized, it destroys. The author returns to the figure repeatedly as a way of forwarding his critiques of Spanish policy: in the foundries of Birmingham and

Sheffield, for example, the same skilled laborers that in a Spanish context would be making trinkets out of precious metals instead make nails, iron plates, and other materials that have immediate utilitarian value. The problem is not with the artisans themselves or their skills, but with the value ascribed to the materials they work with: "El arte de dar al Fierro todas las preparaciones de que es susceptible, es sin comparación mas util que los trabajos finos de Plata y Oro" ("The art of treating iron with all the preparations to which it is susceptible, is without comparison more useful than fine work in Silver and Gold"). If only such priorities as they have in, say, Sheffield and Birmingham were applied in Spain and the work in iron were elevated to its rightful station, profitable gains would be seen throughout the Spanish world.[27] As is the case through much of the text, comparison and circulation is the foundational mode of argumentation; what has worked in England should also be tried in the Spanish American context.

When making its arguments about the importance of farming, even in mercantilistic nations, *Reflexiones* returns again and again to the cases of Britain and the United States. After a general discussion of how other states, for example, had profited from their imperial endeavors, the author notes that while "Se cree generalmente, que el Comercio es el Arco maestro del poder de la Gran Bretaña, la basa mas solida de su riqueza es su *Agricultura*" ("Commerce is generally considered to be the grand arch of the power of Great Britain; there is no doubt but it is one of its principal pillars; but the most solid basis of her riches is her *Agriculture*").[28] Similarly, he states that "Los Estados Unidos de America tienen un Comercio muy extendido, fundado enteramente en los productos de su Agricultura: el alto precio de la mano de obra, o del trabajo no les permitira poseer todavia en muchos años Fabricas de consequencia" ("The United States of America have a very extensive Commerce, founded entirely on the produce of their Agriculture: the high price of labour will not permit them to possess for many years to come manufactories of any consequence").[29] Here, then, he establishes that alongside production, farming has an equal and important role in the development of material gain for the Crown. This is no small argument at all, especially in 1799 when Spain had been experiencing extensive loss of wealth, in part due to the wars with England and France, which occasioned the decree to which this is a response. The argument then is one of recommending a correction of course toward more profitable industries, and in particular of correcting course to more closely follow its competitors as models – "as well in Spain as in her Colonies."

Then, to really drive home the significance and ubiquity of comparison and circulation, he argues again that commerce should exist solely to support other realms, and shall be "rapido, y pronto movimiento de los objectos de Cambio util a co-operadoes de sus funciones, y que como la circulacion e la sangre en el cuerpo humana anima, y vivifica todas las partes que le component" ("that rapid and quick movement of the objects of exchange, useful to the cooperators of its functions, which, like the circulation of the blood in the human body, animates and vivifies each component part").[30] As we see in Puglia, the logic of exchange in *Reflexiones* governs the structure of this argument on commerce, even when the argument itself is calling for the significance of commerce to be (relatively) muted. In particular, the appeal to French, English, and US contexts – with very little specificity about the Spanish case proper – positions this work in the broader republic of letters, and within the universalist Enlightenment tradition from which it draws. The underlying assumption here – and again it is one that very much determines the publication of at least these early Hispanophone texts – is one of a foundational porousness in the cultural relations between England, the United States, and the Spanish Americas. Moreover, this exchange positions England and the United States as models to be followed, peers to which one might aspire and one day even relate, establishing, at least discursively, an accord among the nations of the Americas even before some of those nations have declared independence.

Reciprocity and the Beginnings of Hispanophone US Literature

This accord among nations is the reciprocity to which the author of *Reflexiones* refers, and its promise informs the publication of these earliest texts, beginning with Puglia. While the content and direction of Hispanophone literature in the United States would continue to change over time, the logics of exchange continued to provide a recurring structure. Many of the most prominent and influential proponents of Spanish American independence were influenced by French, English, and US sources. Because the Inquisition (which did not formally conclude until the 1830s) prohibited the publication of seditious or heretical texts, writers expounding the virtues of political independence turned to countries outside their own for the support they needed to foment revolution. Thus the beginnings of pro-independence publications can be found not in Spanish America but in the United States, along with the beginnings of US Hispanophone literature. What John C. Havard describes as the

Hispanicism of the early nation, then, must be considered with a clear understanding of both the political and economic gains inherent in such Hispanicism, considering, for example, the prospects of a newly independent Spanish America open to trade with the United States.[31] Later in the nineteenth century, Hispanophone writers like José Martí would use their positions in a hemispheric republic of letters to challenge those tendencies and fortify independence movements across the Americas against not only Spain but eventually against the United States as well.[32] These earliest works thus not only evidence a literature in transition, as US publishers begin to include Hispanophone writing in their list of books and more and more newspapers and other periodicals include Spanish words within their pages. They also reveal transitions in national cultures, toward an economic vision that is necessarily transnational and driven by exchange and circulation.

Notes

1   Santiago F. Puglia, *El desengaño del hombre* (Philadelphia: Bailey, 1794). The work appeared at roughly same time in English attributed to James Philip Puglia as *A Short Extract (Concerning the Rights of Man and Titles) from the work Man Undeceived* (Philadelphia: Johnston and Justice, at Franklin's Head, 1793). *Reflexiones sobre el comercio de España con sus colonias en América, en tiempo de guerra* (Philadelphia: James Carey, 1799) was translated as *A Spaniard in Philadelphia, Observations on the commerce of Spain with her colonies, in a time of war* (Philadelphia: James Carey, 1800).

2   Doris Sommer, "American Projections of One-derland," in *Latinos: Remaking America*, ed. Marcelo Suárez-Orozco and Mariela Páez (Berkeley: University of California Press, 2008).

3   Steven L. Kaplan and Sophus A. Reinert, "The Economic Turn in Enlightenment Europe," in *The Economic Turn: Recasting Political Economy in Enlightenment Europe*, ed. Kaplan and Reinert (Cambridge: Cambridge University Press, 2019).

4   "Interdependence and Interlingualism in Santiago Puglia's *El desengaño del hombre* (1794)," *Early American Literature* 53.3 (October 2018): 745–772.

5   Rodrigo Lazo, *Letters from Filadelfia: Early Latino Literature and the Trans-American Elite* (Charlottesville: University of Virginia Press, 2020).

6   For expansive and field-defining examinations of Hispanophone US literature, see, among others listed elsewhere here, the following works: Kirsten Silva Gruesz, *Ambassadors of Culture, The Transamerican Origins of Latino Writing* (Princeton, NJ: Princeton University Press, 2001); Anna Brickhouse, *Transamerican Literary Relations and the Nineteenth-Century Public Sphere* (Cambridge: Cambridge University Press, 2004); Raúl Coronado, *A World Not to Come: A History of Latino Writing and Print Culture* (Cambridge, MA:

Harvard University Press, 2013); and the anthology *The Latino Nineteenth Century*, ed. Jesse Alemán and Rodrigo Lazo (New York: NYU Press, 2016).

7 Lazo, *Letters from Filadelfia*, 3.

8 Nancy Vogeley, *The Bookrunner: A History of Inter-American Relations – Print, Politics, and Commerce in the United States and Mexico* (Philadelphia: American Philosophical Society, 2011), 42; and Rodrigo Lazo, "'La Famosa Filadelfia': The Hemispheric American City and Constitutional Debates," in *Hemispheric American Studies*, ed. Caroline F. Levander and Robert S. Levine (New Brunswick, NJ: Rutgers University Press, 2008), 57.

9 Lazo, *Letters from Filadelfia*, 69, 70.

10 Puglia lived the rest of his life in the United States, spending many years in Harrisburg, Pennsylvania, and a short spell in Charleston, South Carolina. In the summer of 1805 Puglia set sail and, over the course of two and a half years, visited Chile, Peru, Mexico, California, and various islands in the Pacific. See Antonio Saborit, "Introduction," in *El desengaño del hombre* (Mexico City: Fondo de Cultura Económica, 2014), xvi.

11 My thinking here (as elsewhere) is greatly indebted to Kirsten Silva Gruesz's *Ambassadors of Culture*. In addition to recovering US Latino literary history from the nineteenth century and its influence on canonical Anglo-American writers, Gruesz expands our understanding of transamerican diplomacy beyond the political as traditionally defined and toward including cultural work such as literature and journalism.

12 Ibid., 62.

13 Puglia, *El desengaño del hombre*, 96, 94.

14 Ibid., 15.

15 The 1793 *A Short Extract (Concerning the Rights of Man and Titles) from the work Man Undeceived* notes that "Walworth" refers to Edmund Burke – though Puglia seems to have confused him with a different author altogether.

16 Puglia, *El desengaño del hombre*, 87, translation mine.

17 Ibid., 81.

18 Emily García, "'The cause of America is in great measure the cause of all mankind': American Universalism and Exceptionalism in the Early Nation," in *American Exceptionalisms*, ed. Sylvia Söderlind and Jamey Carson (Albany: SUNY Press, 2011), 51–70.

19 While the title page lists only "A Spaniard" as author, the work has been variously ascribed to Foronda, Torres, and Yrujo, with perhaps the most recent voice on the subject, Coronado, settling on the latter. Several catalog entries include Puglia as an author, indicating that perhaps he is the "Another Spaniard" cited as translator in the 1800 English edition. Of all of these possible authors, only Yrujo is mentioned directly, which might actually be an indication that he was the author (given the self-promotion evidence by the Marques along with many others in Philadelphia at the time). What is most important to our interests here, however, is the Spanish authorship of both the Spanish and English editions.

20 Coronado categorizes the work as anti-mercantile, and this might be a good
general way to locate it within other works available at the time, though the
argument drawn throughout is a bit more nuanced and at times even contradictory. The work is, most succinctly, a response or, as the title puts it,
"reflexiones"/"observations" on a 1799 decree prohibiting neutral vessels from
entering Spanish ports. This move, as the author states it, occasions compar-
isons of how the Spain treats its colonies in the Americas with how other
European nations – namely, France and England – treat theirs.

21 *Reflexiones sobre*, 13; *Observations on the Commerce of Spain*, 8.

22 *Reflexiones sobre*, 36; *Observations on the Commerce of Spain*, 25–26.

23 *Reflexiones sobre*, 37; *Observations on the Commerce of Spain*, 26.

24 *Reflexiones sobre*, 37; *Observations on the Commerce of Spain*, 26.

25 *Reflexiones sobre*, 23, 30–31, 23.

26 *Reflexiones sobre*, 21; *Observations on the Commerce of Spain*, 21.

27 *Reflexiones sobre*, 18.

28 *Reflexiones sobre*, 25; *Observations on the Commerce of Spain*, 18.

29 *Reflexiones sobre*, 26; *Observations on the Commerce of Spain*, 18.

30 *Reflexiones sobre*, 39–40; *Observations on the Commerce of Spain*, 28.

31 John Havard, *Hispanicism and Early US Literature: Spain, Mexico, Cuba, and
the Origins of US National Identity* (Tuscaloosa: University of Alabama
Press, 2018).

32 José Martí, "Nuestra América," *La Revista Illustrada* (1891).

CHAPTER 12

The Emigrationist Turn in Black Anti-Colonizationist Sentiment

Kirsten Lee

Arise, ye winds, America explore,
Waft me, ye gales, from this malignant shore;
The Northern milder climes I long to greet,
There hope that health will my arrival meet.
—Phillis Wheatley, "To a LADY on her coming to North-America
with her Son, for the Recovery of her Health"[1]

Introduction: Wheatley's Failed Deportation

In an October 1774 letter, Phillis Wheatley updates the British merchant and philanthropist John Thornton on the death of her mistress and her manumission. Praising her "old master's generous behaviour in granting me my freedom," Wheatley nevertheless kindly declines Thornton's offer to help her serve as a missionary on the African continent.[2] She writes, "You propose my returning to Africa with Bristol Yamma and John Quamine ... but why do you hon'd sir, wish those poor men so much trouble as to carry me so long a voyage? Upon my arrival, how like a Barbarian shou'd I look to the Natives."[3] Wheatley's familiarity with Yamma and Quamine, as well as the example of their case more broadly, show a trend of back-to-Africa campaigns for free and/or educated Blacks marketed as missionary efforts in the late eighteenth century.[4] In a February 9, 1774, letter Wheatley actually notes her awareness of Yamma and Quamine, but insists that she cannot join them in their mission, this time referencing her "asthmatic complaint."[5] In her letters Wheatley voices her support for Negro missionary work in Africa, but repeatedly disqualifies herself as a candidate for relocation, for missionary purposes or otherwise. Indeed, Wheatley emphasizes that these two men, Yamma and Quamine, "are desirous of returning to their native country" while remaining silent about whether she wanted to return to her birthplace.[6]

Missionary campaigns such as Yamma and Quamine's illustrate a sustained push in the late eighteenth century to send free Blacks from the thirteen colonies to Africa, either permanently or semi-permanently, but such campaigns have often been studied as a mid-nineteenth-century phenomenon.[7] This essay, however, takes as its focus the heated debates and repeated calls for repatriation and expatriation to African countries that flourished in *early* nineteenth-century Black print. I demonstrate that Black dreams of return to the African continent cannot be reduced to desires for repatriation; rather, as this chapter argues, African American public discourse around various iterations of back-to-Africa movements wove together demands for rights to the protections of national citizenship with aspirations to build a Black nation outside the United States. Indeed, some nineteenth-century Black nationalists saw emigration as both politically necessary and effectively abolitionist. Black Americans enslaved and free had to differentiate their own dreams of establishing a settler state in the Americas from the desires of white colonizationists, who had long proposed the same project of Black emigration. Building a political platform through the press, literary and mutual aid societies, and conventions, African Americans in the early nineteenth century presented emigration as an act of collective self-determination that spatialized their apposite relation to American political subjectivity, performing what Fred Moten calls "the refusal of refused and therefore tainted citizenship."[8]

Scholarship by critics such as Eddie S. Glaude Jr., Eric J. Sundquist, and Elizabeth McHenry has discussed the links between the early Black press and anticolonizationist politics, as well as the reappearance of the Black national periodicals and the surge of emigrationist politics in the 1840s and 1850s. But I propose that it is crucial to study the transition from Black anticolonizationist to emigrationist politics underway between the 1820s and 1830s.[9] In this essay I identify as emigrationist any Black rhetoric that promotes mass Black departure from the United States as a solution to being excluded from protections of liberal personhood defined as citizenship. What differentiates emigrationist rhetoric from its colonizationist antagonist is precisely its foundation in Black-led political organizing and African American reading publics; Black literacy in the nineteenth century is politicized by the fact of its widespread prohibition, so an emigrationist rhetoric treats the fact of its address to a Black reading public as a political act. Emigrationist rhetoric offered free and enslaved Black people in the United States a way to politicize their feeling "part of the home, and yet homeless" and to mobilize around their rights to property, in particular.[10] Looking to the founding of the American Colonization Society (ACS) in

1816 and rhetoric opposing its aims circulating in the 1820s and 1830s shows how Black emigration and separatism were hotly debated topics of national concern, for whites and Blacks alike. Further, the debate between anticolonizationists and colonizationists is one of the defining national debates alongside abolitionism in the early nineteenth century.[11] David Walker's 1829 *Appeal to the Coloured Citizens of the World*, to which this chapter will return, launches a sustained attack on the ACS and its goals. Critics of the ACS like Walker identified Black separatism as a critical counterstrategy to colonizationist discourse – the natural end of which might be mass departure from the United States. Emerging Black emigrationist platforms and societies in the 1820s and 1830s knit together Black longing for return to Africa with a longing for the rights of American citizenship, positing the former as a solution to the latter.

In this essay I look to the development of African American newspapers *Freedom's Journal* and *Rights for All*, the publication of Walker's 1829 *Appeal*, and the 1830 inaugural session of the National Colored Convention to anchor my analysis of a shifting and increasingly formalized Black emigrationist platform in the early nineteenth century. Against critics like Benedict Anderson, who see the newspaper as a vital formation in the project of homogenizing national consciousness, I propose in this essay that we find numerous early claims, circulating in the Black press, to print speech as specifically Black, rather than preserving "white speech . . . as the disembodied, articulate, universal sign of intellect as such."[12] The early nineteenth-century print sphere had Black voices and Black readers, and those Black readers and Black writers addressed each other. Later emigrationist platforms build out this mutual address as a foundation for collective Black self-determination in print and through settlement. Studying the relation between anticolonizationist rhetoric and other rhetorics of liberation draws our attention to how African Americans defined and redefined how to free themselves. Examining the longue durée of Black anticolonizationist sentiment in the United States helps to illustrate how and why rhetorics of return to Africa have had such staying power in the frame of African American print culture.

Colonization and the Rise of the African American Periodical *Freedom's Journal*

By the end of the eighteenth century, there was a flourishing Black print culture in the United States: publications supported by and affiliated with mutual aid societies, print editions of oratory, confessions, and gallows literature populated the print landscape with Black writing. Within this late eighteenth-century print cultural context, colonization was already a subject under genuine debate. In 1792, Afro-Philadelphians petitioned the newly federal government for "federal aid in the cause of black emigration."[13] The petition's fifty-five signatories argue that Black peoples enslaved and free deserve the government's endorsement of "a gradual Emansipation to take place, and . . . an Assalem [Asylum] for such as may meline [malign] who are free, to resort, similor to the one prepared by the British in Serealluone."[14] This petition explicitly refuses to graft Black-led emigration onto existing settlements in West Africa, instead pressing for a realization of the "formal equality" promised under American law.[15] Speaking as one, the signatories thus try to "achieve humanization in writing" by petitioning the state for rights formally promised them and yet held in permanent abeyance by white nationalist agendas.[16] Thomas Jefferson's writings, for example, show his support for African slaves' deportation after their manumission in order to further construct whiteness as a basis for citizenship in the United States.[17] In his 1787 *Notes on the State of Virginia* Jefferson argues that African slaves should be educated, freed, and then "*colonized* to such place as the circumstances of the time should render most proper."[18] He further argues that Blackness itself is "a powerful obstacle to the emancipation of these people," making deportation to an American protectorate their only hope for something like freedom.[19] Refusing colonization schemes designed to further the aims of white American nationalism, Black people pressed state and federal governments to support their own emigration projects from the late eighteenth century onward, among them 1773 and 1787 petitions to Massachusetts General Court by enslaved and free signatories, respectively. *Freedom's Journal*, the first newspaper founded and edited by African Americans, thus entered a print cultural landscape where the relation between Blacks' emancipation and emigration was passionately debated. Periodicals can index this debate not only by presenting a chronology of the conversations on the issue but by rendering in print the "dialogic nature of consciousness, the dialogic nature of human life itself."[20] Examining the run of *Freedom's Journal* illustrates how Black writers and readers over time encountered arguments in favor of both white-affiliated colonization projects and Black-led emigration, giving us an index of the "deep and genuine connection between knowledge and its maps and the economies of dominance and subordination."[21] Importantly, *Freedom's Journal* started out opposing colonization specifically because of its proponents' affiliation with racially integrated coalitions joining white nationalist interests to abolitionist rhetoric, combining "racial 'purification' of a domestic space and imperial power over foreign spaces."[22]

Founded in 1827 by a group of free men of color based in New York City, *Freedom's Journal* ran from 1827 to 1829. Seeking to reach free Blacks across the nation and to promote literacy among the same, the founders selected Samuel Cornish and John B. Russworm as senior and junior editor, respectively. Both men brought to their work at *Freedom's Journal* resumes of activism and leadership within urban Black communities. Cornish was the first African American preacher licensed by the Presbytery of Philadelphia in 1819, and went on to organize the First Colored Presbyterian Church in New York City in 1821, serving as its pastor while continuing his missionary work. Like Cornish, Russworm was a supporter of Afrodiasporans' emigration to Haiti; while a student at Bowdoin College, Russworm made plans to study medicine in order to practice in Haiti.[23] *Freedom's Journal* entered a print cultural landscape in the early nineteenth century of newspapers designed for racial and working-class groups, among them the first indigenous newspaper the *Cherokee Phoenix* (1828) and the laborer periodical the *Journeyman Mechanic's Advocate* (1827, Philadelphia).[24] *Freedom's Journal* circulated in eleven states in the United States, the District of Columbia, Canada, Haiti, and England; the paper's reach in the American South was particularly impressive and tapped into existing antislavery underground distribution networks that were difficult for later newspapers like *The Liberator* to replicate.[25] Estimates of the subscribers to *Freedom's Journal* hover around 800, most of whom are believed to be Black, which is similar to the circulation of other weekly papers of the period.[26] Though some critics remain skeptical about whether there were enough literate Blacks to justify a newspaper, both the rise of colored reading rooms and reading societies in the early nineteenth century and the reality of an enslaved reading public put to rest any such skepticism.[27] Frances Foster Smith points out that "Reliable statistics on African-American literacy are hard to get and even harder to interpret," before acknowledging that *Freedom's Journal* alone could not resolve this difficulty.[28] Frankie Hutton further notes that for early African American newspapers, circulation figures likely do not represent or capture the full scope of their readership, because copies were often shared or accessed through reading rooms.[29] Organizations like the Colored Reading Society in Philadelphia either subscribed to or received free copies of *Freedom's Journal* for their members to read. As Elizabeth McHenry and Kwando M. Kinshasa note, readers who were functionally illiterate could still access the paper by having it read aloud to them, a common practice in the antebellum period.[30] Newspapers provided the African American community a forum in which "multiple readers who possessed a range of literacy levels" could meet and consider the same ideas, in what McHenry calls "literary interaction."[31]

Freedom's Journal stepped into an already developed Black literacy and literary landscape. Indeed as critics Dorothy Parker and Joanna Brooks explain, Blacks did have a print culture and reading community through the late eighteenth century and early nineteenth century, though Parker notes that many of the earliest Negro societies in the United States were for mutual aid rather than literary purposes explicitly.[32] Though the 1830s saw an explosion in both the abolitionist press and the number of Black literary societies, many with libraries or reading rooms as part of their purpose, Blacks had long been organizing for themselves and their rights.[33]

Freedom's Journal formalized a Black public sphere in print, with wide circulation, and that mobilized the multivocal character of periodicals to construct and configure debates by, between, and for Blacks both enslaved and free. The entrance of Black editors into the periodical industry signals a new kind of for-us-by-us aesthetic, where Black writers could include as their object of address other Black people. Put differently, with *Freedom's Journal*, Blacks could see themselves as subjects and objects of address, as both free and enslaved people. Russwurm and Cornish codified this mutual address between Black readers and writers as one of their paper's chief aims; they write in an opening editorial that they wish *Freedom's Journal* to become "a medium of intercourse between [their] brethren in the different states of this great confederacy."[34] In the paper's inaugural issue, Russwurm and Cornish lament in their editorial that "Too long have others spoken for us, too long has the public been deceived by misrepresentations."[35] Both editors state the purpose and ambition of their publication as that of unequivocally promoting the uplift and education of their people, as well as the exposure and analysis of their oppression. They write, "The civil rights of a people being of the greatest value, it shall ever be our duty to vindicate our brethren, when oppressed, and to lay the case before the publick."[36]

In its earliest days *Freedom's Journal* maintained a staunchly anticolonizationist tone, capturing an existing attitude already common among free Blacks. In January 1817, for example, a group of free Black men met in Georgetown, Virginia, to discuss their opposition to the newly founded ACS, asserting their "dislike to colonize in Africa" and calling for "free and independent men of color" to unite in official opposition.[37] Indeed, white abolitionists' hesitation to publicly oppose the ACS drew more attention, both positive and negative, to Black activists and writers who opposed it.[38] Richard S. Newman argues that as a result of this hesitation, Black activists who had been largely segregated in the national reform agenda became "part of mainstream debates over slavery and abolitionism in the 1820s."[39] Editorials and articles in *Freedom's Journal* can help us better understand how these mainstream debates were reconstructed for and by a Black audience. Russworm and Cornish unequivocally state their "decided disapprobation of the [American Colonization] Society" in a September 1827 editorial.[40] The newspaper reserved many columns for debate about colonization, between editors and readers who wrote in commenting on previous issues, as well as reprinting articles on the topic from other publications. In issues that ran before Cornish's departure in 1828, in particular, *Freedom's Journal* reveals Russworm and Cornish writing against colonization by advocating for Black emigration to existing West African colonies and to the Caribbean. In an unsigned editorial likely written by him alone,[41] Russworm expressed his support for the Haitian Revolution and "the establishment of an independent nation by men *of our own colour.*"[42] He posits the Haitian Revolution as the most sublime of his time because it was orchestrated by and for the benefit of "those who but lately were in the bonds of slavery."[43] Here Russworm praises the establishment of a Black nation-state in the Americas without white intervention or design. This praise for Black self-determination, and in particular by enslaved and/or formerly enslaved people for their kinfolk, speaks back to assertions by the ACS that colonization would "procure a proper situation in Africa, [and] the captured negroes should be put under its care." This "captured" could refer to either those kidnapped into slavery or emancipated by deportation; the ambiguous entrapment illustrates how abolitionist and colonizationist talking points become almost indistinguishable in the rhetoric of the ACS.

Genius of Universal Emancipation, an antislavery newspaper whose articles were often reprinted in *Freedom's Journal*, illustrates well how abolitionist and colonizationist rhetoric meld. Founded in 1821 by Benjamin Lundy of Ohio, *Genius of Universal Emancipation* condemned slavery on moral and religious grounds while also promoting the settlement and deportation of freed slaves to Haiti, Liberia, and Canada.[44] Abolition was held out as a potential moral triumph for whites and Blacks alike. In its second issue, an article appears about Reverend Ephraim Bacon's recent trip to Sierra Leone.[45] Reporting on his findings, Bacon finds that "all the colonists enjoyed, very good health" and that crops like coffee, cotton, and tobacco "grow spontaneously."[46] Bacon concludes from his time in Sierra Leone that "The prospects of the colony were considered as very promising, and afford the highest gratification to the agents or colonists."[47] The *Genius of Universal Emancipation*'s vision of colonization makes the resettlement of Blacks in Africa not only morally justified and politically correct, but personally satisfying to all involved as participants or observers. The paper reported favorably on Black passengers' transport to Liberia on April 14, 1823, calling all of the emigrants "very intelligent."[48] The reporter describes a sermon given by Reverend Bishop Richard Allen of Philadelphia and Reverend R. R. Gurley of the Colonization Society, after which, under Dr. Aves's supervision, Peter Galt, Esq., extracted an oath of fealty to the cause of settlement from the twenty-five colored men even when the conditions were hard and their sufferings great.[49] The reporter remarks on this display as "an interesting and impressive scene," simultaneously conveying his ability to judge the higher ideals from a safe distance as well as his approval of its display. This approbation is later reified in the reporter's recounting of a recently emancipated traveler's story:

> Among them is a late slave of DANIEL MURRAY, Esq. whose master not only gave him liberty, but furnished him with support to aid him in the new settlement. – There are good grounds to be confident that Mr. Murray's example will be followed by many, as soon as the colony becomes more settled.[50]

It becomes apparent that the writer's concern is not the welfare of the emancipated slave but the possibility that the example of the combined manumission and resettlement will inspire other slaveholders to do the same for those they hold in bondage. Afrodiasporans entirely fall out of this representation of settlement and its benefits; instead, Blacks appear when they are being complimented for their good conduct, marked by their docility and consent to be governed as well as their willingness to embark on the journey. Indeed, the reporter celebrates the example of the emancipation of Daniel Murray's slave as a way to recruit white slave-owners to the cause of colonization, drawing them into the article with a depiction of Black emigrants as "subjected and practised bodies, 'docile' bodies."[51]

In another instance, the editor of *Genius of Universal Emancipation* prefaces a letter written to the paper on the topic of Haitian emigration by insisting that support for the American colonizationist movement and for abolition are not at odds.[52] The letter writer, signed Benevolus and whose identity is known only to the editor, argues that free Blacks' relocation to Haiti does not ultimately challenge or hurt the goals of the Colonization Society.[53] Benevolus goes on to argue that the ACS, having gone recently into debt "in behalf of this unfortunate race among us," has done more for the abolitionist cause "than all the emancipation societies put together."[54] Benevolus further furnishes arguments that the ACS was key to the slave trade being made illegal.[55] Interestingly, Benevolus makes strong claims for the stability of the labor system even if slaves are manumitted and sent to American colonies in West Africa: "[The colonies] will substitute a legitimate production of African labour for a cruel traffic in the labourers themselves."[56] Benevolus here betrays that his main concern in these debates about colonization is actually not that of emancipation but that of the control of Black laborers, even when legally free. The editor clarifies below the letter that he never opposed Haitian emigration, as Benevolus believed, but instead sees "the great advantages to be realized by a removal of the coloured people to Hayti."[57] On this issue of Haitian emigration, perhaps surprisingly, many other Black Americans agreed.

Early Emigrationist Movements

Haiti holds multiple meanings in the early nineteenth-century Atlantic imaginary. The Haitian Revolution frightened metropolitan and planter class whites as well as imperial powers who found the revolution and its Black-led republic, in the words of Michel-Rolph Trouillot, "unthinkable."[58] Flows of white planter refugees from Saint-Domingue to the United States from 1791 onward carried with them stories of terror about living through the Black uprising.[59] In the same period free and enslaved Blacks in the United States looked to "the trope of San Domingo" as an inspiring example[60] of a revolutionary blow against both white nationalism and chattel slavery. But Haiti carried more than conceptual appeal for Afrodiasporans. A second wave of emigration from the United States to Haiti in the early 1820s mainly included free Blacks, encouraged by Haitian President Jean-Pierre Boyer.[61] Using promises of land and suffrage to attract Black Americans to the island, Boyer calculated that an expatriate community might offer leverage to gain American recognition of Haiti.[62] Beginning his presidential term in 1818, Boyer identified the importance of attracting resources to the island, presenting Haitian emigration as a more attractive option to Blacks than West Africa, calling colonization schemes "a thing impracticable, to say nothing more."[63] Boyer's 1824 promise to Blacks in the United States for "an honourable existence in becoming citizens of the Haytien Republic" should they emigrate was quite effective,[64] drawing thousands of Black emigrants to the island. Leaving out emigration from discussions about the American imperial imagination of, anxiety about, and fear of the Haitian Revolution obfuscates the dynamic flows between the two even during heights of white paranoia about the contagious nature of enslaved peoples' uprisings. Emigration to Haiti (and, to a lesser extent, Canada) in the early nineteenth century shows how Black anticolonizationist sentiment deployed expatriation as a rhetorical and practical strategy for emancipation.

Afrodiasporans in both North America and the Caribbean saw the potential of Black immigration to Haiti to meaningfully curtail American colonizationist efforts. But the collapse of a Black American settlement in the early Haitian republic showed that not all mass Black emigrations would succeed in creating a permanent colony like those in Sierra Leone and Liberia. Nevertheless, Black emigrationists continued to advocate for mass Black relocation to a settler colony under Black leadership, opposing a strengthening anticolonizationist rhetoric supported by a racially integrated coalition like the ACS. Establishing this linked appeal, and making a case for the true self-determination involved in expatriation, was one of the major rhetorical strategies for emigrationists in the early nineteenth century. In an 1818 address to the American Convention for Promoting the Abolition of Slavery and Improving the Condition of the African Race, for example, Prince Saunders instructed delegates in the difference between emigration and colonization, and explained why free Blacks in the United States preferred the former.[65] He advised the Convention that many abolitionists already understand

> that it is time for them to act in relation to an asylum for such persons as shall be emancipated from slavery, or for such portion of the free coloured population at present existing in the United States, as shall feel disposed to emigrate. And being aware that the authorities of Hayti are themselves desirous of receiving emigrants from this country; are among the considerations which have induced me to lay this subject before the Convention.[66]

Though he was largely unsuccessful in garnering the Convention's support, by portraying emigration as desirable for Afrodiasporans in both Haiti and the United States, Saunders recasts the debate about colonization as ultimately a decision about whether international intraracial solidarity would be allowed to flourish. The US-based Haytien Emigration Society (HES) deployed talking points similar to Saunders's, pitching the idea of emigration to free Blacks in the Atlantic world as a means of showing their solidarity with each other and the early Black republic. In 1825 the Society printed an edition of its proceedings, including abbreviated versions of its history, encouraging "All classes and descriptions of Free People of Colour, of *good character*" to accept President Boyer's offer to emigrate and "be received as citizens and children of the Republic."[67] Boyer, Saunders, and emigrationist societies like the HES repurpose metropolitan anxieties about the contagious quality of Black freedom in Haiti to attract Afrodiasporans to relocate to the island as citizens.

Freedom's Journal remained staunchly anticolonizationist for much of its run. Readers wrote to the paper with their own arguments about the relation between anticolonizationist politics and emigration. In the July 11 and 18, 1828, issues of *Freedom's Journal*, "A Coloured Baltimorean" argues that the ACS will not solicit Black input on its plans, confirming the racism of their schemes. In the fist half of his letter he uses a hypothetical republican scenario to illustrate how the ACS bears the same relation to the "free coloured people of the United States, as the latter of the two preceding relations of constituent and representative."[68] Continuing in the metaphor, "A Coloured Baltimorean" rhetorically asks, "[H]ave the members of that society ever come among us for the purpose of eliciting our true sentiments relative to colonization in Africa?"[69] The following week, his letter concludes its response to colonizationist rhetoric by chastising its solicitation of Black donations. In this half of the letter, "A Coloured Baltimorean" accuses those anxious for the removal of Africans and their descendants from the United States of deliberately leaving Black voices out of the public discussion; the writer dares colonizationists to solicit Black commentary on their "*schemes*," writing, "[L]et them call public meetings of our people and find out their true sentiments relative to colonization in Africa."[70] Implying that colonizationists refuse to solicit Blacks' input even as they continue to court their financial support, "A Coloured Baltimorean" requests that "the money collected, not be appropriated in the fitting out [of] new expeditions, but be sent forthwith to supply, the necessaries of the colonists, many of whom … are in suffering circumstances."[71] "A Coloured Baltimorean" thus reveals that Blacks in the United States are getting their own information from colonists already in Africa, much of which contradicts the narratives of success and improvement promoted by the ACS to new recruits. This epistolary circuit connected Black colonists to friends and family stateside, and reveals how their feelings about the colonizationist movement changed, and in many cases soured, over time.

The Skipwith family offers a good example of this epistolary record between Black colonists in West Africa and people in the United States. Peyton Skipwith arrived in Liberia in 1833 after being manumitted by John Hartwell Cocke, having long been a talented stonemason at the Bremo plantation in Virginia.[72] Skipwith, his wife Lydia, and their six children were manumitted by Cocke on the condition of their emigration to Liberia, for which Cocke paid.[73] Skipwith's wife and daughter died within the first year of their arrival in Liberia, but he and the rest of his children stayed, going on to become important local politicians. Even so, Skipwith expressed his ambivalence about staying in the colony, noting that his health may prevent him from permanently living in the settlement. In a letter to Cocke on March 6, 1835, Skipwith writes:

> I have lost my wife she died on July 2d 1834 the rest of my family are tolerable well Sir This is the third letter that I have wrote to you and have received no answer ... I wonce had a [notion] of coming home and still have a notion but I want to go up to Sirrilione as I am advised by doctors to quit laying s[t]one ... If not will return back to America.[74]

Skipwith's letter shows him trying to imagine return as imminent, as a possibility contained in a conditional future that is not reducible to "a nostalgic preference."[75] As David Kazanjian and Randal Miller have shown, Skipwith predicts a future in which he can be a freeman in his country of birth, where he has only ever lived as a slave. He projects a future in which his rights will not be tied to his performance as a laborer, where he can live free and even if he cannot keep "laying s[t]one." Skipwith's correspondence signals that Black settlers imagined "return" not exclusively as a single event or as a return to Africa, but also as their restoration to the United States after having been free(d).[76]

Black emigrants to Haiti also deployed this right-to-return rhetoric, as did Haitian officials. For example, five days before his death on October 8, 1820, King Henri Christophe I prepared a formal agreement with Prince Saunders, committing a ship and $25,000 as an initial investment in the relocation of free Black peoples from the United States to Haiti.[77] According to Saunders's account, Christophe never signed the agreement because "a revolt took place," which "put a period to [Christophe's] existence" and to the royal line.[78] After Christophe's death, Black emigration to Haiti continued to receive support from the republic's national leaders. President Jean-Pierre Boyer focused first on unifying the República del Haití Español (Republic of Spanish Haiti) with both the Republic and Kingdom of Haiti, before turning his attention to attracting Black emigrants from North America.[79]

By 1825, complaints about the location of the three acres Boyer promised to any emigrant willing to "farm government land"[80] grew stronger as available lands quickly ran out around Port-au-Prince after a larger influx than expected. In addition, a smallpox epidemic ravaged Port-au-Prince in winter of 1825, reaching as far as Cap-Haïtien, further polarizing native-born Haitians and American emigrés. The introduction of the disease to the island was blamed on a Philadelphia cohort that reached Port-au-Prince in December 1824, though it cannot exactly be confirmed that it was precisely these emigrants who brought the disease with them.[81] Finding that the Haitian economy would not sustain their entrepreneurial efforts as robustly as they had hoped, many Black emigrants returned to the United States in 1826, among them John Allen of Philadelphia; other settlers moved to the former Spanish colony of Santo Domingo, now known as the Dominican Republic, particularly its northern regions.[82] Further, the December 1826 Haitian general election made it clear that settler Black Americans would not be granted suffrage or the right to serve on juries, the promise of which had drawn them to the island.[83] Though all black-skinned males twenty-one years and older were guaranteed the right to vote in Haitian elections after one year of residency, in 1826 a group of Black Americans in Port-au-Prince showed up at a polling center only to be escorted out without casting a single vote.[84] This political treatment of American settlers revealed Haitians' "reluctance to uphold the promise of Haiti as a Black nation for all descendants of Africa."[85] The legacy of Haitian emigration and its disappointments motivated later Black American emigrationists to push more strongly for building their own settler colonies in places like the western territories of North America, Canada, or Nicaragua. The failed coalition between American emigrants and Haitian citizens points out how Black settlement and emigration were not only issues of intense debate in the early nineteenth century but also issues that, at times, also divided Afrodiasporans.

Many American anticolonizationists, some of them just readers of *Freedom's Journal* rather than affiliated with relevant societies, understood that colonization was ultimately a red herring that misrepresented domestic racism as irreconcilable. Critics of colonization identified that framing ACS-backed colonies as sites for Black freedom mixed white nationalism with emancipation. In a December 1828 letter in *Freedom's Journal*, an unnamed writer elaborates his opposition to the Colonization Society, blaming the organization for deceiving Blacks about the necessary conditions for their liberty by insisting that emigration was a crucial component. The writer condemns the Colony of Liberia for encouraging Black citizens in the United States to make "a deplorable error respecting the true interest of the colored population, and of themselves."[86] Relatedly, a January 1829 article reprinted in *Freedom's Journal* characterized growing support for colonization by slaveholders as an attempt to consolidate and preserve their power: "The southern people seem to be saying to us – 'We will free our slaves, if any body will take them away from us.'"[87] The article also identifies northern abolitionists as complicit both in the institution of chattel slavery and in the white nationalist project of emancipation-by-deportation if they did not refuse the colonizationist co-opting of manumission.

Other Black readers wrote to *Freedom's Journal* in specific opposition to local initiatives to deport colored populations for the good of white inhabitants of the region. Lewis Woodson of Ohio, among the twenty founders of Wilberforce University in 1856, wrote quite vehemently against local whites' fears that Blacks would never be convinced to move out of the country. Woodson objected to a letter written to his local paper (reprinted in *Freedom's Journal*) and proposed patience to white readers, suggesting that any "citizen of Ohio whether a member of the colonization society or not" should be able to see the net benefit of giving local Blacks a county of their own, free from white intervention, which would "constitute such a nursery of people who would be willing ultimately to go to Africa, or Hayti, or Mexico, where they would enjoy political freedom."[88] Woodson rejected in the strongest terms possible eventual repatriation, agreeing that Black people should be given their own land in Ohio, but swearing that this land grant would never convince them to return to Africa. "Africa, is with us, entirely out of the question; we never wanted it: neither will we ever go to it," writes Woodson.[89] His critique is one of the last strong anticolonizationist declarations in *Freedom's Journal.* On February 21, 1829, the paper cautiously announced their changed views on the ACS, stating that "the mist which completely darkened our vision, having been dispelled, we now stand before the community a *feeble advocate* of the society."[90] In its five remaining issues, *Freedom's Journal* became progressively more assertive in espousing their procolonizationist stance. Russworm's gradual conversion to supporting the American Colonization Society, and his eventual departure for Liberia in 1829, preceded the paper's rejection of its earlier anticolonizationist politics, compelling contemporary critics to wonder what exactly prompted him to recast the paper's earlier stance. Some critics identify Russworm's procolonizationist politics as one potential reason for Cornish's departure as senior editor in September 1827.[91] Indeed, the paper that Cornish next started, *Rights for All*, which ran for six issues in 1829, maintained a staunch anticolonizationist stance.

By its final issues *Freedom's Journal* not only embraces colonization but becomes increasingly aggressive and condescending about their subscribers' inability to do the same. The February 21, 1829, editorial, for example, praises the ACS for having "done much in *favor* of emancipation," but mostly relates this to the fact that the Society took slaves "to be landed on the shores of Liberia, to become freemen."[92] By March 7, 1829, the editors ran a piece called "Our Vindication" congratulating themselves for their change of heart about the Society, beginning to insult readers for their lack of comprehension of "the American Settlement" and its importance for Blacks and their children to "enjoy all the rights of freemen."[93] In an article titled "Colonization," which ran in the following week's paper, the editors again assert that emancipation for Blacks as a class depends on their leaving the United States. The editors write that "the universal emancipation desired by *us* and by all our friends, can never take place, unless some door is opened whereby the emancipated may be removed as fast as they drop their galling chains, to some other land besides the free states."[94] The editors go on to suggest that their readers' opposition to colonization results from their failure to understand the situation, which would inevitably be resolved by "a candid investigation."[95] The final issue of *Freedom's Journal* reprinted in full a selection from the ACS's Twelfth Annual Report, on a plan for civil government – including a discussion of voting – in Liberia.[96] With this literal citation of ACS-backed settlement as the surest route to suffrage for free Black Americans, *Freedom's Journal* thus completed its transformation into a supporter of colonization. Efforts to imagine Black liberation outside of, and in specific rebuke to, the American colonization movement would have to find outlets beyond the periodical for the next decade.

David Walker and the Emigrationist Turn

David Walker's anticolonizationist stance treated emigration as a domestic issue of concern for all Black Americans. Walker's "nationalistic geographic imagination" puts forth the idea that Blacks can and should build a settler colony in the Americas, distinct from Haiti.[97] His 1829 self-published *Appeal to the Colored Citizens of the World* circulated in the same "anti-deportation reading network" that extended the reach of *Freedom's Journal* and *Rights for All* beyond known subscribers.[98] A dedicated distributor of *Freedom's Journal*, Walker held an 1827 meeting at his Boston home to encourage his colleagues to provide "aid and support" to the forthcoming periodical a month before its first issue went to print.[99] Walker was born around 1797 in Wilmington, North Carolina, to a free mother and enslaved father. This placed him in a "loophole of retreat" according to the doctrine of *partus sequitur ventrem*, since his legal status was conferred on him by his mother.[100] Walker moved to Charleston in his young adulthood and joined the African Methodist Episcopal Church where he may have witnessed the planning of parishioner Denmark Vesey's 1822 uprising. By 1825, Walker moved to Boston where he was very active in the Black community in back of Beacon Hill. Through his work as an agent of *Freedom's Journal*, the Massachusetts General Colored Association, and the Prince Hall Freemasons, Walker made clear his commitment to anticolonizationist organizing for the betterment of Black life in the United States. His 1829 *Appeal* makes particularly vivid his view that Black liberation required opposing colonizationists by whatever means necessary; in this pamphlet Walker builds his liberationist argument by engaging what Stephen Best calls "blackness as a condition of genealogical isolation" in the United States.[101] In the late 1820s, anticolonizationist rhetoric like Walker's increasingly turns to emigration as a strategy for building a Black settler colony in North America rather than elsewhere.

In the *Appeal* Walker identifies his audience as fellow Blacks in the United States, whom he addresses from the first as his "*dearly beloved Brethren and Fellow Citizens.*"[102] By hailing his Black readers as citizens – even as he goes on to show how white supremacy has profoundly restricted the parameters of that citizenship – Walker invests only in Blacks' collective liberation. He elaborates on this politics of citizenship by linking both himself as speaker and his audience to their status as Americans:

> Having travelled over a considerable portion of these United States, and having, in the course of my travels, taken the most accurate observations has warranted the full and unshaken conviction, that we, (coloured people of these United States,) are the most degraded, wretched and abject set of beings that ever lived since the world began; and I pray God that none like us ever may live again until time shall be no more.[103]

Defining colored people as citizens over and above "*Christian* Americans!," Walker reverses figure and ground in his picture of American citizenship.[104] In Walker's "Preamble," two major themes recur in his reasoning for why opposing slavery cannot wait. First, he argues that chattel slavery in the Americas is unlike any other historical form of slavery, making nineteenth-century abolitionist politics of world-historical importance. Comparing ancient slavery in Greece and Egypt with contemporary European forms of slavery orchestrated by the Spanish and Portuguese, Walker finds the Christian American form of slavery the worst that has ever been. Though he reserves the "we" for his fellow colored people – and in this he leaves open the gender identity of the group to be more than male – Walker at key moments employs the second person to interpellate the white readers he suspects will pick up his text as the perpetrators of the Black suffering described. In closing the "Preamble," Walker specifically addresses "O ye *Christians!!!* who hold us and our children in the most abject ignorance and degradation" with a series of questions about the "cruelties and murders with which you have, and do continue to afflict us."[105] In the "abolitionist geography" Walker sets out, he considers such prefatory questions to be "the suburbs," signaling that the argument that follows in the *Appeal's* remainder will go more to the heart of the matter of both Black suffering and liberation.[106] In this way Walker both anticipates the significance and political appeal of what W. E. B. DuBois later calls "abolition-democracy" and also rejects it as a complete solution to the social problems wrought and sustained by chattel slavery. Instead, Walker posits that only Black self-determination can offer a viable global future[107] since the entire world has been degraded by slavery. Walker's call to his brethren to "Read the history particularly of Hayti" makes his opinion of the stakes of self-determination clear; while Hayti was "butchered by the whites" and its power made precarious by international sanction, Walker sees Black Americans as capable of avoiding such a fate if they remain united.[108]

Walker's *Appeal* has four Articles, each focusing on a different facet of the political economy of racial capitalism and also a different proposal for how Blacks may coordinate their collective power. Articles I–III focus mainly on domestic issues, taking on white nationalism as expressed in American government, education, and Christianity; he famously excoriates Jefferson's *Notes on the State of Virginia* and tells his brethren to read and contest it in word and deed. Walker reminds his Black readers that "We, and the world wish to see the charges of Mr. Jefferson refuted by the blacks *themselves.*"[109] In Article IV, Walker revises his approach to motivate his Black readers by showing them that Black resistance is already in evidence and provides a template for how to protect and manifest a liberated Black future. Walker's tonal and rhetorical shift coalesces through his critique of the American colonizationist movement, insisting that Black liberation can and indeed must happen on American soil. In Article IV Walker ties his calls for Black self-determination in education and politics to plans for a Black separatist society in "our country."[110] In so doing Walker shames Black settlers of West Africa as a disgrace to emancipation and broader Black liberation. "Those who are ignorant enough to go to Africa," Walker writes, "the coloured people ought to be glad to have them go, for if they are ignorant enough to let the whites *fool* them off to Africa, they would be no small injury to us if they reside in this country."[111] In this last section of the *Appeal* Walker ultimately casts Blacks as rightful Americans, and identifies any colored colonizationist as a defectors from both the United States and opponent to "the salvation of his brethren."[112]

Walker uses calls to violent uprising throughout his *Appeal*, but in Article IV those incitements get mobilized to push Blacks to take over America. As Walker sees it, such a courageous takeover not only opposes the colonization movement to deport colored citizens to Africa, but also allies Blacks with indigenous ethnic groups. This move is particularly complicated, because it shows Walker drawing inspiration from Indigenous resistance to white colonization, while also casting Black people as having earned through their labor and suffering recognition as rightful inhabitants of the Americas. Asking a series of rhetorical questions to his brethren, Walker argues that whites have not targeted "the inhabitants of Asia" or "the Aborigines of this country" to enslave because they would rise up and kill their oppressors.[113] Walker accuses his own people of lacking such courage, lamenting, "But my colour, (some, not all,) are willing to stand still and be murdered by the cruel whites."[114] Walker proposes that his brethren can redeem themselves for their passivity by claiming the Americas as their own by force, identifying the Southern Hemisphere as a relatively easy target for as few as 15,000 "Blacks, [who] would almost take the whole of South America," telling his reader to "only look at the thing!!!!"[115] Walker further reminds readers that Blacks outnumber whites in most parts of North America and the Caribbean.[116] But it is the United States that Walker is most intent on claiming as Black land:

> Let no man of us budge one step, and let slave-holders come to beat us from our country. America is more our country, than it is the white – we have enriched it with *our blood and tears*. The greatest riches in all America have arisen from our blood and tears: – and will they drive us from our property and home, which we have earned with our *blood*?[117]

Three things become clear in this passage. First, Walker sees slavery both as the downfall of the United States and as what has made Blacks its most true citizens. Second, Walker sees the lands of North America as reappropriable to Blacks, who have more than earned it with their suffering under white nationalism and slavery. In a moment of failed coalition, Walker struggles to imagine Indigenous reclamation of the Americas, even though he understands Native Americans as the continent's original inhabitants and admires their courage and community. Walker believes not only that Blacks should argue against colonization and its supporters, "who have always been our oppressors and murderers," but that they should insist on their rights to stay in the Americas, with violence if necessary.[118] Walker also sees that the only way Black refusal of the colonizationist imperative might endure is if they claim their rights to "properties and homes" where they already live.[119] Third, Walker argues that the American colonization movement can only ever be a tool of white nationalism because of its affiliation with slaveholders' efforts to purify the United States of its free Blacks. Walker expresses anger and pity for Blacks who consent to white-backed colonization schemes, who "do not know that the sole aim and object of whites, [is] only to make fools and slaves of them, ... and to make them work to support them and their families."[120] Walker thus sees the colonizationist movement as an attempt to both keep control over Black labor and to protect American citizenship and the rights pertaining thereto for whites. Because Walker understands procolonizationist politics as fundamentally a dispute about property rights, and white anxieties about a growing population of Blacks who were no longer were legally property in the Caribbean and United States, he sees Black assertion of their right to ownership of "property and homes" as one of their surest strategies to contest "the colonizing trick."[121]

In so doing Walker identifies emancipation as at odds with colonization, by design, incredulously repeating the white argument "That we ought not to be set free in America, but ought to be sent away to Africa!!!!!!!"[122] Walker warns white Americans that if they continue to promote colonization they will cause Blacks to "obtain our liberty by the crushing arm of power," demanding that they "tell us now no more about colonization, for America is as much our country, as it is yours."[123] Walker holds that either God or the "oppressed, degraded and wretched sons of Africa" will strike against the United States for its white nationalism, though he goes back and forth on which he thinks is surer to happen first.[124] But though Walker keeps the United States as his main target of critique, he also promises that white slaveholders and their supporters are all subject to the coming Black revolution that will "root some of you out of the very face of the earth!!!!!!"[125]

Conclusion: The National Colored Convention Movement and the Settler Dream of Black Nationalism

Anticolonizationist thought occupied a central place in African American activism, abolitionism, and print culture in the 1810s and 1820s. But the 1830 inaugural National Colored Convention in Philadelphia focused its program of uplift on emigration and creating a Black nation-state within North America without the aid or design of whites. The Convention promoted self-determination for growing numbers of manumitted and self-emancipated Blacks in the United States through a vision of the Black colony as a mobile form of sociopolitical organization, allied to emigration but ultimately built on community and mutual aid.

The National Colored Convention drew delegates from Pennsylvania, New York, Maryland, Delaware, and Virginia, electing John Bowers as president and Abraham D. Shad and William Duncan as vice presidents. According to later accounts, one of the Convention's first actions after the election of its officers was "the formation and establishment of a Parent Society in the city of Philadelphia, for the purpose of purchasing land, and locating a settlement in the Province of Upper Canada," open to only "Persons of Colour."[126] The Convention quickly created a "Committee on the condition of the Free People of Colour of the United States."[127] The first finding reported by the Committee advocated that an emigrationist platform was critical to secure Black freedom: "in the opinion of this Convention, it is highly necessary that the different Societies engaged in the *Canadian Settlement*, be earnestly requested to persevere in their praiseworthy and philanthropic undertaking; firmly believing, that, at a future period, their labours will be crowned with success."[128] The Committee viewed the ACS "with unfeigned regret," believing its efforts to be "an immense and wanton waste of lives and property."[129] Though the Conventional Address included further criticisms of colonization, the speech focused more on claiming the United States as "our own native land, ... the birthplace of our *fathers*," and on encouraging Blacks to seek "asylum in the Canadas":[130]

> Our prospects are cheering; our friends and funds are daily increasing; wonders have been performed far exceeding our most sanguine expectations: already have our brethren purchased eight hundred acres of land – and two thousand of them have left the soil of their birth, crossed the lines, and laid the foundation for a structure which promises to prove an asylum for the coloured population of these United States.[131]

The remainder of the Address depicts education and mutual aid as the surest steps toward Black freedoms, specifically petitioning delegates and their respective communities for support for the Canadian undertaking.[132] Right before the Address comes to a close, the Convention again briefly acknowledges the American Colonization Society, noting that "they are pursuing the direct road to perpetuate slavery ... in this boasted land of freedom."[133] In speaking to the ACS, the Convention politely requests that "we would in the most feeling manner, beg of them to desist; or, if we must be sacrificed to their philanthropy, we would rather die at *home.*"[134] Two significant things happen here. First, the delegates insist that they and their colored Fellow-Citizens claim the United States as home, and as their home by birth. Second, the Convention refuses to make the ACS the main subject of discussion or critique of the Address, instead keeping focus on its hoped-for Canadian settlement and on a Black community built on self-determination, mutual aid, and shared dreams of freedom. The concluding paragraph of the Address calls for Blacks to support the Black press, education of their brethren, temperance, and "the production of freemen wherever it can be had."[135] By making emancipation a collective activity performed by the Black community, the Convention pivots from its critique of the false liberation peddled by the ACS to an affirmation that Black liberation can be achieved only by the community for the community. The first Colored Convention, and the emigrationist politics articulated as its platform, linked the "by-us, for-us" sensibility of Black periodical and pamphlet print cultures to Black-led settler projects of self-determination.

Notes

1 Phillis Wheatley, *Poems on various subjects, religious and moral. By Phillis Wheatley, Negro servant to Mr. John Wheatley, of Boston, in New-England* (Philadelphia: reprinted, and sold by Joseph Crukshank, in Market-Street, between Second and Third-Streets, 1789), 41.

2 Phillis Wheatley, *Collected Works*, ed. John C. Shields (New York: Oxford University Press, 1988), 183.

3 Ibid., 184. See David Kazanjian, *The Colonizing Trick: National Culture and Imperial Citizenship in Early America* (Minneapolis: University of Minnesota Press, 2003), 91–93, 124–126.

4 Vincent Caretta, *Phillis Wheatley: Biography of a Genius in Bondage* (Athens: University of Georgia Press, 2011), 159–165. See Richard West, *Back to Africa: A History of Sierra Leone and Liberia* (New York: Holt, Rinehart and Winston, 1971). See also Kenneth C. Barnes, *Journey of Hope: The*

Back-to-Africa Movement in Arkansas in the Late 1800s (Chapel Hill: University of North Carolina Press, 2004).

5 Wheatley, *Collected Works*, 175.

6 Ibid. See Joseph Yannielli, "African Americans on Campus, 1746–1876," *Princeton & Slavery*, Princeton University, accessed November 18, 2021, https://slavery.princeton.edu/stories/african-americans-on-campus-1746-1876. See also Carretta, *Phillis Wheatley*. Stolen from Anomabu (now in Ghana) and shipped to Newport, Rhode Island, Yamma and Quamine purchased their freedom in 1773 and departed for Princeton in November 1774 after a transatlantic fundraising campaign to support their education and future mission work. Neither ultimately returned to Africa. In Quaque's case, after becoming the first African to be ordained as an Anglican priest in 1765, the Society for the Propagation of the Gospel (SPG) paid for his transport to his native land the next year. Quaque and his wife stayed in Africa for the next fifty years, while the SPG boasted of him as their "Missionary, Cathecist and Schoolmaster to the Negroes on the Gold Coast in Africa" (qtd. Carretta, *Phillis Wheatley*, 162).

7 Critics such as Eddie S. Glaude Jr., Lisa A. Lindsay, Emma J. Lapsansky-Werner, and Margaret Hope Bacon have written about back-to-Africa campaigns as a mid- to late nineteenth-century trend. Conversely, critics like Ousmane K. Power-Greene and David Kazanjian place the origins of anticolonizationist sentiment more squarely in the early nineteenth century.

8 Fred Moten, *The Universal Machine* (Durham, NC: Duke University Press, 2018), 93.

9 Ousmane K. Power-Greene, *Against Wind and Tide: The African American Struggle against the Colonization Movement* (New York: New York University Press, 2014), 17–45.

10 Imani Perry, *Vexy Thing: On Gender and Liberation* (Durham, NC: Duke University Press, 2018), 48.

11 Noted abolitionist William Lloyd Garrison, for example, supported the ACS in its early days, but became one of the Society's most vocal critics in print, publishing a 1832 pamphlet titled *Thoughts on African Colonization*.

12 Kazanjian, *Colonizing Trick*, 10.

13 Richard S. Newman, Roy E. Finkenbine, and Douglass Mooney, "Philadelphia Emigrationist Petition, circa 1792: An Introduction," *The William and Mary Quarterly* 64, no. 1 (2007): 162 [161–166].

14 Ibid., 165.

15 Kazanjian, *Colonizing Trick*, 137.

16 Ronald A. T. Judy, *(Dis)Forming the American Canon: African-Arabic Slave Narratives and the Vernacular* (Minneapolis: University of Minnesota Press, 1993), 69.

17 See Thomas Jefferson, "A Bill Declaring Who Shall Be Deemed Citizens of This Commonwealth" and "Report of the Commissioners for the University

of Virginia," both in *Writings*, ed. Merill D. Peterson (New York: Library of America, 1984), 48–49 and 131–147.

18 Jefferson, *Writings*, 264, my emphasis. Kazanjian, *Colonizing Trick*, 102ff.

19 Jefferson, *Writings*, 270.

20 Mikhail Bakhtin, *Problems of Dostoeysky's Poetics*, trans. Caryl Emerson (Minneapolis: University of Minnesota Press, 1984), 293.

21 Hortense Spillers, *Black, White, and in Color: Essays on American Literature and Culture* (Chicago: University of Chicago Press, 2003), 183.

22 David Kazanjian, "Racial Governmentality: Thomas Jefferson and African Colonisation in the United States before 1816," *Alternation* 5, no. 1 (1998): 46. https://hdl.handle.net/10520/AJA10231757_83.

23 Jacqueline Bacon, "The History of *Freedom's Journal*: A Study in Empowerment and Community," *The Journal of African American History* 88, no. 1 (2003): 1–20 [11]. See David Scott, "That Event, This Memory: Notes on the Anthropology of African Diasporas in the New World," *Diaspora* 1, no. 3 (1991): 261–284; Brent Hayes Edwards, "The Uses of Diaspora," *Social Test* 19, no. 1 (2001): 45–73; Stephanie E. Smallwood, *Saltwater Slavery: A Middle Passage from Africa to American Diaspora* (Cambridge, MA: Harvard University Press, 2008). I use the term "Afrodiasporan" to emphasize the multinational sensibility and possibility of Black movements in the Americas and Atlantic world. My use of this term builds on work by Brent Hayes Edwards, Stephanie E. Smallwood, and David Scott.

24 Bacon, "The History of *Freedom's Journal*," 4.

25 Ibid., 8.

26 Ibid., 7.

27 See Nat Turner, *The Confessions of Nat Turner, The Leader of the Late Insurrection in Southampton, Va.* (Baltimore: Published by Thomas R. Gray, 1831), 8ff. See also Mary Prince, *The History of Mary Prince, a West Indian Slave* (London: Published by F. Westley and A. H. Davis, 1831), 17. Nat Turner in his *Confession* talks about the unknown or unremembered "manner in which he learned to read and write" and reports "no recollection whatever of learning the alphabet" (p. 8). It is possible that Turner is obscuring the origins of his literacy skills in order to protect whoever taught him or how he learned as a child, as those people could be presumably still alive and likely enslaved at the time of publication. Mary Prince in the 1805 narrative similarly describes learning to read as a child, though she names the source: "The Moravian ladies (Mrs. Richter, Mrs. Olufsen, and Mrs. Santer) taught me to read in class" (17).

28 Frances Smith Foster, "A Narrative of the Interesting Origins and (Somewhat) Surprising Developments of African-American Print Culture," *American Literary History* 17, no. 4 (2005): 714–740 [720].

29 Qtd. Bacon, "The History of *Freedom's Journal*," 7.

30 Elizabeth McHenry, *Forgotten Readers: Recovering the Lost History of African American Literary Societies* (Durham, NC: Duke University Press, 2002), 53–54; Kwando M. Kinshasa, *Emigration vs. Assimilation: The Debate in the African-American Press* (Jefferson, NC: McFarland, 1988), 114–117.

31 McHenry, *Forgotten Readers*, 85.

32 Dorothy B. Parker, "The Organized Educational Activities of Negro Literary Societies, 1828–1846," *The Journal of Negro Education* 5, no. 4 (1936): 555–576 [555].

33 Matt Sandler, *The Black Romantic Revolution: Abolitionist Poets at the End of Slavery* (New York: Verso, 2020), 8–9.

34 "To Our Patrons," *Freedom's Journal*, March 3, 1827.

35 "To Our Patrons," *Freedom's Journal*, March 16, 1827.

36 Ibid.

37 Qtd. in Power-Greene, *Against Wind and Tide*, 1.

38 Richard S. Newman, *The Transformation of American Abolitionism: Fighting Slavery in the Early Republic* (Chapel Hill: University of North Carolina Press, 2002), 96–100. See also Benjamin Quarles, *Black Abolitionists* (New York: De Capo Press, 1991).

39 Newman, *Transformation*, 96.

40 "Colonization Society," *Freedom's Journal*, September 14, 1827.

41 Winston James, *The Struggles of John Brown Russworm: The Life and Writings of a Pan-Africanist Pioneer, 1799–1851* (New York: New York University Press, 2010), 141.

42 Ibid., 148, my emphasis.

43 Ibid., 142.

44 *Genius of Universal Emancipation* was originally purchased by Benjamin Lundy in 1821 from Elihu Embree.

45 "African Colonization," *Genius of Universal Emancipation*, August 1821.

46 Ibid., 28.

47 Ibid., 28.

48 "Liberia, the United States Colony of Africa," *Genius of Universal Emancipation*, May 8, 1823.

49 Ibid.

50 Ibid.

51 Michel Foucault, *Discipline and Punish: The Birth of the Prison*, trans. Alan Sheridan (New York: Vintage Books, 1991), 138.

52 "Emigration to Hayti – No. IV: To the Editor of *The Genius of Universal Emancipation*," *Genius of Universal Emancipation*, February 1825, 69.

53 Ibid., 70.

54 Ibid., 70.

55 Ibid., 71.

56 Ibid., 71.

57 Ibid., 72.

58 Michel-Rolph Trouillot, *Silencing the Past: Power and the Production of History* (Boston: Beacon Press, 1995), 70–107.

59 Eric J. Sundquist, *To Wake the Nations: Race in the Making of American Literature* (Cambridge, MA: Belknap Press of Harvard University Press, 1993), 32.

60 Ibid., 32.

61 See C. L. R. James, *The Black Jacobins: Toussaint L'Ouverture and the San Domingo Revolution* (New York: Vintage Books, 1963); Susan Buck-Morss,

Hegel, Haiti, and Universal History (Pittsburgh: University of Pittsburgh Press, 2009); Sara Fanning, *Caribbean Crossings: African Americans and the Haitian Emigration Movement* (New York: New York University Press, 2015); Leonora Sansay, *The Secret History; or the Horrors of St. Domingo*, ed. Michael Drexler (Peterborough: Broadview, 2008).

62 Power-Greene, *Against Wind and Tide*, 27–28; Fanning, *Caribbean Crossings*, 11–12.

63 Jean-Pierre Boyer and Daniel Loring Dewey, *Correspondence Relative to the Emigration of Hayti, of the Free People of Colour, in the United States* (New York: Printed by Mahlon Day, 1824), 7.

64 Ibid., 8.

65 Power-Greene, *Against Wind and Tide*, 24.

66 Prince Saunders, *A Memoir Presented to the American Convention for Promoting the Abolition of Slavery, and Improving the Condition of the African Race, December 11th, 1818* (Philadelphia: Printed by Dennis Heartt, 1818), 13.

67 Haytien Emigration Society, *Information for the Free People of Colour Who Are Inclined to Emigrate to Hayti* (Philadelphia: Printed by J. H. Cunningham, 1825), 7.

68 "American Colonization Society," *Freedom's Journal*, July 18, 1828. The letter is reproduced across the July 11 and 18, 1828, issues, though only the latter is discussed in detail here.

69 Ibid.

70 Ibid.

71 Ibid.

72 Kazanjian, *Brink of Freedom*, 66; Anne E. Bromley, "UVA Building Named for Former Slave and Stonemason Peyton Skipwith," *UVA Today*, University of Virginia, April 13, 2017, https://news.virginia.edu/content/uva-building-named-former-slave-and-stonemason-peyton-skipwith.

73 Bromley, "UVA Building Named."

74 Randal M. Miller, ed., *"Dear Master": Letters of a Slave Family* (Ithaca, NY: Cornell University Press, 1978), 59.

75 Kazanjian, *Brink of Freedom*, 67.

76 Ibid., 68ff.

77 Power-Greene, *Against Wind and Tide*, 21; Henri Christophe, *Henry Christophe and Thomas Clarkson: A Correspondence*, ed. Earl Leslie Griggs and Clifford H. Prator (Berkeley: University of California Press, 1952), 125, 226.

78 Christophe, *Henry Christophe*, 227.

79 Fanning, *Caribbean Crossings*, 43–44; Power-Greene, *Against Wind and Tide*, 27–28.

80 Fanning, *Caribbean Crossings*, 100.

81 Ibid., 102.

82 Ibid., 111–112. Note that though many Black settlers abandoned Haiti by 1826, some stayed and farmed the allotments promised to them, while holding the titles to their land.

83 Ibid., 112.

84 Ibid.

85 Ibid., 113.

86 "The [Illegible] Society," *Freedom's Journal*, December 20, 1828, p. 4.

87 "Emancipation and Colonization," *Freedom's Journal*, January 2, 1829.

88 "From the *Ohio Monitor*," *Freedom's Journal*, January 31, 1829.

89 Ibid., 2.

90 "Liberia," *Freedom's Journal*, February 21, 1829, p. 6, my emphasis.

91 Bacon, "The History of *Freedom's Journal*," 2, 11–12; Parker, "Organized Educational Activities," 559; Jacqueline Bacon, "Acting as Freemen': Rhetoric, Race, and Reform in the Debate over Colonization in *Freedom's Journal*, 1827–28," *Quarterly Journal of Speech* 93, no. 1 (2007): 58–83 [61].

92 "Liberia," *Freedom's Journal*, February 21, 1829.

93 "Our Vindication," *Freedom's Journal*, March 7, 1829.

94 "Colonization," *Freedom's Journal*, March 14, 1829.

95 Ibid.

96 "Plan for the Civil Government of the Colony of Liberia," *Freedom's Journal*, March 28, 1829.

97 Chris Apap, "'Let No Man of Us Budge One Step': David Walker and the Rhetoric of African American Emplacement," *Early American Literature* 46, no. 2 (2011): 319–350 [322].

98 Gordon Fraser, "Distributed Agency: David Walker's *Appeal*, Black Readership, and the Politics of Self-Deportation," *ESQ* 65, no. 2 (2019): 221–256 [224].

99 Qtd. in Bacon, "The History of *Freedom's Journal*," 5.

100 Harriet Jacobs, *Incidents in the Life of a Slave Girl, Written by Herself*, ed. L. Maria Child (Boston: Published for the Author, 1861), 173.

101 Stephen Best, *None Like Us: Blackness, Belonging, Aesthetic Life* (Durham, NC: Duke University Press, 2018), 10.

102 David Walker, *David Walker's Appeal: In Four Articles, Together with a Preamble, to the Coloured Citizens of the World, but Particularly, and Very Expressly, to Those of the United States*, ed. Sean Wilentz (New York: Hill and Wang, 1995), 1.

103 Ibid., 1.

104 Ibid., 1.

105 Ibid., 5, 6.

106 Martha Schoolman, *Abolitionist Geographies* (Minneapolis: University of Minnesota Press, 2014), 5; Walker, *Appeal*, 6.

107 W. E. B. DuBois, *Black Reconstruction in America, 1860–1880*, ed. David Levering Lewis (New York: Free Press, 1998), 184.

108 Walker, *Appeal*, 20.

109 Ibid., 14–15, original emphasis.

110 Ibid., 64.

111 Ibid., 64.

112 Ibid., 64.

113 Ibid., 63.
114 Ibid., 63.
115 Ibid., 63.
116 Ibid., 62–64.
117 Ibid., 65.
118 Ibid., 64.
119 Ibid., 65.
120 Ibid., 64.
121 Ibid., 67.
122 Ibid., 66.
123 Ibid., 70.
124 Ibid., 71.
125 Ibid., 72.
126 *Constitution of the American Society of Free Persons of Colour, for Improving Their Condition in the United States; for Purchasing Lands; and for the Establishment of a Settlement in Upper Canada. Also the Proceedings of the Convention, with Their Address to the Free Persons of Colour in the United States* (Philadelphia: Printed by J. W. Allen, 1831), 5.
127 *Minutes and Proceedings of the First Annual Convention of the People of Colour, Held by Adjournments in the City of Philadelphia* (Philadelphia: Published by Order of the Committee of Arrangements, 1831), 4.
128 Ibid., 4.
129 Ibid., 5.
130 Ibid., 12.
131 Ibid., 13.
132 Ibid., 13.
133 Ibid., 15.
134 Ibid., 15, my emphasis.
135 Ibid., 15.

CHAPTER 13

The Black Child, the Colonial Orphan, and Early Republican Visions of Freedom

Anna Mae Duane

In a 1789 letter, Thomas Jefferson mused that "as far as I can judge from the experiments which have been made, to give liberty to, or rather, to abandon persons whose habits have been formed in slavery is like abandoning children."[1] Nearing the end of his life, Jefferson saw freedom as requiring precisely such an act of child abandonment. In 1824, frightened by the prospect of a prolifically reproducing enslaved population, Jefferson imagined that the only way forward would be to sever ties between parents and children. Always attentive to numbers, Jefferson speculated that if the "whole annual increase" of African Americans were "to be of 60 thousand effective births, then 50. vessels of 400. tons burthen each, constantly employed in that short run, would carry off the increase of every year, & the old stock would die off in the ordinary course of nature." Carrying off the "increase" – the children of African American parents – as part of a colonization scheme would, Jefferson acknowledged, "involv[e] some constitutional scruples." And, he admitted, "the separation of infants from their mothers too would produce some scruples of humanity." But to let such scruples stand in the way "would be straining at a gnat, and swallowing a camel." Better to dismiss such misplaced sentimentality, Jefferson reasoned, and move forward with a plan that, in the end, would render African Americans "perhaps more good than evil" by bestowing on them the blessings of freedom and nationhood.[2]

Jefferson's choice to draw on the figure of the orphan to meditate on freedom and futurity should come as no surprise to literary historians who have long noted two intertwined realities of the early republican era: the late eighteenth- and early nineteenth-century US was, in fact, a country dominated by young people, and writers often imagined the nation's future, and what freedom could look like within that future, through the image of childhood.[3] In particular, orphanhood emerged in a host of early republican stories as an emblem of independence, a literary legacy that has been largely embraced by later generations. Mid-twentieth-century literary critics have lauded how early Americans valorized the parentless youth as an "American Adam" unshackled to the past or, to use Leslie Fiedler's phrase, "an outcast or orphan" who found freedom in disconnection.[4] As Jefferson's link between slavery and orphanhood suggests, the fortune-seeking orphan we have come to embrace as an American touchstone has often provided a deceptive gloss over the difficulties raised by the actual orphans created by the era's embrace of slavery and dispossession.

Even as the early US was swept up by stories that imagined the future of an "infant nation," set adrift, the possibilities offered by the child were expanded or circumscribed by which actual children were claimed or rejected as part of the nation. This essay explores this tension between the figurative and literal child by examining how formulations of the "child," the "slave," and the "orphan" shaped manumission laws, local school curricula, and locally produced literature in early republican New York City. These terms – often-used political metaphors for the infant nation – became, once grounded in local practice, sites capable of opening radical possibilities. More specifically, I focus on points of exchange between the American Colonization Society and students at the New York African Free School (1783–1833) to offer a case study in the complex inter-change between metaphorical and actual children. Reading these texts together suggests that, embedded within the character of the self-reliant orphan that became central to the stories early Americans told them-selves, and that literary historians have – at times – conflated with our understanding of the young nation itself, is a struggle over the meanings of freedom as it emerges in the prospect of a free Black child.[5]

The postrevolutionary moment in which Jefferson wrote his first letter generated a reading public fascinated by stories that transformed the figure of the orphan from an emblem of trauma into a subject that taught the nation that filial disregard was the path to freedom. Enlightenment phi-losophy that aligned the acquisition of reason with coming of age lent itself exceptionally well to depictions of the American colonies as a restless youth on the verge of independence.[6] Seduction novels featured daughters who effectively disinherited themselves in order to pursue their desires. Richardson's *Clarissa* – notably, the best-selling novel of 1775 – featured a young girl whose refusal to adhere to her father's wishes required leaving his home entirely. Similarly, Charlotte Temple, the protagonist of Susannah Rowson's popular seduction novel, followed her inclination to accompany a soldier to the United States, leaving her family of origin behind. In both cases, the women's desires for disentanglement proved deadly. Although seduction heroines were almost certain to meet an early death, early republican readers seemed thrilled by their misadventures.

Stephen Burroughs and Benjamin Franklin offer two more sanguine views of the alienated child. Although ostensibly a tale of misadventure, Burroughs's memoir offered readers a glimpse of the radical possibilities open to a self-made "outcast among mankind" who needed to create his own path "without any regard to family, blood, or connexion."[7] Benjamin Franklin's *Autobiography* goes a step further, depicting Franklin's early disobedience and natal alienation as building blocks of greatness. The *Autobiography* depicts a teenaged Franklin lying about his identity and illegally breaking his apprenticeship agreements. Franklin, unlike Charlotte Temple, immediately finds friends and fortune in his new city, with nary a backward glance at the large family he left behind.[8]

Revolutionary-era white Americans may have embraced the idea of casting the nation as a colonial youth throwing off the reins of oppressive paternal care, but even the most progressive among them were largely unable to imagine Black freedom outside a carefully curated maturation process.[9] Eighteenth-century white legislators in the Northeast, faced with the contradictions slavery posed to a nation allegedly founded on the principal of expanded freedom, seemed quite sure that slavery simply could not be ended abruptly. "To set them [slaves] afloat at once would, I really believe, be productive of much inconvenience & mischief," George Washington wrote the Marquis de Lafayette in 1786, "but by degrees it certainly might, & assuredly ought to be effected & that too by Legislative authority."[10] As François Furstenberg has demonstrated, Washington's fears about the "mischief" that would occur by freeing slaves before they had been properly prepared for the honor fell in line with antislavery thinking both in the United States and abroad, as evidenced in the writing of Nicolas de Condorcet, a French philosopher who exerted considerable influence on Jefferson, Lafayette, and others. While he offered sharp critiques of slavery, Condorcet nonetheless warned against "changes too brusque." Instead of racing to enact universal liberty, he insisted that those currently enslaved would be better served by a "slow march of emancipation."[11] The presently enslaved, in this vision, were ruined by bad habits, chained to a past that would forever shape their future. In order to imagine the freedom of Black people, white elites in the northern states felt compelled to imagine a future generation, yet unborn perhaps, that would somehow be able to carry the burdens that those currently enslaved would not be able to bear.

When legislators in Pennsylvania, New York, New Jersey, Connecticut, and Rhode Island began to construct a legal structure through which Black freedom might be realized, they placed their collective faith in infant Black children.[12] New York's 1799 manumission law, for instance, initially freed only those enslaved people who were born on or after July 4 of that very year. Notably, the states did not free these newborns immediately. Freedom could come only after the children had reached a maturity that lawmakers imagined would be carefully nurtured through an extensive educational process. As a member of the New York Manumission Society explained, such a plan would "PROVIDE FOR THE INTELLECTUAL AND MORAL CULTIVATION of slaves, that they may be prepared to exercise the rights, and discharge the duties of citizens, when liberty shall be given them; and which, having thus fitted them for the station, will confer upon them, in due time, the privileges and dignity of other freemen."[13] This cultivation would apparently require decades, a process that might begin with infants, but would extend long past adolescence. (Most laws did not call for emancipation until the children were in their mid- to late twenties.) If the newly emancipated nation enjoyed thinking of itself as an orphan, freeing itself from the fetters of tyranny, New Yorkers were quite insistent that the few enslaved Black children who were being considered for eventual freedom would have to be carefully, scrupulously monitored from birth to adulthood.[14]

The decision to invest in the education of the youngest of African Americans perhaps comforted legislators who imagined that they would be overseeing a generation of Émiles, who, like Rosseau's famous pupil, would find their intellect and interior states unerringly molded by cultured adults.[15] For a brief moment, it might seem, some Black children in northern states might be imagined as the collective blank slate that Revolutionary thinkers had embraced, untethered to the traumas of their parents' history. During the first two decades of the nineteenth century, the global embrace of what would come to be called the Lancasterian model of education seemed to herald a future in which *all* students could be detached from the mistakes of the past. Imagining a method of educating the world's poor orphans, Englishman Joseph Lancaster had promised that his system would free the world from troublesome factions. The New York African Free School enthusiastically embraced the Lancasterian model early in the nineteenth century, perhaps in the hopes that Lancaster's system would help to dissipate any fractious feelings harbored by their students. In Lancasterian classrooms, students largely taught one another, leaving the schoolmaster to loosely supervise large groups of students. Because students were tasked with each other's instruction, Lancaster argued, their education could be free of ideology, leaving the prejudices and legacies of the adult schoolmaster behind. "[W]hen the pupils, as well as the schoolmaster, understand how to act and learn on this system," Lancaster promised, "the system, not the master's vague, discretionary, uncertain judgment, will be in practice."[16] The great enthusiasm for the Lancasterian system throughout the United States testified to the allure of producing a generation of students free from the "uncertain judgments" of adult prejudice. As with the manumission laws that postponed all enslaved people's freedom in order to foreground childhood education, the Lancasterian philosophy undergirded lofty ideals with material rewards that benefited the powerful. The idea that Black children needed tutelage to earn freedom allowed slavery to stay in place for another generation, and the idea that fewer teachers generated less prejudice also allowed schools to be run on a shoestring budget.

In many ways, the writers of gradual manumission laws had anticipated Lancaster's faith in students' capacity to be teachers. By investing in the "cultivation" of Black youth, they were effectively betting on Black children's ability to benefit from an education that would remake them as unequivocal Americans. They also invested in the capacity of Black students to change the minds of prejudiced white people around them.[17] Such persuasion often involved inviting the public to performances held by schools that showcased their African American students' remarkable progress.[18] Those performances, and the educational process that produced them, were designed to convince both the students and the white adults who would eventually rule on their fate that a new future was possible. In 1763, Benjamin Franklin visited a schoolhouse in Philadelphia and expressed his admiration for the Black students' "considerable Progress in Reading," noting that they "behav'd very orderly, showd a proper Respect and ready Obedience to the Mistress." After witnessing the students' deportment, Franklin wrote that the school visit had changed his opinion about "the natural capacities of the black Race."[19] He was not alone. In 1818, a visitor to the New York African Free School wrote a letter to the editor of the *American Monthly Magazine*, declaring that he "saw enough to convince the most skeptical that the colored race is abundantly imbued by nature with every intellectual and moral faculty."[20]

Of course, investing students, especially Black students, with the power to educate adults was a double-edged sword. If good students could sway prejudiced onlookers to embrace equality, then bad students could exert dangerous influence over children and adults alike. Robert Finley, the eventual founder of the American Colonization Society, was well acquainted with how quickly students might master a teacher. As his friend and memoirist Isaac Brown recalled in 1819, Finley faced difficulties as a young grammar school teacher who struggled "to introduce order and establish discipline" among unruly students. Despite his best efforts, the students remained "irregular and insubordinate in their temper and manners." Although Finley "proceeded with energy," the students "manifested a refractory temper, resisted his regulations, and, on being urged to comply, broke out into open rebellion, in hopes of intimidating the youthful instructor and constraining him to connive at their idle and disorderly habits."[21] As Christopher Castiglia has argued, "[Finley's] battle is ultimately about influence and imitation; the fear is . . . that the teacher will be taught, that Finley might be made to 'connive' at the behavior of his pupils."[22] What, Finley later worried, would educated Black children be able to "connive" the rest of the country into believing? Ideally, the generation of Black children educated for freedom would in fact prove to be a testament to the Enlightenment faith in pedagogical transformation. Finley feared, however, that rather than these children becoming disconnected from their parents' historical trauma, they would be motivated to avenge it. "The evil," Finley warned in 1816, "increases every year, and the gloomy picture grows darker continually, so that the question is often and anxiously asked – *What will be the end of all this?*"[23]

Faced with an uncertain future, Finley, the former schoolmaster, joined forces with public education advocates such as Charles Fenton Mercer to graft the figure of the plucky American orphan on to the fantasy of a colonizing Black child. In 1816, Finley founded the American Colonization Society, which declared that the education Black children were currently receiving should be deployed in Liberia, not America.[24] In other words, Finley's vision reimagined education's ability to culturally dislocate Black children and replaced it with colonization's capacity to physically dislocate the next generation.

The American Colonization Society has long functioned as a curious footnote in studies of American literature and culture, a colonialist cul-de-sac that was always already doomed to fail. And in truth, it fell far short of its ambitions. Only a fraction of the nation's four million enslaved African Americans would ever take the journey to Liberia. Yet we ignore the power that the colonizationist narrative had during the early republic at our peril. Among liberal white elites, the story the ACS told was incredibly persuasive. White Abolitionists William Lloyd Garrison, Gerrit Smith, Samuel J. May, and Arthur and Lewis Tappan were originally supporters of African colonization, although most of them would eventually embrace immediate emancipation at the behest of Black colleagues.[25] As late as

1852, the best-selling antislavery novel *Uncle Tom's Cabin* dispatched its Black protagonists either by death (Uncle Tom) or emigration to Africa (Topsy and George Harris). As late as 1862, Abraham Lincoln felt compelled to meet with Black leaders to try to encourage them to lead a colonization party to Liberia or Central America.[26]

Regardless of the ACS's appeal to white elites, the Society had to reach an audience beyond white donors and benefactors if it wanted to achieve its goal of mass Black emigration. The story the ACS told about colonization was arguably the first official narrative that white Americans crafted specifically for a Black audience. Notably, the ACS insisted that their plan had to be carried out voluntarily – Black Americans would have to be convinced, not coerced, to believe that dislocation from their native country offered them the best possible future. It "will not do," read a missive from the president of the American Colonization Society in 1817, "to ship these unfortunate people out of our territory merely because we are afraid of them, or because they may grow troublesome here. This would be as flagrant an act of injustice to them, as that which brought them, or their ancestors from Africa for the purposes of rendering them slaves." Therefore, it is "evident that their departure must be the result of a voluntary disposition."[27] At a meeting at the Hartford colonization society, members worried aloud about the hurdles of convincing a skeptical Black public. Because of the "abundant cause" Black people had "to distrust the white men's professions," colonizationists knew that they would have to "convince them by our kindness, of the purity of our motives, and the blessings we mean to confer upon them." Only then would Black freed people be willing to "change their state of comparative insignificance and misery, for independence and happiness."[28]

Convincing Black people of the "blessings" of colonization would require significant outreach, in newspapers, in public meetings, and, of course, in schools. Because gradual manumission laws had prioritized the education of younger people, the ACS's most likely readers of their promotional narratives, would, in practice, be Black youth and children, reading newspapers and missives out loud in family settings.[29] As Beverly Lyon Clark reminds us, family reading sessions were the norm throughout the nineteenth century. As late as 1873, Black print culture testified to the importance of child readers, as a columnist in Black publication *The Christian Recorder* depicted Black children reading the newspaper to their parents: "Fathers and mothers that cannot read, when the work's day is done, press the school children or some friend into service and the *Christian Recorder* is read in the family circle. The sayings of the different writers are commented on, the news is discussed, and pleasant instructive evenings are spent."[30] In the ACS's case, the schoolchildren pressed into service were also the target audience for their colonizationist sales pitch.

One of the most prominent characters in that pitch was the orphan. In this case, however, the meaning attached to that character would be calibrated differently for white and Black audiences in ways that echoed Jefferson's shift from paternalistic concern for unattached children to his withering disdain for the sentimentalism he imputed to Black families who resisted familial separation. For white audiences, the ACS picked up on the antislavery strain that held up the separated child as a tragedy that could, with colonization, be repaired by returning African Americans to their "mother country." In 1825, an ACS advocate assured readers that "the design of this association" was "to listen to the sorrows of Africa's widowed mothers and orphan children" and "to restore them to the land of their ancestors."[31] Here the harms of slavery, the story suggested, could be addressed, and perhaps even written over, by acknowledging the rupture of families on a historical and global scale.[32]

In the discourse directed at Black audiences, however, the ACS sought to remake the orphan created by slavery's greed into an inspirational character. Drawing from sources ranging from the biblical Exodus story to the United States' own colonial beginnings, the ACS sought to instruct Black audiences to recast the Black orphan as a heroic figure, whose youth and vigor invites an entirely new start.[33] Henry Clay was one among many ACS members who invited Black freed people to imagine themselves in the mold of America's colonial forefathers, who voluntarily left the past behind to embrace the freedom waiting for them on other shores. For Clay, the settlement of Africa would offer a chance to both repeat and improve on the settlement of America. "What brought our fathers voluntarily to these shores, then savage and forbidding, not less savage and forbidding perhaps than Africa itself?" he asked. The answer was apparent: "to render themselves more happy."[34] Although Clay and others worried about the reluctance of African Americans to leave behind the only country they had ever known, and all their relations, Clay assured them that such loss was a small price to pay. "He has placed a false estimate upon liberty," he insisted, "who believes that there are many who would refuse the boon, when coupled even with such a condition."[35]

At a later meeting of the Colonization Society of Kentucky, Clay imagined a "United States of Africa" in which, once again, the choice to leave one's birth nation would result in a new order. This United States of Africa would "assume [America's] likeness, bask in the beams of her splendour, reflect back the glory of her greatness, and attain and exercise all her moral and intellectual and physical energies."[36] This narrative repurposing African Americans' loss of natal ties as a second American coming would shape the rhetoric of the ACS for years to come. Later ACS advocates would declare that African Americans' decision to leave country and kin behind was reenacting American origin stories anew. According to ACS member B. B. Thatcher, their journey was nothing short of "the renewal on the African shore, in 1820, of the splendid drama acted on the 'stern and rock-bound coast [of New England] *two centuries before*." [37] The 1820 ship ferrying an early cohort of African American colonists to Liberia would be nicknamed the "Mayflower 2."

The confused and conflicted reimagining of Black orphanhood as a vector to both individual freedom and retroactive national redemption resonates powerfully in a text inspired by students at the New York African Free School. *The Life and Adventures of Olaudah Equiano; or Gustavus Vassa, the African: From an Account Written by Himself* was adapted by Abigail Mott, a Quaker teacher and antislavery advocate. It was published by Samuel Wood in 1829.[38] This decidedly minor version of a major text offers a powerful glimpse into the uneasy imaginings of freedom in the early republic centered around educating a Black child who functions as both a muse and an epistemic absence. Mott's text first evokes the Black child reader, and then denies that child's engagement with the material within its pages, rendering the book an orphan text in itself, cut off from its intended readerly home. In the preface, dated 1825 (four years before the book's actual publication date), Mott explains that the text was inspired by her visits to the "African Free School in New York" where she had "observed tickets given to the pupils as rewards for attention to their studies," which had "became a sort of currency" that students could turn in in exchange for toys or other valuables. Such observation led Mott to "believe that there is scarcely anything which can be given to a child as a premium for good behavior which has a better tendency than a book." "This belief," she explains, "prompted me to attempt an abridgment of the Memoirs of Gustavus Vassa, the African," because a text containing "many interesting circumstances, may not be thought unsuitable for distribution in those schools."[39] Notably, by the 1820s the school's white schoolmaster and board members had largely embraced the tenets of the American Colonization Society and encouraged students to consider leaving New York for a new start in Liberia, which makes Mott's decision to create a text focusing on the middle passage particularly interesting.[40]

Soon after Mott's declaration that her visit to Black schoolchildren prompted her to adapt Equiano's *Narrative*, she refuses to gesture directly to the children who inspired her work. "Whether or not the design of these extracts meet the approbation of the Trustees of the African Schools," Mott notes, "I think it will be an interesting little work for children of any class, and I have therefore placed it in the hands of the publisher."[41] In an era in which authors often directly addressed their proposed readers, Mott relinquishes any imaginative connection with them on the first page. Her resignation in placing the text "in the hands of the publisher" splinters authorial intention from readerly reception.[42]

The dislocation invoked in the book's preface continues throughout the text as both editor and publisher create content that denies the presence of the free, literate Black child that allegedly inspired the book's existence. Like the plans conjured by the American Colonization Society, Mott's version of Equiano's *Narrative* cannot quite bring itself to fully acknowledge or understand the audience it is designed to serve, or the nation that speaks to them. Rather than adapting the eighteenth-century slave narrative for young New Yorkers in the late 1820s, this text – both Equiano's adapted narrative and the appendix that accompanies it – seems to want to transport its audience back to a time before most of them were born, and a place it was unlikely any of them had ever seen.[43] To begin with, Mott's version of Equiano's journey from slavery to freedom disrupts the typically linear slave narrative form that intertwines a enslaved child's journey to freedom with their path to maturity. Instead, this adaptation emphasizes the picaresque aspects of Equiano's tale to render his story as a life marked by constant motion. Equiano's journey through orphanhood, to the middle passage, to his enslaved youth, and to eventual freedom in Great Britain is compressed into a scant twenty-five pages, nine of which describe his residence in Africa. In rapid succession, we learn of several roundtrips to the West Indies, trips to Portugal, a stop in Greenland, and several trips to England. In Mott's hands, Equiano's incessant wandering is not the byproduct of being torn from his original home, but instead emerges as a function of his adventurous wanderlust. The moment in which Equiano gains his freedom, rather than occupying the centerpiece of the narrative, is merely one more stop in his picaresque tale. When he purchases himself – an act itself made possible by the industry he deploys in his many travels – his first thought is about taking yet another sea voyage. The entreaties of his former master to remain where he is causes Equiano a "hard struggle" because he "longed to go to London and see my old Captain Pascal."[44] While the original narrative emphasizes Equiano's self-identification as an

Englishman, in this adaptation, England emerges as just one stop in a seemingly endless journey.

The appendix – which takes up roughly a third of the entire page count of the text – further disrupts the sense of historical progression one might expect from abolitionist materials. By Mott's account, she created the text in 1825, two years before universal manumission in New York state. When it was published in 1829, that landmark day had come and gone. Yet the materials appended to Equiano's narrative cast the slavery struggle starkly in eighteenth-century terms. After the termination of Equiano's *Narrative*, readers are told that "The publisher here thought it proper to enlarge this small work by adding the following remarks upon the Slave Trade: not with a view to excite the indignation of any, but to give the young and the uninformed a correct idea of what the poor inhabitants of Africa suffer."[45] What follows is a tract stridently urging action to render to transatlantic slave trade illegal, something that had occurred nearly twenty years earlier. In fact, the Black community would hold annual parades celebrating this event. One of the New York African Free School's first school masters, an African American named John Teasman, likely lost his job for having the temerity to take to the streets for precisely such a parade.[46] In any case, those who had been "young and uninformed" when the tract was first published would be well into middle age by its inclusion in this book.

Whether or not the students of the New York African Free School actually read this book, the sense of temporal and national dislocation it offered would be profoundly familiar to them, and to many in the generation who had come of age in the era of gradual manumission.[47] Even as they aged into the freedom that antislavery legislators had imagined for them in 1799, Black children in New York City were interpellated by the ACS into a story that told them that somehow they still had not met their mark. The colonizationists who held positions as teachers and board members at the school collectively imagined movement out of slavery, not as a bildungsroman in which a youth grows into their place in the world, but rather as a speculative picaresque in which both time and space shift positions, in which origins are reproduced and improved upon, and in which the ending point is continually deferred.

We do not know how individual Black children at the New York African Free School responded to Mott's convoluted text. But we can trace the resistance those children and their community expressed in the face of colonizationist stories that were held up as a liberatory education. In 1833, students boycotted the school because of the schoolmaster's

"colonizationist views," demanding Black instructors replace white colonizationist teachers, and they succeeded.[48] The American Colonization
Society's vision, packaged in the hopes of convincing Black children to
validate America's violent colonialist origins as their own path to freedom,
was refuted in both figurative and material terms. Not only did the New
York African Free School community's boycott collectively silence those
who told colonialist stories in the children's schools, but nationally only a
few thousand (out of over four million enslaved people) would take the
American Colonization Society up on their offer to reenact Plymouth
Rock on African shores. Jefferson's vision of a generation who would
willingly leave their parents to embrace his vison of independence would
never come to pass. Instead, vocal Black resistance to the ACS would
eventually convince many white abolitionists, Garrison among them, to
change their stance on colonization and instead demand immediate
emancipation.[49]

While Abigail Mott and the text she created in response to seeing Black
schoolchildren seem unable to embrace Black child readers, or at least to
claim them as an audience, scholars can turn our attention to how
metaphors of childhood presided over intense debates about shifting
national and racial identity in the early republic. In particular, attending
to Americans' fascination with a particular form of orphanhood offers
insight into how deeply both literature and the law were shaped by the
very enslaved and dispossessed children we have largely written off as
invisible in early republican letters. Seeking out children's responses,
especially Black children's responses, to early republican and antebellum
depictions of them requires expanding our own critical repertoire to seek
out different texts, but also to privilege the alternate creative genealogies
they represent. Children's literature, family reading, collective authorship,
and vibrant editorial practices of reprinting and reframing existing texts all
offer us a way to rethink how we imagine authorship itself.[50]

By engaging in reading practices that explore the intersections of children's literature, educational treatises, and legal edicts, we can complicate
the conventional wisdom that has suggested it was impossible to imagine
children, especially Black children, as participants in the stories that shaped
their lives in the early republic. In the cluster of texts I have examined here,
we can glimpse how Black children's work as students and their overwhelming rejection of the colonizationist story designed for their consumption helped to change the trajectory of how freedom was defined for
them and for others in the years going forward. Indeed, many of the
children who were instructed by colonizationist teachers at the school

would go on to lead the charge for universal emancipation as young adults. Bruce Dorsey has argued that "colonizationists contributed to the development of a white discourse on race, sex, gender, and civilization that shaped the underpinnings of white supremacy and white male dominance for the remainder of the nineteenth century."[51] By looking for, and foregrounding, Black rejection of this discourse – a discourse that often placed children at its center – scholars can complicate the figure of celebrated American orphan, whose independence so easily maps onto celebrations of masculinist colonial adventuring. In its place, we can begin to excavate an alternate case for freedom that emerged in minoritarian communities that rejected the false bargain that equated liberty with alienation and removal.

Notes

1 Thomas Jefferson to Edward Bancroft, January 26, 1789. *Founders Online*, National Archives, https://founders.archives.gov/documents/Jefferson/01-14-02-0266.

2 Thomas Jefferson to Jared Sparks, 4 February 1824, *Founders Online*, National Archives, https://founders.archives.gov/documents/Jefferson/98-01-02-4020.

3 Some of the scholarship on the resonance of the child in early America includes Courtney Weikle-Mills, *Imaginary Citizens: Child Readers and the Limits of American Independence, 1640–1868* (Baltimore: Johns Hopkins University Press, 2012); Jay Fliegelman, *Prodigals and Pilgrims: The American Revolution against Patriarchal Authority 1750–1800* (Cambridge, UK: Cambridge University Press, 1982); John Demos, *A Little Commonwealth: Family Life in Plymouth Colony* (Oxford and New York: Oxford University Press, 1970/2000); Gillian Brown, *The Consent of the Governed: The Lockean Legacy in Early American Culture* (Cambridge, MA: Harvard University Press, 2001); Gillian Avery, *Behold the Child: American Children and Their Books, 1621–1922* (New York: Vintage, 1994); Sari Edelstein, *Adulthood and Other Fictions: American Literature and the Unmaking of Age* (Oxford and New York: Oxford University Press, 2018); K. Sánchez-Eppler, *Dependent States: The Child's Part in Nineteenth-Century American Culture* (Chicago: University of Chicago Press, 2005); Robin Bernstein, *Racial Innocence: Performing American Childhood and Race from Slavery to Civil Rights* (New York: NYU Press, 2011); Caroline Levander, *Cradle of Liberty: Race, the Child, and National Belonging from Thomas Jefferson to WEB Du Bois* (Durham, NC: Duke University Press, 2006).

4 Richard Warrington Baldwin Lewis, *The American Adam* (Chicago: University of Chicago Press, 2009); Leslie Fiedler, *Love and Death in the American Novel* ([Normal, IL]: Dalkey Archive Press, 1997).

5 Leslie Fiedler and F. O. Matthiessen – and the generations of responses their work has inspired – offer salient examples of how American critics have

canonized texts featuring alienated/orphaned children. Francis Otto Matthiessen, *American Renaissance: Art and Expression in the Age of Emerson and Whitman* (Oxford and New York: Oxford University Press on Demand, 1968). For a more recent examination of how early Americans viewed national progress and citizenship through the linear growth imagined in childhood, see Edelstein, *Adulthood and Other Fictions*; Corinne Field, *The Struggle for Equal Adulthood: Gender, Race, Age, and the Fight for Citizenship in Antebellum America* (Chapel Hill, NC: University of North Carolina Press, 2014); Weikle-Mills, *Imaginary Citizens*.

6 Levander, *Cradle of Liberty*; Shirley C. Samuels, *Romances of the Republic: Women, the Family, and Violence in the Literature of the Early American Nation* (Oxford and New York: Oxford University Press on Demand, 1996); Anna Mae Duane, *Suffering Childhood in Early America: Violence, Race and the Making of the Child Victim* (Athens, GA: University of Georgia Press 2010).

7 Stephen Burroughs. *Memoirs of Stephen Burroughs: To Which Are Added, Notes, and an Appendix* (Albany, NY: Published by B. D. Packard, 1811), 5, 48.

8 For an illuminating comparison of Franklin's tale of runaway rebellion and that found in slave narratives, see David Waldstreicher, *Runaway America: Benjamin Franklin, Slavery, and the American Revolution* (New York: Hill & Wang, 2004.)

9 For work on the early republican equation of growing up and acquiring citizenship, see Brown, *The Consent of the Governed*; Weikle-Mills, *Imaginary Citizens*.

10 George Washington to Lafayette, 10 May 1786, *Founders Online*, National Archives, https://founders.archives.gov/documents/Washington/04-04-02-0051. Original source: *The Papers of George Washington*, Confederation Series, vol. 4, *2 April 1786 – 31 January 1787*, ed. W. W. Abbot (Charlottesville: University Press of Virginia, 1995), 41–45.

11 Nicolas de Condorcet, *Réflexions sur l'esclavage des nègres*, 51–52 ("changes too brusque"), 66 ("slow march of emancipation"), 31–32. Cited in François Furstenberg, "Atlantic Slavery, Atlantic Freedom: George Washington, Slavery, and Transatlantic Abolitionist Networks," *WMQ* 68.2 (2011): 276.

12 The effects of these gradual manumission laws were often long delayed and the motivations behind them clouded. See Joanne Pope Melish, *Disowning Slavery: Gradual Emancipation and "Race" in New England, 1780–1860* (Cornell University Press, 1998).

13 Samuel Miller, "A Discourse, Delivered April 12, 1797, at the Request of and before the New-York Society for Promoting the Manumission of Slaves, and Protecting such of Them as Have Been or May Be Liberated" (1797) (Ann Arbor: Text Creation Partnership, 2011). https://quod.lib.umich.edu/e/evans/N24540.0001.001?view=toc.

14 Sarah L. H. Gronningsater, "Born Free in the Master's House: Children and Gradual Emancipation in the Early American North," in *Child Slavery before and after Emancipation: An Argument for Child-Centered Slavery Studies*, ed. Anna Mae Duane (Cambridge, UK: Cambridge University Press, 2017), 123–150.

15 Jean-Jacques Rousseau, *Émile; or, On Education: Includes Émile and Sophie; or, The Solitaries* (Hanover, NH: University Press of New England, 2010). For a study of how Lockean and Rousseauian ideas about education shaped the early republic, see Holly Brewer, *By Birth or Consent: Children, Law, and the Anglo-American Revolution in Authority* (Chapel Hill, NC: University of North Carolina Press, 2012).

16 Joseph Lancaster, *The British System of Education: Being a Complete Epitome of the Improvements and Inventions Practised by Joseph Lancaster: To Which Is Added, a Report of the Trustees of the Lancaster School at Georgetown, Col.* (1812), 93.

17 Paul J. Polgar, "'To Raise Them to an Equal Participation': Early National Abolitionism, Gradual Emancipation, and the Promise of African American Citizenship," *Journal of the Early Republic* 31.2 (2011): 230.

18 As Carolyn Eastman has demonstrated, a major evaluation tool for early republican schools, black and white, was the appreciation of an audience who would attend public student demonstrations. Carolyn Eastman, *A Nation of Speechifiers: Making an American Public after the Revolution* (Chicago: University of Chicago Press, 2009).

19 Benjamin Franklin to John Waring, December 17, 1763, in *Papers of Benjamin Franklin*, 45 vols., ed. Leonard W. Labaree et al (New Haven: Yale University Press, 1959-present), 10:395–396.

20 Qtd. in Charles C. Andrews, *The History of the New York African Free Schools* (New-York: Mahlon Day, 1830), 49.

21 Isaac V. Brown, *Memoir of the Reverend Robert Finley* (New-Brunswick: Terhune and Letson, 1819), 17.

22 Christopher Castiglia, "Pedagogical Discipline and the Creation of White Citizenship: John Witherspoon, Robert Finley, and the Colonization Society," *Early American Literature* 33.2 (1998): 201.

23 Robert Finley, "Thoughts on the Colonization of Free Blacks" (1816), in *The African Repository and Colonial Journal* (Washington City: American Colonization Society, 1834), 334.

24 Charles Fenton Mercer, *A Discourse on Popular Education* (Princeton, NJ: DA Borrenstein, 1826).

25 Bruce Dorsey, "A Gendered History of African Colonization in the Antebellum United States," *Journal of Social History* 34.1 (2000): 80.

26 "Address on Colonization to a Deputation of Negroes," August 14, 1862, in *Collected Works of Abraham Lincoln*, vol. 5, ed. Roy P. Basler (New Brunswick: Rutgers University Press, 1953).

27 "From the President of the American Colonization Society," *New York Advertiser*, reprinted in *Boston Recorder*, July 22, 1817.

28 *Constitution of the Hartford Auxiliary Colonization Society: A List of Officers Chosen at the Organization of the Society; Together with an Address to the Public* (Hartford, CT: Printed by Lincoln & Stone, 1819), 13.

29 For more on Black reading practices in the first half of the nineteenth century, see Karen Chandler, "'Ye Are Builders': Child Readers in Frances Harper's Vision of an Inclusive Black Poetry," in *Who Writes for Black Children?:*

African American's Children's Literature before 1800, ed. Kate Capshaw and Anna Mae Duane (Minneapolis: University of Minnesota Press, 2017).

30 "Fancy Etchings," *Christian Recorder*, February 20, 1873; letter, January 18, 1877, quoted in Carla Peterson, "Frances Harper, Charlotte Forten, and African American Literary Reconstruction," in *Challenging Boundaries: Gender and Periodization*, ed. Joyce W. Warren and Margaret Dickie (Athens, GA: University of Georgia Press, 2000), 44.

31 *Saratoga Sentinel*, November 22, 1825

32 In this respect, ACS discourse actually lined up with a long-standing tradition in antislavery writing, particularly writing by formerly enslaved authors. In African American writing of the era, the act of familial separation often marked the passage from a state of freedom into intractable slavery.

33 For more on the influence of the American Colonization Society on both white and black antislavery activism, see Beverly C. Tomek, *Colonization and Its Discontents: Emancipation, Emigration, and Antislavery in Antebellum Pennsylvania*, vol. 3 (New York: NYU Press, 2011).

34 *The Second Annual Report of the American Society for Colonizing the Free People of Colour of the United States*, 10 vols. (1818–1827) (Washington, DC: Davis and Force, 1819), 110.

35 Ibid.

36 Clay, "Address Delivered to the Colon. Society of Kentucky," in *Proceedings of the First Annual Meeting of the NJ Colonization Society* (1825), 31; *18th Annual Report of the American Society for Colonizing the Free People of Color of the US* (Washington, DC, 1835), 25–26.

37 "Eighteenth Annual Meeting of the American Colonization Society," *African Repository and Colonial Journal* 11 (1835): 38.

38 For two excellent analyses of this text, see Martha J. Cutter, "The Child's Illustrated Antislavery Talking Book: Abigail Field Mott's Abridgment of Olaudah Equiano's Interesting Narrative for African American Children," and Valentina K. Tikoff, "A Role Model for African American Children: Abigail Field Mott's Life and Adventures of Olaudah Equiano and White Northern Abolitionism," both in Capshaw and Duane, eds., *Who Writes for Black Children?*

39 Abigail Mott, *The Life and Adventures of Olaudah Equiano; or, Gustavus Vassa, the African: From an Account Written by Himself* (New-York: Mahlon Day, 1829), 5.

40 Charles Andrews, the schoolmaster, singles out a bright student who chooses to leave for Liberia as an exemplar in his *History of the New-York African Free Schools* (New-York: Mahlon Day, 1830), 119. New York Public Library Digital Collections. https://digitalcollections.nypl.org/items/510d47db-cbb8-a3d9-e040-e00a18064a99.

41 Mott, *Life and Adventures of Olaudah Equiano*, 5.

42 While Mott crafted the adaptation, it is unclear whose choices guided the inclusion of the materials in the appendix, which comprises nearly a third of the book itself, and offers a decidedly outdated view of the slavery debate. It is quite possible that both the text and the images for the appendix were chosen by Samuel Wood, the publisher of several abolitionist books for children.

43 As critics of adaptation have noted, one of the most common motivations to adapt a text is to "update a source by situating the story in a more contemporary and hence more accessible setting." Tara Collington, "The Chronotope and the Study of Literary Adaptation: The Case of Robinson Crusoe," in *Bakhtin's Theory of the Literary Chronotope: Reflections, Applications, Perspectives*, ed. Nele Bemong et al. (Gent: Academia Press, 2010), 179.

44 Mott, *Life and Adventures of Olaudah Equiano*, 17.

45 Ibid., 25.

46 Robert J. Swan. "John Teasman: African-American Educator and the Emergence of Community in Early Black New York City, 1787–1815," *Journal of the Early Republic* 12.3 (1992): 331–356; Anna Mae Duane, "'Can You Be Surprised by My Discouragement?' Education and Colonization at the New York African Free School," in *Warring for America*, ed. Nicole Eustace and Fredrika J. Teute (Williamsburg, VA and Chapel Hill, NC: Omohundro Institute of Early American History and Culture and University of North Carolina Press, 2017).

47 As Brigitte Fielder has argued, the literary life of Black children in the nineteenth century often involved moments of fraught racial cross reading, as they encountered texts written by white authors for white children out of which they had to draw their own meanings. Brigitte Fielder, "'No Rights That Any Body Is Bound to Respect': Pets, Race, and African American Child Readers," in Capshaw and Duane, eds., *Who Writes for Black Children?*

48 James McCune Smith, Introduction to *A Memorial Discourse* by Henry Highland Garnet (Philadelphia: Joseph M. Wilson, 1863) 23. Also see Records, New-York Society for Promoting the Manumission of Slaves, and Protecting Such of Them as Have Been, or May Be Liberated, 1785–1849, vol 8, p. 78, New-York Historical Society.

49 Garrison would acknowledge the influence of Black thinkers on his change of heart in his *Thoughts on African Colonization; or, An Impartial Exhibition of the Doctrines, Principles and Purposes of the American Colonization Society: Together with the Resolutions, Addresses, and Remonstrances of the Free People of Color* (Boston: Garrison and Knapp, 1832).

50 For work on Black print culture in early America, see P. Gabrielle Foreman's work with the Colored Conventions Project (ccp.org) and Eric Gardner, *Black Print Unbound: The Christian Recorder, African American Literature, and Periodical Culture* (Oxford and New York: Oxford University Press, 2015). For work that focuses particularly on Black children, see Nazera Sadiq Wright, *Black Girlhood in the Nineteenth Century* (Urbana, IL: University of Illinois Press, 2016); Crystal Webster, *Beyond the Boundaries of Childhood: African American Children in the Antebellum North* (Chapel Hill, NC: University of North Carolina Press, 2020); Capshaw and Duane, eds., *Who Writes for Black Children?*; Richard Bell, *Stolen: Five Free Boys Kidnapped into Slavery and Their Astonishing Odyssey Home* (New York: 37 Ink, 2019).

51 Bruce Dorsey, "A Gendered History of African Colonization in the Antebellum United States," *Journal of Social History* (2000): 77–103.

PART III

Methods for Living

CHAPTER 14

The Affective Postwar

Michelle Sizemore

Which War?

Wars remain durable period markers for nineteenth-century American literary history, notwithstanding appeals in recent years to rethink periodization, most notably the divide before and after the Civil War.[1] For scholars of earlier periods, our literary demarcations are shaped and punctuated by other wars. Rescaling for the long nineteenth century usually involves a war on either or both ends; *J19: The Journal of Nineteenth-Century Americanists*, for example, sets its dates from the end of the Revolutionary War to the beginning of World War I (1783–1914). Conflicts such as the French Revolution (1789–1799), the Haitian Revolution (1791–1803), the War of 1812 (1812–1815), the Creek War (1813–1814), the First Seminole War (1817–1818), and a host of uprisings from Shay's Rebellion (1786–1787) to Nat Turner's Rebellion (1831), while they do not delimit a time period in the same way, nevertheless serve as touchstones for literary criticism of the early long nineteenth century.

This is why, when asked to contribute an essay on the postwar period for a volume covering the years 1770–1828, "Which war?" was the first question that came to mind. This question was amiss, clearly. The American Revolution has long been the ballast in narratives of historical progress, the pivot from before to after – from colony to nation, from monarchy to republic, from founding to nation-building. Fewer literary scholars today would subscribe to these neat nationalistic accounts of American history, nor to their attendant Edwards-to-Emerson or American Renaissance literary and cultural histories. We now recognize that "literary history is messy," to borrow Cody Marrs and Christopher Hager's opening proposition for a collection on the myriad timelines of American literature.[2] Taking a cue from those essays, this chapter proposes an alternative timeline for "postwar," one that complements and extends the 1783 Treaty of Paris's termination of the Revolutionary War.[3] An "affective postwar," I argue, must encompass subsequent invocations of the Revolution, an event generating national feelings long after its conclusion. Within the parameters of this volume, the affective postwar stretches through the War of 1812, the Era of Good Feelings, and the Semicentennial – a timeline demonstrating a *longue durée* of feeling that extends Revolutionary history beyond its origins to the spikes in patriotism attending US commemorative culture.

Affects overcome periodization by lengthening the duration of an event.[4] The Revolution fomented patriotic feelings that reemerge in subsequent instances of nationalism hearkening to American independence, as recently as President Trump's 2020 "Salute to America" July 4 event.[5] And while patriotism may seem the least likely of political feelings to yield new insights given its widely accepted definition as love of country, there are more layers to probe.[6] This essay examines an overlooked connection between patriotism and paranoia. As a certain strain of Revolutionary War fiction attests, love of country breeds both suspicious minds and suspicious affects. John Neal's *Seventy-Six* (1823) is a full-tilt exploration of enmity's growth from patriotic love. In this historical romance, the affective bonds of homosocial fraternity and heterosexual romance function as analogous expressions of patriotism. As these personal-national relationships intensify, they become ridden with anxieties about betrayal and humiliation: enemies may be lurking in the guise of lovers and friends.

The argument unfolds in three stages. The first section makes the case for conceiving of paranoia as a set of affects in addition to the mental properties for which it is more commonly understood. The section ends by outlining the affective linkages between paranoia and patriotism. The second section demonstrates these affective linkages ("paranoid patriotism") in *Seventy-Six*, and what is more, the transmission of paranoid patriotism among persons. The third section contends that style serves as the means of transmitting the paranoid affects engendered by patriotism. This observation is significant because literary criticism has traditionally emphasized paranoia's affinities with narrative, particularly conspiracy theory. More recently, literary critics point to the continuities between paranoia and interpretation, namely, the hermeneutics of suspicion or the paranoid's search for coherent explanation and order.[7] Neal's novel insists that we also recognize paranoia as a trait of style.

Paranoia's Affects

In common usage, paranoia is the unrealistic belief that others want to do us harm. Derived from ancient Greek (*para nous*), the term originally denoted madness, the condition of being outside or beside one's mind. Paranoia-as-delirium returned as a medical term in the middle of the eighteenth century, eventually becoming associated with delusions resulting from fever. The scientific community maintained the understanding of paranoia as exclusively a symptom of psychosis until the 1990s as researchers began accounting for the pervasive low-level paranoia experienced by millions of people, not just the clinically ill. Today it is customary for psychologists and cultural critics to conceive of paranoia on a spectrum of the everyday ("a coworker gave me a strange look") to the extreme ("the US government caused the romaine lettuce crisis"). Experts also now tend to agree that one can be paranoid even if one's suspicions are founded, hence the expression "even paranoids have enemies." Just because you're paranoid doesn't mean they aren't after you.[8]

Even as this quick rundown illustrates, discussions of paranoia continue to give priority to its cognitive dimensions – from the American Psychological Association's definition of the "paranoid state" as "a condition characterized by delusions of persecution or grandiosity" to cultural studies' and literary studies' repeated investigations of conspiracy theory, the paranoid search for explanation in an unintelligible world.[9] Moreover, studies of paranoia often assume this mental condition belongs to the persecutory fantasies of a single mind, or else attribute the paranoia of multiple individuals to group psychology. And yet paranoia is not simply a psychopathological property of the mind; it is also a property of bodies and social environments, as much as these factors have been undertheorized. Discerning paranoia's affective features brings us closer to an understanding of the affiliation between paranoia and patriotism.

A number of philosophers and political theorists who write on patriotism rely on love of country and affection for fellow citizens in their definitions, even if emotion is not usually the explicit focus of their inquiry. Benedict Anderson proclaims that "nations inspire love, and often a profoundly self-sacrificing love" in *Imagined Communities* – a work generally remembered for its influential account of nationalism, not for the related discussion of patriotism.[10] Most scholars who write about patriotism differentiate between an inclusive version of patriotism they deem as necessary for democracy and an exclusive version of patriotism fraught with oppositional (and often xenophobic, ethnocentric, or racist) tendencies.[11] It is the exclusive version of patriotism that concerns us here. Political theorist Steven Johnston argues that patriotism is fundamentally narcissistic, a self-directed love ensuring internal objects of affection and securing eternal truths about the nation's virtue. In his study, the patriot's hyper-self-consciousness resembles the paranoid's, whose well-documented traits include suspicion, centrality, and hostility.[12] Although Johnston never labels patriotism as paranoid, he points to overwhelming similarities: "Patriotism ... seems to suffer from a self-conscious self-consciousness. As it attends to social and political life, it ineluctably turns inward and fixes on self-generated preoccupations: us and them, loyalty and enmity, fidelity and betrayal."[13] These oppositions are attributable to the nature of patriotic love, an emotion burdened by the specter of its loss. Patriotic love conditions enmity. Always at peril of diminishment or loss, patriotism must be protected and proven: a dual mandate delineating them from us, disloyal from devoted, patriot from pretender, enemy from friend. The paranoid streak in patriotism, then, arises as a preemptive defense against its own destruction, not by foreign powers but by domestic operatives. Hence, the suspicion born from perennial uncertainty over others' love of nation. Who is a true patriot?

Paranoid Patriotism in John Neal's *Seventy-Six*

John Neal provides some answers. *Seventy-Six* is a historical romance set during the Revolutionary War and published in 1823 with the nearing semicentennial; it is the third of Neal's nine novels and a singular contribution to the heap of "loving tribute to the old Revolutionaries" paid by the nation mid-decade.[14] Narrated by an aging Jonathan Oadley to his children, the story follows a young John and his brother Archibald into battle – of both the military and courtship kind. Throughout, the Oadley brothers fight the British forces and fend off suitors of the Arnaud sisters, their New Jersey neighbors and love interests. Like other examples of Revolutionary fiction from the period, *Seventy-Six*'s romances and rivalries serve as allegories for political relations.[15] The amorous affairs of multiple romantic partners stand in for state affairs, where betrayal and suspicion throughout gives way to fidelity and trust in the end. This gloss is rather more tidy than the sprawling two volumes teeming with characters, skirmishes, side plots, minute descriptions of horses, and em dashes (more on this later) – writing Neal himself characterized in his preface as "rambling incoherency."[16] But it is enough to keep us focused on the paranoid operations of the novel.

Enemies abound in *Seventy-Six*. The ambiguity of the opponent is especially noteworthy. Of the 150 times the word "enemy" appears, only twice are the British directly mentioned. In the rare moments a military enemy gets a face and a name, it is the brutally violent Hessians. More often, though, the line between enemy and friend is gauzy thin. The Continental Army confiscates its countrymen's stores; defectors raid farms and destroy property. Within the army, the New Jerseyans sometimes fight beside and sometimes stand against the Virginians. Men in the same battalion who were once neighbors and confidants vie for the same love interest. Under these circumstances the Oadleys sense that anyone can become an enemy at any moment. Strangers, neighbors, and acquaintances are all regarded with distrust. Growing suspicion contributes to the Oadleys' increasingly defensive posture and moments of full-blown paranoia. For instance, John advances a wacky conspiracy theory to explain the capture of General Charles Lee by British forces, supposing that Lee, instead of bringing relief to General Washington as ordered, had gone rogue and was plotting "a *coup de main* upon the extended outposts of the enemy." Why? To steal the glory from Washington, his competitor for accolades and career advancement. "Lee," John conjectures, "was willing to sacrifice Washington to *his* popularity."[17] There is no evidence to support this theory either in the novel or in the historical record.

Up to this point, we have been following a fairly standard interpretation of political paranoia: a threat posed by a vague but omnipresent enemy. Suspicious thinking culminates in a conspiracy theory framed as a Manichean struggle between good and evil: Washington versus Lee, the American Cincinnatus versus "the Caesar of America," republicanism versus totalitarianism.[18] From here, it would be a matter of course to claim paranoia as integral to xenophobic patriotism and show how the infiltration of so-called un-American influences consolidates national identity. *Seventy-Six* certainly bears out all of these readings, but much more is to be gained by drilling down on the unexpected bits offered by the novel.

For Neal, paranoia consists of acute anxiety, irritability, and hostility, a feeling-state prompted by possible betrayal and humiliation in a military hierarchy where status depends on reputation as much as merit. Losing face and losing status loom as constant threats. Archy, for instance, competes with Clinton, his military commander and love rival, for the affections of the mutually admired Lucia Arnaud. During Clinton's first convalescence at the Arnaulds, Archy begins to suspect that Lucia has fallen for the handsome officer (he's right), which causes him to launch into a highhanded, self-pitying speech before Lucia, Clinton, and John in which he "pray[s] for [Lucia's] happiness" but also predicts she will eventually be sorry with her choice. Twice he stops mid-sentence to warn Clinton not to interrupt him, the second time, infuriated: "Clinton, by God! – I will not be interrupted (striking the hilt of his sword) and if you interfere again, man as you are – tall as you are, I will bring your forehead to the dust."[19] John notes that "Clinton retreated a pace or two, tapped the hilt of his sabre with his fingers – and smiled – damn him, I could hardly keep my own sword in its sheath."[20] It is not clear whether Clinton actually interrupted Archy, but Archy and John perceive an affront. And not just here. The brothers are always on the lookout for a slight or an insult, especially from Clinton, and especially Archy, always coiled and ready to spring. In an effort to redeem Lucia's honor, and his own, Archy kills Clinton in a fencing match–turned-duel at the end of the first volume.

Anxiety, irritability, and hostility have long been associated with paranoia, as well as hypersensitivity, anger, and fear. With a few notable exceptions, however, affects are still considered secondary to cognition, less a component of paranoia's constitution than a trigger or a symptom.[21] Neal is perceptive in recognizing that specific feelings and energies are fundamental to the condition, spreading among people, creating a climate. Note how anxiety and hostility move from Archy to John in this scene, from Archy's perception of Clinton's disrespectful interruption to John's perception of Clinton's mocking smile. How does this work? The novel's explanation of paranoid transmission may well be its most innovative contribution on the subject.

In one sense, affective transfer is a basic premise of affect studies. "Affect," as Gregory Seigworth and Melissa Gregg put it, "is found in those intensities that pass body to body."[22] Yet there are particularities in the manner in which certain affects move, in this case the anxiety, hostility, and irritability accompanying paranoia. In recent years, psychologists have also begun to argue that affects travel, that subjects are not affectively and energetically self-contained as psychological theory has long presumed. Teresa Brennan suggests that the "transmission of affect" occurs through a combination of sociological, psychological, and physiological factors. Neurologists' physiological explanation for shared affect is "entrainment" – a process by which two or more persons' hormonal and nervous systems are brought into alignment. Chemical entrainment works through sending and receiving pheromones, whereas nervous or electrical entrainment works through the synchronization of physical motion, pulsation, utterance, intonation, even brain waves.[23]

Obviously, Neal did not have modern science to explain how one feels another's feelings, but he does sense that one body's movements can influence the movements of another and in turn attune the pair's feelings. It would take neurologists and kinesiologists another 200 years to explain how this mode of corporeal intelligence relies on touch, sight, and sound, in addition to bodily movements and gestures, particularly the emulation of rhythm. In Brennan's words, "Rhythm has a unifying, regulating role in affective exchanges between two or more people" and fosters a "sense of well-being."[24]

Far from a chronicle of well-being, *Seventy-Six* showcases the *arrhythmic* fits attending paranoia. The novel is rife with spasmodic bodily movements. Whether the action relates to valor on the field or the mundane business of writing a letter, characters conduct themselves with jarring, contorting, and fitful gesticulation. Such movements accompany conflict and foster a general sense of ill-being, assisting in the diffusion of paranoia's elemental affects. Observe in the previous passage Archy's explosive "striking the hilt of his sword," a motion matched by Clinton's imperturbable light finger-tapping. Regardless of physiological or a psychosociological explanation, paranoia is mimetic, a generator of symmetries.[25]

Paranoid Style

Style, I argue, is the term we should appoint in literary studies to the linguistic and performative modes through which affect is transmitted and characters and readers are brought in and out of alignment. In *Seventy-Six*, *paranoid* style names the swift and erratic motions of bodies and words, motions that generate anxious, irritable, and hostile affects; it also names the aggressive and antagonistic relations preceding and proceeding from these affects. This definition of "paranoid style" is distinct from the classic definition offered in Richard Hofstadter's 1964 *Harper's* article, "The Paranoid Style in American Politics," cited for decades by almost everyone who writes about American paranoia. Hofstadter describes "the paranoid style" as a "style of mind" distinguished by "heated exaggeration, suspiciousness, and conspiratorial fantasy."[26] Paranoid style here refers to *bodies'* resonances and articulations and to the stylistic features of written and verbal expression. The aesthetic category of style offers new insight to paranoia, namely, how it comes to saturate an environment, buzzing in the atmosphere, accumulating among people. For paranoia rarely belongs to one person. More often it is the shared property of a community (think Infowars) and style is a crucial means of transmission. As such,

I recommend a shift in literary analysis of paranoia from individual characterological traits and narrative elements to stylistic features that sync characters with each other and the larger organizations of which they are a part – in the case of *Seventy-Six*, military personnel with the military complex.

Neal's distinctive manner of expression – his hectic movement of bodies and words through space – has long absorbed critics, though commentary has been confined to his hurling of words, not bodies.[27] Indeed, Ned Watts and David Carlson have aptly described Neal's long fiction as showcasing a "hyperkinetic and sometimes hyperbolic sense of energy."[28] Contemporary critics were not so forgiving. For a reviewer in *The Rover*, "His style is eccentric, and frequently faulty."[29] For a reviewer in *Zion's Herald*, Neal's style is the mark of "a madman."[30] Even Poe, who praised Neal's literary "genius," betrays exasperation in an 1849 article in the *Southern Literary Messenger*: "I hardly know how to account for the repeated failures of John Neal as regards the *construction* of his works.... He seems to be either deficient in a sense of completeness, or unstable in temperament; so that he becomes wearied with his work before getting it done. He always begins well – vigorously – startlingly – proceeds by fits ... but his conclusions are sure to ... [fall]-off."[31] Poe's complaint is that Neal runs out of steam, that he fails to sustain his vigor from start to finish, whereas other critics find that Neal's writing suffers from too much oomph or pizzazz, or that it pitches rapidly and wildly forward with "fatal facility."[32] Whatever the objection, something about the energy is off, and his readers come away irked.

Readerly irritation is partly the result of vigor-induced cacophony. When words dart, lop, scramble, and detonate on the page, they tend not to create a regular cadence. Flip through the book and find a cornucopia of asterisks, exclamation points, and four- and five-hyphened dashes, often compressed into a single passage. At the beginning of the second volume, for instance, sectional rivalries within the army intensify. Archy warns Copely, a Yankee officer, about a Virginian "conspiracy" designed to "provoke" and "insult" him, possibly to injure him.[33] After a duel between Copely and the corresponding Virginian officer, in which the latter dies, John descends into a frenzied dream:

> At dead of midnight, I heard a trumpet, as I though, sounding to battle. I arose, pained and dizzy, – unwilling to go out – and desirous to skulk, if I could, into the holes of the rocks. Then I thought that it began to rain fire upon me; and the earth shook, and battalions of men, armed all over in shining mail, spattered with blood, came, parading, column after column,

from the earth – nation after nation – each of loftier, and yet loftier stature still, – warlike – and terrible, like the buried Apostles of liberty: and then, all at once, there was a tremendous explosion, and I felt myself sinking in the swamp – the loose earth quivering like jelly, at every tread, and cold serpents and bloated toads all slipping about me, so thickly, that, set my naked foot, wherever I would, something that had life in it — some fat icy reptile would stir under the pressure – and then I was entangled in the thorny creeping tendrils of many a plant that encumbered my path; dead bodies lay in my way; I was pinioned hand and foot, and serpents fed upon my blood, and vultures flapped over me. And then, out of the east, there blazed all at once, a light, like a million of rockets, that blinded me. And then, I felt a hand – the hand of a murderer about my throat – God! – *that* could be no dream, it was too distinct! Even in my sleep, I felt it, and started broad awake. My heart stopped – stopped, as if struck with death! a hand *was* upon my head! – feeling about my hair; as if to get a good hold. I shuddered – gasped – "Archibald!" said I, "*dear* Archibald!" (Archibald had been suspected of walking in his sleep, since the death of Clinton.)[34]

Visually, we immediately notice choppy disjointed sentences and chaotic word arrangements. Aurally, we perceive the dissonance of this jerky stopping and starting. Neal's prolific dashes work to achieve this dissonance, sometimes keeping rhythm, as Emily Dickinson's do, but more often forging irregular patterns and measures. The dysprosody and confusion of this passage appropriately convey John's disturbance during a dream where he is persecuted by a shape-shifting enemy. Even subconsciously he feels someone is out to get him. After all, from the outset of volume 2, John is preoccupied with restoring the Oadley name after Archy slays Clinton, and as the last two lines suggest, on some level John feels his own brother is not to be trusted.[35] Moreover, dashes disrupt and reassemble conventional relationships between words, extending, with the help of many commas and semicolons, the narrator's description of flight and pursuit into a single breathless sixteen-line sentence. If dashes rush together otherwise unrelated topics (battalions, toads, murderers), they also place emphasis on certain words by setting them apart (— "nation after nation" — and — "warlike" —). This dramatic accenting establishes tonal relations between the words, encouraging them to be comprehended together extra-semantically as notes of higher emotional pitch. Of course, these adverbs? adjectives? – it is unclear whether they modify the "battalions of men" or the way the men "parad [e]" – and the string of other modifiers in the passage could almost as easily be read vertically up and down as horizontally left to right, as columns just as well as lines.

Once again, Poe weighs in. In an 1848 *Graham's* essay devoted to punctuation, he criticizes the modern editor for subduing the use of the em dash by substituting a comma here, a semicolon there, as the result of the em dash's "excessive employment about twenty years ago." The culprit, he explains, was John Neal, who "exaggerated its use into the grossest abuse."[36] Of punctuation, he rues, "There is no treatise on the topic – and there is no topic on which a treatise is more needed." Actually, an astonishing amount had been written on punctuation by Poe's time. In *A Treatise on English Punctuation*, John Wilson devotes an entire section to each punctuation mark, relaying his annoyance in "Remarks on the Use and the Abuse of the Dash" at the em dash's indiscriminate employment.[37] "[S]urely," he writes, "the unnecessary profusion of straight lines, particularly on a printed page, is offensive to good taste, is an index of the dasher's profound ignorance of the art of punctuation, and, so far from helping to bring out the sense of an author, is better adapted for turning into nonsense some of his finest passages."

If possible, opinions on the topic appear as impassioned now as they were then. A 2012 article in *The Atlantic* covers a current quarrel over the em dash. For every Ben Yagoda and Jen Doll who praise the *double-hyphened* horizontal line for its versatility and defiance, there's a Philip Corbett who tells people to please stop. The use of the em dash "can seem like a tic," Corbett warns us; "worse yet, it can indicate a profusion of overstuffed and loosely constructed sentences, bulging with parenthetical additions and asides."[38] Doll, the author of *The Atlantic* article, whose title is "The Singular Beauty of the Em-Dash," openly sides in its favor, declaring "She's a lover – not a fighter." By "lover," Doll means the em dash "is something of an attention-grabber, and can be a bit touchy-feely, but she only means to help people connect."[39]

It is the reverse in *Seventy-Six*. As long as we are personifying punctuation marks, Neal's em dash is more aptly "a fighter" – a pugilist with fists up and chin out.[40] After all, the *OED* tells us, the verb "to dash" is "to strike with violence so as to break into fragments"; "to drive impetuously forth or out, to cause to rush together"; "to put down on paper, throw off, write, or sketch, with hasty and unpremeditated vigor."[41] Neal's punctuation and other elements of style parry and push away. Along with the ugly feelings I have been describing, this antagonistic manner of relation is a hallmark of paranoid style if style is considered, in part, "the protocols for making social relationships," as Nancy Armstrong and Len Tennenhouse have recently discussed.[42]

In fact, *Seventy-Six* is framed by paranoia *about style* in a series of prefatory exchanges between writers and hypothetical critics. We know

Neal's idiosyncratic expression was part of his aspiration to create a distinctive American literature, but his American innovations bring with them some insecurities if his narrator in *Seventy-Six* is any indication. In the first chapter, Oadley ostentatiously announces his style: "My style may often offend you. I do not doubt that it will. I hope that it will. It will be remembered the better."[43] Oadley anticipates and even welcomes objections from his readers. And yet welcoming readers' attacks seems a fairly standard strategy of defense. It is as though Oadley aims to lessen the sting of criticism by getting there first. In his preface to *Seventy-Six*, Neal owns the "incompetency" of his writing, fully expecting those "who have been bothered and frightened with the rambling incoherency, passion and extravagance of *Logan*" (published the year before) to come after him again. This time he hopes they "may have an opportunity of getting in a better humor with the author and, if possible, themselves."[44] However self-aware and playful the preface, there is a tinge of defensiveness, which only becomes magnified next to the novel's characters, who spend a fair amount of time imagining insults and avoiding humiliation at all costs.[45]

Antagonism structures the relationships between the characters and propels the plot. *Seventy-Six* opens with the disintegration of the patriarchal household and the Oadley brothers' introduction into a more impersonal military hierarchy. The novel revolves around men who learn to navigate the military's chain of command even as they fight for the nonauthoritarian governance of a democratic society. The persistent conflict is one of male rivals competing for rewards distributed variously according to democratic and antidemocratic values. The ranks to which the men are recommended on the meritocratic basis of skills, intelligence, and courage are constantly threatened by the dictates of personal loyalty, favoritism, and cronyism. What is more, this alternative set of guidelines for security of position, not to mention future promotion, relies on the codes and conduct of a privileged fraternity absolutely mystifying to John. In this system of precarity, one is always liable to lose his footing as John's anxiety dream about "sinking in a swamp" provocatively suggests. His sense of vulnerability is so acute that five decades after the war his narrative of wartime experience is motivated by anticipation of persecution – posterity's "insult and derision" of the heroes of '76.[46] Paranoia results in the patriotic narrative that sets things right.

Thus in probing the question "Who is the true patriot?," Neal's novel markedly departs from the meaning the term held in its eighteenth-century setting. In 1776, a patriot was an American revolutionary committed to a specific set of political principles, among them, the defense of liberty and the opposition to British authority.[47] By 1823, a patriot had come to mean someone with an affection and special concern for the *patria*, regardless of the native country's distinguishing attributes; hence, *Seventy-Six*'s subtitle, "Our Country! – Right or Wrong," which suggests the characters' partiality for their country *as their country*, apart from its merits or any ethical considerations.[48] Further, the true patriot must prove his love of country. Such demonstrations in the novel can be explained in part by what scholars identify as a "touchstone" of patriotism: "love expressed in action" or "what one is prepared to do for" one's country.[49] Whether expressed through civic engagement such as attending a parade or self-sacrifice such as joining the military, patriotic acts are generally understood as volitional acts.[50]

In an opening scene, Archy resolves to enlist with the army against his father's wishes and urges the paterfamilias to sell the farm, strap on a knapsack, and trek with his sons through the backcountry to recruit for Washington. These overtures, as Archy puts it, to "give up all you have to your country" are recognizable as decisive acts of patriotism.[51] Simultaneously, Neal draws to our attention the involuntary registers of patriotism – the love of country native to a native countryman and the attendant paranoia for safeguarding it. Paranoid patriotism is involuntarily transmitted via hormonal and nervous systems, via unconscious bodily motors and movements. The mimetic character of paranoia is part and parcel of the paranoid style of embodied characters and prose. If the tics and twitches of the characters evince paranoid patriotism, so too do the tics and twitches of the composition. For Neal, words are the extension of bodies, living speech, "talk[ing] on paper"; and though not involuntary in the same way as a muscle contraction, they are spontaneous sentiments erupting from the body.[52] The novel suggests that its various involuntary, almost instinctive, stylistic manifestations and transmissions of love of country are innate. The authenticity of one's patriotism is proven, finally, if it is a reflex of the body, an involuntary and instantaneous jolt of the bones, muscles, and vocal cords.

If paranoid style describes a manner of relation between characters, and also between writers and readers, then it also describes a manner of relation between writing and reading. Paranoid writing may very well call for paranoid reading – a new mode of paranoid reading. The New Historicist legacy of "paranoid reading" (a.k.a., "the hermeneutics of suspicion," a.k.a., "symptomatic reading," "critique," "ideology critique") has been thoroughly taken to task over the past few years. These efforts have brought a disciplinary self-awareness to what had become a default reading practice and offer a range of alternatives for "the way we [should] read now."[53] While something may certainly be gained from uncovering the many hidden agendas, enemies, and conspiracy theories in Neal's paranoid text, this essay has instead made the case for attending to the paranoia of surfaces rather than of depths.

It is important to pay attention to the affective landscape of the long nineteenth century because affects and emotions shape history and possess a history themselves. Although historians who research the emotions of the American Revolution limit their studies to the time frame of colonial crisis, war, and the formation of the new republic (1760s–1790s), it is evident that an affective postwar stretches beyond these years to the nineteenth century and into the twenty-first.[54] The patriotism occasioned by the Revolution, in wartime and in commemoration, gives rise to paranoia as war with external enemies (Americans vs. British) becomes a "war" over nation-building from within (Americans vs. Americans).

Notes

1 Christopher Hager and Cody Marrs, "Against 1865: Reperiodizing the Nineteenth Century," *J19: The Journal of Nineteenth-Century Americanists* 1.2 (Fall 2013): 259–284.

2 "Introduction," in *Timelines of American Literature*, ed. Cody Marrs and Christopher Hager (Baltimore: Johns Hopkins University Press, 2019), 1.

3 In particular, see Jesse Alemán's "The Age of US Latinidad," in Marrs and Hager, eds., *Timelines* (159–169). Alemán stresses the inaccuracy of the "antebellum literature" designation, which uses the Civil War as a point of reference for a cluster of decades (1820–1860) that saw numerous wars.

4 Although there is no strict consensus on the criteria differentiating affect from emotion, scholars do agree on a difference, and for the purposes of this essay, "emotions" are social feelings that require a subject, that is, a person who feels the feeling. Emotions like love, hate, and envy are possessed by the feeler, the person experiencing love, hate, or envy. Emotions are social in the sense that they belong more fully within the realm of signification and epistemological coherence. In Brian Massumi's words, emotions are more "socio-linguistically fixed" (88). "Affects" are less so. Though affects are by no means code-free or meaningless, they exist prior to ideology – that is, "prior to intentions, meanings, reasons, and beliefs – because they are nonsignifying autonomic processes that take place below the threshold of conscious awareness and meaning" (Ruth Leys, "The Turn to Affect: A Critique," *Critical Inquiry* 37.3 [2011]: 437). Affects are pre-personal and pre-social. "Feelings," it should be noted, will be the generic term, here, to encompass affects, emotions, and other modes of sensibility. See Brian Massumi, "The Autonomy of Affect," *Cultural Critique* 31 (1995): 83–109; Lawrence Grossberg, "Mapping

Popular Culture," in *We Gotta Get Out of This Place: Popular Conservatism and Postmodern Culture* (New York: Routledge, 1992), 69–87; Eric Shouse for a short accessible set of definitions: "Feeling, Emotion, Affect." *M/C Journal* 8.6 (2005), http://journal.media-culture.org.au/0512/03-shouse.php; Leys, "The Turn to Affect: A Critique."

5 In his speech, Trump invokes the Heroes of '76 to bolster a version of patriotism that demands unquestioning loyalty to country and intolerance of criticism due to America's unparalleled greatness: "Thanks to the courage of those patriots of July 4th, 1776, the American Republic stands today as the greatest, most exceptional, and most virtuous nation in the history of the world.... We will never allow an angry mob to tear down our statues, erase our history, indoctrinate our children, or trample on our freedoms." Donald Trump, "Remarks by President Trump at the 2020 Salute to America," www.whitehouse.gov/briefings-statements/remarks-president-trump-2020-salute-america/ (accessed November 1, 2020).

6 Mary G. Dietz, "Patriotism: A Brief History of the Term," in *Patriotism*, ed. Igor Primoratz (New York: Humanity Books, 2002), 201–215.

7 For a small sampling on this topic, see Eve Sedgwick, "Paranoid Reading and Reparative Reading; or, You're So Paranoid, You Probably Think This Essay Is about You," in *Touching Feeling: Affect, Pedagogy, Performativity* (Durham, NC: Duke University Press, 2003); Robert Levine, *Conspiracy and Romance* (Cambridge: Cambridge University Press, 1989); Samuel Chase Coale, *Paradigms of Paranoia: The Culture of Conspiracy in Contemporary American Fiction* (Tuscaloosa: University of Alabama Press, 2005); Mike Davis, *Reading the Text That Isn't There: Paranoia in the Nineteenth-Century Novel* (Abingdon: Routledge, 2014); *Conspiracy Nation: the Politics of Paranoia in Postwar America*, ed. Peter Knight (New York: NYU Press, 2002); George E. Marcus, *Paranoia within Reason: A Casebook on Conspiracy as Explanation* (Chicago: University of Chicago Press, 1999); Leo Braudy, "Providence, Paranoia, and the Novel," *ELH* 48.3 (1981): 619–663.

8 Daniel Freeman and Jason Freeman, *Paranoia: The Twenty-First Century Fear* (Oxford: Oxford University Press, 2008).

9 "Paranoid State." *APA Dictionary of Psychology*. https://dictionary.apa.org/paranoid-state (accessed May 12, 2020).

10 Benedict Anderson, *Imagined Communities: Reflections on the Origins and Spread of Nationalism* (London: Verso, 1983), 141. This oversight may be due to Anderson's conflation of patriotism with nationalism except when patriotism receives direct mention, tellingly, in the title to chapter 8, "Patriotism and Racism." The declaration that nations inspire love serves to dissociate nationalism from what Anderson sees as its prevailing "near-pathological" characterization, its alleged "roots in fear and hatred of the Other, and its affinities with racism" (141). For discussions on the confusion of nationalism and patriotism, see Maurio Viroli, *For Love of Country: An Essay on Patriotism and Nationalism* (Oxford: Clarendon Press, 1995), and John Schaar, "The Case for Patriotism," in *Legitimacy in the Modern State* (New Brunswick, NJ: Transaction Publishers, 1989), 285–311.

11 See Robert Pinsky, "Eros against Esperanto," Hilary Putnam, "Must We Choose between Patriotism and Universal Reason?," and Charles Taylor, "Why Democracy Needs Patriotism," all in *For Love of Country: Debating the Limits of Patriotism*, ed. Martha Nussbaum and Joshua Cohen (Boston: Beacon Press, 1996).

12 Robert S. Robins and Jerrold M. Post, *Political Paranoia: The Psychopolitics of Hatred* (New Haven, CT: Yale University Press, 1997).

13 Steven Johnston, *The Truth about Patriotism* (Durham, NC: Duke University Press, 2007), 26.

14 Andrew Burstein, *America's Jubilee* (New York: A. A. Knopf, 2001), 6. For work on Neal, see the excellent essay collection *John Neal and Nineteenth-Century American Literature and Culture*, ed. Ned Watts and David Carlson (Lewisburg, PA: Bucknell University Press, 2012); Paul Gilmore, "John Neal, American Romance, and International Romanticism," *American Literature* 84.3 (2012): 477–504; Fritz Fleischmann, "'A Likeness, Once Acknowledged,' John Neal and the 'Ideosyncrasies' of Literary History," in *Myth and Enlightenment in American Literature*, ed. Dieter Meindl and Friedrich W. Hurlacher (Erlangen: Universitätsbund Erlangen-Nürnberg, 1985); Donald Sears, *John Neal* (Boston: Twayne Publishers, 1978).

15 See Shirley Samuels, *Romances of the Republic* (New York: Oxford University Press, 1996).

16 John Neal, *Seventy-Six* (Bainbridge, NY: York Mail-Print, 1978), i.

17 Ibid., vol. 1, 138.

18 Ibid., vol. 1, 138.

19 Ibid., vol. 1, 120.

20 Ibid., vol. 1, 120.

21 For work that recognizes the affective components of paranoia, see Eve Sedgwick "Paranoid Reading and Reparative Reading," and Sianne Ngai, *Ugly Feelings* (Cambridge, MA: Harvard University Press, 2005).

22 Gregory Seigworth and Melissa Gregg, "An Inventory of Shimmers," in *The Affect Theory Reader*, ed. Gregory Seigworth and Melissa Gregg (Durham, NC: Duke University Press, 2010), 1.

23 Teresa Brennan, *The Transmission of Affect* (Ithaca, NY: Cornell University Press, 2004), 60–73.

24 Ibid., 71.

25 Eve Sedgwick characterizes paranoia as "contagious," arguing that it "is drawn toward and tends to construct symmetrical relations, in particular, symmetrical epistemologies." This claim founds the proposition that paranoia is "reflexive and mimetic," that it "seems to require being imitated to be understood, and it, in turn, seems to understand only by imitation." Sedgwick's account is clarifying to my discussion, though I view paranoia's reflexive and mimetic qualities more as pre-conscious registering than conscious "understanding" ("Paranoid Reading and Reparative Reading," 126, 131). Anna Gibbs argues that a range of affects participate in "mimetic communication." See her Anna Gibbs, "After Affect: Sympathy, Synchrony, and Mimetic Communication," in Seigworth and Gregg, eds., *The Affect Theory Reader*, 186–205.

26 Richard Hofstadter, "The Paranoid Style in American Politics," *Harper's* (November 1964): 77.

27 Maya Merlob, "*Celebrated Rubbish: John Neal and the Commercialization of Early American Romanticism,*" in Watts and Carlson, eds., *John Neal and Nineteenth-Century American Literature and Culture,* 99–122.

28 Ned Watts and David Carlson, "Introduction," in *John Neal and Nineteenth-Century American Literature and Culture,* xxv.

29 "John Neal" (1843), *The Rover : A Weekly Magazine of Tales, Poetry, and Engravings, Also Sketches of Travel, History and Biography (1843–1845).* August 30,   http://ezproxy.uky.edu/login?url=https://search-proquestcom.ezproxy .uky.edu/docview/127988498?accountid=11836 (accessed November 30, 2019).

30 "John Neal" (1835), *Zion's Herald (1823–1841).* October 28, http://ezproxy .uky.edu/login?url=https://search-proquest-com.ezproxy.uky.edu/docview/ 127253532?accountid=11836 (accessed November 30, 2019).

31 Edgar Allan Poe, "Marginalia" (1849), *The Southern Literary Messenger; Devoted to Every Department of Literature, and the Fine Arts (1848–1864),* http://ezproxy.uky.edu/login?url=https://search-proquest-com.ezproxy.uky .edu/docview/126334240?accountid=11836 (accessed November 30, 2019).

32 Sears, *John Neal* 34.

33 Neal, *Seventy-Six,* vol. 2, 45–46.

34 Ibid., vol. 2, 54–55.

35 Ibid., vol. 2, 16.

36 Edgar Allan Poe, "Marginalia" (1848), *Graham's American Monthly Magazine of Literature, Art, and Fashion (1844–1858),* http://ezproxy.uky.edu/login?url= https://search-proquest-com.ezproxy.uky.edu/docview/124729848?accoun tid=11836 (accessed November 30, 2019).

37 John Wilson, *A Treatise on English Punctuation,* 4th ed. (Boston: John Wilson & Son, 1855), 174.

38 Philip B. Corbett, "Dashes Everywhere," *New York Times,* April 5, 2011.

39 Jen Doll, "The Singular Beauty of the Em-Dash," *The Atlantic,* October 23, 2012.

40 In fact, James Russell Lowell, in his satire *A Fable for Critics,* attributes to Neal a "pugilist brain" and accuses him of breaking "the strings of his lyre . . . by striking too hard." "He has so much muscle and loves to show it, / That he strips himself naked to prove he's a poet." James Russell Lowell, *A Fable for Critics* (Boston: Putnam, 1848), 62–63.

41 *OED Online,* "dash, v." Oxford University Press, www-oed-com.ezproxy.uky .edu/view/Entry/47368?rskey=iFFShc&result=4 (accessed December 1, 2019).

42 Nancy Armstrong and Leonard Tennenhouse, *Novels in the Time of Democratic Writing: The American Example* (Philadelphia: University of Pennsylvania Press, 2018), 19. For a recent full-length study of style, see Ezra Tawil's *Literature, American Style: The Originality of Imitation in the Early Republic* (Philadelphia: University of Pennsylvania Press, 2018).

43 Neal, *Seventy-Six,* vol. 1, 17.

44 Ibid., preface.

45 Neal himself was famous for self-directed criticism. After *Seventy-Six's* publication, Neal poses in *Blackwood's* as a British critic reviewing American literature in a series of five essays. Among other writers, the critic pays special attention to none other than John Neal, doling out both compliments and criticism of his oeuvre in another preemptive strike at would-be attackers. John Neal, *American Writers: A Series of Papers Contributed to Blackwood's Magazine (1824–1825)*, ed. Fred Lewis Pattee (Durham, NC: Duke University Press, 1937).

46 Neal, *Seventy-Six*, vol. 1, 15.

47 Dietz, "Patriotism," 208.

48 "Our country, right or wrong" was a widespread saying coined by US naval officer Stephen Decatur in a toast he gave in 1816: "Our country! In her intercourse with foreign nations, may she always be in the right; but our country, right or wrong!" James T. De Kay, *A Rage for Glory: The Life of Commodore Stephen Decatur, USN* (New York: Simon and Schuster, 2004), 173. Social and psychological research distinguishes between "blind patriotism," an uncritical love of country represented here, and "constructive patriotism," a critical love of country. In political philosophy, the term for the former is "extreme patriotism."

49 Primoratz, *Patriotism*, 10.

50 Polycarp Ikuenobe, "Citizenship and Patriotism," *Public Affairs Quarterly* 24.4 (2010): 297–318; Sean Richey, "Civic Engagement and Patriotism," *Social Science Quarterly* 92.4 (2011): 1044–1056.

51 Neal, *Seventy-Six*, vol. 1, 26.

52 Ibid., 17. In the preface, Jonathan Oadley reveals his goal as a narrator is to "talk on paper" and indicates his approval of ordinary conversational vernacular. For Neal on interchangeability of spoken and written American English, see "Speculations of a Traveller Concerning the People of the United States: With Parallels," *Blackwood's Edinburgh Review* 16 (July, 1824): 91–97. Neal advances colloquialism as a trait of national literature, a style he hoped would be emulated. In the early national period, as Ezra Tawil argues, style resolved the settler-colonial dilemma of imitation. American writers could stylistically innovate an inherited English language since style is manner, not form or content. Tawil, *Literature, American Style*, 32.

53 Stephen Best and Sharon Marcus, "Surface Reading: An Introduction," *Representations* 108.1 (2009): 1–21.

54 See Nicole Eustace, *Passion Is the Gale: Emotion, Power, and the Coming of the American Revolution* (Chapel Hill, NC: Omohundro Institute of Early American History and Culture and University of North Carolina Press, 2008), and Sarah Knott, *Sensibility and the American Revolution* (Chapel Hill, NC: Omohundro Institute of Early American History and Culture and University of North Carolina Press, 2009).

CHAPTER 15

Revolutionary Lives
Memoir Writing and Meaning Making during the American Revolution

Michael A. McDonnell and Marama Whyte

Introduction

Elizabeth Fisher had not long turned seventeen when the war came. She had just given birth to a son and spent the past few months confined at home with a "broken breast." But at 6 a.m. on a summer morning in 1777 there was a knock on the door, and Fisher found her house surrounded by patriot riflemen who were looking for her much older husband, an ex–British Army soldier. When they discovered he was not there, they told Fisher to get out of the house or they would burn her in it. She grabbed her seven-month-old son, stood aside, and watched in horror as the riflemen looted her house and then burned it down. Fisher was forced to walk some twenty-two miles with her son that day to get help. She spent the rest of the war as a refugee in army camps and then in exile in Montreal.

Elizabeth Fisher's war story, laid out in a memoir she wrote in 1810, does a great deal to complicate our often-anodyne notions of a benign American Revolution. She tells a less-known tale of betrayal, violence, deprivation, and separation during the conflict. Taken as a whole, her memoir interrupts our notion of the Founding era more generally. Fisher was born amid the violence of a previous global war, the Seven Years' War. Her mother died three days after giving birth to her. She endured a succession of cruel and abusive caregivers who betrayed her, and then ended up in an unhappy marriage. Her father was an intermittent presence in her life, often traveling between North America and Britain. Fisher herself ended up torn between living in Montreal and returning to the new United States. Eventually, her stepbrother (a relative of the prominent family of John Jay of New York) accused her of forging deeds to lands given her by her father. In her late forties, Fisher spent over five years in a New York State jail. Even after she was pardoned, she wrote that her own children "seem to have forgotten that I am their mother," and refused to visit her. When Elizabeth Fisher sat down to write her story out in 1810, three years after her release from jail, her narrative of the Founding era was halting and uncertain. At the very least, it pushed awkwardly against the ideal of republican motherhood that flourished in the post-Revolution period.[1]

Fisher was not alone in writing her story – and writing out a different kind of story than the one with which we are more familiar. In the years and decades following the end of the Revolutionary War, dozens of ordinary Americans engaged in different ways with what, in retrospect at least, we might call the burgeoning genre of memoir writing. They did so for different reasons, and in different ways. Some wrote to justify compensation claims from the British, others to flesh out their Revolutionary War pension claims. Some wrote to try and make a little money in the face of impoverished circumstances, while others simply wanted to make sure their children knew their stories. All of them, however, undermined or complicated more well-known narratives about the Revolutionary era that dominated the mainstream print culture. They did so by joining with Elizabeth Fisher in emphasizing themes of betrayal, deprivation, division, violence, and chaos. As often, though, these memoir writers disrupted seamless narratives that centered a linear progression from patriot resistance to British tyranny, to battlefield glories of heroic leaders, to Independence and a new nation. Instead, most memoir writers eschewed discussion of formal politics, and focused instead on the hardships of an international war in which they found themselves inadvertently enmeshed, or downplayed the conflict altogether in favor of more salient themes and topics particular to their own lives. Collectively and over many decades, these memoir writers drew on and enriched a new medium of storytelling that ultimately reveals a more complicated national founding story.

The Memoirists

Most stories from the Revolutionary era originate from a relatively narrow band of surviving sources, written mainly by literate elites at the time. These include letters, pamphlets, petitions, newspapers, and the written texts produced – the Declaration of Independence, the US Constitution, the Federalist Papers, and others, along with a myriad of new laws, regulations, and policies produced at the state and local levels. A little later, some of these participants wrote histories of the Revolution, or told stories of their participation in it that were widely circulated. Most of this extant literature from the era came from the quills and presses of those most heavily invested in seeing through the patriot movement and the establishment of stable new polities.[2] The most powerful and lasting stories have come from the so-called Founding Fathers, whom we now know wrote with future readers in mind, aware that if they lost the war of words, posterity would judge them, perhaps even more harshly than the British, who would judge them first.[3]

Others wrote as well, of course, and there are thousands of letters and diaries, public petitions and memorials from ordinary folk who found themselves caught up in the chaos of a Revolution. Historians have done a wonderful job of piecing together these sources – as well as the sources written about them (probate inventories, enslaved runaway advertisements, court records, muster lists, etc.) – to give us a much richer and more inclusive history of the era. But the *meaning* made of the swirl of events by ordinary colonists has been more elusive. We have fragments and half-told stories, not whole-life biographies with accompanying boxes of correspondence. And the stories are further limited by uneven literacy rates over this era, access to the materials of production, and archival processes. Even among the relatively prosperous Euro-American settlers, the production of history was – and still is – subject to the operation of often unseen and unequal levers of power.[4] The larger contours of the origin story set down by elite and partisan participants at the time has had a powerful hold on the national imagination.

That hold might be best seen in the few instances where we do have richer, more complete stories that reveal alternative meanings that participants gave to this era. Some we have ignored. Boston King's revealing journey toward liberty, published in 1796, is hardly known – because as an enslaved African American in South Carolina, he found liberty within the British empire.[5] Abigail Abbot Bailey is also unknown outside specialist historiographical circles.[6] The story she told in 1815 hardly touched on the celebrated events of the Revolution. Instead she focused on her spiritual trials and the horrific domestic violence she and her daughters suffered at the hands of a Continental Army officer.[7] Hardly a good premise for a founding story, it seems. Other stories have been co-opted to "fit into" a larger, more established narrative, in much the same way that veterans of the conflict had to bend their stories to make compelling claims for pensions.[8] Authorities wanted to know from these aging veterans which prominent field officers they served under, and in which well-known battles they participated. They did not want to hear about the boredom, hunger, cold, sickness, violence, and terror that were at the center of many veterans' stories. Many still don't want to hear those stories.[9]

Still, there were many who wrote their stories. Some were compelled to do so. The first cluster of what might be called memoirs emerged even as the war still raged. Several colonists who found themselves on the wrong side of local squabbles were soon labeled tories, or loyalists, and hounded out of their homes, communities, and former colonies. They wrote out their stories of betrayal, often in exile, in order to seek justice – and compensation – from the government to whom they had stayed loyal. Following the war, and perhaps more surprisingly, another cluster of African Americans wrote out or told their stories to others. Some, like Boston King, wanted to shed light on the physical and spiritual journey toward freedom; others, like Jeffrey Brace of Vermont, wanted to call attention to the hypocrisies of a new nation dedicated to equality that would deny African American veterans of the conflict their basic rights as citizens.[10]

A steady drip of memoirs, both published and unpublished, were written in the decades following the Revolution, punctuated by further clusters triggered, it seems, by external events. The War of 1812, for example, saw a rise in the number of memoirs from elites and nonelites alike, and the numbers kept steady as the nation approached its Jubilee celebrations in 1826. Overlaid with public commemoration activities was the introduction of new pension schemes – most notably in 1818 and expanded in 1834 – that coaxed aging veterans to tell their stories once again. Some wrote to claim those pensions; others wrote in frustration because the pension claim process did not allow them to tell their full story. The most well-known example of this was Joseph Plumb Martin. His pension application of 1818 is a mere paragraph. He then sat down to write his much lengthier and more garrulous account of his wartime service and published it in 1830.[11] Most of the veterans wrote their accounts to try to earn a little money to supplement their meager pensions – few really profited.[12]

Revolutionary War veterans' accounts continued to roll off the presses as some of the public, at least, grew anxious about the loss of this senescent cohort. Still, not all were published immediately – nor did the authors intend them to be. A significant number of memoir writers explicitly noted they only wanted their children to know their stories, or to learn from them. Another cluster was published posthumously as the Civil War loomed. Antiquarians and historians published another group of memoirs through the late nineteenth and early twentieth centuries – helping to bring to light previously buried (or boxed up) manuscripts. It seems safe to say that there has been enough interest in most of these Revolutionary era memoirs that those that ended up in archives or at historical societies have been published in one form or another. Still, what is unclear is how many more memoirs like that of Elizabeth Fisher or Abigail Abbot Bailey – which deviate substantially from topics traditionally considered interesting by historians and even archivists – still lie neglected in the corners of archives or attics.

Because these memoirs arose for different reasons, and across time, they vary a great deal in form and substance. Some were told to third parties, while at least a few are written in the third person. If editors were involved, they usually introduced the memoirs, but on occasion, there are clear signs of silent – and not so silent – editorial interventions. Despite these differences, their value lies in the fact that they were generally free-form, self-generated attempts to make sense of one's life, to make meaning out of it. The complexities and variabilities within the source base go some way to explain why the historiography on nonelite and loyalist memoirs of the Revolution remains thin, and why so few scholars have made use of this remarkable group of sources.[13] But while historians and literary scholars have long contested the definitions of autobiography, biography, memoir, reminiscences, and other subcategories, most might agree with William L. Andrews, who, in his study of African American autobiography, noted, "Whatever else it is, autobiography stems more often than not from a need to explain and justify the self."[14] And those disparate late eighteenth- and early nineteenth-century memoir writers, in their varied forms and diverse styles, were among the earliest group to try to explain themselves. In that respect, those who wrote about their Revolutionary-era experiences were also engaging in a Revolutionary act.

War Stories

What kind of picture of the Revolutionary era emerges from the pages of these neglected memoirs? What stories did they tell? What meaning did they make of these tumultuous years?

Some memoirists recalled familiar starting points and claimed they were motivated by lofty political sentiments. Levi Hanford of Connecticut turned sixteen in September 1775, and found himself eligible for military service. Writing in the third person, he recalled the "bravery and valor" of the patriots at Lexington and Concord, and was "Roused by the common feeling and stimulated by the example of those around him, but no more so than the natural emotions of his own patriotic heart."[15] William Chamberlin emphasized reason over emotion in his decision to side with the patriots when he recalled that between 1770 and 1774, the dispute between Britain and the colonies was "becoming very serious and threa[t]ning." The newspapers were filled with alarming reports, and essays called on the people "to defend their natural and inalienable rights against the encroachments of a lawless power." But even the bookish twenty-year-old Chamberlin hinted at more than a defense of rights as his reason for joining a militia company in April 1775. His family had been rocked by a typhoid epidemic in 1767, and his father had mounting medical bills to pay on top of the deaths of at least one daughter. William had to labor hard, cutting cedar timber in the swamps. Then, a hoped-for inheritance from his uncle failed to materialize. By the time the war began, Chamberlin had had enough of laboring. He was thoroughly "Tired of this kind of life" when the troubles with Britain began.[16]

Other memoirists framed the conflict as a religious contest. Jacob Ritter of Pennsylvania confessed that when he was about sixteen, he was drawn into "solemn silence, and stood alone in the woods, when a sight and sense came over me of the horrors of war." He struggled to understand the meaning of this sensation but noted that there was a common talk at the time of whigs and tories. Four years later, there was a muster of militia in his neighborhood and the minister of the Lutheran church to which he belonged preached the propriety and necessity of "standing in defence of our country against her enemies." Ritter joined up: "I was persuaded against my better judgment, to join the army; and taking up my musket, I entered the American service."[17] Daniel Barber of Massachusetts, on the other hand, thought that "real fears of Popery" in New England had influenced many "timorous pious people to send their sons to join the military" and they had been particularly roused by the Quebec Act. He thought many believed King George had thus become a "traitor[,] . . . was secretly a Papist; and whose design it was to oblige this country to submit itself to the unconstitutional power of the English monarch."[18]

For the most part, though, few memoirists recalled prewar religious or political impulses, remembered imperial debates, or expressed partisan sentiments. Most of the memoirists were very young when swept up in the unfolding Revolution. Almost none started their accounts with the Great Awakening, Seven Years' War, or Stamp Act – traditional starting points for many historians today. Many instead began their stories emphasizing their own acts of rebellion. John Greenwood, for example, took advantage of the confusion at the start of the war to run away from an apprenticeship under his uncle, far from his own family in Boston.[19] Samuel Dewees recounted a prewar childhood spent in Pennsylvania in "every species of poverty," struggling against "the tides of ill fortune in a cold, oppressive, and unfriendly world." He was bound out and separated from his family and suffered ten years under a master who treated him with the "most brutal and wanton cruelty." When war came, Dewees jumped at the chance to run away and enlist.[20]

Boston King, an enslaved African American in South Carolina, also recalled a prewar life of misery. He was hired out by his master to a cruel carpenter, who "severely" beat him "without mercy" for trivial mistakes. As patriot elites put the finishing touches on the Declaration of Independence, announcing that all men were created equal, King noted the assaults continued apace. Falsely accused of stealing some nails, he was "beat and tortured most cruelly, and was laid up three weeks before I was able to do any work." Eventually, when the British came south later in the war, King faced the "severest punishment" when he was late bringing back a horse. To escape the "cruelty" of his patriot master, he "determined to go to Charles-Town, and throw myself into the hands of the English." King recalled that "they received me readily, and I began to feel the happiness of liberty, of which I knew nothing before."[21]

Others saw opportunities in the conflict. Daniel Trabue and his brother enlisted in the army in Virginia in 1776, but only because there was no other way to make money; there was no market for their goods: "At this time no sail for produce." So they "concluded we would Join a company that was a going to the North under General Washington" and pick up the generous bounty offered for doing so.[22] Other memoirists waited for opportunities to join privateers at sea before joining the conflict. Even the celebrated George Robert Twelves Hewes, whose patriotic presence at the Boston Tea Party Alfred F. Young has written about, spent most of the war years plying the seas for profits.[23] John Joseph Henry of Pennsylvania "panted after military glory" and "clandestinely" joined the army after his father tried to push him into another unpromising job. He had already been bound out to an uncle who had moved him to Detroit, only to see the business fail. Henry had to walk all the way back to Lancaster – some 500 miles – on his own.[24]

Many memoirists had no choice but to join the fighting. Jonathan Elkins had just moved to Peacham, Vermont, with his father to help clear a newly purchased lot of land as the war broke out in April 1775. At the age of fourteen, he found himself on the front lines of a war not of his making, threatened by Native peoples and eventually British troops making their way southward from Canada.[25] Jeffrey Brace had even less choice. Brace's Connecticut master sent the enslaved African American into the army in his place – as a substitute. Years later, Brace recalled with irony that he joined the Continental Army as a "Poor African Slave, to liberate freemen, my tyrants." Years later, he was still enslaved despite his service to the new nation: "Thus was I, a slave for five years fighting for liberty."[26]

Many of the young, eager soldiers who marched off to battle with thoughts of politics, glory, plunder, or promotion soon ran headlong into the realities of an eighteenth-century war. Daniel Barber recalled the warmth and emotion of the send-off from his hometown of Simsbury, Connecticut, in 1775, and the anticipation of his comrades, most of whom had never before been more than "twenty miles from home." On the road to Boston, the inhabitants of Connecticut were "very polite" and greeted them with "tokens of joy and gladness." But as they crossed into Massachusetts, the youthful army was treated with suspicion – as if they were a "banditti of rogues and thieves." The inhabitants there had already suffered at the hands of soldiers marching ahead of them.[27]

A few months later, and to Barber's north, sixteen-year-old John Joseph Henry, who counted himself among the "enthusiastic whigs," marched into the woods of Maine with "my whole soul . . . bound up in the cause." But Henry's decision to join the ill-fated invasion of Canada soon became a journey into the heart of darkness. The soldiers suffered dreadfully from disease and hunger, resorting to eating dogs and fighting over the roots of weeds. They experienced dysentery, and assumed they would die. Henry's recollections were full of shame. He recalled passing a New England man struggling in the three-foot-deep cold waters – "lean and wretched from abstinence." Yet no one would help. "Death stared us in the face," Henry recalled: "I gave him a sincere sigh at parting." Henry put his own life first. He could not step out to help him, he reasoned, "for to lose my place in the file, might have been fatal." The column moved on. "This pitiable being died in the wilderness," alone. He was one of many. Henry could only try to erase his shame by telling his story.[28]

Others also wrote of hunger and deprivation, but especially diseases. William Chamberlin, who had already seen his family suffer from the ravages of typhus before the war, found himself retreating from the Quebec campaign amid an epidemic of smallpox. His comrades had picked it up in Montreal, he thought, and it was now almost "useless to try to avoid it." As they fled up the Champlain Valley, they arrived on an island "covered with the people sick with the small-pox in its various stages." There was "no possibility of escaping the contagion." They had inadequate food and medicine, and were sleeping out on the ground. Chamberlin tried to inoculate himself by cutting his arm and rubbing "some of the infection" into it. He then set off again in a boat full of infected soldiers, "one of whom was blind with the disorder, and two or three afterwards died." Chamberlin thought that at least a third of his comrades who set out with him in the spring of 1776 never returned.[29] Boston King, the escaped slave from South Carolina, was also struck down with smallpox while with the British. They immediately abandoned him and other infected African Americans. King recalled they "suffered great hardships" and were often left without food or water while ill. He was saved only by an anonymous Samaritan who brought him a few things he needed.[30]

More recent works have drawn on some of the memoirs to highlight the diseases and deplorable conditions that ravaged the prison camps and ships on all sides of the conflict.[31] Yet some memoirists blamed their own officers for the miseries they endured. When eighty-four-year-old Samuel Dewees wrote out his war story, he spent some eighty pages detailing the harsh punishments meted out by the Continental Army officers whom he thought were supposed to protect them. One incident stood out with remarkable clarity. The veteran fifer recalled that in early June 1781, when he was about twenty years of age, he was forced to watch as a group of his comrades in arms, fellow Continental soldiers, were shot to death. Dewees noted with a shudder that the force of the close-range musket shots blew the head off of one of his friends. The fence behind the men was "covered over with blood and brains." In Dewees' eyes, the soldiers had lost their lives for the most trivial of offenses. Two of them had made the mistake of speaking to their superior officers using "indecorous language." They could hardly have believed their indiscretions would lead to their death. They did. And young Samuel Dewees, who had shared food, drink, and wartime trials with each of them would not – could not – forget them.[32]

The violence of the war stood out for both soldiers and civilians alike. John P. Becker of Schoharie, New York, was one of the few non-veterans who wrote a memoir. He was only ten when war broke out. But he later recalled his cold and selfish neighbors as Burgoyne advanced down the Hudson Valley in 1777 and everyone scattered. In the aftermath of the campaign, Becker came across the wounded on both sides. He recalled recoiling at the "sight of these wretched people, pale and lifeless . . . and the sound of groaning voices as each motion of the litter renewed the anguish of their wounds, filled me with horror and sickness of heart." He also remembered with horror the hanging of seven "disaffected" men by a "mob" after a public brawl. In retrospect, he queried the point of it all and noted that "we were much affected with what we saw . . . and the remembrance cannot be effaced."[33]

Many memoir writers recognized the violence as the tragic product of a civil war. Like Becker, John Joseph Henry observed the most "disgusting and torturing sight" – of carriages laden with the dead of both sides going to the "dead house" where they were "heaped in monstrous piles . . . their limbs distorted in various directions." "Curse on these civil wars which extinguish the sociabilities of mankind, and annihilate the strength of nations."[34] Others recalled vivid moments of recognition of the tragic consequences of that violence. When John Peters found himself fighting for the British at the battle of Bennington in 1777, he remembered the moment during the fierce fighting when someone rushed at him yelling, "Peters, you damned Tory, I have got you!" before skewering him with his bayonet. Luckily, though it pierced him just below his left breast, the bayonet was "turned by the bones." Pinned, Peters recognized his attacker as "an old schoolmate and playfellow, and a cousin of my wife." His own musket loaded and primed, he faced an awful choice: "Though his bayonet was in my body I felt regret at being obliged to destroy him."[35]

Many of those caught up in this most uncivil war recalled being betrayed by their patriot neighbors, but many felt betrayed by the British, too. Elizabeth Lichtenstein was a refugee with the British army at Portsmouth, Virginia, in November 1780. Then the British forces decided to pull out of the town. Eliza remembered in vivid detail the shock that many of the inhabitants felt at the decision, taken "just as the poor people came forward to show their loyalty, in the hope that the British would remain permanently there." Her landlady, a Mrs. Elliott, was speechless at the news, "scarce in her senses from the shock" until she could finally lament that this was the third time they had been left by the British troops "to the rage and persecution of the Americans."[36]

Others unwillingly experienced the war as a truly international conflict. Some ventured beyond colonial borders to engage in brutal wartime events. At the age of seventeen, Nathan Davis from Mansfield, Connecticut, enlisted in the army for three years. He soon found himself on General Sullivan's infamous campaign across Iroquoia, torching farms, villages, and crops of Native Americans whom Davis believed had been "induced by the English to take up arms against America." On the march across what is now Upstate New York, Davis remembered an "inhospitable wilderness," which was of course a rich and fertile home for Native peoples, and remembered seeing "here and there . . . a human skeleton bleaching in the woods" – a relic of previous skirmishes. He detailed the destruction wrought by the troops, threats against Indian women, and their terrorization of so-called loyalist prisoners. When provisions ran out,

Davis recalled that they were promised a share of the plunder, at which "every eye brightened and sparkled with vengeance."[37]

Other memoirists were flung further afield. After nineteen-year-old Jonathan Elkins of Peacham got dragged into the conflict, he was taken prisoner by a party of pro-British settlers and Indians and whisked away in captivity to St John's, Canada. There he was violently sick for weeks, put in manacles that turned his hands black, and suffered a dangerous trip to Quebec in which he almost drowned. He then starved in a Quebec prison before being sent to Portsmouth, England, via Cork, Ireland, and thence to Mill Prison in Plymouth. He suffered greatly throughout and at several points thought he was on the verge of death by disease, starvation, and the hangman for treason.[38] Joshua Davis also found himself at sea at the age of nineteen, on board a privateer sailing out from Boston in 1779. Within three months he was a prisoner on board a British ship at Newfoundland. He spent the rest of the war as an impressed sailor on various British ships, fighting his countrymen and their French allies, before ending up in Mill Prison at Plymouth, like Jonathan Elkins. But unlike Elkins, who was exchanged after Cornwallis' defeat at Yorktown, Davis was betrayed again by the British and had to serve even more time as an impressed sailor.[39]

The separations endured by some of the veterans of the conflict were everywhere felt across and within families, too – but particularly loyalist families whom patriots forced to uproot. We already noted Elizabeth Fisher's disrupted life across the Revolutionary era. Elizabeth Lichtenstein also experienced the war in exile and apart from her family members. Her war story was of a young girl coming of age amid an uncivil conflagration. Though she met her husband, William Martin Johnston, because of the conflict, these were not happy recollections of a newlywed. Her memory of those years was dominated by painful separations, first from her father and then from her husband, followed by months of anxiety and uncertainty about their safety as she received reports of other deaths in the extended family. Elizabeth and her growing family spent much of the war years as refugees from the conflict. She moved from place to place, taking shelter in barns, on board ships, and in the homes of strangers, even while pregnant and then with infants in tow. She was driven out from her hometown of Little Ogeechee in Georgia, survived the siege of Savannah, traveled to New York, sojourned at Portsmouth in Virginia, went to Charleston after it fell to the British, and was forced to leave again when the British evacuated the town.[40]

The end of the Revolutionary War did not bring peace to many of the memoirists. Boston King recalled an anxious and uncertain conclusion to the Revolutionary conflict. He found himself in New York City at war's end, among the British and loyalist refugees – some of whom were there with their still enslaved workforce. News of the peace "issued universal joy among all parties, except us, who had escaped from slavery, and taken refuge in the English army." King's recollection of this moment gives us a glimpse of the harrowing irony of the end of the American Revolution for many African Americans:

> for a report prevailed at New-York, that all the slaves, in number 2,000, were to be delivered up to their masters, although some of them had been three or four years among the English. This dreadful rumour filled us all with inexpressible anguish and terror, especially when we saw our masters coming from Virginia, North-Carolina, and other parts, and seizing upon their slaves in the streets of New-York, or even dragging them out of their beds. Many of the slaves had very cruel masters, so that the thoughts of returning home with them embittered life to us. For some days, we lost our appetite for food, and sleep departed from our eyes.

In the end, the British did give escaped slaves like King his freedom, but King and his wife had to endure some severe hardships in a cold climate in Nova Scotia, and the British were unwilling to help get them established. Eventually, King traveled back to West Africa where – after losing his wife to new diseases there – he eventually made peace with both God and Europeans – albeit an uneasy one.[41]

There were more struggles to come for many after the war. Patriot soldier Joshua Davis, who spent many difficult years in prison and impressed on British ships, found himself stranded in London at the end of the war. He labored hard for almost five years before he could secure passage back to his family, arriving back in Boston on December 30, 1787 – some eight and a half years after he left. Davis then tried to go into business with the hope of making up his "lost time." He worked hard for some years, "but by repeated misfortunes, I am nearly reduced to the situation I was in when robbed in Ireland." In 1811, unable to labor any longer, and angry that the British were again impressing American sailors, he thought he would "put my scraps of half-worn papers together, in order to inform mankind how I and many of my fellow countrymen have fared, and do still fare on board of his majesty's ships of war." Even then, his experiences had left physical scars too difficult to overcome. He said he could have "swelled my narrative to a volume, but being lame in my left side, it is with difficulty that I can write at all."[42]

Jeffrey Brace, the African American from Connecticut who had to sue his master for his freedom even after five years of service in the patriot army, continued to struggle in the postwar years. Brace headed to Vermont, undoubtedly aware that it was the first state formally to abolish slavery. But his white neighbors reneged on work contracts and bilked him out of what little land he could purchase. He married a widowed African woman, Susannah, but neither of them could prevent her children being taken away from them and bound out as servants. Brace and his now-growing family continued to move further north, away from unscrupulous fellow citizens. He finally purchased some land on the shores of Lake Champlain, but three years later his wife died unexpectedly, and Jeffrey began to go blind. He asked someone to help prepare his memoir, in which he railed bitterly against hypocritical white Christians, and hoped that God would yet bring a Revolution to come. Over a decade later, Brace applied for a war pension. His application relied on testimony from neighbors that he had no property of any kind left, and had been supported for some time by public and private charity. Nor were any of his family well off enough to support him. One deponent told the court the total value of Brace's property in 1821 was "Nothing."[43]

Conclusion

If the memoirists collectively told a story of an uglier, more violent, divisive, and expansive Revolution than the story often told in our popular texts and textbooks, it is worth noting that they also struggled to make sense of it, even in retrospect. As they sat down to reflect on their experiences – whether it was a few years, or a few decades, after the end of the Revolution – they often struggled to find meaning in it all. John P. Becker noted that his family had lost so much during the war, and postwar opportunities never materialized. The sacrifices made by his family seemed in vain. He queried the point of it all: "Is much public happiness then bought at the price of individual wretchedness? Must blood and tears and sorrow be the result of even the most just and righteous controversies?" He wrote his memoir, he said, with death and "consolation" only a few days away.[44]

John Joseph Henry admitted he could not tell every "dreadful tale of incidents," as he wrestled with his own shameful behavior in the war. Through tear-filled eyes, Henry tried to assert he would serve again if he had to, but hoped his story would inspire his readers "with a disgust, towards war of any kind."[45] Similarly, Nathan Davis regretted his participation in the campaign against the Iroquois. Writing about the time of Jacksonian Removal, probably between 1825 and 1831, and nearing age seventy, he noted that even during the campaign, it did not "altogether escape our reflection what must be the inevitable consequence resulting from the destruction of all the sustenance of a multitude of natives." Davis reasoned that they had been compelled to do it out of revenge for Indian atrocities. But now he wasn't sure. The poor soldiers who had served had been forgotten, he said, and, in turn, "[we have become] the oppressors of the weak; and the defenceless Creek and Cherokee feel the full force of our insatiable avarice. May God save our country from ruin."[46]

Others turned to God after the war to save themselves from ruin. Jacob Ritter left his pro-patriot Lutheran congregation, joined the Quakers, and became a pacifist.[47] Daniel Barber left the Episcopal Church and became a wandering itinerant Catholic in his later years, eschewing all claims to a worldly life.[48] Henry Holcombe even broke all ties to his Revolutionary past. He had been born into a well-to-do South Carolina family and had purchased an officer's commission at the age of seventeen in 1777. At some unknown point, he resigned his commission and was then ordained as a minister in 1785.[49] He was in the vanguard of what historians have come to call the Second Great Awakening – the Protestant religious revival that swept the fledgling nation in the wake of the Revolution. Ritter, Barber, and Holcomb suggest that many tried to find meaning in God because it could not be found in the Revolutionary past.

Yet Henry Holcombe went even further. By 1812, when the Baptist minister wrote his memoir – divided into a series of letters – he was already on the path to pacifism. He significantly downplayed his military career and the Revolution in his life story. He hardly mentioned it. Instead, he offered a narrative of religious conversion and of his later career. When he finally mentioned the war, Holcombe wrote that while he once venerated Washington's piety, he now thought a Christian would be ridiculed in an army camp. He organized the Pennsylvania Peace Society in 1822, and became an even more ardent pacifist by the time of his death in 1824.[50]

That Holcombe hardly mentioned the Revolution, that Boston King wrote his story of the era in Bristol, England, and that Elizabeth Fisher – with whom we started this essay –saw it only as one in a series of traumatic disruptions, redraws our attention to the fact that many participants did not see this moment as primarily a nation-making event. They suggest that if we move beyond mining these memoirs for stories about the war alone, we may find the Revolution significantly decentered. Yet we should also remember that even the grizzled veterans who did write mainly about their Revolutionary War experiences struggled to make sense of the violence, the terror, the deprivation, and the upheaval of this most uncivil conflict. No doubt their inability to spin a more coherent or appealing yarn contributed to the relative obscurity to which the memoirists have been assigned. Few had their stories published in their lifetimes; only a handful were read beyond their own families. How many other unfinished notes or scrawled manuscripts were used for kindling, or yet still molder in chests and boxes?

This obscurity may have come at a cost, and might still be costing us. Perhaps these ordinary memoirists represent only a handful of people who lost out in the boisterous jostling of colonies, empire and a new nation, cut adrift and exceptional in their experiences. Or perhaps they represented a much greater number of people whose voices have been drowned out by the more successful spin that patriots and nationalists – with greater access to the public and private presses – were able to put on the chaotic events of the late eighteenth century when establishing a new nation that entrenched slavery, sanctioned the dispossession of Native peoples, and excluded more people from civil society than it included. Some 250 years later, as the same nation seems once again at war with itself, the stories of Elizabeth Fisher, Boston King, and John Joseph Henry might yet remind us of the consequences in not acknowledging a more complicated, expansive, and turbulent history – and not recognizing our often common and shared trials, tribulations, and trauma.

Notes

1 Elizabeth Fisher, *Memoirs of Mrs. Elizabeth Fisher of the City of New-York . . .* (New York: Printed for the author, 1810), 3–4, 16–18, 20–21, 38–39, 44–45. In her edition Sharon Halevi notes the many ways Fisher's account illuminates common understandings of the Revolution. Sharon Halevi, *The Other Daughters of the Revolution: The Narrative of K. White (1809) and the Memoirs of Elizabeth Fisher (1810)* (Albany: State University of New York Press, 2006).

2 With some important exceptions, they also tend to be an even more select group who ended up on the side of the winners in that contest – the patriots. Eileen Ka-May Cheng has noted these exceptions, and that some loyalists did eventually manage to weave their stories into the more conservative view of the Revolution which emerged over time. Eileen Ka-May Cheng, *The Plain and Noble Garb of Truth: Nationalism and Impartiality in American Historical Writing, 1784–1860* (Athens: University of Georgia Press, 2008), 208–236.

3 Even patriot newspapers were heavily implicated in the literal stitching-together of a powerful story of self-defense against tyranny; see Robert G. Parkinson, *The Common Cause: Creating Race and Nation in the American Revolution* (Chapel Hill: University of North Carolina Press for the Omohundro Institute of Early American History and Culture, 2016). See

also Michael A. McDonnell, "War Stories: Remembering and Forgetting the American Revolution," in *The American Revolution Reborn*, ed. Patrick Spero and Michael Zuckerman (Philadelphia: University of Pennsylvania Press, 2016), 9–28; Michael A. McDonnell, Clare Corbould, Frances M. Clarke, and W. Fitzhugh Brundage, eds., *Remembering the Revolution: Memory, History, and Nation Making from Independence to the Civil War* (Amherst: University of Massachusetts Press, 2013).

4 See Michel-Rolph Trouillot, *Silencing the Past: Power and the Production of History* (Boston: Beacon Press, 1995).

5 Boston King, "Memoirs of the Life of Boston King, a Black Preacher . . .," *The Methodist Magazine* (March–June 1798), Arizona State University, Antislavery Literature Project, www.latinamericanstudies.org/slavery/Boston_King.pdf (accessed September 24, 2020). King's memoir has been taken up in specialist circles; see Alan Gilbert, *Black Patriots and Loyalists: Fighting for Emancipation in the War for Independence* (Chicago: University of Chicago Press, 2012); Mary Louise Clifford, *From Slavery to Freetown: Black Loyalists after the American Revolution* (Jefferson: McFarland & Company, 1999); James W. St. G. Walker, *The Black Loyalists: The Search for a Promised Land in Nova Scotia and Sierra Leone, 1783–1870* (Toronto: University of Toronto Press, 1992); Phyllis R. Blakely, "Boston King: A Black Loyalist," in *Eleven Exiles: Accounts of Loyalists of the American Revolution*, ed. Phyllis R. Blakely and John N. Grant (Toronto: Dundurn Press Limited, 1982), 265–287.

6 See Lisa M. Logan, "Territorial Agency: Negotiations of Space and Empire in the Domestic Violence Memoirs of Abigail Abbot Bailey and Anne Home Livingston," in *Women's Narratives of the Early Americas and the Formation of Empire*, ed. Mary McAleer Balkun and Susan C. Imbarrato (Hampshire: Palgrave Macmillan, 2016), 215–227; Sharon Halevi, "'A variety of domestic misfortunes': Writing the Dysfunctional Self in Early America," *Early American Literature* 44.1 (2009): 95–119; Roxanne Harde, "'I consoled my heart': Conversion Rhetoric and Female Subjectivity in the Personal Narratives of Elizabeth Ashbridge and Abigail Bailey," *Legacy* 21.2 (2004): 156–171.

7 Abigail Abbot Bailey, "The Memoirs of Abigail Abbot Bailey" (1815), in *Religion and Domestic Violence in Early New England: The Memoirs of Abigail Abbot Bailey*, ed. Ann Taves (Bloomington: Indiana University Press, 1989), 51–198.

8 Not all memoirs have been neglected by scholars, or by readers at the time. At least some of those written by patriot elite men have long been in print and circulation, and have been used more commonly – they have helped create the narrative bedrock of the story of the American Revolution.

9 In a telling example, David McCullough used John Greenwood's memoir to add color to his history of the Continental Army, but carefully left out the details which did not fit his narrative such as Greenwood enlisting as a last resort after finding himself "without a friend or a house to shelter me for the

night," and almost deserting after three weeks. McDonnell, "War Stories," 15. See also William Huntting Howell, "'Starving Memory': Anti-Narrating the American Revolution," in McDonnell et al., eds., *Remembering the Revolution*, 93–109.

10 *The Blind African Slave, or Memoirs of Boyrereau Brinch, Nicknamed Jeffrey Brace*, ed. Karl J. Winter (Madison: University of Wisconsin Press, 2004).

11 Joseph Plumb Martin, *A Narrative of Some of the Adventures, Dangers, and Sufferings of a Revolutionary Soldier* . . . (Hallowell: Glazier, Masters & Co., 1830).

12 Michael A. McDonnell and Briony Neilson, "Reclaiming a Revolutionary Past: War Veterans, Pensions, and the Struggle for Recognition," *Journal of the Early Republic* 39.3 (2019): 467–501.

13 Some scholarship does gesture to loyalist memoirs; see Rebecca Brannon, *From Revolution to Reunion: The Reintegration of the South Carolina Loyalists* (Columbia: University of South Carolina Press, 2016); Jim Piecuch, *Three Peoples One King: Loyalists, Indians, and Slaves in the Revolutionary South, 1775–1782* (Columbia: University of South Carolina Press, 2008). Edward Larkin in his chapter on "Loyalism" in the *Oxford Handbook of the American Revolution*, ed. Jane Kamensky and Edward G. Gray (Oxford: Oxford University Press, 2012), 291–310, also calls for a new reading of the loyalists and looks at several important war stories told by loyalists. The failure to engage more fully with writing by nonelite women and African Americans may be in part because, as Susan Stanford Friedman has argued, "individualistic models of the self," which remain popular in scholarship on autobiography, are fundamentally inapplicable to women and minorities because they ignore "the importance of a culturally imposed group identity" for marginalized groups. Susan Stanford Friedman, "Women's Autobiographical Selves: Theory and Practice," in *The Private Self: Theory and Practice of Women's Autobiographical Writings*, ed. Shari Benstock (Chapel Hill: University of North Carolina Press, 1988), 34. Sarah J. Purcell, *Sealed with Blood: War, Sacrifice, and Memory in Revolutionary America* (Philadelphia: University of Pennsylvania Press, 2002), and Alfred F. Young, *The Shoemaker and the Tea Party: Memory and the American Revolution* (Boston: Beacon Press, 1999), both refer to the existence of the memoirs but do not engage much with them. The notable exceptions are Stephen Carl Arch, *After Franklin: The Emergence of Autobiography in Post-Revolutionary America, 1780–1830* (Hanover, NH: University Press of New England, 2001), and Susan Clair Imbarrato, *Declarations of Independency in Eighteenth-Century American Autobiography* (Knoxville: University of Tennessee Press, 1998). Other scholars have worked to reintroduce memoirs into the historical record: Emmy E. Werner, *In Pursuit of Liberty: Coming of Age in the American Revolution* (Washington, DC: Potomac Books, 2009); Joyce Appleby, ed., *Recollections of the Early Republic: Selected Autobiographies* (Boston: Northeastern University Press, 1997); J. Todd White and Charles H. Lesser, *Fighters for Independence: A Guide to Sources of Biographical Information on Soldiers and Sailors of the*

American Revolution (Chicago: University of Chicago Press, 1997); John C. Dann, ed., *The Revolution Remembered: Eyewitness Accounts of the War for Independence* (Chicago: University of Chicago Press, 1980).

14 William L. Andrews, *To Tell a Free Story: The First Century of Afro-American Autobiography, 1760–1865* (Urbana: University of Illinois Press, 1988), 1. See also Elizabeth W. Bruss, *Autobiographical Acts: The Changing Situation of a Literary Genre* (Baltimore: Johns Hopkins University Press, 1976); Ruth Banes, "The Exemplary Self: Autobiography in Eighteenth-Century America," *Biography* 5.3 (1982): 226–239; Sidonie Smith and Julia Watson, *Reading Autobiography: A Guide for Interpreting Life Narratives* (Minneapolis: University of Minnesota Press, 2001); Gabriel Cervantes, "Learning from Stephen Burroughs: Republication and the Making of a Literary Book in the Early United States," *William and Mary Quarterly* 73.4 (2016): 711–740, here 720–721.

15 Charles I. Bushnell, ed., *A Narrative of the Life and Adventures of Levi Hanford* ... (New York: Privately printed, 1863), 9.

16 William Chamberlin, "Letter of Gen. William Chamberlin," *Proceedings of the Massachusetts Historical Society*, Second Series 10 (1986): 492–493.

17 *Memoirs of Jacob Ritter, a Faithful Minister in the Society of Friends*, ed. Joseph Foulks (Philadelphia: T. E. Chapman, 1844), 12–13.

18 Daniel Barber, *The History of My Own Times*, Part 2 (Washington City: Printed for the author by S. C. Ustick, 1828), 17–18. Daniel Trabue also recalled years later that in Chesterfield County, the Baptists and Presbyterians supported the patriot movement, but the Anglican parson had told his father that "the people was Deluded by some of their Leaders" and warned that the "negros would also rise in Rebellion ... if the people Did Rebel," and they would "suffer much by high Fines and Taxes, etc." Chester Raymond Young, ed., *Westward into Kentucky: The Narrative of Daniel Trabue* (Lexington: University Press of Kentucky, 2004), 42.

19 Isaac J. Greenwood, ed., *The Revolutionary Services of John Greenwood* ... (New York: De Vinne Press, 1922), 5.

20 John Smith Hanna, ed., *A History of the Life and Services of Captain Samuel Dewees* ... (Baltimore: Robert Neilson, 1844), 31–32.

21 King, "Memoirs," 106–107. See also Fisher, *Memoirs*, 3–15.

22 Caroline Cox, "Public Memories, Private Lives: The First Greatest Generation Remembers the Revolutionary War," in McDonnell et al., eds., *Remembering the Revolution*, 113, 116; Young, ed., *Westward into Kentucky*, 43, 67–68; Michael A. McDonnell, *The Politics of War: Race, Class and Conflict in Revolutionary Virginia* (Chapel Hill: University of North Carolina Press for the Omohundro Institute of Early American History and Culture, 2010), 260, 358–359.

23 A Citizen of New-York [James Hawkes], *A Retrospect of the Boston Tea-Party, with a Memoir of George R.T. Hewes* ... (New York: S. S. Bliss, 1834).

24 John Joseph Henry, *An Accurate and Interesting Account of the Hardships and Sufferings* ... (Lancaster: William Greer, 1812), 7.

25 Jonathan Elkins, "Reminiscences of Jonathan Elkins," *Proceedings of the Vermont Historical Society* (1912–1920), 187.

26 Brace filed a pension application in 1818, when new legislation allowed it, giving us some corroborating evidence of his military career. *Memoirs of Boyrereau Brinch*, 53–54, 67–68, 159, 166. For other memoirs detailing enforced choices, see also Elizabeth Lichtenstein Johnston, *Recollections of a Georgia Loyalist*, ed. Arthur Wentworth Eaton (New York: Bankside Press, 1901); "Narrative of Loyalist John Peters, Lieutenant-Colonel of the Queen's Loyal Rangers in Canada, Written in Letter to a Friend in London, Pimlico [Eng.], June 5, 1786," *Daily Globe* (Toronto), July 16, 1877, 3 (with thanks to T. Cole Jones for providing a copy); Frances Mary Stoddard, ed., *An Account of a Part of the Sufferings and Losses of Jolley Allen ...* (Boston: Franklin Press, 1883); *Narrative of the Exertions and Sufferings of Lieut. James Moody ... ,* ed. Charles I. Bushnell (New York: Privately printed, 1865).

27 Barber, *History*, Part 1, 14–15.

28 Henry, *Account*, 125, 200.

29 Chamberlin, "Letter," 497–498. See also Thomas Painter, *Autobiography of Thomas Painter, Relating His Experiences during the War of the Revolution* (Washington, DC: Privately printed, 1910), 47–48; Nathaniel Segar, *A Brief Narrative of the Captivity and Sufferings of Lt. Nathan'l Segar ...* (Paris, ME: Printed at the Observer Office, 1825), 8–9.

30 Ironically, smallpox may have saved his life. As he was recovering, patriot forces drew up nearby, and would have almost certainly been keen to recover lost property. But they feared getting infected, and left King and his sick comrades alone. King, "Memoirs," 107.

31 See Judith I. Madera, "Floating Prisons: Dispossession, Ordering, and Colonial Atlantic 'States,' 1776–1783," in *Buried Lives: Incarcerated in Early America*, ed. Michele Lise Tarter and Richard Bell (Athens: University of Georgia Press, 2012), 175–202; Edwin G. Burrows, *Forgotten Patriots: The Untold Story of American Prisoners during the American Revolutionary War* (New York: Basic Books, 2008); Robert E. Cray, Jr., "Commemorating the Prison Ship Dead: Revolutionary Memory and the Politics of Sepulture in the Early Republic, 1776–1808," *William and Mary Quarterly* 56.3 (1999): 565–590.

32 Hanna, ed., *History*, 228–231.

33 John P. Becker, *The Sexagenary; or, Reminiscences of the American Revolution* (Albany: J. Munsell, 1866), 34, 40, 58–59, 73, 82–85, 96, 100, 134–135.

34 Henry, *Account*, 134. See also Moody, *Narrative*, 8–9, 11–12.

35 "Narrative of Loyalist John Peters," 3.

36 Johnston, *Recollections*, 66–67. For a short biography and further details of Eliza's life in exile, see Maya Jasanoff, *Liberty's Exiles: American Loyalists in the Revolutionary World* (New York: Alfred A. Knopf, 2011), xii, and passim.

37 Nathan Davis, "History of the Expedition against the Five Nations, Commanded by General Sullivan, in 1779," *The Historical Magazine and*

Notes and Queries, Concerning the Antiquities, History and Biography of America 3, 2nd series (1866): 198–201.

38 Elkins, "Reminiscences," 195–208.

39 Joshua Davis, *A Narrative of Joshua Davis, an American Citizen . . .* (Boston: Printed by B. True, 1811), 13–15, 24–27, 33–34. See also Charles I. Bushnell, ed., *The Narrative of John Blatchford, Detailing His Sufferings in the Revolutionary War . . .* (New York: Privately Printed, 1865), 22 and passim.

40 Johnston, *Recollections*, 61–66, 211, and passim.

41 King, "Memoirs," 157. For King's postwar reconciliation with Europeans and his spiritual journey, see Clare Corbould and Michael A. McDonnell, *To Choose Our Better History: African Americans and the American Revolution from Independence to Today* (New York: The New Press, forthcoming), chap. 2.

42 J. Davis, *Narrative*, 72.

43 *Memoirs of Boyrereau Brinch*, 166, 171, 177, 214–215, and passim. Other veterans, including Daniel Trabue and Nathaniel Segar, similarly found little to sustain them in the new republic; see Cox, "Public Memories, Private Lives," 113, 116; Young, ed., *Westward into Kentucky*, 43, 67–68; McDonnell, *Politics of War*, 260, 358–359; Segar, *Narrative*, 29–31.

44 Becker, *Sexagenary*, 34, 40, 58–59, 73, 82–85, 96, 100–103, 134–135, 153–157, 213.

45 Henry, *Account*, 143.

46 N. Davis, "History," 203–205. John Joseph Henry wanted to believe he had fought "for freedom" but he was bedeviled by his recollections of the realities of the war; see Henry, *Account*, 7. Loyalist John Peters also seemed to struggle to reconcile his decisions; see "Narrative of Loyalist John Peters," 3.

47 *Memoirs of Jacob Ritter*, 21–38.

48 Barber, *History*, Part 3, 11–12.

49 Henry Holcombe, *The First Fruits; in a Series of Letters* (Philadelphia: Ann Cochran, 1812), 21, 44, 45.

50 Holcombe, *First Fruits*; John B. Boles, "Henry Holcombe, a Southern Baptist Reformer in the Age of Jefferson," *The Georgia Historical Quarterly* 54.3 (1970): 381–407, here 400–403.

CHAPTER 16

Literature of Poverty and Labor

Lori Merish

There is a well-known literature about labor in the early republic, one that celebrates the working *man* as both bedrock of republican virtue and key to national prosperity. "Those who labour in the earth are the chosen people of God," Thomas Jefferson famously pronounced; similarly, J. Hector St. John de Crèvecoeur identified the agrarian labor of the small freeholder as the engine of both economic and moral development, producing a harmonious, egalitarian, pastoral world of plenty where "the useless become useful, and the poor become rich."[1] But the best-known literary narrative of American labor from this period is Benjamin Franklin's *Autobiography*, which memorably depicts Franklin's experience as indentured servant and apprentice, as well as his success as a master artisan, entrepreneur, and public figure on the national and international stage. Foregrounding an indefatigable industriousness that became legendary – Max Weber would proffer Franklin as living embodiment of the Protestant ethic of industry and self-restraint – he narrates his rise, as he explains in the narrative's opening lines, "from the Poverty and Obscurity in which I was born and bred, to a state of Affluence and some Degree of Reputation in the world." His industry is the basis of his accumulated wealth as well as social visibility and esteem, his "Character and Credit."[2] The economic and social mobility he charts has a geographic dimension: it originates in his flight from an oppressive apprenticeship under his brother in Boston to freedom, independence, and prosperity in Philadelphia. The most prominent early American narrative of labor is a Philadelphia story.

This essay centers on Philadelphia for reasons beyond the long shadow cast by Franklin over my topic. As Samuel Otter notes, Philadelphia's cultural consequence in early America has been wrongly neglected, in part because of the rapid development of New York in the post-Revolutionary era.[3] This is certainly true in terms of class and labor history; New York has dominated accounts of the decline of the artisanal system of production and the rise of wage labor, and the history of working-class parties and political activism. New York also regularly features in the literary history of labor, class, and poverty, in scholarship that examines sensationalist narratives of urban misery and the obscene gap between rich and poor in the antebellum era, and in studies of naturalist narratives of Bowery degradation and devastation. But besides being a vital literary and cultural center and the new nation's capital and largest city until 1790, Philadelphia was a major port of immigration and the site of the nation's largest and most established free Black community. Positioning itself as a short companion piece to Otter's magisterial *Philadelphia Stories*, and drawing on the rich social history of poverty in late eighteenth- and early nineteenth-century Philadelphia, this essay takes up narratives of the "free" laboring poor, especially the mobile poor, both Black and white. Turning away from narratives of industrious self-making such as Franklin's or expressions of artisanal republicanism such as William Manning's, I examine stories of a group frequently sidelined in critical discourse.[4] Giving the lie to the nationalist mythology of upward mobility and ready success, these narratives showcase the misery and struggles, as well as the creativity, resilience, and sometimes oppositional power of the most marginal in the new economy. Far from being culturally invisible, the laboring, mobile poor were highly visible in eighteenth-century picaresque fiction, in what Matthew Pethers describes as colonial narratives of transportation and "bound labour" and in the robust performance cultures – including underclass and "rogue performances" – of the Atlantic world.[5] That cultural visibility was arguably tied to their political marginality: Pennsylvania, like most states, retained a property requirement for the franchise in its first state constitutions; and while the state – unlike its neighbors New Jersey and Delaware – did not add a pauper exclusion when eliminating the property requirement for white men in 1828, in Pennsylvania and Philadelphia the poor, especially the mobile poor, remained politically marginalized.[6] Illustrating how, in Peter Stallybrass and Allon White's words, what is "*socially* peripheral is ... frequently *symbolically* central,"[7] this political and social marginality helped foster intense cultural interest in the identities, motivations, and what often seemed the inscrutable interiority of the poor, notably lodging that fascination in the poor's *voice*.

This fascination with the voice of the poor was evident throughout early national culture. It conjoined a desire to access what Shane White calls the "edgy street culture" of the poor with a wish to impose discipline on poor subjects by making them transparent and intelligible. Describing the widespread solicitation of story in early national New York, White offers the following example: "'Tell us your history,' intoned the magistrate in a Police Office in late 1827, addressing a 'tall, well looking mulatto man' arrested as a possible runaway from New Orleans.... In a variety of situations, blacks were forced to recount their stories in order to prove that they were free and to justify their presence in the city."[8] But it was not only African Americans who were required to deliver such narratives; the poor of all races were routinely called on, in the language of an 1820 Pennsylvania law, to make a satisfactory "account of themselves." The era is replete with examples of what Carolyn Steedman calls "enforced narratives," in which modernity's "autobiographical imperative" takes an especially severe form. Steedman explains how, starting during the Renaissance, "the emerging administrative state" in England demanded that it was "the poor [not the elite] who tell their story, in vast proportion to their vast numbers.... Under legislation of 1661, magistrates were required to inquire into the origins of those who might become applicants for poor relief," creating a robust archive of "formulaic self-narration." In this way, "multitudes of men and women surveyed a life from a fixed standpoint, told it in chronological sequence, gave an account of what it was that brought them to this place, this circumstance now, telling the familiar tale for the justice's clerk to transcribe."[9] This system traveled to the colonies: in Philadelphia, enforced narratives were delivered in alms-houses, jails, and private charity societies, as well as in street encounters; informal "interviews" with the urban poor were featured in newspaper and magazine sketches and would become a standard motif in urban reform and sensational literature in the antebellum era.[10]

These enforced narratives are continuous with other forms of self-narration, from written "begging letters" to published "beggar narratives" and other autobiographical texts. Mechal Sobel observes that between 1740 and 1840, the churches and later the new state encouraged the written reevaluation of life experience in journals and autobiographies; writing a self-narrative "became virtually a ritual act, and as a result myriad life narratives were written by 'ordinary' people, black and white, male and female."[11] Karen Weyler calls such authors "outsider authors," "those Americans without the advantages of an elite education, social class, or connections, who relied largely on their own labor for subsistence" and "experienced significant constraints on their liberty and labor." In the late eighteenth century, outsider authors might publish as-told-to personal narratives such as Deborah Sampson's *The Female Marine* (itself produced in support of a petition for an invalid's pension) or engage in other forms of collaborative life writing.[12] Such texts call our attention to the vibrant oral culture of early America and the especially rich, complex interrelationship between oral and literary culture in this period. In this essay, I take up a variety of poverty narratives as particular examples of "outsider authorship"; I then explore how oral testimonials of the poor shaped the "dialogic" form of the early American novel.[13] Illuminating what one scholar calls the "porous boundaries" between print and oral performance cultures during this era, poverty testimonials become entry points through which vernacular oral performances of the poor could be imported into the fictional text.[14]

Down and Out in Philadelphia: Narratives of the "Lower Sort"

The laboring poor were conspicuous in Philadelphia during this period, partly due to the rapid increase in poverty that attended population growth (the product of increased immigration from abroad, especially Ireland, and also from other states), economic crises, and economic transformation (the gradual decline of slavery and indentured servitude and the rise of wage labor).[15] A major port of entry, Philadelphia's population grew from 20,000 in 1760 to 70,000 in 1800. While some gloried in this growth as the basis of national prosperity, the increase in population also created tension and anxiety, especially since institutions of slavery, apprenticeship, and indentured servitude (which allowed masters to regulate and control unfree laborers) were in decline, while revolutionary ideology and expanding political rights unsettled established norms of class deference. Wealthy residents and visitors to the city complained about the "children, dogs, and hogs" who threateningly swarmed the streets; chimney sweeps "clothed in rags" who were "most unpleasant to the sight"; indentured servants who presented "a most revolting scene of want and misery"; and almshouse residents who comprised a picture of "all that misery and disease can assemble."[16] Such accounts drew on a vocabulary of "taste" that, according to Grant Kester, justified increased residential class segregation in nineteenth-century cities and worked to contain the traumatizing visibility of labor and urban poverty.[17] Certainly, poverty during this era wore a plainly visual aspect; drawing on records of the Philadelphia Almshouse and other city institutions, Simon Newman has elaborated how "status, class and poverty were embodied" in the appearance of the poor, whose "very bodies" could reveal how "the lives . . . of the poor had been molded" by circumstance while functioning as "texts" that encoded "the struggle between coercive power and personal independence."[18] The era's vocabulary of "sorts" (replacing "orders" and "estates") reveals a broad impulse among the propertied to impose social order on seeming urban disorder, to put the growing population of the "masterless" lower sort in their place. As social historians note, this was the era of the "birth of the asylum" and institutions such as almshouses, prisons, and hospitals (some transformed by overhauled poor laws) that were intended to properly control and regulate the lower sort.[19] And the view of the poor was hardening, under pressure of liberal political economy, which fostered a new skepticism and distrust of the urban poor: rather than deserving pity and warranting charity, the poor were increasingly deemed "thriftless" beings "to be taken up, incarcerated, punished, and corrected."[20] While the language of the aesthetic and the visual are pronounced in representations of the poor, the oral performances of the poor, especially their personal narratives, became a significant locus of cultural interest. The revolutionary culture of voice and political agency – as well as emerging structures of biopolitical discipline and self-regulation – made the self-narratives of the poor a charged and contested cultural site.[21]

My first text is a "begging letter," one of several epistolary pleas for relief written by Irish immigrants during this era and submitted to Matthew Carey's Hibernian Society, an Irish-American mutual aid group.[22] A striking thing about these letters is that they (unlike almshouse interviews and many other species of poverty testimonials) are self-authored, not transcribed by an interviewer.[23] As their name suggests, the letters assume the form of a plea; the unconventional, phonetic spelling suggests a lower-class version of the eighteenth-century aphorism that to write a letter is but to "talk upon paper." Some of the letters' authors, including the "friend[less]" unemployed hosier Thomas McMahon, request relief because of unemployment; others write from debtor's prison, like William Sohterin, who, in soliciting legal assistance and interim support for his wife and children, expressed confidence in his "Claim to [Carey's] Assistance" due to shared background. But Stephen Egan Fotterall presents the most detailed poverty narrative in this collection of three dozen letters.[24] Fotterall was born in Dublin, on July 4, 1772, and was likely Catholic, though in his petition Fotterall claimed he was "brought up in Belfast in the Countey of Antrim" – perhaps out of deference to the primarily Scotch-Irish composition of Philadelphia's Irish aid societies. Fotterall allegedly served in the British army in Dublin; perhaps hoping to escape the army, he determined in 1788, at age fifteen, to bind himself to a shipmaster for a five-year term of indentured servitude in the United States.[25] Traditional structures of deference clearly inform Fotterall's act of writing: naming his letter a "humble petition" by a "humble petitioner,"

Fotterall alternates in his text between a stance of humility and assertions of betrayal and outrage. Like the English pauper letters examined by Thomas Sokoll, the letter balances "deferential rhetoric" with bluntness and a "self-confident attitude."[26] In Fotterall's case, that confidence was likely leavened by the Revolutionary discourse of the rights of the common man, as well as a traditional understanding of the right of the poor to material sustenance associated with what E. P. Thompson calls a "moral economy" – an understanding plainly held by the 1793 Philadelphia almshouse inmate described by an admissions officer as "impudent[ly]" insisting upon "every accommodation of Cloathing &c. (with insolence) *as a matter of right.*"[27] Fotterall explains to Carey that "Captain Blair then commander of the Ship, Rising Sun ... [had] promised if I would Bind Myself for five Years to him that he would put me in Gurney & Smiths Office to Act as a Clerk." Fotterall "embraced" the proposal, despite efforts of "all my Relations" who strongly opposed the plan. But perhaps because indentured servitude was in decline, when he reached Philadelphia he "was Sold to a Mr Hubley who Lived at the Middle Ferry on Schuylkill," and "Lived with the utmost discontent."

Having defined his indenture as a consensual act of will, as a proposal that involved promises by his employer and his own assent, he chafes against the effort to dispossess him of all bodily autonomy: it was not uncommon for indentures to be sold, but – as with pauper auctions – such transactions reveal overlapping "geographies" of Black and noncitizen white bound labor during this period.[28] "Never been used to Such buissnes as I had for to doe there which time Mr. Hubley cannot say but I behaved both faithful & Honest to him." Feeling "so ill used," he determines to escape: when sent by Hubley to deposit $10 in a Philadelphia bank, he "took the oppertunitey of leaving him and sending him a Letter to acquaint him that I was a Goeing to try to get home to Ireland and that I would Remit him what he had Lost by me which was the Remaining part of my time" plus the ten dollars of stolen cash, noting that Hubley had "paid fifteen pounds penselvenia Currensy for my time." The letter to Hubley – like the subsequent letter to Carey – affirms the agency that "embrac[ing]' the proposal had signified at the start. Fotterall leaves for Norfolk; unable to find a ship sailing for Ireland, he takes a job as a clerk for eight months and sends Hubley the full fifteen pounds he owes, believing that repayment will cancel all debts. He writes to Carey that he expected the payment "would satisfy him for my time having lived with him for better than two years and promised to remit him more when I could afford it." Perhaps like some runaway slaves in the era of gradual emancipation, Fotterall was banking on the phasing-out of indenture, expecting that his former master would "give up the indenture" and take what he could get, and using funds (here accumulated through fugitive "free labor") to purchase his freedom. But when Fotterall returns to Philadelphia after eight months and visits Hubley, the latter reclaims possession of him, retrieving a "Constable and Sent me to Gaole which place I now Remain being Commited here as a Run away Servent." Debtor prison could confine the poor for extended periods; runaway servants were also jailed. "Having No friends nor relations in America to assist Me," Fotterall appeals to the Hibernian Society. Repeating the phrase "distressed situation" twice, Fotterall crafts his letter as a plea, addressing Carey's "kind[ness]" and sense of justice, as well as feelings of ethnic/national kinship. And his appeal is successful: the well-connected Carey does indeed intervene to secure the young man's release. At the same time, the letter attests to the ways that, in self-emancipating through physical escape and thus claiming mobility as a class weapon, Fotterall refuses disposal of his body by those with power, leveraging his labor to accumulate money to pay his debts while employing his voice to contest forms of class control. In her study of the significance of correspondence in and for early national literature and culture, Elizabeth Hewitt examines the social import of letters in creating social networks and eliciting a "community of readers"; through his epistolarity, Fotterall mobilizes such a network, transforming "friend[lessness]" into kinship and Irish-American solidarity.[29]

My second text is not a self-authored letter but an "enforced narrative" – the poverty testimonial of James Huston, related to the Guardians of the Poor (city officials responsible for administering poor relief) during his admissions interview at the Philadelphia Almshouse.[30] Huston was an African American sailor, one of the most common occupations of African American low-wage laborers in the late eighteenth century. Because of the seasonal nature of the work, the occupation was also precarious, and mariners comprised a significant proportion of the almshouse population. According to his testimony, Huston was born enslaved under the name of James Davis in Delaware around 1786 and self-emancipated (in the words of his testimonial, "left his master") and fled to Pennsylvania around 1800. Once in Pennsylvania, he changed his name, and in Delaware County, one Joseph Hatton, a Quaker, "bought his freedom." The narrative that follows reveals the precarity of African American freedom during this period (when, for example, free Blacks might be kidnapped and sold into slavery or wrongly imprisoned as suspected fugitives) as well as the ways indentured servitude could mirror the circumstances of enslavement. According to Huston, it was "in consideration" of Hatton's actions that he "bound himself by an indenture to serve ... Hatton" for seven years. Two years later, however, Huston's indenture was sold to a man named Caleb Ayers, "with whom he lived one year." At that time, "by consent of his master," Huston traveled to Haiti "as a sailor" and remained "about a year," earning enough to "pa[y] his master for the balance of his time" – thus purchasing the remainder of his indenture. Huston's interest in Haiti may have been piqued by ongoing discussion of the new republic among African Americans in Philadelphia and President Jean-Pierre Boyer's invitation to Black Americans to emigrate and resettle there. Philadelphia was also becoming less hospitable to free Blacks, as laws were proposed several times between 1807 and 1813 to close the city to free Black immigrants. In 1813, a bill was introduced to require registration of all people of color and provide for the sale of any Black person convicted of a crime.[31] It was sometime around 1810 when Huston traveled from Philadelphia harbor to "Hayti as a sailor" with Ayers's consent; like Fotterall, he understood indenture as a strategy of mobility.

Huston's plan eventually worked, and he later returned to Pennsylvania to become a free man. He remained in the city, "liv[ing] at various places, but not a year together with any one person" – suggesting the transience of the professional seafarer – and was thus unable to establish legal residency under the settlement laws. Huston's narrative reveals how "lifelong transiency and, for many, vagrant destitution were part of the legacy of release from slavery and indentured servitude"; it also highlights the way that "mobility and stasis [have been] two powerfully intertwined forces" in African American narratives.[32] Before long, poverty and illness prompted Huston's entrance into the Philadelphia Almshouse in December 1826, abruptly curtailing his agency and strategic mobility. His appearance in the almshouse was not surprising; professional sailors were among the poorest of urban laborers. Their work was hard and dangerous; vulnerable to injuries and especially contagious disease and illness, their bodies were "shaped, bent, and broken by the rigors of life and work at sea."[33] The Guardians of the Poor who conducted Huston's entrance interview described him as a "Blk. Single man" who was too "sick" to travel – that is, unfit to be removed to his last place of official residence (Delaware County, the site of his indenture). Without kin, and without legal settlement, he was vulnerable to such removal, or to imprisonment as a vagrant in the Walnut Street jail. Designed to protect poor relief coffers filled with taxpayer funds from the needs of "strangers," or those without a "personal

or professional connection to a community," poor laws enforced concepts
of acceptable and "illicit mobility" among the poor.[34] According to Gary
Nash, of all groups, "blacks were most vulnerable to arrest for vagrancy
because Philadelphia was the destination of many runaway slaves, and dark
skin gained no one favors" in an era of increasing racial hostility.[35] Spared
warning out, he would have received negligible medical care at the almshouse. Whereas Fotterall had been able to use his story to mobilize the care
of fictive kin, the racial and class inscription and institutional control
of Huston's body-as-text overwhelms the generativity and efficacy of
his voice.

Authors of published "beggar narratives" differently transformed personal narratives of economic hardship into material support. As Ann
Fabian notes, "Storytelling beggars, carrying the books and briefs that
detailed their woes, wandered from the courts of the old world into the
marketplace of early nineteenth-century America. With help from political
allies, wealthy patrons, sympathetic co-religionists, commercial scribblers,
and friendly printers, people who had been reduced to begging got stories
made up as books, using print to achieve their own ends and turning
narratives of misadventure into commodities that could be transferred and
sold." They testified to "the effects of an expanding maritime economy
that tied men and women of the east coast into an Atlantic world where
some prospered but others were sent wandering in search of money or
work."[36] Beggar narratives highlight the interchange between the oral and
the written. Especially given increasing distrust of "beggar imposters" in
the early decades of the nineteenth century, street beggars, relating oral
stories of economic distress to solicit charity, often carried written creden-
tials and testimonials to support authenticity. While I have not located a
full-length beggar narrative by a Philadelphia author within the time frame
of this study, Philadelphia does figure centrally in an episode that exemplifies the genre's rich interchange between orality and writing. Moses
Smith, a poor cooper from Long Island, participated in Francisco de
Miranda's ill-starred initial attempt to lead Spain's South American colonies to independence. Convicted of piracy by a colonial court and sen-
tenced to ten years' hard labor, he tunneled out of a "foul and
unwholesome dungeon[]" and escaped.[37] A kind American captain took
him as far as Maryland; with the help of his friends, he "drew up a short
advertisement" about his South American adventures to be published in
the Baltimore newspaper (103). With just ten shillings to his name, he
begins telling his tale to gain funds to complete his journey. Recognizing
the need of the poor wanderer to present a good account to oneself, his

serial retellings of his story to "such as were disposed to hear it" are animated by a hope for "sympathy" for the fact that "it was the story nearest to my heart and ... tongue," and also by the need to disarm suspicion and out of fear of further captivity: "it was necessary to account for my condition and appearance, which was too like that of a convict escaped from legal coercion" (104). He eventually gathers enough support to make his way by stage to Philadelphia. When he spots men in the stage office reading the Baltimore paper and "engaged in conversation about the paragraph we had inserted" (108), he hails them, presenting himself as a celebrity of sorts. Accepting the published text as a kind of beggar credential, they "generously pressed upon" him sufficient funds to continue on to New York and "procure" some new clothing. The text stages repeated, reversible interchanges between orality and writing that blurs the distinction between them, seemingly demonstrating the inseparability of embodied author from written text. Folding this episode into his story, he goes on to publish his "adventures and sufferings" in a book-length narrative; he recruited enough subscribers to publish two editions.

Fabian notes that beggars' attempts to fashion stories worthy of aid set up an interesting literary dilemma: How was one to distinguish between impostors who wove a good tale and professional writers "who made a living arranging words"? Such questions peaked in the antebellum decades; in Britain, groups like the Mayhew Mendacity Society sought "to protect a credulous public from imaginative schemes hatched by the clever poor" by ferreting out impostors; in America, stories such as John Greenleaf Whittier's "The Yankee Gypsies" warn of the existence of an industry of commercial writers who "manufacture beggar-credentials at the low price of one dollar per copy ... to suit customers."[38] Magazine sketches from the early national era stage a range of poverty encounters while fashioning images of the itinerant poor as authorial persona. Kristie Hamilton tracks the importance of the sketch as genre in early America, linking its popularity and commercial profitability to "the explosion of magazine and newspaper publication and the growth of public education." She notes that the sketch was a preferred genre for young and inexperienced authors, and created space for nonelite authorship.[39] A number of early national sketches strikingly align the author with the figure of the impoverished wanderer. In an "original" series entitled "Tortoise," written for Philadelphia's *The Eye: by Obadiah Optic*, one "Tim Titular" quickly identifies himself as "a person of a restless habit" who "with hasty step" leaves "the *seat* of literature to mix in the bustle of the busy world." He is immediately "accosted by a pauper, with 'Please your Honour!' – his hat and staff in one hand, and presenting a paper with the other"; he takes it and quickly reads that the old man before him was a soldier in the Revolutionary War, now infirm and reduced to indigence. Giving "him the price of a beggar's blessing," and receiving in return more words ("he was not illiberal in his measure of what cost him nothing"), the writer returns to his study, and considers that "the beggar's petition" is more moving than anything he has penned. This celebration of the beggar's literary "skill" alternates with distrust of his possible inauthenticity ("had I the abilities of this beggar . . . never would I degrade such talents by using them to mask idleness . . . in the character of honest indigence"). But these thoughts are interrupted when he "hear[s] a confused noise in the street"; "anxious to 'Catch the manners living as they rise,'" he hastily concludes the sketch – again embracing, for further literary inspiration, the urban itinerancy he had interrogated.[40]

Other, more polemical short pieces, such as "Poverty No Disgrace" (signed "Pauper Superbus") published in Philadelphia's *Weekly Magazine*, ground the pauper's literary authority and "credit" in classical republicanism's distrust of wealth and luxury. The sketch contrasts "the ancient and philosophic spirit, which chose, and gloried in" poverty, with the modern spirit, "which avoids and is ashamed of it," noting that "poverty hurts our credit only on the 'Change" and affirming that "the indigence of Socrates reflected lustre upon his doctrines. Is there a soul who would not prefer a [Socratic] pedigree" and disinterested pursuit of truth to "the whole lineage of Attalus?"[41] A series of sketches by "Proteus" (written for the *Philadelphia Repository*) stage poverty encounters that recount the oral narratives of mendicants and voice traditional, plebian values of the moral economy. Affirming a republican commitment to exposing and reforming vice, the author in one sketch learns from his host at dinner that the loaf of bread is "*too light,*" and determines to visit the baker to investigate possible "fraud" and defend the assize (regarding the law defining the "just price" for bread). Early the next morning, he spies the baker hide underweight loaves from the inspecting officer and he exposes these "fraudulent dealings." The distraught baker confesses, begs forgiveness, and promises "uprightness and honesty"; the officer imposes the standard fine but accepts the apology, assuring the baker that the event will not be made public. But the author publishes the sketch as "warning to bakers of Philadelphia" that he might unexpectedly "come upon them" and that "they shall be exposed without reserve" if they attempt "similar tricks."[42] Anticipating the urban writings of another Philadelphia author,

Edgar Allan Poe, where flânerie sometimes transforms into detection, these sketches ground their literary and at times moral authority in the persona of the itinerant poor.

Early American novels by local authors bore the imprint of these poverty narratives. Dana Nelson has explored how the oral culture of the "commons" and "moral economy" shaped early American literature. Joseph Shapiro, drawing on Fredric Jameson's narrative theory, tracks voices of class protest in early American fiction, contending that lower-class voices in these novels are circumscribed, discursively marginalized through active, moralizing, and didactic speechifying on the part of bourgeois characters.[43] Elsewhere, I have examined how oral testimonies of poverty are embedded across antebellum literature and culture.[44] In the remainder of this essay, I briefly consider how novels by Philadelphia authors are marked by the widespread poverty narratives considered above. Sometime Philadelphia resident Hugh Henry Brackenridge's picaresque novel *Modern Chivalry* includes poverty testimonials, especially prostitute narratives, that resemble the almshouse testimonials discussed above. But I focus below on two novels from the turn of the century: Charles Brockden Brown's *Wieland; or, The Transformation* (1798), in which fascination with and anxiety about the power of the voice of the poor itinerant takes center stage; and Martha Meredith Read's *Monima; or, The Beggar Girl: A Novel Founded on Fact* (1802), which explores the special pressures on, and cultural resonance of, the poverty testimonials of impoverished women.

Wieland features the voice of the poor as both fascinating presence and dangerous gothic power. Indeed, the novel foregrounds the creative agency and feared duplicity of the voice of the poor while ultimately rerouting its unruly power through the disciplinary structure of the confessional mode. Brockden Brown's Carwin embodies various threating qualities that were attributed to the poor during this era: inadequate control over bodily and sexual appetites (he threatens Clara with rape and is suspected by Pleyel of facilitating her "fall") as well as unreadability and inscrutability. Like "Proteus," above (the mythological reference denotes both shapeshifting and prophecy), he assumes a power of surveillance and transformation. But he is especially characterized through a powerful voice, which possesses a "magical and thrilling power"; Pleyel imagines that Carwin's "eyes and voice had a witchcraft in them."[45] Carwin thus evokes anxieties about the possible duplicity and inauthenticity of the voice of the poor and fears of its unleashed social power. Carwin's voice of course moves Wieland to commit murder; like the city's poor who, some commentators claimed, "fill[ed] the air with profane and indecent language" that "contaminated" those of higher rank,[46] Carwin's voice seems a carrier of the class contagion of both vice and criminality. As he tells Clara during the scene in which he confesses his manipulation of her family, "'You are not apprized of the existence of a power which I possess.... It enables me to mimic exactly the voice of another, and to modify the sound so that it shall appear to come from what quarter, and be uttered at what distance I please'" (223). Carwin's ability to produce "counterfeit" (210) sounds and his extraordinary power of "biloquism" – the ability to detach his voice from the location of his body and shape it to imitate the sounds of others – furnishes an extreme example of social unintelligibility associated with the poor transient. In a powerful reading of Carwin as vagrant, Sal Nicolazzo argues, "While the textual arms of regulatory institutions, such as runaway advertisements and almshouse records, rely on the bodies, habits, and voices of the poor to fix and disclose consistent and traceable identities, Carwin's body defies such a goal through its ability to transform a feature taken to be so central to consistent identification."[47] Carwin's confession to Clara enacts his renunciation of the "magical ... power" (78) of his voice, performing a commitment to disciplinary self-monitoring and subjective transparency and marking his reform as a free white man. As Nicolazzo notes, while racial minorities and formerly enslaved people were commonly targeted by vagrancy laws and imprisoned, and while Irish immigrant vagrants were sometimes forcibly sent home, Carwin benefits from histories of whiteness, and is given leave at the end of the text to wander through the wilderness. Transforming a dispossessed white male vagrant into a frontiersman, Brockden Brown plots Carwin on a trajectory through which the impoverished, transient, white male subject is at once reinvented and redeemed.

Martha Read's *Monima* foregrounds the prominence of class and class struggle in the early republic. The novel opens in Philadelphia, with sixteen-year-old Monima and her aged father consuming their "last morsel," and Monima announcing that she "will go seek for work" to support them.[48] When her father warns that they are alone in a large city ("we are utter strangers[;] who can depend on your honesty without recommendation?") the virtuous Monima vows they "must trust to providence" (13). Highlighting the "friendless" (193) condition of the poor in the City of Friends, Read stresses the pronounced class barriers in the "walking city" and its inhospitability to the poor from the outset: Monima goes out in search of work, while a "storm beat in torrents off the habitations that wore opulence in their aspect, yet forebade all entrance, to the almost houseless wanderer" (14). The novel as a whole follows elaborate melodramatic plot lines that stretch to France and the West Indies, employing the conventional melodramatic character of a vicious aristocrat – the "haughty" (20) Pierre DeNoix – who has persecuted Monima's family on two continents and seeks the daughter's sexual ruin. Like the Revolutionary-era seducers discussed by Cathy Davidson, he manipulates language and story (orally and in writing) to secure his nefarious ends. But especially in the sections of the novel set in Philadelphia, the text – "founded up on fact," as its subtitle declares – attests to the realities of life for the poor under conditions of urban "friendlessness"; unlike *Wieland,* the novel is centered in the experience of the poor character(s) and presents a rich testimony to lived conditions of urban impoverishment. The text registers the vulnerability of the poor to physical confinement and punishment (debtor's prison, almshouse, and workhouse); early on in the text Monima is arrested for disturbing the peace and deposited in the city workhouse (31). Distraught at the thought of her father's suffering and unable to work, she receives "several lashes of the rod of correction" (38). The novel depicts her persecution in the criminal justice system, as Monima is accused twice of theft – of a watch and expensive fabric she is sewing – and nearly imprisoned. Even after it becomes clear that she has been unfairly accused, she must pay court fees, staging the increasing, stereotypic association of poverty with criminality.[49] Accused of theft and called before the constable, bystanders remark that "she looks beggarly enough to be [a thief]" and that "she seems ... to be one of that tribe, that do not much like work" (234).

But the novel especially highlights the precarious nature of the *voice* of the poor in this urban setting: Monima repeatedly attempts to deliver her poverty narrative, but finds an unreceptive audience. The motif is established in the first chapter, when she visits wealthy Mrs. Sontine's house to appeal for work. "I have an old father who depends on me for subsistence," Monima begins, when Mrs. Sontine cuts her off: "I have no work for you. It's because I have a French name, that every one comes here for work, but one would have enough to do, to maintain every French beggar" (16).[50] On the street, she finds no listening ear, and "no eye was found open enough to read her sorrows in her dejected countenance" (18). She applies at several houses, but is "repelled, either with indifference or contempt" (19). Later, turning to the "last refuge of the wretched" (46), begging, she finds the "unpitying scorn" of the wealthy an impediment to tale telling: "she made several attempts to claim charity, but the cool contempt, with which she was regarded, repulsed her voice, and instead of telling her woe-fraught tale . . . she only asked for work" (85). The response is glossed as coldness (the "keen insolence" of "sentimental lad[ies]" [256]), even sadism (some "laugh at the pitiful figure she made" [227] and "delighted to sport with the feelings of the poor" [39]), as well as narcissistic enjoyment of one's own elevated status: neighbors provide occasional "little kind-nesses" while requiring, by "repeated insinuations of the mighty favors they had conferred, to be a slave at their command, and repay them by incessant labour, and servile humility" (222–23). The novel castigates characters who dismiss poor women as idle, depraved, and improvident, bringing poverty on themselves– as would later Philadelphia writers such as T. S. Arthur – and takes aim at the greedy and hard-hearted rich for causing the pauperism they condemned. "No one could trust the 'mean-looking creature' [Monima] with work; and yet each one exclaimed against her indolence, in passing her prime, engaged in claiming charity, when she looked great and able enough to work" (251). As Monima asks a minister who betrays this mindset, "How is the cause of honesty to be served if all those who, from their poverty appear to be lazy, should be excluded from all employ; this would necessarily make honest people to be thiev[e]s!" (236).

Unlike the other narratives considered in this essay, *Monima* centers on *women's* experience of poverty: featuring a female protagonist, a working-woman, Read showcases the economic struggles of the female breadwinner (women headed one of every eight households in the city in the 1790s), while shining her light on the plight of the poor Philadelphia needle-woman decades before Matthew Carey made the figure famous.[51] In particular, the text highlights how sexuality haunts the scene of relief for women; entitlement to relief increasingly depended on one's sexual stand-ing. With the rising moralization of poverty, respectability was newly conditioned on female sexual restraint, and welfare institutions were tasked with reforming poor women in accord with a new "sexually inert" model of womanhood. Female vagrants could be arrested and charged with prostitution, and, once deemed lewd or disorderly, could be bound out or imprisoned, and whether the Guardians deemed a woman worthy of outdoor relief or consigned her to almshouse or prison depended in part on one's perceived "respectability" and/or sexual story.[52] Monima's voice is circumscribed by the power of others to talk *about* her. A group of young sailors tell a story about her that nearly results in her arrest (445), and her enemies' accusation that she is a "kind of bad girl" who "goes to meet gentlemen" (249) nearly leads to her homelessness, prompting neglect by neighbors that makes her more economically vulnerable (251). The text depicts the special import of clothing for poor women and girls: Monima's rags are an "obstacle to her preferment" (257), while her attractive form can sexualize the scene of relief (so that male generosity is discounted as sexual interest). And while Monima is plainly inscribed as poverty's victim, and while the novel figures her paternalistic "rescue" from poverty by a wealthy white man who becomes her husband, she asserts agency and fights back in striking ways. She supports her father for years, repeatedly facilitates their escape from captivity by their persecutors, and – in a plot twist worthy of Laura Jean Libbey – shoots her captor and would-be rapist De Noix before successfully fleeing him. After 1828, during the Jacksonian era expansion of white male democracy, the poverty of what were called "able-bodied" white males became increasingly problematic; in opposition to the newly enshrined ideal of white male "independence," women and African Americans were defined as the personification of dependency. The year 1828, the end date of this essay and the year Pennsylvania adopted its new constitution enshrining "universal" white male suffrage, was also the year Philadelphia passed its new poor law, which eliminated outdoor support and required that all support of paupers be confined to institutional settings – a change that severely delimited the agency of the poor and plainly circumscribed the power of poor subject's voice and narrative.[53] In tandem with the rise of carceral and biopolitical institutions aiming to exert greater control over the lives of the poor, the rise of sentimentalism and related languages of moral reform reshaped poverty discourse by the 1820s, sedimenting particular narrative constructs of the poor and marginalizing literary space for broadly subversive class meanings evident, for example, in picaresque fiction. (In antebellum sentimental fiction, notably, it is the poor *female* orphan whose story is most frequently told.) In the process, in both the United States and in Britain, the poor "lost much of their impish vitality... their individuality fad[ing] into pale images of want and deprivation."[54] The agency apparent in Read's characterization of the impoverished needlewoman is largely erased in Matthew Carey's influential portraits of pitiable, sentimentalized figure of the poor Philadelphia seamstress – but that agency is crucial to recollect in any literary history of poverty in the United States.

Notes

1 Thomas Jefferson, *Notes on the State of Virginia*, ed. William Peden (New York: Norton, 1972), 164–65; J. Hector St. John de Crèvecoeur, *Letters from an American Farmer*, ed. Albert E. Stone (New York: Penguin, 1981), 80.

2 *Benjamin Franklin's Autobiography*, ed. J. A. Leo Lemay and P. M. Zall (New York: Norton, 1986), 1, 49.

3 Samuel Otter, *Philadelphia Stories: America's Literature of Race and Freedom* (New York: Oxford University Press, 2010).

4 On the general inattention to poverty in scholarship about US literature, see Gavin Jones, *American Hungers: The Problem of Poverty in U.S. Literature, 1840–1945* (Princeton, NJ: Princeton University Press, 2008); Michael Merrill and Sean Wilentz, eds., *The Key of Liberty: The Life and Democratic Writings of William Manning, "A Laborer," 1747–1814* (Cambridge, MA: Harvard University Press, 1993).

5 Matthew Pethers, "Transportation Narratives," in Nicholas Coles and Paul Lauter, eds., *A History of American Working-Class Literature* (New York: Cambridge University Press, 2017); Peter P. Reed, *Rogue Performances: Staging the Underclasses in Early American Theatre Culture* (New York: Palgrave, 2009); Elizabeth Maddock Dillon, *New World Drama: The Performative Commons in the Atlantic World* (Durham, NC: Duke University Press, 2014).

6 Claire Lyons notes, "all men over age 21 who paid taxes gained the vote ... The poor were still excluded from the franchise, [though] most artisans and mechanics now had a direct political voice." *Sex among the Rabble* (Chapel Hill: Omohundro Institute of Early American History and Culture University of North Carolina Press, 2006), 209 n. 38.

7 Peter Stallybrass and Allon White, *Politics and Poetics of Transgression* (Ithaca, NY: Cornell University Press, 2006), 194.

8 Shane White, *Stories of Freedom in Black New York* (Cambridge, MA: Harvard University Press, 2007).

9 Carolyn Steedman, "Enforced Narratives: Stories of Another Self," in *Feminism and Autobiography: Texts, Theories, Methods*, ed. Tess Coslett, Celia Lury, and Penny Summerfield (New York: Routledge, 2000), 28–30.

10 Lori Merish, "The Poverty of Sympathy," in *Philanthropic Discourse in Anglo-American Literature, 1850–1920*, ed. Frank Q. Christianson and Leslee Thorne-Murphy (Bloomington: Indiana University Press, 2017), 13–29.

11 Mechal Sobel, *Teach Me Dreams: The Search for Self in the Revolutionary Era* (Princeton, NJ: Princeton University Press, 2000), 3.

12 Karen A. Weyler, *Empowering Words: Outsiders and Authorship in Early America* (Athens: University of Georgia Press, 2013), 4-5.

13 In *The Dialogic Imagination*, Bakhtin theorizes the novel form as defined by an incorporation and orchestrating of competing "social speech types" or voices. On the class dialogism of the early American novel, see Joe Shapiro, *The Illiberal Imagination* (Charlottesville: University of Virginia Press, 2014). Poverty testimonials form an important, unstudied dimension of the "heterogeneous polyphony" of the novel during this period (66).

14 If the mouth of the poor was, for Thomas Malthus, the seat of threatening oral desires among those who "live from hand to mouth," the verbal generativity and ingenuity of the poor was often envisioned as equally transgressive, constituting an object of both fascination and disciplinary regulation.

15 Indentured servitude was in legal decline during this era, with states gradually limiting its applicability to certain groups. Kristin O'Brassill-Kulfan, *Vagrants and Vagabonds: Poverty and Mobility in the Early American Republic* (New York: New York University Press, 2019), 97, and John K. Alexander, *Render Them Submissive: Responses to Poverty in Philadelphia* (Amherst: University of Massachusetts Press, 1980), 26–47.

16 Robert Waln, *The Hermit in America on a Visit to Philadelphia* (Philadelphia: M. Thomas, 1819), 72; *The Cries of Philadelphia: Ornamented with Elegant Wood Cuts* (Philadelphia: Johnson and Warner, 1810), 32; Henry Bradshaw Fearon, *Sketches of America* (London: Longman, Hurst, Rees, Orme, and Brown, 1818), 150; Brissot de Warville, *New Travels* (London: J. S. Jordan, 1792), 206, as seen in Simon Newman, *Embodied History: The Lives of the Poor in Early Philadelphia* (Philadelphia: University of Pennsylvania Press, 2003), 1-2.

17 Grant Kester, "'Out of Sight Is Out of Mind': The Imaginary Space of Postindustrial Culture," *Social Text* 35 (1993): 72–92.

18 Newman, *Embodied History*, 3, 11, 12.

19 See, for example, Newman, *Embodied History*; Billy G. Smith, ed., *Down and Out in Early America* (University Park: Penn State University Press, 2004), and Seth Rockman, *Scraping By: Wage Labor, Slavery, and Survival in Early Baltimore* (Baltimore: Johns Hopkins University Press, 2009).

20 Newman, *Embodied History*, 41. On these shifts in attitude, see Merish, *Archives of Labor: Working-Class Women and Literary Culture in the Antebellum United States* (Durham, NC: Duke University Press, 2017).

21 In focusing my archive for this piece, I leave to the side such genres as folk ballads and criminal autobiographies (published as sermons, broadsides, pamphlet narratives) – forms that have already received significant critical attention. See, e.g., Joanna Brooks, *Why We Left: Untold Stories and Songs of America's First Immigrants* (Minneapolis: University of Minnesota Press, 2013); Daniel A. Cohen, *Pillars of Salt, Monuments of Grace* (Boston: University of Massachusetts Press, 2006).

22 Pauper and begging letters are a valuable record of the lived experience and narratives of the poor during this era; they have received attention by historians, but not by literary scholars. Noting that pauper letters are "rooted in the oral rhetoric of people's everyday day life," Thomas Sokoll argues that the "rhetorical habitus expressed in pauper letters is . . . the outcome of two forms of rhetorical performance, of 'scriptual' and 'vocal' expertise." "Writing for Relief: Rhetoric in English Pauper Letters, 1800–1834," in *Being Poor in Modern Europe: Historical Perspectives 1800–1940*, ed. Andreas Gestrich, Steven King, and Lutz Raphael (Bern: Peter Lang, 2006), 108-9.

23 Unlike the "threatening letters" discussed by E. P. Thompson, which were always anonymous, begging letters were tied to a particular subject, a way for poor subjects to record their own self-narratives. And whereas almshouse testimonials were inscribed by another, these autobiographical narratives are

inscribed by the poor subject herself. On threatening letters in the United States, see Leon Jackson, "The Spider and the Dumpling: Threatening Letters in Nineteenth Century America," in *The Edinburgh Companion to Nineteenth-Century American Letters and Letter-Writing*, ed. Celeste-Marie Bernier, Judie Newman, and Matthew Pethers (Edinburgh: Edinburgh University Press, 2016), 152–68. Jackson notes, "The practices that fall under the rubric of social crime – poaching, squatting, filching, smuggling, and bootlegging, to name but a few – were often understood by their practitioners as customary in nature and as reflecting a moral, rather than a profit-driven, economy; and they were often defended or abetted by recourse to threatening letter" (156).

24 These letters are among Carey's papers held at the Historical Society of Pennsylvania. Several of the letters, including Fotterall's, appear in Kerby A. Miller, Arnold Schrier, Bruce D. Boling, and David N. Doyle, eds., *Irish Immigrants in the Land of Canaan: Letters and Memoirs from Colonial and Revolutionary America, 1675–1815* (Oxford: Oxford University Press, 2003), 287–303.

25 See the editors' discussion of this letter in ibid., 296–97. Fotterall's letter appears on pp. 277–79.

26 Sokoll, "Writing for Relief," 102.

27 Quoted in Newman, *Embodied History*, 37.

28 O'Brassill-Kulfan, *Vagrants and Vagabonds*, 95.

29 Elizabeth Hewitt, *Correspondence and American Literature, 1770–1865* (Cambridge: Cambridge University Press, 2004), 2.

30 Examination of James Huston, Examination of Paupers 1826–31, Guardians of the Poor, Almshouse Records, Philadelphia City Archives. See the discussion of this narrative in O'Brassill-Kulfan, *Vagrants and Vagabonds*, 84.

31 Lyons, *Sex among the Rabble*, 355.

32 O'Brassill-Kulfan, *Vagrants and Vagabonds*, 97; Edlie Wong, *Neither Fugitive nor Free* (New York: New York University Press, 2009), 97, as seen in O'Brassill-Kulfan, *Vagrants and Vagabonds*, 201 n. 7.

33 Newman, *Embodied History*, 106.

34 O'Brassill-Kulfan, *Vagrants and Vagabonds*, 14, 2.

35 Gary Nash, *Forging Freedom: The Formation of Philadelphia's Black Community, 1720–1840* (Cambridge, MA: Harvard University Press, 2003), 157. O'Brassill-Kulfan notes that Blacks and vagrants were often conflated, as vagrants conjured up in white minds "images of shoeless travelers, black-faced Jim Crow on the stage, and roughly clad fugitive slaves on the roads" (90).

36 Ann Fabian, *The Unvarnished Truth: Personal Narratives in Nineteenth Century America* (Berkeley: University of California Press, 2000), 11.

37 Moses Smith, *History of the Adventures and Sufferings of Moses Smith* (Albany, NY: Packard & Van Benthuysen, 1814), 124. All further references to this edition appear parenthetically within the text.

38 Fabian, *The Unvarnished Truth*, 43–45.

39 Kristie Hamilton, *America's Sketch Book: The Cultural Life of a Nineteenth Century Genre* (Athens: Ohio University Press, 1998), 14. On the sketch, an

important early national genre with "truth baked into it and often present [ing] a proto-documentary stance toward its subject," see Lydia G. Fash, *The Sketch, the Tale, and the Beginnings of American Literature* (Charlottesville: University of Virginia Press, 2020).

40 *The Eye*, 1.6 (February 11, 1808): 70.

41 *Weekly Magazine* 2.18 (June 2, 1798): 155.

42 *Philadelphia Repository and Weekly Register* 4.12 (March 24, 1804): 93. On uprisings in Philadelphia involving the price of bread and the actions of monopolizers and forestallers in raising prices (especially the Fort Wilson Riot), see Alexander, *Render Them Submissive*, 33–36.

43 Dana Nelson, *Commons Democracy: Reading the Politics of Participation in the Early United States* (New York: Fordham University Press, 2015); Shapiro, *Illiberal Imagination.*

44 Merish, "The Poverty of Sympathy."

45 Charles Brockden Brown, *Wieland, or The Transformation*, ed. Fred Lewis Pattee (New York: Harcourt Brace Jovanovich, 1926), 78, 141. All further references to this edition appear parenthetically within the text.

46 See Alexander, *Render Them Submissive*, 5.

47 Sal Nicolazzo, *Vagrant Figures: Law, Literature, and the Origins of the Police* (New Haven, CT: Yale University Press, 2021), 169.

48 Martha Read, *Monima, or The Beggar Girl: Founded on Fact* (New York: P. R. Johnson, 1802), 13. All further references to this edition appear parenthetically within the text.

49 Alexander, *Render Them Submissive*, 66–67. Although the Pennsylvania Constitution of 1776 made some changes involving imprisonment for debtors, people who owed only small debts continued to suffer confinement for long periods. Those found innocent of criminal charges but unable to pay the cost of prosecution were still clapped into jail as debtors, and were also required to pay the costs of their own maintenance while in prison, all of which further victimized the poor. Between 1780 and 1790 (a decade when criminals were more likely to be incarcerated than in colonial days), the number of debtors in the city and county jail of Philadelphia outnumbered criminals 4,061 to 3,999.

50 Like Fotterall's letter, the novel highlights the role of ethnic communities (including mutual aid societies like Carey's) in poor relief and communal survival. In ethnically diverse Philadelphia, "people lived chiefly among their own kind"; Monima is "forlorn, unallied, poor and insulted" not because she lacks family, but because she is "a French b—h" (31) and "a total stranger to the surrounding neighbours and inhabitants" (221) in an anglophone city where much depended on one's social network. Against Franklin's narrative of self-making, Read made it clear that no one in Britain or the United States, however capable, could make it entirely on their own – a fact especially true of poor women. As historian Karin Wulf shows, single women in Philadelphia depended on family, friends and neighbors to survive (*Not All Wives* [Ithaca, NY: Cornell University Press, 2000]). On Read's gendered economic narrative, see Eve Tavor Bannet, "Shifting Cultures and Transatlantic Imitations:

The Case of Burney, Bennett, and Read," in *The Edinburgh Companion to Atlantic Literary Studies*, ed. Leslie Elizabeth Eckel and Clare Frances Elliott (Edinburgh: Edinburgh University Press, 2016), 75–87. In addition, and though this is not my focus here, Read situates her heroine in a complex novelistic plot that casts immigration as precarity and downward mobility. Monima's beggarly state proceeds from the fact that she and her father immigrated to America with the wave of French refugees fleeing the revolution in Santo Domingo. The novel figures the complex mobility of the poor in the Atlantic world.

51 Billy G. Smith, *The "Lower Sort": Philadelphia's Laboring People, 1750–1800* (Ithaca, NY: Cornell University Press, 1990).

52 Lyons, *Sex among the Rabble*, 289; Newman, *Embodied History*.

53 For one obvious example, see the discussion of the evolving treatment of women's bastardy testimonials in Lyons, *Sex among the Rabble*, 354–92, and Merish, *Archives of Labor*.

54 Lynn Hollen Lees, *Solidarities of Strangers: The English Poor Laws and the People, 1700–1948* (Cambridge: Cambridge University Press, 1998), 94.

CHAPTER 17

Neuroqueering the Republic
The Case of Charles Brockden Brown's *Ormond*

Sari Altschuler

> Through diagnosis, autistics are storied into autism, our bodyminds
> made determinable and knowable through the criteria of neurodeve-
> lopmental disability.... Even when autism is depicted as a condition
> that resists the narratable (... an unfortunately typical move), the
> narrating impulse remains entrenched in the act of diagnosing
> unto itself.
>
> —Melanie Yergeau, *Authoring Autism* (2018)

Just after Constantia Dudley decides–at long last and with a heavy heart–
not to marry Ormond, he appears before her for what will be their second-
to-last conversation. Ormond discerns that she has already made her
decision and rants about what he has determined are the obstacles to
their union. Constantia, for her part, studiously avoids "his incoherences,"
but Ormond will not let her diffuse the situation (244). Instead, he directs
her to "look at me; steadfastly" (245). "Catch you not," he asks, "a view of
the monsters that are starting into birth *here?*" as he touches his forehead
(245). As candid as he is with her in this moment, true representation of
his mental state is, he explains, impossible: "Should I paint them to you
verbally, you would call me jester or deceiver. What a pity that you have
not instruments for piercing into my thoughts!" (245). The problem is one
of "incredulity," he explains, although that word alone seems insufficient
for what he describes. It is not simply that Ormond's audience *will not*
believe he has thought the things he has thought or done the things he
claims to have done – but that they cannot (245). Ormond presses the
point by way of example:

> "To-morrow I mean to ascertain the height of the lunar mountains by
> traveling to the top of them. Then I will station myself in the track of the
> last comet, and will wait til its circumvolution suffers me to leap upon it;
> then, by walking on its surface, I will ascertain whether it be hot enough to
> burn my soles. Do you believe this can be done?... Do you believe, in

consequence of my assertion, that I design to do this, and that, in my apprehension, it is easy to be done?"

"Not unless I previously believe you to be a lunatic,." (245)

Having demonstrated his point, Ormond concludes it futile to describe his mind to her or to anyone else, since "the hearer will infer nothing from my speech but that I am either a lunatic or liar" (245).

If we take Ormond at his word, which is to say, not metaphorically, it is possible to see his remarkable clarity about his situation. Ormond is not wrong. Most readers and critics wrestle with the question of how to read Ormond with criticism toggling between the poles of "lunatic" and "liar." Constantia herself dismisses Ormond's speech as crazy talk, full of "wild" "incoherencies" (250). Scholars like Sidney Krause, for example, likewise read Ormond's "lunar mountains" as an elaborate metaphor for his plans to rape Constantia – "that he *will* indeed be forced to attempt the incontemplatably monstrous, and hence impossible, and hence lunatic."[1] Ed Cahill likewise glosses most Brown scholarship as following the "conventional critical model of psychological transformation in Brown's novels," which charts "a unilateral movement from aesthetic pleasure to insanity."[2] Conversely, critics like James Russo insist Ormond is a liar. Firmly convinced that duplicity lies at the heart of the novel, Russo argues that in a story rife with so many "incoherencies," we should always critically incline toward deception.[3]

And yet these poles – lunatic or liar – are insufficient. While many readers of Ormond both within the novel and in contemporary criticism ultimately announce themselves for one or the other, declaring what has *really* been going on with Brown's titular character, the options seem depressingly flat. Ormond certainly thinks so, but, reconsidering, many critics would probably agree. As Christopher Lukasik explains, the problem of reading Ormond lies at the heart of the novel: "The ability to penetrate Ormond's performances and discern his permanent character becomes one of the central, if more difficult, tasks in the novel."[4] "Reading him correctly confounds a number of characters," Lukasik continues, "yet, discerning Ormond's character is not just a problem for the persons within [Sophia Courtland's] story, it is a problem for her as the author of that story, and thus, for the readers of her narrative as well" (485).[5] I will have more to say about Sophia's ways of reading later, but I would like to frame the problem differently: What happens, this essay asks, if we consider that problem to be historical rather than purely interpretive? What I mean is this: What if Ormond is right, and it is not possible for the words he uses to adequately convey his mind, at least not in the 1790s? Furthermore, what if the problem is, fundamentally, about the problem of knowing other minds – a problem that, at its root, threatened to undermine the nascent republican project in the United States?

In what follows, I consider Brown's *Ormond* as an imaginative experiment with neurodiversity, considering, in particular, what it means to know, as we now do, that different brains work differently, without having a language for naming that difference.[6] Here I am most interested not in questions of intelligence or of mental health per se (there is other wonderful work being done on these topics in the period)[7] but in fundamental neurological difference.[8] The novel's logic puts pressure on the interpretive binary between intentional bad behavior and madness in the late eighteenth century to suggest the different formations of bodyminds – in contemporary terms *neurodiversity* – that were surely present, if not thinkable as such. (In using the term *bodyminds*, I am drawing on work in disability studies that underscores the need to think about bodies and minds as inextricably connected, particularly important in discussions of neurodiversity.) We need not insist, in other words, on recovering prehistories of autism, schizophrenia, or obsessive compulsive disorder to recognize that brains – and thus cognition – have always existed in a variety of forms.

The early national period is not an arbitrary moment for undertaking this task. Rather, the utopian Enlightenment beliefs that helped birth the new nation created a new and pressing need to understand how the bodyminds of all potential citizens might work. The United States was a new nation politically organized through republicanism in which representative – white, propertied – men were expected to represent the needs of "the people" more broadly and trusted with governance. American bodyminds simply required the right education and training to become, in Benjamin Rush's words, "republican machines" that are able "to perform their parts properly, in the great machine of the government of the state."[9] *Ormond* troubles these idealistic formulations. As the neuroqueer reading I propose here reveals, republicanism was structured by a presumption of neurotypicality or, at the very least, by a belief that bodyminds were more or less versions of the same form. *Ormond* presents a fascinating example of a novel working to represent fundamentally different bodyminds during a time when there were not yet adequate narrative means for doing so.

Representing Disability and Neurodiversity
in the Eighteenth-Century Novel

Disability scholars have long asserted disability's central role in literature of all times and places, even if the broader field of literary criticism has taken longer to recognize disability's centrality.[10] Of the eighteenth century specifically, Lennard Davis has argued that disability played a fundamental role in the development of the novel, identifying a formal convention that protagonists "be typical" and "also have bodies and minds that signify their averageness. The protagonists of British novels are British, look typical, and embody the virtues that England values. Love stories may offer a cross-national or class liaison but usually end up ratifying the norm."[11] For Davis, protagonists exemplify normality in British novels written between 1720 and 1870, and they are "virtually" never "in some way physically marked with a disability" (328). Arguing that this highlights the funda-mental logic of the form, Davis continues: "on some profound level, the novel emerges as an ideological form of production whose central binary is normal-abnormal" (329). In this formulation, protagonists are "normal" but temporarily disabled by circumstance, telegraphing the work of the novel, more generally in which "plot functions . . . by *temporarily deforming or disabling the fantasy of nation*, social class, and gender behaviors that are constructed as norms. The *telos* of plot aims to return the protagonists to this norm by the end of the novel" (330, first emphasis added).

While I deeply admire Davis's efforts to demonstrate disability's central-ity to literary studies – it has been one of my goals as well – as I have argued elsewhere, the role of disability in novels of this period is more complicated than he suggests, at least in the American context.[12] Disability, as we are used to understanding it, does not often appear in US fiction before 1816. Where it does – particularly in representations of physical disability – it does not carry the narrative significance that later representations do, and the word *disability* itself operates differently in these texts.[13] The difficulty of squaring early claims about disability's centrality with disability's apparent absences in the first decades of US literature is one reason why disability studies perspectives have arrived so late to the study of early American literature. Understanding how ability and disability function in literature of the period – its appearances, its absences, and its differences in any given period – is crucial even as we strategically adopt a self-consciously anachronistic lens through which to view that literature anew.

According to Davis, even if early novels do not represent disability explicitly, they celebrate "the incipient impulse" of the norm, a description that is likewise a poor fit for novels like *Ormond*. Here Davis charts a history that has come to be practically doctrine in disability studies: that with the emergence of a collection of events, including the rise of industrial capitalism, statistics, and the liberal subject in the 1840s, the idea of the norm became hegemonic. The novel anticipates this shift with plots that move protagonists from normal to abnormal and back again. This sounds good, but, as careful historical work by Peter Cryle and Elizabeth Stephens has recently suggested, the idea of norm did not emerge as a hegemonic concept in the nineteenth century. Rather, it took until the twentieth century to do so.[14]

In place of Davis's model, we ought to use what a number of disability studies scholars have recognized as one of disability's hallmark features: its diversity. As Rachel Adams, Benjamin Reiss, and David Serlin explain,

> The meanings we attribute to disability are shifting, elusive, and sometimes contradictory. Disability encompasses a broad range of bodily, cognitive, and sensory differences and capacities. It is more fluid than most other forms of identity in that it can potentially happen to anyone at any time, giving rise to the insiders' acronym for the nondisabled, TAB (for temporarily able-bodied).... Disability can be situational; it can also wax and wane within any particular body. Disability brings together people who may not agree on a common definition or on how the category applies to themselves and others.[15]

It is this "broad range" that literary criticism ought to embrace when considering disability – that is, the multiplicity within the singularity of the term itself; the corporeal, social, and historical contingency; and the tension between the specificity of particular disabilities and the universality of disability itself as an identity category. Here disability functions differently as an analytic than other kinds of identity-based frameworks we bring to bear on literary studies in that it brings together people joined by common experiences of marginalization and prejudice but whose embodied experiences and perspectives differ – often radically. In this essay I take up the challenge to read for the "elusive[ness]," in the terms of Adams, Reiss, and Serlin, of neurological difference in the late eighteenth century.

Reading Neurodiversity in *Ormond*

Before embarking on the task at hand, I want to be clear that while the problem of engaging a different bodymind is at the core of *Ormond*, the novel, like others of the period, is studiously uninterested in what it understands as disability.[16] There is no better example of Brown's lack

of interest in disability than Stephen Dudley's blindness, which has great
potential, from a contemporary perspective, to serve as an organizing
metaphor for a novel whose subtitle underscores the importance of "witnessing," but Brown does not give it this narrative weight.[17] Dudley's
character well exceeds this physical attribute, in large part because, as
I have argued elsewhere, the early national novel was heavily invested in
the mutability and rehabilitative potential of citizens; it was not interested,
as later novels would be, in fixed physical impairments (like Captain
Ahab's or Ethan Frome's legs) that metaphorically explain those characters
as a whole or link them inexorably to tragic outcomes.[18]

Where Brown shows little interest in physical disability, he is quite
interested in cognitive difference.[19] The narrator, Sophia Courtland, presents her friend Constantia Dudley as a woman whose quest for a suitable
mate depends on her evaluation of each suitor's moral and intellectual
qualities. For this reason she judges Ormond's mistress Helena an inappropriate match and considers him as a possibility for herself. Nevertheless,
the novel assures us, time reveals all, and, where Ormond begins as an
interesting and unique thinker, the question of whether he is a lunatic or a
liar grows increasingly pressing as the novel continues. Since the novel is,
after all, centrally concerned with proving Constantia's virtue – it is framed
as a letter to her potential suitor, essentially to guarantee she is still chaste –
the plot becomes increasingly wrapped up in the mental life of Ormond.
Narratively, one is quite dependent on the other: the argument for
Constantia's chastity relies on her ultimate evaluation of Ormond's mental
difference. Constantia might have fallen for Ormond but, as Sophia tells it,
does not because she judges him, on prolonged and reasoned evaluation, to
have outlandish ways of thinking that make him an unfit match.
Constantia rationally rejects his bodymind and thus preserves her virtue.

Nevertheless, the grounds on which Constantia should reject him
remain difficult to parse. In her opening letter to Constantia's suitor
I. E. Rosenberg, Sophia Courtland introduces Ormond as a "a contradictory or unintelligible being" (37). Unable to fully understand him, Sophia
demurs that she will "pretend not to the infallibility of inspiration. He is
not a creature of fancy" (37). Using a convention of the period in which
proof of accurate depiction is formally supported by unfolding a narrative
sequentially, as it occurred, she records details only as they appear to her
and in the order that she learned them.[20] However successful this strategy
may be on other counts, Sophia simultaneously registers its failures to
account fully for Ormond. For, even as she makes a claim for "facts," she
nevertheless admits that empirical accounting is incongruous with the

story she sets out to tell (37). To excuse this she argues that "harmonious congruity" is the effect of "poetical taste," not reason (37). Her access to materials may be "singularly fortunate and accurate," but it is not "unerring" nor "complete" (37). In a sense, then, her narration presents a paradox: in order to account most fully for a bodymind like Ormond's, she must use ways of knowing that cannot fully account for Ormond. Through the naïve empiricism of her narration (she imagines she can know all through factual evidence), Ormond is rendered "contradictory or unintelligible," even though Ormond has detailed his thoughts precisely (37). Marking the unnarratability of neurodiversity according to her system of understanding, Sophia lays bare the rational failures of late eighteenth-century empiricism itself. She marks a site where purportedly unvarnished facts are not themselves self-explanatory. Ormond himself issues just such a critique. While telling Constantia of the lunar mountains and comet temperatures he means to "ascertain," he adopts the language of empiricism only to lament, "What a pity that you have not instruments for piercing into my thoughts!"

Here we might build on Ed Cahill's observation that Brown eschews binaries when it comes to the mind.[21] If, as Cahill suggests, the mind is a complex entity for Brown, one dependent on faculties and experiences – and one that is always evolving – we might press further to consider not only the varieties of mind Brown explored in novels like *Ormond* but also the limits of that exploration. For, if Ormond is semi-legible only as an "impenetrable," "contradictory or unintelligible being" who possesses "a mind of uncommon energy," as Sophia Courtland describes him, that is a statement about the limits of her own understanding rather than his (131, 37, 131).

Taking the idea of Ormond's neurodiversity further, we might recognize that Brown's text itself identifies in his character a number of characteristics we recognize today as belonging to neurodiverse individuals including obsession, unconventional – or even anti-conventional – thought and behavior, difficulty imagining the thoughts and responses of others, grand claims, detail-oriented mental processing, and an expanded sense of possibility. Here are some examples: a relentless neglecter of, Ormond acts "not in compliance with the dictates of custom," "conform [ing]" only to "his own opinions" (128). He possesses a sense of "reason" that is internally consistent but dangerous to others. At times he describes himself as a bad reader of the minds of others, one who had "frequently been made [duplicity's] victim" (130). At other times he grandiosely asserts that he knows all, even before it has occurred. These latter assertions echo his claims about summiting lunar mountains and riding comet trails that likewise demonstrate an expanded sense of possibility. His more plausible, impressive political actions likewise demonstrate this broader sense of what is possible. Additionally, his power of knowing resembles those associated with contemporary autism-spectrum disorders as a character who does not gloss scenes but rather "carrie[s] away with him a catalog of every thing visible" (146). Near the end of the novel Ormond obsesses over Constantia almost to the exclusion of everything else. William Huntting Howell argues that Ormond may himself have been modeled on a "multilingual polymath" named Servin, the description of whom comes strikingly close to something like neurodiversity, his immoral character diagnosed by Benjamin Rush as originating in "an original defect in . . . the brain."[22]

It is tempting to diagnose these characteristics in a contemporary fashion – autism, mania, obsession, compulsion, schizophrenia – but this too would be an error on at least three counts. (1) These characteristics do not line up with a particular contemporary diagnosis, even if (2) a retrospective diagnosis were desirable, which is it not. Retrospective diagnosis, after all, risks reducing the traits of a character from the past anachronistically to a contemporary category. (3) It is less fruitful to think about diagnosing Ormond than it is to think about the opportunities opened up by thinking Ormond neurologically queer.

We ought to consider Ormond, who himself makes the case for his bodymind difference as difference rather than disability, on his own terms. He is, if anything, represented as hyper-able. An insatiable evaluator of the abilities of others, he judges his mistress Helena is an imperfect mate for him because she is hampered by "the imbecility of her sex," a "capacity . . . limited by nature" wedded to his belief in the "incurable imperfection of the female character" (141, 141, 134). In fact, having never met "a female worthy of his confidence," he believes "the intellectual constitution of females was essentially defective" (132). His discovery of Constantia's abilities attracts him to her as his only equal match. Like Weiland or Edgar Huntly, other Brockden Brown characters who arguably also possess neurologically diverse bodyminds, Ormond queers ability, as often as not, in demonstrating his own extensive ability rather than his impairments. This, among other reasons, is why I want to read him as neurodivergent and not disabled. He may be socially disabled according to our current understanding – he is, after all, represented as unfit for marriage because of his bodymind – but his abilities are distinct rather than lesser and do not fit categories of disability as it was understood in the eighteenth century.[23]

The Problem of Neurodiversity

This problem of neurodiversity is not something the eighteenth-century novel, *pace* Davis, is supposed to raise. Davis's account would have the narrative arc look something like this: Constantia Dudley, who represents the national norm, is "disabled" by some kind of life circumstance and then cured when her ability is restored in the end. Along the way, any actually impaired character (Ormond) would be killed or cured so that the foundational norm can be restored.[24] So far, so good. But any Brown critic will tell you, none of his novels is this straightforward. Instead of neatly resolving issues of difference, *Ormond*'s plot becomes consumed with its inability to narrate Ormond's difference.

This fixation is most obvious in the title of the work, which is, after all, *Ormond* and not *Constantia*. As the plot unfolds, it focuses less completely on Constantia's virtue and more on Ormond's inexplicable difference, even though Constantia's contested virtue is, after all, the reason for the story. Even when Ormond does die in the end so that Constantia may remain virtuous, he does so by Constantia's hand. If the only way to dispense with the narrative force of Ormond is an act of violent erasure, then, of course, this is no act of erasure at all. Left holding the bloody penknife, Constantia does not rid the world of Ormond's difference but rather weds herself to it. In killing Ormond, she draws attention to her complicated relationship with him, a good deal of which Sophia admits she does not know. How is the reader of Sophia's letter to interpret the state of Constantia's mind, as that reader encounters her alone at night, standing over the bodies of her two persecutors, Ormond and Craig?

Constantia herself provides unsatisfying answers. When Sophia asks about the state of her mind she replies, "Alas! I know not! My deed was scarcely the fruit of intention. It was suggested by momentary frenzy.... My stroke was desperate and at random" (273–274). Removing her mind from the equation, Constantia leaves the question for her body, or at least her instinctual or nonrational mind, alone to answer. In so doing, she raises more questions about her own bodymind than she answers, a bizarre plot twist for a story that is meant to assure its reader of Constantia's admirable rationality and unshakable virtue.[25] This act instead risks making her as unknowable as Ormond.

The reader is, arguably, as jarred by Constantia's bodymind in this moment as they have been by Ormond's. Logical questions immediately arise: How can a story about the suitability of a young woman for marriage end by revealing her a murderer? Who is the "demon" Constantia claims barred the door so that no one could witness the scene (272)? What does Constantia mean when she tells Sophia that she is "lost," even as she claims not to have been raped and that she had no choice but to kill him? And how are we to read Sophia's preemptive remark to Constantia that she hopes "nothing has happened to load you with guilt or with shame" when she finds Constantia locked in a room with two dead bodies (273)? The key appears to lie less in Sophia's attempt to cover up what has happened with her words than in her reading of Ormond's body and mind. In her final description of Ormond, Sophia leaves the reader with an image of his enigmatic "secret" wound and "smile of disdain" that refuse, to the last, narrative resolution (273).

Cripping the Republic

Brown scholars have often narrated the ways in which his novels resist such closure as a comment on the instability of the moment. But while Brown's unsettling plots, of course, register a broader unease in the 1790s and are a hallmark of gothic writing,[26] they are also directly connected to questions of difference in the 1790s. Americans wondered whether the various crises of the 1790s like the Whiskey Rebellion and the Alien and Sedition Acts represented fundamental community differences – of will, of beliefs, of region, of ability, of interests, of perspectives, or, more generally, of mind – that might doom the republican experiment. This question had been less pressing under the British monarchy than it would be later, when paradigms – most infamously, race science – rendered the classification of different bodyminds natural, but in the 1790s Americans still held on to the idea that a single body could stand in for all others that were versions (if less perfect versions) of it. In other words, in the 1790s, the idea of a representative US government was premised on the idea that the bodyminds of white, propertied men could stand in for those of all Americans, and the stability of US national enterprise was built on the regularity of these representative bodyminds, which is to say that they all operated according to a similar, predictable logic. It is this fantasy that *Ormond* presses against; its titular character and its narrative disjunctures raise the possibility that perhaps republicanism is, after all, an ill-fated fantasy.

Such concerns are entangled with the project of understanding Ormond. Sophia Courtland herself underscores the connections between Ormond and the nascent republic when she explains to Rosenberg (a German suitor) that her factual report should describe not only Ormond but the "modes of life" and "character" of individuals in America (37–38).

"Society and manners constitute your favourite study," she writes, "and I am willing to believe that my relation will supply you with knowledge, on these heads" (38). Should he find her account "unsatisfactory," she exhorts him to "go and examine for yourself" (38). Yet what could Rosenberg expect to find? Ormond exists, by her own account, beyond the power of observation. To see him for yourself is, pointedly, *not* to know him but rather to understand the limits of the Enlightenment epistemology that undergirded the republic.

When Sophia connects Ormond's story to that of the nation, she underscores the urgency of determining who exactly "the people," on whom the government was based, were, as well as the immediate danger Ormond poses. As William Huntting Howell argues, Ormond's function in the text "threatens to dissolve the entire social contract" (170). The threat here is not solely individual; rather, Brown connects Ormond to certain strains of republican thought. "His political projects," Sophia forecasts, "are likely to possess an extensive influence on the future condition of this western world" (126). His role in the Bavarian Illuminati serves as a particular pressure point; the secret transatlantic group rumored to be at work in the United States sought to direct the course of republican politics by "employing, for a good purpose, the means which the wicked employed for evil purposes," a 1798 critic explained.[27] Ormond is thus introduced as an agent of republicanism but is quickly revealed to imperil the system. How was the United States, founded as a country by and for the people, to regulate bodyminds that not only refused to conform but endangered the polis? And what if, at some basic level, these bodyminds revealed that "the people" were not one, knowable entity but a heterogenous and opaque group?

If we locate this problem of individual difference at the center of *Ormond*, we might profitably read the novel's narrative incompleteness differently – through what Tobin Siebers calls "disability aesthetics."[28] According to Siebers, disability aesthetics "refuses to recognize the representation of the healthy body – and its definition of harmony, integrity, and beauty – as the sole determination of the aesthetic. Rather, disability aesthetics embraces beauty that seems by traditional standards to be broken, and yet it is not less beautiful, but more so as a result" (3). Using disability aesthetics, we might not shun but rather embrace incompleteness, brokenness, and fragmentation as a way of grappling toward a new kind of representation, something beyond what can be narrated in available paradigms and something that would account for some of the haunting power of Brown's novels. In this I depart from Cathy Davidson's nationalist claims that the fiction of the revolutionary age "carved out its literary territory in the here-and-now of the contemporary American social and political scene and commented upon and criticized that scene, but left the solution of these problems up to the individual reader – the indeterminacy of the solution as basic to the form as the incisiveness of its critique."[29] Instead, I ask us to consider that the "indeterminacy of the solution" may instead be a part of the art that we might better leave unresolved. Embracing the disability aesthetics of novels like *Ormond* means living with the incompleteness of narrative and recognizing its attempt to reach for a description of bodyminds that captured the formidable imaginary of its writer but could not yet be narrated. In this view, Brown's narrative captivated readers beginning in the early national period not because of its beautiful narrative completeness but because it takes on the complex contours of the republican project and particularly the diversity of the individuals that necessarily comprised it. Any imperative we feel as critics to find a resolution to the question of Ormond's difference is an extratextual ableist imperative – one that might, in a better world, be resisted.[30] We might, in other words, read *Ormond* for the ways in which the text "crips" standard Enlightenment narratives about the republic.[31]

A Usable Past: Reading for Neuroqueerness before Diagnosis

I am arguing here not for intent but for potentiality. Ormond's neurodiversity – insistently *not* disability – does important work. In resisting a diagnosis of "lunacy" that might excuse his criminal behavior, the novel will not let readers acquit Ormond.[32] But, insofar as "liar" is also insufficient for encapsulating Ormond's thoughts and actions, readers are pushed to seek a third term – one grounded in individual difference.

Here we might take our cue from Melanie Yergeau's vision of "neuroqueer futures." In *Authoring Autism*, Yergeau laments that "through diagnosis," which is to say since the early twentieth century when autism was first diagnosed, "autistics [have been] storied into autism, our bodyminds made determinable and knowable through the criteria of neurodevelopmental disability" (2). "Even when autism is depicted as a condition that resists the narratable (which … is an unfortunately typical move)," she continues, "the narrating impulse remains entrenched in the act of diagnosing unto itself" (2). Proposing a different model, Yergeau seeks *neuroqueer* futures in which "neuroqueer subjects" act as "verbed forms," "accurately and radically conceived in cunning movements," like the ones she practices in authoring and narrating her account of autism (27).

Still, for Yergeau, the past is depressing, full of "violent ephemera" in search of a "cure" (30). While we must not deny the horrors and atrocities committed and narrated into being, especially in the twentieth century when autism was first diagnosed as such, perhaps there is more reason for hope reaching back in time. That is, if diagnoses like *autism* and *Asperger's syndrome* are, at root, neurotypical attempts to account for neurodiverse bodyminds with eugenicist origins, it is worth reaching back to accounts that predate the narratives these labels have structured.[33] It is this kind of "neuroqueer" history I am after, building on Yergeau's productive term to signal the ways neurodiverse bodyminds "queer" rhetorical traditions and, for the purposes of this essay, narrative ones.[34] To be clear: if we take as a given that neurodiversity existed in the past – that bodyminds were diverse and did approach the world differently – then we must believe that we can find traces of them.

To do so is *not* a utopian move. I do not wish to naively imagine a world in the past where neurodiversity was wholly embraced rather than stigmatized, and this is not a past *Ormond* offers. After all, late eighteenth-century Americans believed their social and political worlds depended on the ability of one representative figure to stand in for all others and that many others (women, children, enslaved individuals) were lesser forms of that representative individual who could not be trusted to represent themselves. Nevertheless, what *Ormond* shows us is that there were attempts to grapple with cognitive difference, even if, as Brown's gothic style suggests, representing this kind of difference was deeply threatening.

Still, we can and should read for a neuroqueer history here against the grain. *Ormond* offers us the chance to recuperate the neurological variability of the past. Brown's attempt furthermore suggests the potential it holds for recuperating representations – or failed representations – of diverse bodyminds before contemporary diagnoses existed. Brown's works, so uncertain of the Enlightenment project or the predictable sameness of human minds, offer a number of sites for thinking beyond the poles of liar and the lunatic – for thinking neurodiversity. The stakes in Brown's world of a vision that includes this kind of variety are profoundly radical and figured in the novel most often as a direct danger to the republic. Nevertheless, this kind of reading has the potential to be useful to us in the twenty-first century. If we take Ormond seriously as a neurodivergent figure and invest in the novel's articulated frustrations with problems of representation that attend such characters, we can begin to trace a new history for neuroqueerness in American literature. And if we situate

Ormond's neurodiverse bodymind at the center of its narrative, as it turns out it already is, rather than resisting or attempting to dispense with the troubles it raises, we might, alternatively, let it queer our readings and recuperate other histories of bodyminds in American literature and culture obscured by unwittingly ableist forms of criticism and history.

Notes

1 Sydney J. Krause, "Ormond: Seduction in a New Key," *American Literature* 44.4 (1973): 570–584, here 579.
2 Cahill himself finds this trajectory "somewhat misleading"; Edward Cahill, "An Adventurous and Lawless Fancy: Charles Brockden Brown's Aesthetic State," *Early American Literature* 36.1 (2001): 31–70, here 56. For another provocative reading of Ormond, see, for example, William Huntting Howell's reading that Ormond is less human than he is a dangerous "republican machine." His actions lack "humanity," as he acts with a "mechanical inevitability." William Huntting Howell, *Against Self-Reliance: The Arts of Dependence in the Early United States* (Philadelphia: University of Pennsylvania Press, 2015), 186. "What Ormond considers to be selfless, disinterested, and ineluctable acts – recalling the republican mantras of political and economic dispassion and the necessitarian philosophy of mechanic causality," Howell explains, "Constantia not surprisingly considers abominations" (187). Developing the disability aesthetics argument I will make later in this essay, we might use this reading of Ormond's perceived lack of humanity as further evidence of his neurodiversity that builds from Melanie Yergeau's argument that neurologically divergent individuals, particularly autistics, are often represented as lacking humanity, especially because of the ways they seem to repeat things mechanistically, which invalidates them as rhetors, or individuals capable of crafting their own arguments. As Yergeau explains, rhetorical skill has long been associated with being human. See, especially, her introduction to *Authoring Autism: On Rhetoric and Neurological Queerness* (Durham, NC: Duke University Press, 2018).
3 James R. Russo, "The Tangled Web of Deception and Imposture in Charles Brockden Brown's *Ormond*," *Early American Literature* 14.2 (1979): 205–227.
4 Christopher Lukasik, "'The Vanity of Physiognomy': Dissimulation and Discernment in Charles Brockden Brown's *Ormond*," *Amerikastudien/ American Studies* (2005): 485–505, here 485.
5 Hannah Walser's dissertation also treats this problem of knowing other minds in *Ormond*, although she is most interested in Constantia's consciousness. Hannah Walser, "Mind-Reading in the Dark: Social Cognition in Nineteenth-Century American Fiction" (PhD dissertation, Stanford University, 2016), 36–38.

6 By "imaginative experiment," I mean "both the various ways in which doctors and writers used their imaginations to craft, test, and implement their theories of health and the role literary forms played in developing that work." Sari Altschuler, *The Medical Imagination: Literature and Health in the Early United States* (Philadelphia: University of Pennsylvania Press, 2018), 8. *Ormond* is not Ralph James Savarese's "neurocosmopolitan" novel, which adopts "an attitude toward cognitive difference much like that of the conventional cosmopolite toward cultural difference," although this might be a useful way of understanding what Brown's novel cannot do. Ralph Savarese, "Neurocosmopolitan Melville," *Leviathan* 15.2 (2013): 7–19. Also see Ralph James Savarese's *See It Feelingly: Classic Novels, Autistic Readers, and the Schooling of a No-Good English Professor* (Durham, NC: Duke University Press, 2018) for recent thinking about how to read literature from neurodiverse perspectives, especially in collaboration with autistic readers.

7 See, especially, Lindsey Grubbs's recent dissertation "The Politics and Poetics of Diagnosis in Nineteenth-Century American Literature" (PhD dissertation, Emory University, 2019); and Ittai Orr's dissertation, "American Intelligences: Varieties of Mind before IQ" (PhD dissertation, Yale University, 2020).

8 For scholarship on neurodiversity in antebellum literature, see Savarese's "Neurocosmopolitan Melville" and Ittai Orr's "Robert Montgomery Bird's Neurodiversity Hypothesis," *American Quarterly* 71.3 (September 2019): 719–740. Orr locates an "early example of neurodiversity thinking" in Bird's 1836 novel *Sheppard Lee*. I am interested here in a moment prior when brain differences cannot be narrated as such, but literature nonetheless grapples with them.

9 Benjamin Rush, *Essays, Literary, Moral and Philosophical* (Philadelphia: Printed by Thomas and Samuel F. Bradford, 1798), 14–15. For a reading of *Ormond* as a critique of this mechanical imaginary, see Howell's *Against Self-Reliance*, where he explains that the issue is not that a person "is a damaged machine but that he (or anyone) is imagined to be a machine in the first place: Ormond . . . represents the cultural perils of casting persons as particularly sophisticated automata" (172).

10 In their groundbreaking book, *Narrative Prosthesis: Disability and the Dependencies of Discourse* (University of Michigan Press, 2000), for example, David Mitchell and Sharon Snyder describe meeting a Japanese scholar interested in disability in American literature. When questioned, the scholar cannot think of a single example of disability in Japanese literature, but, "Upon further reflection, he listed several examples and laughingly added that of course the Nobel Prize winner Kenzaburo Oë wrote almost exclusively about the subject," leading them to conclude that without a critical apparatus for analyzing disability, "readers tend to filter a multitude of disability absently through their imaginations" (51). Similarly, Rosemarie Garland Thomson observed in *Extraordinary Bodies: Figuring Physical Disability in American Culture and Literature* (Columbia University Press,

1997) that disabled bodies appear in a variety of literary traditions "from folktales and classical myths to modern and postmodern" texts (10).

11 Lennard J. Davis, "Who Put the 'the' in 'the Novel'?: Identity Politics and Disability in Novel Studies," *Novel* 31 3 (1998): 317–338 [328]. Hereafter page numbers are cited parenthetically.

12 The arguments in this paragraph appear in full in my 2014 essay "Ain't One Limb Enough: Historicizing Disability in the American Novel," *American Literature* 86.2 (2014): 245–274. Davis's argument is, of course, a bit more complicated. The essay would like both to point out the limitations of identity politics but also to argue that there is a serious argument to be made for situating disability at the heart of "the" novel. Davis, "Who Put the 'the' in 'the Novel'?"

13 Davis's argument depends on collapsing any new life event, or "abnormality," into a disability – a problematic move, but one rooted in eighteenth-century thinking. After all, Samuel Johnson's 1755 dictionary defined disability less in terms of a mental or somatic qualities than situational ones. Disability was, for Johnson, "want of power to do any thing; weakness; impotence" or "want of proper qualifications for any purpose; legal impediment." The examples Johnson offered considered the "disabilities" that could be produced situationally by particular kinds of reading, argumentation, and legal or clerical decisions. Likewise, "to disable" could mean to physically impair, but it could also refer to impairments that related to finance, tactical positioning, and sovereignty, as Johnson's examples illustrated. In *Ormond, disability* is used in these ways. Stephen Dudley is not described as "disabled" by his blindness, but Constantia is "disabled from furnishing pecuniary aid" when her father forbids her from helping a sick family (72) and Ormond inquires whether he should "disable" himself by marrying a woman who is not his equal (135).

14 See Peter Cryle and Elizabeth Stephens. *Normality: A Critical Genealogy* (Chicago: University of Chicago Press, 2017), where they persuasively argue that the concept emerges from its niche, discipline-specific use only in the last century.

15 Rachel Adams, Benjamin Reiss, and David Serlin, eds., *Keywords for Disability Studies* (New York: New York University Press, 2015), 5–6.

16 For more on how disability functioned as a word and concept in the late eighteenth century, see Sari Altschuler and Cristobal Silva "Early American Disability Studies." *Early American Literature* 52, no. 1 (2017): 1–27.

17 When Dudley is conned out of his fortune by Thomas Craig, he might still rebuild it and rectify his error, but his blindness disables him such that his daughter Constantia must work to keep both of them alive. His shame at the situation causes him to change both their names and to leave New York for Philadelphia, removing them from proximity to friends who might otherwise offer to help the family. This is an event that sets the plot of *Ormond* into motion, but the novel spends little time examining it. Readers quickly forget about Dudley's blindness – that is, until Ormond cures and kills him in what

amounts to a bizarre subplot that only strengthens Constantia's conviction (rather than decides it) that she will not give herself to Ormond. The degree to which disability does not become metaphor in Brown's novels is certainly refreshing for disability studies scholars who have long decried the flattening work of disability's representations.

18 See Altschuler, "Ain't One Limb Enough."

19 See Greta LaFleur, "'Defective in One of the Principle Parts of Virility': Impotence, Generation, and Defining Disability in Early North America," *Early American Literature* 52.1 (2017): 79–107, here 92–95, for more on the ways in which we might rethink disability in eighteenth-century America more generally, where categories like "defective" and "capable" were compatible.

20 For another example of this claim, see Matthew Carey's "A Short Account of the Malignant Fever" (1793), which he published in various installments, adding as he gained new information.

21 Edward Cahill, *Liberty of the Imagination: Aesthetic Theory, Literary Form, and Politics in the Early United States* (Philadelphia: University of Pennsylvania Press, 2012), 32. Hereafter page numbers are cited parenthetically.

22 Howell, *Against Self-Reliance*, 171; quoted at 171.

23 Again, for this, see Altschuler and Silva, "Early American Disability Studies."

24 Garland-Thomson lays out this "kill or cure" logic in her essay "The Cultural Logic of Euthanasia: 'Sad Fancyings' in Herman Melville's 'Bartleby,'" *American Literature* 76.4 (2004): 777–806.

25 As Peter Jaros has observed, the text itself plays with Constantia's characterization. Her very name appears inconsistently, sometimes as Constantia and sometimes as Constance (personal communication).

26 This move is less strange than it may seem at first since the disabled bodymind has been central to the gothic. As Martha Stoddard Holmes explains, "Since the gigantic, spectral body parts that appear in Walpole's *The Castle of Otranto* (1764), fiction, poetry, drama, and film have reiterated a connection between disabled embodiment and the Gothic" ("Disability," in William Hughes, David Punter, and Andrew Smith, eds., *The Encyclopedia of the Gothic* [Chichester, UK: Wiley-Blackwell, 2012], 181). There is, according to Holmes, an intimate connection between disability and the gothic, which draw "elements of the Gothic, carried by disabled bodies" into "a number of other novels" (ibid., 181). The gothic "build[s] on ... the capacity of the human body itself to become alien over the course of a normal lifetime," Holmes writes. This is a natural feature of human bodies, but nondisabled readers often resist the vulnerability of their own bodyminds. Because of our own alienation from our own mortal frailty, disability functions representationally to "collaps[e] the familiar and the strange ... Before experiencing disability, however, we may think of it as epitomizing the unfamiliar (a perception reinforced by Gothic narrative's frequent use of disability as a marker for intense alterity)" (ibid., 183).

27 John Robison, *Proofs of a Conspiracy against All the Religions and Governments of Europe, Carried on in the Secret Meetings of Free Masons, Illuminati, and*

Reading Societies (Philadelphia: Printed for T. Dobson, 1798), 290. Mary Chapman footnotes this in her edition of *Ormond*, p. 126.

28 Tobin Siebers, *Disability Aesthetics* (Ann Arbor: University of Michigan Press, 2010). It is worth noting, as long as we are focused on formal features of the novel, that the intersections of disability and the gothic remain more generally undertheorized. For what does exist, see Holmes, "Disability"; David Punter, "'A foot is what fits the shoe': Disability, the Gothic and Prosthesis," *Gothic Studies* 2.1 (2000): 39–49; and the recent special issue on "Disabled Gothic Bodies," ed. Stevi Costa, *Studies in Gothic Fiction* 6.1: 4–85. Unfortunately, these discussions mostly focus on twentieth- and twenty-first-century literature. Also see Mitchell and Snyder's discussion of Byron's *The Deformed Transformed* in *Narrative Prosthesis*.

29 Cathy N. Davidson, *Revolution and the Word: The Rise of the Novel in America* (Oxford and New York: Oxford University Press, 2004), 303.

30 For an excellent account of the diagnostic features of Brown's narrative in *Weiland* with regard to mental health, see Grubbs, "The Politics and Poetics of Diagnosis."

31 For a discussion of "crip" as an adjective, noun, and verb, see McRuer, who describes its "fluid and ever-changing" character, its challenge to compulsory norms, and its radical potential. Robert McRuer, *Crip Theory: Cultural Signs of Queerness and Disability* (New York: New York University Press, 2006), 34. Also see Carrie Sandahl's essay "Queering the Crip or Cripping the Queer?: Intersections of Queer and Crip Identities in Solo Autobiographical Performance," *GLQ: A Journal of Lesbian and Gay Studies* 9.1 (2003): 25–56. Yergeau builds on this discourse of "cripping" when she suggests the transformative work of "neuroqueering" (*Authoring Autism*).

32 On the crisis of the insanity defense in the late eighteenth century – especially acquittal without confinement – see Richard Moran's "The Modern Foundation for the Insanity Defense: The Cases of James Hadfield (1800) and Daniel McNaughtan (1843)," *The Annals of the American Academy of Political and Social Science* 477.1 (1985): 31–42; and Nigel Walker's "The Insanity Defense before 1800," *The Annals of the American Academy of Political and Social Science* 477.1 (1985): 25–30.

33 See, e.g., Edith Sheffer, *Asperger's Children: The Origins of Autism in Nazi Vienna* (W. W. Norton, 2018).

34 See, e.g., Yergeau, *Authoring Autism*, 18–19.

CHAPTER 18

A Queer Crip Method for Early American Studies

Don James McLaughlin

[T]he pleasure is in the fit – temporary and unburdened.
            —Travis Chi Wing Lau, "The Pleasure of Fit" (2019)

Take back your hands. Hold out your dominant hand, palm up.
Your other hand curls into a fist, except for your pointer and your
middle finger. Rest those two fingers on your dominant palm. This is
the sign for "lie," as in lying down. Imagine those fingers as your legs,
your body.
                    —Ross Showalter, "Night Moves" (2020)

In the early United States, Knickerbocker[1] poet Fitz-Greene Halleck
became known for the intimate friendships with men that he documented
in verse. Biographers have enjoyed illustrating this reputation by way of
the candid, playful, though no less despondent resentment he displayed
when his best friend and fellow poet Joseph Rodman Drake quit his
bachelorhood to marry Sarah Eckford in 1816. Halleck never married.
Nor did he try to conceal the betrayal he felt. To his sister Maria, Halleck
grumbled:

> [Drake] has married, and, as his wife's father is rich, I imagine he will write no
> more. He was poor, as poets, of course, always are, and offered himself a
> sacrifice at the shrine of Hymen to shun the "pains and penalties" of poverty.
> I officiated as groomsman, though much against my will. His wife is good
> natured, and loves him to distraction. He is, perhaps, the handsomest man in
> New York, – a face like an angel, a form like an Apollo, and, as I well knew
> that his person was the true index of his mind, I felt myself during the
> ceremony as committing a crime in aiding and assisting in such a sacrifice.[2]

The poet's spectacular pettiness notwithstanding, the marriage was not as
catastrophic as Halleck predicted. He and Drake kept writing poetry
together, and their lives remain entwined in literary history. So great an
impression did Halleck and Drake's relationship make on contemporaries
that they are said to have inspired Bayard Taylor's *Joseph and His Friend*

(1870), a book frequently hailed as one of the century's most significant queer novels.[3]

While Halleck continues to be remembered for advancing a national tradition of queer love poetry, a key aspect of the erotics of his verse has consistently been glossed over. Halleck was partially deaf, and he wrote with attention to his deafness. He lost hearing in his left ear in 1792, at the age of two. Observing the toddler playing by himself one day, two inebriated militiamen decided it would be amusing to "astonish" the "little fellow" by "discharging their guns, loaded only with powder," next to his head; the practical joke terminated "the hearing in his left ear for life."[4] Surviving accounts indicate that his right ear was also somewhat affected, and his hearing continued to diminish in adulthood as his career progressed. Halleck sought and became disillusioned with medical solutions as a young man. Months prior to Drake's death, Halleck wrote to his sister, "My deafness has lately been accompanied with a dizziness and a constant pain in the head," leaving him certain "that the applications made by my quack doctor would not avail me."[5] A longtime churchgoer, Halleck grew frustrated with the inaccessibility of the service to the hard of hearing and eventually ceased attendance. Before abstaining from church for good, Halleck was known to occupy himself during a too-silent sermon by reciting "inaudibly" to himself "poems or favorite chapters of the Bible, which he had committed to memory."[6] Even when he possessed enough hearing to make out the sermon as a child, this had been his preferred style of engagement, "recalling some of his favorite poems, in lieu of listening to a dull sermon."[7] As with his fondness for handsome men, Halleck's hearing loss became an important facet of his celebrity, during his lifetime and posthumously. Still, scholars have yet to unite these formative elements – his queerness and deafness – to examine the way Halleck's poetry aestheticizes a composite queer disabled sensibility.

This chapter sketches a queer crip method for the study of early American literature and culture. Far beyond Halleck, queer and disability histories have too rarely combined forces. Queer historians have often predicated the politics of biographical recuperation on ableist logics of physical and intellectual meritocracy. Meanwhile, recent colonial and early national disability histories have situated the affordances of preindustrial familial work – that is, the revelation that disabilities tended to be actively assimilated into the division of domestic labor in earlier periods – within the narrow purview of heterosexist kinship. A critical question arises: What divergent intimacies and life histories become accessible when we break from these siloed schemas?

Intersections between disability and queerness have elicited greater consideration from scholars of contemporary media. In *Crip Theory*, Robert McRuer uses the term "compulsory able-bodiedness" to denote an ideology, akin to Adrienne Rich's concept of "compulsory heterosexuality,"[8] which presumes certain thresholds of physical ability (the capacity for heterosexuality included) to constitute innate ideals to which all bodies aspire.[9] Fault lines spread through the refusals of real bodies to acquiesce: "precisely because these systems depend on a queer/disabled existence that can never quite be contained, able-bodied heterosexuality's hegemony is always in danger of collapse."[10] From this vantage point, queer crip reciprocities have been understood to materialize through the work of critique – that is, the function of critique to refract social norms through prisms of deviant and extraordinary embodiment, thus making visible normativity's interior tensions and dependencies. This critical lexicon informs recent historical work as well. In his essential book *Novel Bodies*, Jason Farr shows how eighteenth-century British novels "establish queer, disabled embodiment as an ambivalent experience marked by the exquisite pleasure of transgression and the enduring social and physical pain of disability," thus evincing how "the British literary history of sexuality is thoroughly reliant on impaired bodies for its discursive contours."[11] Across this work, excavating the contingencies of normative discourse facilitates the denaturalization of ableist, homophobic, and transphobic regimes of representation.

This scholarship has developed an invaluable vocabulary around the common positionalities linking queer and disabled subjects. However, the task of historicizing disability, sexual difference, and gender variance introduces complicating quandaries that remain underexplored. One is the straightforward issue of anachronism. Are disability and queerness really useful categories of analysis for early American studies? Building on previous research, the present chapter maintains that both categories prove useful to the extent that they can be decoupled from presentist connotations. As Greta LaFleur explains, sexuality did not cohere in its modern post-sexological iterations in the eighteenth century; nevertheless, "there was still sex," including a science of sex.[12] Moreover, as Thomas A. Foster writes, "same-sex sex becomes more consistently and firmly, if still inconsistently, attached to personhood and identity" across the colonial and early national periods.[13] Likewise, Sari Altschuler and Cristobal Silva assert that while early American ideas of disability did not possess the cultural and legal cohesion the concept holds today, disability history may still address itself to the question of "which conditions were disabling in the period," as well as to "how historical epistemologies and reading practices of disability can help us evaluate the period anew."[14] Interfusing these foci, this chapter takes particular interest in how people in the early United States posed deviating bodies, behaviors, and desires within, against, on the peripheries of, and beyond their sociolinguistic milieu.

A related impasse has been that intersectional work funneled through a multipurpose theory of social constructionism, which foregrounds norms to demonstrate how their dominance has been propped up by ideology, has sometimes risked ensnaring queer disabled subjects within the same prejudicial paradigms they challenge. For good reason, queerness and disability have been explored together in light of their subjection (and resistance) to what disability theorist Eunjung Kim has termed "curative violence," meaning "the exercise of force to erase differences for the putative betterment of the Other," which, in its insatiable appetite for conformity, "ends up destroying the subject in the curative process."[15] To be sure, the same medical model that distorts the meaning of disability in this way, as a state needing to be "fixed," is complexly imbricated with late nineteenth- and twentieth-century treatments of same-sex desire and transgender consciousness as psychopathologies in need of therapeutic correction. Yet this same chronological overlay begs the question: How should the constitutive reciprocities of queerness and disability be conceived of prior to the compounded consolidation of the medical model of disability with the field of sexology?

In making notes toward an answer, I chart a national iconography of queer disability in the early United States, which at once interacts with and exceeds the logic of pathologization. A word on the subject of American literature "in transition" becomes necessary. In disability history, the period 1770–1826 tends to be described across the Atlantic world as a shift from charity to the augmentation of medical and institutional powers – in Henri-Jacques Stiker's words, a purported "humanization of the lot of the aberrant," reified through "the realization of the medical profession's great dream to care for the ill and in so doing to become the adjudicators of ... norms of life and of health."[16] In the American colonies, diverse impairments confronted a range of responses. As Kim E. Nielsen writes, "bodily variations were relatively routine and expected – and accommodations were made ... to integrate individuals into community labor patterns."[17] Towns used almshouses to manage individuals without familial support; in the late colonial and early national periods, institutions used to confine the "insane" paved the way for the rise of the asylum. Nielsen emphasizes further how stigmatization took new shape in the early United States via "the legal and ideological delineation of those who embodied ableness and thus full citizenship, as apart from those ... considered deficient and defective."[18] Instructive as these generalizations are in establishing collective context, a queer crip historical method requires that we pursue also the embodied rebellions, kinships, and pleasures of figures who carved out spaces and livelihoods suited to their unique ambitions. Accordingly, the interlocutors at the heart of this chapter reveal departures unbidden across three domains: (1) the discursive tools of queer crip self-fashioning, (2) erotic built environments, and (3) the queerly disabled sensoria of early American letters.

   1. *Early Americans laid claim to intersections between disability, gender variance, and sexual difference as sites of self-fashioning.* In May 1782, a man named Robert Shurtliff, roughly 5'7" in stature, joined the Light Infantry Company of the 4th Massachusetts Regiment of the Continental Army. An elite troop, the Light Infantry Company selected members for their pronounced height and strength. Later in 1782, Shurtliff took two musket balls to the thigh and received a cut on the forehead. For reasons obscure to his compatriots, Shurtliff insisted on removing the musket balls himself. Allowing a doctor to intervene was too great a risk because of an undisclosed factor: Shurtliff served as a wartime alias for a person known elsewhere as Deborah Sampson.[19] Women took on numerous roles critical to the success of the revolution – in relaying intelligence, in service roles as camp followers, and on the battlefield in extenuating emergencies – but they were denied enlistment. Adopting a male persona constituted the only avenue to serve officially in combat. In and outside the army, for persons who took on the dress and identity of a gender other than the one they were assigned at birth, medical attention signified prohibitive perils. When Shurtliff became ill in 1783, it was a Philadelphia physician who discovered the cloth he used to bind his chest, first removed Shurtliff to his family's home to protect the patient's privacy, and at last broke confidentiality in a letter to General John Paterson, at which point Sampson was honorably discharged. Earlier, following his injuries in 1782, Shurtliff had succeeded in removing one musket ball from his thigh, just below his groin, with a sewing needle and penknife. Buried too far in to be retrieved, the second musket ball stayed lodged in Sampson's thigh.[20]

   Because Sampson reassumed her previous name after the war, her orientation toward gender has attained significance in commodious and competing ways. Sampson has been hailed as a woman patriot who refused to be precluded from fighting for liberty, thus attesting to the unfoundedness of sex-based discrimination in the military.[21] In their play with the changeable accoutrements that make gender legible and fungible, Sampson emblematizes a profound legacy of soldiers who have transitioned in military history and the barriers nonbinary veterans have faced historically.[22] Furthermore, LaFleur has revealed how Herman Mann's biography of Sampson implements botanical sexual science to supply a lexicon expressive of her romantic involvements with other women.[23] Alongside this scholarship, the injuries Sampson incurred during the war have tended to be interpreted, straightforwardly, as a sign of the soldier's bravery, rather than a concerted nexus of self-fashioning. In fact, much of Sampson's energy following the war was spent in efforts to obtain her place on the Invalid Pension Roll, a fight she became one of the first women in the United States to win in 1805. An important historiographical question surfaces at this intersection: Why has Sampson's decades-long investment in being recognized by Congress with the status of "invalid" been treated as separate from the complexity of her gender or, more precisely, been discussed as a fixed impairment effectively posterior to the gender variance that has made Sampson's story such a popular subject of recovery?

Historians have neglected to theorize an emancipatory dynamic: it was Sampson's unwavering resolve to earn recognition as a veteran invalid that, in turn, gave her an opportunity to maintain the identities of both Sampson and Shurtliff for multiple decades after the revolution ended. Mann's account insinuates that Sampson had mixed feelings on being discharged. Not fully prepared "to close the last affecting scene of her complicated, woe-fraught revolution of her sex!," Sampson made a detour. Retreating to a "sequestered hamlet in Massachusetts," they borrowed "the name of her youngest brother" Ephraim and "passed the winter as a man of the world, and was not awkward in the common business of a farmer."[24] This detail makes for a noteworthy caveat, suggesting a predisposition to live as a man disconnected from the apology of patriotic zeal.

Just the same, it would be a mistake to require this singular disclosure to acknowledge how Sampson's gender variance continued to unfurl following her time as a soldier. As Jodi Schorb has observed, Mann's biography itself represents a strategic reclamation of gender multiplicity. Early in her struggle to procure an invalid pension for her military service, Sampson – by then married to a man with the surname Gannett – sought out Mann, "a local editor eagerly hoping to build his reputation as a printer," to discuss the possibility of collaboration.[25] Convinced that Sampson deserved to be compensated for wartime injuries, Mann commenced interviews with the veteran by 1793. When *The Female Review* was published in 1797, all 1,500 copies sold. Intent on proving the veracity of Sampson's honor, while also indulging in the sensational appeal of gender subterfuge, the narrative became indispensable to broadcasting Sampson's story.[26] Within just two months of publication, Sampson took off for New York City to seek the assistance of the poet and editor Philip Freneau in drafting her first direct petition to Congress. Freneau not only agreed to help; he published an ode to Sampson a week after the application had been submitted, proclaiming, "Now for such generous toils, endured, / Her day of warfare done, / In life's decline at length reward / This faithful amazon."[27] The poem took care to highlight the modesty of her request in comparison with her physical sacrifice: "She asks no thousands at your hands, / Though mark'd with many a scar."[28] This initial application failed, but the publicity laid the groundwork for a triumph in 1805. Throughout these ventures, an identity composed at the convergence of gender variance and disability became a lifelong project.

Invalid pensions for Revolutionary War veterans mark a founding moment in the development of a disabled American identity, defined as a status produced at the intersection of national belonging and physical impairment. Laurel Daen has demonstrated how this inceptive language of disability in the United States, inaugurated in the 1780s and 1790s, hinged on evaluating veterans' capacity for labor. "Federal invalid pension legislation authenticated the definition of disability as laboring incapacity and the assessment of disability by degree," resulting in a spectrum from full to fractional pensions, "and veterans and deponents molded the language of their applications to these specifications."[29] For Daen, the postrevolutionary bureaucracy erected to grant and deny pension applications based on one's capacity for labor reveals further how disability gained legibility in the United States as a requisite component of the nation-state.[30] Wartime service that impaired the viability of future work was understood to function proleptically, to constitute a hazardous labor on behalf of independence deserving of posterior remuneration. Sampson's ongoing efforts to garner recognition as a veteran invalid illuminate how she used this same constellation of disability, nationhood, and labor to disseminate records of a life story catalyzed by gender variance.

Sampson's recapitulations of her military past proliferated. One of her most efficacious exploits was the speaking circuit she commenced from 1802 to 1803. These productions – which spanned a dozen cities from Boston and Worcester to Albany and New York City, likely attracted between 1,500 and 2,000 attendees, and received mostly glowing approbation – combined oration with a sensational reveal she knew audiences craved. The address sustained an artful defense of her decision to defy "the tyrant bands which held my sex in awe, and clandestinely, or by stealth, grasp...an opportunity which custom and the world seemed to deny, as a natural privilege."[31] Such lines formulate a poignant parallelism – the despotic subordination of the colonies coextensive with prejudicial obstacles she faced in the female sphere. Recounting scenes of service, Sampson also took care to disclose the lasting consequences of her injury: "A dislocated limb draws fresh anguish from my heart!"[32] Following the speech, Sampson would exit the stage and promptly return as Shurtliff. "Equipped" in "complete uniform," Sampson proceeded to perform "the *Manual Exercises*" they had learned on enlistment. In Boston this performance included being joined "by a company of officers," all "conclud[ing] with the song and chorus, *God Save the Sixteen States*."[33] The pageantry and pathos of the spectacle gave Sampson an enviable platform for substantiating her claim to compensation.

The composite Sampson–Shurtliff persona featured on tour complemented the epistolary campaign she launched to make her particular narrative of veteran impairment convincing to Congress. The 1803 petition that first succeeded in begetting an invalid pension is not known to have survived, but an accompanying document did. One of the best avenues for understanding Sampson's self-fashioning is the way she built her reputability through a network of allies extending from her person: the effusive biographer she found in Mann, the poet-advocate Freneau, and, in coordination with the 1803 petition, the champion she secured in Paul Revere, whose 1804 letter in support of Sampson's claim became instrumental in winning her favor with the Boston congressman William Eustis.

In the essay "Getting Comfortable," writer Laura Hershey contemplates how a writing praxis developed in conjunction with her spinal muscular atrophy underscores the affordances of physical dependency. In Hershey's context, laying bare the "tedious" minutiae of communicating to caregivers what she needs to achieve a comfortable writing posture fortuitously illustrates the creative potential she derives from a "disembodied mind" and "discombobulated body."[34] Sampson routed her public persona through an analogous web of attendants. Revere's letter, for one, reads not just as a vote of confidence but as a calculated extension of Sampson's invalid form. "I have been induced to enquire her situation, and Character, since she quitted the Male habit, and Soldiers uniform," Revere writes. "Humanity, & Justice obliges me to say, that every person with whom I have conversed about Her, and it is not a few, speak of Her as a woman of handsom talents, good Morals, a dutifull Wife and an affectionate parent."[35] In essence, the letter frames Revere's evaluation of Sampson's eligibility as a series of movements undertaken to acquaint himself with and confirm her good character. Unquestionably, it was this hustle for an expansive advocacy that resulted in Sampson's victory: in the first judgment, $4 monthly, representing 80 percent of the $5 maximum.

Crucially, Sampson's efforts to solicit recognition as an invalid veteran transpired as an ever-unfolding recollection of Sampson's gender transgressions. In accounting for these interlocking aspects of Sampson's identity, a compelling phrase stands out from a follow-up petition Sampson submitted in 1818, designed to take advantage of the first general pension act providing annual stipends to any veteran who had served nine months and could prove they were in "reduced circumstances." "Deborah Gannett . . . maketh oath," she wrote, "That she served as a private soldier, under the name of Robert Shurtleff [*sic*] – in the war of the revolution, upwards of two years in manner following, *viz* – ." The "*viz* –" operates like a colon, commanding witness of her autobiography, a condensed account of her enlistment, military service, injury, and departure – days Sampson had described during her tour as the period she "became an actor in that important drama."[36] The language of performativity echoes a rhetoric of visual revelation Sampson used recurrently. "The curtain is now up," she told audiences on tour, "A scene opens to your view."[37] This is the literal meaning of the Latin shorthand *viz*, too. Generally used as a synonym of "that is to say," *viz* designates more precisely an abbreviation of the word *videlicet* (formed from the verbs *videre*, meaning "to see," and *licet*, meaning "it is allowed"), thus encapsulating candidly Sampson's tactical deployment of her public image: my audience *is permitted to see* (Figure 18.1). Sampson's play with an optics of exposure can be traced back to the start of her military career, where she went so far as to select a surname that seems quite obviously, however astoundingly, a brazen homophone for the very situation she guarded against, namely a "shirt-lift," which turned out to predict the conditions of her discharge. Sampson's *viz*, her appropriation of the rhetoric of revelation – the showing of scars, her jarring juxtapositions of "manly elocution"[38] and traditional domestic duty – becomes in her postwar efforts a meticulous style of self-fashioning, choreographed to manage reception of her iconic status as gender-crossing invalid hero/ine.

2. *Eighteenth- and early nineteenth-century built interiors provided material resources for the enactment of queer kinship.* For Sampson, an identity devised at the confluence of gender variance and disability found social intelligibility through the nation-state and bureaucratic assessment.

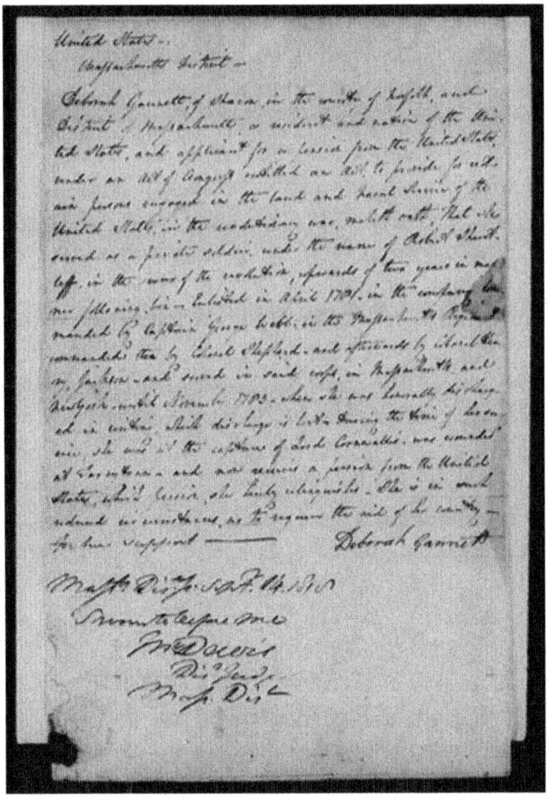

Figure 18.1   Deborah Sampson Gannett. "Revolutionary War Pension
and Bounty Land Warrant Application File S32722. Deborah Gannett, Mass."
https://catalog.archives.gov/id/54636851. Courtesy of the National Archives

Honing a queer crip historical method for early American letters requires
that we dedicate as much attention to ontologies of impairment, debility,
and chronic illness as states of being and becoming that create their own
conditions for sociality outside the optics of medical and political autho-
rization. In *The Matter of Disability*, David T. Mitchell, Susan Antebi, and
Sharon L. Snyder observe how the social model of disability, used today to
reconfigure disability as a "social disadvantage" constructed through envi-
ronmental obstructions to access, has in some cases yielded adverse side
effects.[39] In stepping through the distortive looking glass of prejudice to
understand ableist ideology, the social model has, at times, essentially
inverted that same object of critique: "Within this scenario of deviant

matter, disability has little to offer beyond functioning as a vehicle for exposing certain arrays of disadvantageous material expressions, or at most, an embodiment through which to know the world's exclusions, intolerances, and inhumane discriminations."[40] In its place, Mitchell, Antebi, and Snyder propose a posthumanist, neomaterialist disability studies, beginning with the premise that "the alternative modes of becoming that even the most severe impairments offer involve the promise of an alternative agency that reshapes the world and opens it up to the other modes of (non-normative) being."[41] A queer crip historical method extends this intervention by taking seriously the agential force of disability-as-materiality – meaning both the materiality of the body and the diverse animate and inanimate actors at work in a posthumanist redefinition of the terrain of disabled ontology – with the aspiration of resurrecting the amalgamative force of crip erotic becomings past.

Consider, as an example, the relationship of Charity Bryant and Sylvia Drake, two women remembered today for pioneering a long-term, same-sex companionship at the turn of the nineteenth century. In early 1807, Bryant met Drake during an extended visit to Weybridge, Vermont, the latter's hometown; by mid-spring they had developed strong affections for each other. By July, they were cohabitating. A brief 1844 memoir by Bryant recalls the advent of their domestic partnership straightforwardly: "On the 3rd day of July 1807," Sylvia "consented to be my *help-meet* and came to be my companion in labor."[42] As biographer Rachel Hope Cleves observes, Bryant's use of the term "help-meet" serves to sanctify their devotion as a reverberation of the Hebrew story of creation, in which God fashions Eve from Adam's rib to address the dilemma of human loneliness.[43] In the words of the King James translation of Genesis 2:18, "And the Lord God said, It is not good that the man should be alone; I will make him an help meet for him." Cleves notes further that the crossed-out prepositional phrase "in labor" is evocative for the way it insinuates a prioritization of "love" over "economic need."[44] In January 1809, a year and a half later, Bryant and Drake moved into a new twelve-by-twelve-foot single-room home, erected in Weybridge especially for them, which they used as their living quarters and tailoring shop. The two women shared a bed, made structural additions to their home in the years to come, and became a revered couple (Figure 18.2). As Bryant's nephew, the poet William Cullen (of the same surname), wrote in 1850,

> If I were permitted to draw aside the veil of private life, I would briefly give you the singular ... history of two maiden ladies who dwell in this valley. I would tell you how, in their youthful days, they took each other as

Figure 18.2   This double silhouette depiction of Charity Bryant and Sylvia Drake (circa 1805–15) represents a fashionable form of portraiture in the early United States, sometimes used to portray persons joined in marriage. The frame has been created from braided human hair, which unites in a heart between them. Courtesy of the Collection of the Henry Sheldon Museum, Middlebury, Vermont

> companions for life, and how this union, no less sacred to them than the tie of marriage, has subsisted, in uninterrupted harmony, for forty years, during which they have shared each other's occupations and pleasures ... slept on the same pillow and had a common purse, and adopted each other's relations.[45]

Following Bryant's death in 1857 and Drake's death in 1868, Drake was interred next to Bryant, with a single headstone raised above them, Drake's name resting on Bryant's, their union commemorated through the transparent convention of a shared marital plot.

Two interlinked aspects of the Bryant–Drake partnership provide an opportunity both to supersede the presentist intrigue that has dominated recuperations of their story and to grasp how their companionship nurtured an experimental union of queer and disabled ontologies. In her adolescence and adulthood, Bryant became known for having a dominant personality ("enterprising and spirited in temper," in William Cullen's words),[46] which became diversely manifest in her relationship with Drake, leading one contemporary to observe tersely, "Miss Bryant was the man."[47] Cleves proposes that Bryant thus shares certain traits in common with an eighteenth- and nineteenth-century social type known as the "female husband," a term historian Jen Manion defines as persons who, while "assigned female at birth," "assumed a legal, social, and economic position reserved for men: that of husband."[48] As Manion's definition would suggest, this concept is helpful but not fully adequate to the nuance of Bryant's self-presentation, considering the way she pursued a romantic partnership with Drake, legible as marriage, while also inhabiting a female gender. In addition to embracing a dominant personality characterized by masculine and feminine qualities alike, Bryant cultivated a selfhood enlightened by physical difference: a corporeal state troubled by the tuberculosis that steadily weakened her mother Silence Bryant's health at the time of Charity's birth, caused Silence's death when Charity was just one month old, and was understood to have passed on to Charity an enervated constitution, which she would write about and remain sensitive to across her life.[49] A poem by her older sister Anna shows this awareness was shared by relatives: "You drew in trouble with your earliest breath, / And liv'd the long expected prey of Death! / For wasting sickness nipt your infant bloom / And mark'd you out a victim for the tomb."[50] Indeed, the sickroom into which Charity was born foreshadows the domestic space she created with Drake, which evolved to normalize and shelter chronic illness. In William Cullen's autobiography, a reflection on the kinds of care customized at the Weybridge tailor shop immediately follows the equivalence drawn between their bond and the institution of marriage. Just as their "uninterrupted harmony" endured "in health," so was it enlarged in the way they "watched over each other tenderly in sickness; for sickness has made long and frequent visits to their dwelling."[51] As the "health" of the "head of the family" declined – beginning in 1824, especially, when Charity experienced an attack of severe pain in the left side of her head, which, with symptoms suggesting Bell's palsy, paralyzed her face on the same side – "she was tended by her gentle companion, as a fond wife attends her invalid husband."[52]

A piece of invalid furniture at the center of Bryant and Drake's home survives in the collections of the Henry Sheldon Museum of Vermont History. Stretching over five feet in length and painted olive green, the

Figure 18.3   Early nineteenth-century adult cradle owned by Charity Bryant and Sylvia Drake. Courtesy of the Collection of the Henry Sheldon Museum, Middlebury, Vermont.

object represents a fixture of the material culture of disability in early America known as an "adult cradle" (Figure 18.3). As foremost expert Nicole Belolan explains, adult cradles looked and functioned "like over-sized baby cradles," featuring "two sideboards, a headboard, and a foot-board," placed upon two rockers.[53] Popular from Maine to North Carolina from 1780 to 1840, adult cradles "provided comfort, therapy, and, most importantly, socialization" for people living with both "acute and chronic disability," from painful toothaches and headaches to "the disabling disease of gout," "the wasting disease of tuberculosis," and "open sores." Of the comfort they brought to their users, socialization was central. Sometimes built with handles at the head and foot, adult cradles were portable and often placed at the hearth, with sides low enough to survey the surrounding room. As Belolan explains, "they illustrate the point that in the late eighteenth and early nineteenth centuries people with disabilities were not shut away from the rest of the family," but were instead "integrated" into "everyday life." Adding firsthand experience to her understanding of these objects, Belolan clarifies that, to be used properly, adult cradles required collective participation: "I discovered that I could not rock myself unless I tried really hard, so even that requires another person to be there with you to help you rock." The dissatisfying stasis and contingent mobility of the adult cradle made it a nexus of mutual touch, an impetus to the recognition of discomfort and a reciprocal ritual of affection.

These properties of the adult cradle shed light on its purpose in the Bryant–Drake home. Built out of pine boards by Charity's cousin Asaph Hayward as a gift, the adult cradle sat before Bryant and Drake's hearth (at other times in their chamber)[54] with a magnetic allure, radiating a proclivity for pacifying motion emanating from the rounded base of its rockers. We know from a description penned by the Hagar family – who owned the land Bryant and Drake rented, came into possession of the cradle after Bryant's death, and subsequently donated it to the Sheldon Museum – that the bed held a "fat feather" mattress on a "straw tick."[55] Drake's diary reports that they allowed visiting friends to take naps in the cradle.[56] On August 25, 1823, Drake looked forward to resting her "aching face in the cradle as soon as I can leave the work."[57] On days of intensified sickness, such as September 23, 1823, Drake did not distinguish between work time and cradle time: "Feel quite sick have all that I need brot to the cradle."[58] Taken altogether, surviving letters and diary entries indicate that Drake and Bryant used the cradle in both positions, as rocker and recipient of the rocking, and that Charity rocked Sylvia while the latter did her tailoring work.

The Weybridge adult cradle concretizes the need for a new materialist disability theory. In conversation with Jane Bennett, Olga Tarapata has coined the term "unique mattering" to account for the ways in which "interactions with prostheses, wheelchairs, braces, and other devices" unfold as a "symmetrical, rather than hierarchical, interrelation between human and nonhuman actors," thus recasting disability as a relational dynamic of "agential embodiment."[59] Relatedly, in their "Crip Technoscience Manifesto," Aimi Hamraie and Kelly Fritsch call for a broad-based crip technoscience theory, which, against the banal appropriation of disability as "an object of innovation discourse" and curative consumption, takes for its starting point the reality that "Disabled people are experts and designers of everyday life" – "already making, hacking, and tinkering with existing material arrangements" in forms "committed to interdependence as political technology."[60] A relic of the vast genealogy subtending these commitments, Bryant and Drake's cradle stands out for its sensuality as a desiring actor in their company – "desiring" defined as a state inclined toward interaction, which, in this inclination, seeks the convergence of neighboring bodies. Cleves proposes that Bryant and Drake may have consciously seen the domain of sickness as a special opportunity for intimate touch, a connection substantiated by Drake's reference in her diary to shared "lie-downs" they took outside of sleep, "perhaps leaving a cryptic reference to erotic encounters."[61] Whether or not rocking one another in the adult cradle itself provided a medium of explicit sexual gratification for Bryant and Drake, we should be willing to acknowledge this corresponding aspect of the cradle's resting potential.

Without a doubt, the adult cradle's capacity to facilitate sexual pleasure is imperative to understanding the object's latent affordances in the realm of invalid furniture. The adult cradle demarcated a prerequisite relationality, anticipating its proper experience, thus making it an object wellsuited for early national iterations of what Tobin Siebers has called a "sexual culture for disabled people," meaning a set of practices channeled through the diverse sites of eroticism made possible by disability.[62] Most importantly, observing how the sensuality of the adult cradle surfaced through a triangulated cooperation of animate and inanimate actors opens an aperture onto a history of queer and disabled lovemaking, one where pain and pleasure cohabitated, their margins blurred – bodies pulled on each other, returned pressure, and assented – beyond the reach of identitarian validation.

3. *The knowledge and praxis of queer disabled intimacy shaped early American literature in the form of deviant sensory relations.* But how much sense can we make of the traces left by desiring bodies? What are the stakes of this work? And what ecstasies that spring from the fact of disabled intimacy remain stubbornly enigmatic under the gaze of the historian-interloper? One reason this historical approach can be difficult to put into practice is that it spawns a paradox inherent in the limitations it attempts to transcend: in unshackling responsible history-telling from the hard edges of naming, recovering the materiality of queer crip ontologies relies (partially but inevitably) on resituating the past from the vantage point of a certain transhistorical congruence. Acknowledging this constraint, one can still pursue methods of recovery based on both recognition and self-displacement. In its attention to the variable interface between stimulus and sensation (including the interface between the literary record and sensations imparted to belated readers at a distance), the history of the senses offers a particularly useful frame for seeking out both the resonance and unbridgeable differences of queer crip knowledges as they move between subjects over space and time. Your smells, tastes, are not identical

to my own. So much more removed am I likely to be from the smells and tastes of queer crip forebears.[63] Yet your words, their words, conjure for me a sensorial corridor in common and in so doing achieve a fresh synchronicity.

Enter Fitz-Greene Halleck. Despite the lack of sustained scholarship on the subject, the connection between Halleck's iconicity and his partial and, eventually, profound deafness has endured in popular recollections. In a recent, idiosyncratic tribute, a social media icon named Fitz-Greene Halleck the Deaf Cat, black with a white neck and muzzle, amassed 12,200 followers on Facebook from 2015 until he passed suddenly in 2018.[64] In another evocative recollection, Edward Miner Gallaudet, founder of the first college for the Deaf in the United States (known initially as the Columbia Institute for the Deaf and later Gallaudet University, renamed after his father Thomas Hopkins Gallaudet, another pioneer of Deaf education), recalled seeking out the poet in his youth, while trying to find his own calling. Gallaudet was taken with Halleck's eloquence. The poet was born too early to have been given the option of learning a standardized sign language when he was young,[65] and little is known about the effects his partial deafness had on his style of communication as a child. However, Gallaudet treats the meeting as an impactful one. "[Halleck] showed the fire of genius in his conversation," Gallaudet noted, "and the interview was one long to be remembered."[66] Recorded by an activist who pledged his life to advocating for the necessity of accessible and separate institutions of Deaf education, the anecdote is significant for the way it deploys the nineteenth-century discourse of "genius," advancing a minority group's cause by citing evidence of that group's capacity for exceptional intellect and achievement.[67]

There is evidence to suggest further that Halleck has long been read for the way his poetry incorporates a hard of hearing sensorium. In 1911, founder of the New York School for the Hard of Hearing Edward Bartlett Nitchie published an essay in Alexander Graham Bell's journal *The Volta Review: A Monthly Devoted to the Problems of Deafness* titled "What Poetry Means to Me," which asserts for its central, unequivocal claim, "I have often thought of poetry as the special possession of the deaf."[68] In contrast to sonic music, Nitchie explains,

> The finer beauties of the music of poetry . . . are all mine.... I can conceive of no more haunting melodies in music than are to be found in the poetry of Poe, no more sublimity of rhythm than is to be found in some of the wonderful passages of Whitman, no more sweetness of tune than Tennyson gives us in "The Brook."... I verily believe that because I am denied the full

enjoyment of other music, I enjoy poetry's music more than do those who hear. I concentrate the pleasures of both into the pleasures of one.[69]

In this insistence on a deaf music culture, carved out in the space where Deaf readerships and prosody meet, Nitchie's essay anticipates sites of reception being innovated by Deaf and hard of hearing listeners today, for instance, the deaf-accessible Good Vibrations Music Fest in San Antonio, Texas, which syncs vibrating Subpac backpacks and lightshows, or TL Forsberg's visual performances of music through ASL interpretive dance. Nitchie goes on to qualify that, even as poetry achieves its perfect reception in the deaf reader, lyric represents a humanizing medium, moreover, in the way it unites readers across divergent paths of access. It is here, in shifting to poetry's capacious commonality, that Nitchie turns climactically to Halleck. "All truly great poetry," he explains, "must answer to this test of Fitz-Greene Halleck's appreciation of Burns: 'His that music to whose tone / The common pulse of man keeps time.'" Taken from the poem "Robert Burns; To a Rose Brought from Ayrshire, Burns's Residence," the lines position Halleck not just as a poet who perfectly encapsulates the common music of poetry – the "common pulse of man," routed through metric time – but equally as an ideal reader: a poet who understood, like Nitchie, that poetry is the "special possession of the deaf." Nitchie uses the music of Halleck's iambic tetrameter to frame the essay's persuasive apogee: "No other art so genuinely expresses the universal feelings of the race, and by no other are our hearts made to beat in such perfect time with the pulse-beat of humanity."[70]

In this reading, Nitchie frames Halleck's verse as exemplary of a musical tactility liberated by Deaf reception. The deaf percussionist Dame Evelyn Glennie puts it this way in the "Hearing Essay":

> Hearing is basically a specialized form of touch. Sound is simply vibrating air which the ear picks up and converts to electrical signals, which are then interpreted by the brain. The sense of hearing is not the only sense that can do this, touch can do this too. If you are standing by the road and a large truck goes by, do you hear or feel the vibration? The answer is both.... For some reason we tend to make a distinction between hearing a sound and feeling a vibration, in reality they are the same thing.... Deafness does not mean that you can't hear, only that there is something wrong with the ears. Even someone who is totally deaf can still hear/feel sounds.[71]

Reading poetry extends this musical tactility to the power of the written word to impart rhythm to the body, to impel the body's own rhythms to align or contend with the beat of meter, percussive consonants, and the pace of punctuation. There's nothing to suggest that Nitchie saw Halleck as a queer poet simultaneously. Nonetheless, Nitchie's reading illuminates how Halleck transmitted romantic poetry to other men through a sensorial order informed by hearing loss. As Erica Fretwell reminds in her dazzling history of the scientific study of sensory perception, at such thresholds of communication the senses do not merely impart knowledge of the world; they "structure the ontological possibilities and pitfalls of becoming a particular historical body-subject" and "occasion further meditations on the perceptual habits and sensory ways of being that might be cultivated to instantiate alternative selves or social collectivities."[72]

The most famous poem Halleck wrote for Drake deserves reconsideration for the way it commemorates and grieves the loss of queer intimacy through an exquisitely orchestrated Deaf prosody. In 1820, the adoration that had once showed itself in the bitter visage of the groomsman adapted to a sadder occasion: Drake fell ill with tuberculosis and died at the age of twenty-five. In the elegy penned in the wake of that loss, "On the Death of Joseph Rodman Drake," Halleck combines a meditation on the failure of words to capture their object with an aesthetic grounded in musical tactility:

> When hearts, whose truth was proven,
>   Like thine, are laid in earth,
> There should a wreath be woven
>   To tell the world their worth;
>
> And I who woke each morrow
>   To clasp thy hand in mine,
> Who shared thy joy and sorrow,
>   Whose weal and woe were thine;
>
> It should be mine to braid it
>   Around thy faded brow,
> But I've in vain essayed it,
>   And feel I cannot now.
>
> While memory bids me weep thee,
>   Nor thoughts nor words are free, –
> The grief is fixed too deeply
>   That mourns a man like thee.

The wreath Halleck "should" be the one to braid – an abstract laurel the poem "essay[s]" "in vain" to weave – takes inspiration from the corporeal memory of arms and fingers braided together, the friend's hand "clasp[ed]" "in mine." The poem's ABAB rhyme scheme, conveyed through a variation on common meter, carries the imagery of a braided laurel further, each rhyming strand broken by, because interspersed with, a partner thread. Halleck insinuates it is because their hands can no longer tangibly interlock that the braided wreath the poem begins to weave cannot be completed; untimely abridgments gesture to a love unfinished, such as the open-ended dash following the melancholic confession, "Nor thoughts nor words are free, – ." Halleck dreamed that a physical reunification would genuinely come to pass: he plotted their reunion in his will, requesting that he be buried next to Drake or that Drake's body be disinterred and buried next to him (a dream that came close to happening, but ultimately did not).[73] Most striking in the elegy is the foreshortening of, yet perpetual yearning for, a common meter, literary romanticism's preferred ballad form, defined by its alternation between iambic tetrameter and iambic trimeter. For the attuned reader, each of the first and third lines approaching tetrameter is revealed to consist of just seven beats, allowing one to interpret the lines' concluding amphibrach (a metrical foot taking the form ˘ / ˘) as, instead, a complete iamb followed by half an iamb, unpartnered. Having suspended his readers in the unfinished music of the first and third lines, Halleck proceeds by descending cathartically into perfect trimeter in the second and fourth lines, the companionship of the terminal iamb restored. The "common pulse of man" Halleck references in his tribute to Burns accrues significance in the elegy for Drake in this interweaving of forestalled completion and the dream of its return: the heartbeat that skips in the suddenness of loss – the lover's heartbeat silenced, the heart of the poet incorporating its absence – succeeded by an intermittent recovery of the lover's echo.[74]

"Still every feature I retain, / And every gesture trace"

This chapter has endeavored to outline a framework for a queer crip historiographical mode that departs from traditions preoccupied with either shoring up or reversing the terms of pathology. Elaborating such a methodology is necessary for the way it prioritizes embodied knowledge and simultaneously dismantles the presumption that early Americans would not have understood their lives in terms of disability or minoritarian iterations of gender presentation and sexual intimacy. Deborah Sampson/Robert Shurtliff, Charity Bryant, Sylvia Drake, and Fitz-Greene Halleck all took evident pride in the way they pioneered personhoods, routine affections, and sensorial literary aesthetics that melded disabled becomings with a defiant freedom in the making of queer and gender variant existence.

Nevertheless, in concluding, it will be useful to answer more intentionally the question of what it means to conceive of history using a dyadic queer crip analytic. As discussed earlier, disability studies scholars have pointed out a counterintuitive similarity between medical and social models of disability in recent years: if the medical model depends on circumscribing disability with the language of diagnosis, the social model turns the diagnosis outward, reading disability as a state of inaccessibility in need of repair. This shift has been immeasurably generative in theory and political advocacy, but it also foregrounds an orientation of negation, risking neglect of the way disability itself comprises world-making ontologies, often pointedly in spite of one's built environment. Reflecting on this limitation, Siebers has argued not for jettisoning the social model, but instead for rebuilding it through a frame he terms "complex embodiment."[75] Against a unidirectional rhetoric of diagnosis, Siebers defines complex embodiment as a model for theorizing "the body and environment as mutually transformative."[76] He explains,

> The theory of complex embodiment returns the social to the social model, but this theory does not conceal disabled subjectivity. Instead it places a premium on the disabled subject as a knowledge producer – and to such an extent that people with disabilities are identified as such by their possession and use of the knowledge gathered and created by them as longtime inhabitants of nondisabled society.[77]

I extend Siebers's intervention by proposing that this shift in perspective promises further to return the social to an embodied historicism, both informed by and irreducible to the tenets of social constructionism.

A queer crip method dedicated to centering the self-fashioning, material gratification, and aesthetic sensoria of historical interlocutors prepares us to consider how complex embodiment changes in dialogue with disparate contexts. It reminds that there is much we can learn by telling stories of local, microhistorical transition – what we might describe, borrowing the imagery of Drake and Bryant's vocation, as a focused tailoring of one's environment, associations, and resources. Untethered to diagnosis, a queer crip history of early American literature and culture demands an exploration of the way queer disabled subjects come into being and build community through their possession of knowledges generated wherever impairment and debility open new conditions for gender variance and queer relationality. Is this historiographical mode disabled and queer in content only? Hardly. In decisively inhabiting queer, disabled embodiment, it revels in theatrical disclosures of bodymind variance. It appreciates its own function as a desiring actor in the enabling of exploratory kinships. And it honors, concurrently, the diachronically transmissible sensorial deviations and fiercely opaque lacunae that animate the experience of early American letters.

An early poem by Halleck offers a final example of what this method achieves in practice. Written to his friend Carlos Menie, a Cuban visitor to Halleck's hometown of Guilford, Connecticut, shortly after Menie returned to Cuba, the poem captures Halleck's effort to recover his friend's presence despite the distances, geographical and temporal, separating them. Straining to overcome their physical divide, Halleck employs a true common meter, situating the poem's sensorial order, once again, in a reliable pulse. The speaker recollects the sensation of his heart and his lover's beating in synchrony: "Ah, yes! that gentle heart I know, / At friendship's touch it beats; / I feel the sympathetic glow, / My breast the throb repeats." Halleck entwines this metrical tactility with an emphasis on visual memory, summoning mental recollections of the lover's body as an avenue for overcoming the obscuring effects of time's progression in the wake of Menie's departure.

> Time, whose destroying, wasting hand
> Bears all before its sway,
> As marks imprinted on the sand
> The ocean sweeps away –
>
> Yet hath its circuit rolled in vain
> Your memory to efface
> Still every feature I retain,
> And every gesture trace.

Here and elsewhere, Halleck imagines himself as a kind of steadfast historian, positioning his visual recall of Menie's face, and elsewhere his "pleasing form," as a defense against the sea's imagery of cyclical erasure, the "circuit" of the tide "rolled in vain." Halleck treats this historical work itself as ecstatic, the throb of the heart transfigured into pulsating ejaculation, at once orgasmic and exclamatory: "Oft in the stillness of the night, / When slumbers close mine eyes, / Your image bursts upon my sight; / I gaze in glad surprise!" The significance of the speaker's sensorial design becomes clearest when we contextualize it within an embodied knowledge spoken in concert with Halleck's hearing loss. In the poem to Menie, this embodied knowledge incorporates the writing of history itself. Halleck requests of the lover-interlocutor not just that he think back on their companionship in times of "solitude" but that he endeavor, moreover, to inhabit the lover's distinctive knowledge of him – a knowledge he imagines will "oft intrude" upon the consciousness of his reader, "When the calm mind is free."

Notes

1 Named after Washington Irving's pseudonymous historian-avatar Diedrich Knickerbocker, the Knickerbocker School comprised a cluster of early nineteenth-century authors based in New York City, known especially for their satire and romanticism.

2 Fitz-Greene Halleck, "Letter to Maria, Jan. 29, 1817," in *The Life and Letters of Fitz-Greene Halleck*, ed. James Grant Wilson (New York: Appleton & Co., 1869), 184.

3 See John W. M. Hallock, *The American Byron: Homosexuality and the Fall of Fitz-Greene Halleck* (Madison: University of Wisconsin Press, 2000), 10, 151–174.

4 Wilson, ed., *Life and Letters*, 40–41.

5 Ibid., 235. Halleck's frustration with phony cures for deafness resonates powerfully with Jaipreet Virdi's account of the discourse generated by the myriad family remedies, patent medicines, and restorative tonics attempted in earlier periods: "Quackery and distrust … characterized this commerce in deafness cures, as did hope and desire. Commercial processes were expressions of how to normalize hearing loss" (32). For more on this subject, see Jaipreet Virdi, *Hearing Happiness: Deafness Cures in History* (Chicago: University of Chicago Press, 2020).

6 Wilson, ed., *Life and Letters*, 562.

7 Ibid., 562.

8 Adrienne Rich, "Compulsory Heterosexuality and Lesbian Existence," *Signs* 5, no. 4 (Summer 1980): 631–660.

9 Robert McRuer, *Crip Theory: Cultural Signs of Queerness and Disability* (New York: NYU Press, 2006), 2.

10 Ibid., 31.

11 Jason Farr, *Novel Bodies: Disability and Sexuality in Eighteenth-Century Literature* (Bucknell, PA: Bucknell University Press, 2019), 1.

12 Greta LaFleur, *The Natural History of Sexuality in Early America* (Baltimore: Johns Hopkins University Press, 2019), 10, 11.

13 Thomas A. Foster, "Introduction" in *Long Before Stonewall: Histories of Same-Sex Sexuality in Early America* (New York: NYU Press, 2007).

14 Sari Altschuler and Cristobal Silva, "Early American Disability Studies," *Early American Literature* 52, no. 1 (2017): 12.

15 Eunjung Kim, *Curative Violence: Rehabilitating Disability, Gender, and Sexuality in Modern Korea* (Durham, NC: Duke University Press, 2017), 14.

16 Henri-Jacques Stiker, *A History of Disability*, trans. William Sayers (Ann Arbor: University of Michigan Press, 1999), 104.

17 Kim E. Nielsen, *A Disability History of the United States* (Boston: Beacon Press, 2012), 39. See also Sarah F. Rose, *No Right to Be Idle: The Invention of Disability, 1840s–1930s* (Chapel Hill: University of North Carolina Press, 2017).

18 Nielsen, *Disability History*, 50.

19 In using pronouns for Shurtliff/Sampson, I have chosen to alternate between male and female pronouns according to their self-presentation in the contexts discussed, and to use a neutral pronoun when discussing both identities together.

20 As Alfred F. Young has discussed, accounts documenting Sampson's injuries are contradictory across a number of details. For a discussion of competing records, see Alfred F. Young, *Masquerade: The Life and Times of Deborah Sampson, Continental Soldier* (New York: Vintage Books, 2004).

21 "Mythbusting the Founding Mothers," National Women's History Museum (website), July 14, 2017, www.womenshistory.org/articles/mythbusting-founding-mothers.

22 See, for instance, Alex Myers's novel *Revolutionary*, which retells Sampson's story in the form of fiction.

23 Greta LaFleur, "Precipitous Sensations: Herman Mann's *The Female Review* (1797), Botanical Sexuality, and the Challenge of Queer Historiography," *Early American Literature* 48, no. 1 (2013): 93–123.

24 Herman Mann, "The Female Review (1797)," ed. Ed White and Duncan Faherty, *Just Teach One*, no. 9 (Fall 2016): 58.

25 Jodi Schorb, "Mann Seeking Woman: Reading *The Female Review*," *Just Teach One*, no. 9 (Fall 2016): 2.

26 Mann, "Female Review," 59.

27 Philip Morin Freneau, *The Poems of Philip Freneau: Poet of the American Revolution*, 3 vols., ed. Fred Lewis Pattee (Princeton, NJ: University Library, 1907), 3:183.

28 Ibid.

29 Laurel Daen, "Revolutionary War Invalid Pensions and the Bureaucratic Language of Disability in the Early Republic," *Early American Literature* 52, no. 1 (2017): 141–167 (144).

30 Ibid., 162.

31 Deborah Gannett, "An Address Delivered at the Federal-Street Theatre, Boston" (March 22, 1802), in *Weathering the Storm: Women of the American Revolution*, ed. Elizabeth Evans (New York: Charles Scribner's Sons, 1975), 322.

32 Ibid., 324.

33 *Columbian Minerva*, March 23, 1802.

34 Laura Hershey, "Getting Comfortable," in *The Right Way to Be Crippled and Naked: The Fiction of Disability*, ed. Annabelle Hayse, Sheila Fiona Black, and Michael Northen (El Paso, TX: Cinco Puntos Press, 2017), 130, 131.

35 Paul Revere, "Letter to William Eustis," February 20, 1804, Massachusetts Historical Society, Boston.

36 Gannett, "An Address," 322.

37 Ibid., 323.

38 "A Correspondent," *Hampshire Gazette*, September 1, 1802.

39 David T. Mitchell, Susan Antebi, and Sharon L. Snyder, "Introduction," in *The Matter of Disability: Materiality, Biopolitics, Crip Affect*, ed.

David T. Mitchell, Susan Antebi, and Sharon L. Snyder (Ann Arbor: University of Michigan Press, 2019), 5.

40 Ibid., 6.

41 Ibid., 9.

42 "Account of Her Travels," Charity Bryant, April 9, 1844, Charity Bryant-Sylvia Drake Papers, Henry Sheldon Museum of Vermont History, Middlebury.

43 Rachel Hope Cleves, *Charity and Sylvia: A Same-Sex Marriage in Early America* (Oxford: Oxford University Press, 2014), 101.

44 Ibid., 102.

45 William Cullen Bryant, *Letters of a Traveller; or, Notes of Things Seen in Europe and America* (New York: G. P. Putnam & Co., 1855), 136.

46 Ibid., 136.

47 Cleves, *Charity and Sylvia*, 132.

48 Jen Manion, *Female Husbands: A Trans History* (Cambridge: Cambridge University Press, 2020), 1.

49 Cleves, *Charity and Sylvia*, 3–5.

50 Anna Bryant Kingman, "A Sister's Farewell," qtd. in ibid., 5.

51 Bryant, *Letters of a Traveller*, 136.

52 Ibid., 136.

53 Nicole Belolan, "The Material Culture of Living with Physical Disability at Home, 1700–1900," YouTube video. Daughters of the American Revolution Museum, April 11, 2017, 16:46–23:31. www.youtube.com/watch?v=mPv9pzPrbRM&feature=youtu.be.

54 Sylvia Drake's Diary, entry for August 25, 1823. Courtesy, Henry Sheldon Museum, Middlebury, VT.

55 "Large-Sized Cradle Rocked Grown Poet Bryant to Sleep," *The Burlington Free Press and Times*, July 6, 1936.

56 Sylvia Drake's Diary, entries for March 9, 1821; October 30, 1822; and August 7, 1835. Courtesy, Henry Sheldon Museum.

57 Sylvia Drake's Diary, entry for August 25, 1823. Courtesy, Henry Sheldon Museum.

58 Sylvia Drake's Diary, entry fpr September 23, 1823. Courtesy, Henry Sheldon Museum.

59 Olga Tarapata, "Unique Mattering: A New Materialist Approach to William Gibson's Pattern Recognition," in Mitchell et al., eds., *The Matter of Disability*, 74.

60 Aimi Hamraie and Kelly Fritsch, "Crip Technoscience Manifesto," *Catalyst: Feminism, Theory, Technoscience* 5, no. 1 (2019): 4, 2, 12.

61 Cleves, *Charity and Sylvia*, 183.

62 Tobin Siebers, "A Sexual Culture for Disabled People," in *Sex and Disability*, ed. Robert McRuer and Anna Mollow (Durham, NC: Duke University Press, 2012).

63 While editing this paragraph, I had the privilege of hearing Ben Friedlander's excellent paper "The Dandy's Dissent" at the 2020 Virtual C19 Conference,

which argues for interpreting the decline of critical attention to Halleck as a consequence of his refined, highly particularized taste, so essential to winning admirers in his day, which now leaves readers feeling unmoored. Unlike my usage above, Friedlander means "taste" in the sense of aesthetic acumen; nonetheless, the argument can be adapted to apply here, since Friedlander's point is that appreciating Halleck (his satires especially) often requires reckoning with the loss of an impeccable sensibility, once "world-building," which grips us with its passion, yet does not strike with the force of its prior cohesion.

64 "Fitz-Greene Halleck the Deaf Cat," Facebook.com, April 5, 2015–December 9, 2018, www.facebook.com/fitzgreenehalleck/.

65 Edward's father Thomas would establish the American School for the Deaf in Hartford, Connecticut, in 1817.

66 Maxine Tull Boatner, *Voice of the Deaf: A Biography of Edward Miner Gallaudet* (Washington, DC: Public Affairs Press, 1959), 32.

67 For phenomenal work on early national and antebellum discourses of intellect and genius, see the scholarship of Rachel Walker and Ittai Orr.

68 Edward Bartlett Nitchie, "What Poetry Means to Me," *The Volta Review: A Monthly Devoted to the Problems of Deafness* 13, no. 1 (April 1911): 89–90.

69 Ibid., 89.

70 Ibid., 89.

71 Dame Evelyn Glennie, "Hearing Essay" (1993), January 1, 2015, www.evelyn .co.uk/hearing-essay/.

72 Erica Fretwell, *Sensory Experiments: Psychophysics, Race, and the Aesthetics of Feeling* (Durham, NC: Duke University Press, 2020), 26.

73 Hallock, *The American Byron*, 91.

74 Derek Mong has disputed the hypothesis that the iamb (iambic pentameter especially) originates in the human heartbeat, arguing that the postulation mistakenly "hears the heart, an organ we all share, through an Anglophone ear." While I respect Mong's point that the relationship between the iamb and the heart is not a singular metrical tradition (and that one should be alert to xenophobic claims to the contrary), the language of Mong's rebuttal neglects the relation's capacity for deviant alterity – in Halleck's case, the iamb's capacity to denote a deaf, tactile music of bereavement accessed not by the ear, but through queer touch – crafted through an oscillating sensation of beats withheld and sequentially fulfilled. For Derek Mong's article, see "Iambic Pentameter Has Nothing to Do with Your Heart," *Kenyon Review*, April 16, 2016.

75 Tobin Siebers, "Returning the Social to the Social Model," in Mitchell et al., eds., *The Matter of Disability*.

76 Ibid., 42.

77 Ibid., 47.

Index

353

Printed by Printforce, United Kingdom